European Union: International Law and Politics

European Union: International Law and Politics

Edited by
Melba Wasson

Willford Press
www.willfordpress.com

Published by Willford Press,
118-35 Queens Blvd., Suite 400,
Forest Hills, NY 11375, USA

ISBN: 978-1-64728-446-6

Cataloging-in-publication Data

European union : international law and politics / edited by Melba Wasson.
p. cm.
Includes bibliographical references and index.
ISBN 978-1-64728-446-6
1. International law. 2. World politics. 3. European Union. 4. European Union countries--Politics and government. 5. International relations. 6. International organization. I. Wasson, Melba.
KJE947 .E97 2023
341.242 2--dc23

For information on all Willford Press publications visit our website at www.willfordpress.com

Willford Press

Contents

Preface

The European Union (EU) refers to an economic and political union comprising twenty seven member states mainly situated in Europe. A harmonized system of rule is applicable on all member states, where the states have agreed to operate as one, creating a single internal market. EU policies strive to ensure free flow of services, people, capital, and goods within the internal market place. They also emphasize on preserving common policies in trade, fisheries, agriculture and regional development, and enact laws relating to justice and home affairs. The EU consists of seven major decision-making bodies, which include institutions such as the EU court of justice, European court of auditors, the European council, the European commission, the European central bank, the European parliament, and the Council of the European Union. This book provides comprehensive insights into the field of international law and politics with respect to the European Union. It is a resource guide for experts as well as students.

The researches compiled throughout the book are authentic and of high quality, combining several disciplines and from very diverse regions from around the world. Drawing on the contributions of many researchers from diverse countries, the book's objective is to provide the readers with the latest achievements in the area of research. This book will surely be a source of knowledge to all interested and researching the field.

In the end, I would like to express my deep sense of gratitude to all the authors for meeting the set deadlines in completing and submitting their research chapters. I would also like to thank the publisher for the support offered to us throughout the course of the book. Finally, I extend my sincere thanks to my family for being a constant source of inspiration and encouragement.

Editor

1

Hungary's Latest Experiences with Article 2 TEU: The Need for 'Informed' EU Sanctions

Beáta Bakó

Contents

B. Bakó (✉)
Department of Law, European University Institute, Florence, Italy

Abstract This contribution will concentrate on the Hungarian situation by analysing the generalised practice of targeted legislation and the different causes for legal uncertainty on the constitutional level. The European Parliament initiated an Article 7 TEU sanctioning procedure against Hungary in September 2018 and several infringement proceedings have been launched by the Commission. Unfortunately, these EU responses were not able to grasp the gist of the Hungarian developments. Even the so called Sargentini report of the European Parliament—intended to be a comprehensive analysis of the rule of law deficiencies in Hungary—could not identify the most significant patterns of the Hungarian rule of law decline. This reveals a central shortcoming of EU sanctioning mechanisms employed against 'backsliding' Member States: the need for 'informed' sanctions. Some recent legislative proposals for measuring the rule of law illustrate, that the need for such informed sanctions has been realised by EU institutions. However, the question of 'how' is still unanswered. Taking the case of Hungary as an example, I will finally recommend some aspects to be considered in order to grasp the patterns of 'systemic' rule of law decline.

> Polak, Węgier, dwa bratanki / I do szabli, i do szklanki
> Lengyel, magyar, két jó barát / együtt harcol, s issza borát[1]

1 Introduction

Today, this proverb of Polish-Hungarian friendship has developed a new meaning, as Hungary and Poland 'fight together' against the EU and its founding values as listed (but not defined) in Article 2 TEU. Both countries are shifting towards an extreme version of what Richard Bellamy termed 'political constitutionalism'.[2] Against 'legal constitutionalism' and judicial review as one of its key features, Richard Bellamy argues that the democratic mechanisms and decision-making by majority rule offer superior and sufficient methods for upholding rights and the rule of law. The absence of popular accountability renders judicial review a form of arbitrary rule which lacks the incentive structure democracy provides to ensure rulers treat the ruled with equal concern and respect. According to Bellamy, one of the key legal constitutionalist methods is establishing boundaries for the political sphere by 'designating certain values . . . as beyond the realm of politics.'[3]

Applying Bellamy's words to the current debates revolving around the 'Copenhagen dilemma', it is hard to decide whether the current events should be framed in political or legal terms. Indeed, it seems that Article 2 TEU is at the interface of the

---

[1] 'Polish and Hungarian are two *brothers* [Polish]/two *good friends* [Hungarian]; they fight and drink together.'

[2] About constitutionalism as understood in the EU legal order see e.g. Glencross (2014), pp. 1165–1167; Walker (2007), pp. 254–267.

[3] Bellamy (2007), p. 147.

political and legal realm. While the EU's founding values are clearly beyond the realm of day-to-day politics, the contours of their exact meaning and their enforcement could hardly be more politicised: Article 7 TEU is commonly labelled as a 'nuclear option'.[4] Just like nuclear weapons, pressing the button is exclusively up to politicians. In this light, the defence of the Union's common values faces a twofold risk: first, the risk of becoming a highly politicised question, and second, the risk of losing the bigger picture in narrow and particularized judicial proceedings.

On one hand, politicians usually do not decide in line with constitutional concepts and ideas but rather in line with their *interests*. An important interest that concerns all EU Member States is to maintain peaceful relations and not to give reason for any kind of 'revenge' or 'retaliation'. The recent procedures against Poland and Hungary are testimony to this: After Poland,[5] a second Article 7 TEU procedure was launched against Hungary.[6] Yet, nothing moved forward in the Council. Indeed, the risk of 'mutual indulgence'[7] has increased especially after the Polish and the Hungarian governments enormously contributed to the nomination of the surprise candidate for the presidency of the Commission.

On the other hand, the infringement procedures brought by the Commission were unable to sufficiently address the gist of the illiberal developments in the respective Member States. They were instead, focused on particularized, individual details while leaving the systemic patterns aside.

The Hungarian example perfectly illustrates these shortcomings. Taking Hungary as a case study, this paper will reveal that systemic patterns might be complex and not always visible in the Member States. First, this contribution systematizes the developments in Hungary and reveals two crucial threats to the rule of law: on one hand, the Hungarian government established a skilfully designed, complex and nuanced system of legislation targeting specifically its 'enemies' and 'friends'. On the other hand, there are serious malfunctions on the constitutional level like the questionable use of constitutional amendments as an instrument of every-day politics and the declining role of the Constitutional Court (see Sect. 2). This analysis demonstrates how difficult it is for EU institutions to grasp these developments—especially in a highly politicised (Art. 7 TEU) or particularized legal procedure (Art. 258 TFEU). Seen in this light, it becomes clear that the developments in Hungary were only partially addressed by the Commission's infringement procedures (see Sect. 3) and the Article 7 TEU procedure initiated by the European Parliament (see Sect. 4). These procedures concentrate on specific laws without having the bigger picture in mind. What could be responses to these shortcomings? I argue that there

---

[4]Critically on the 'nuclear myth', see Kochenov (2017).

[5]Proposal for a Council decision on the determination of a clear risk of a serious breach by the Republic of Poland of the rule of law (2017/0360(APP), 20. December 2017.

[6]European Parliament resolution of 12 September 2018 on a proposal calling on the Council to determine, pursuant to Article 7(1) of the Treaty on European Union, the existence of a clear risk of a serious breach by Hungary of the values on which the Union is founded (2017/2131(INL)), P8_TA(2018)0340.

[7]von Bogdandy et al. (2012), p. 497.

should be no procedures against 'backsliding' Member States without a profound legal assessment involving independent experts beforehand—in a nutshell: there is a need for more 'informed' EU sanctions. Some recent legislative proposals reflect the need for 'measuring' the rule of law. However, it is important that any system of indicators should follow a comprehensive approach (see Sect. 5).

2 The Big Picture: Targeted Legislation and Constitutional Malfunctions

2.1 Lex Friends and Lex Enemies

Targeted legislation can take different forms and shapes. In the first years after setting up the new constitutional system in January 2012, several independent state institutions were affected by organisational changes and this was a proper occasion to dispense with independent officials, like the data protection ombudsman (see Sect. 2.1.1), the president of the Supreme Court and 'communist judges' in general (see Sect. 2.1.2). As the years passed and the new constitutional system was consolidated, targeted legislation has diverged from constitutional institutions to everyday subjects: some of them were also useful in the political communication of the governing parties (see Sects. 2.1.3–6).

2.1.1 Turning the Data Protection Ombudsman into an Authority Influenced by the Government

As the new Hungarian Fundamental Law entered into force in January 2012, the office, and together with that, the term of the former data protection ombudsman was terminated and a new Data Protection Authority was established.[8] Contrary to the ombudsman who had been elected by the parliament, the president of the National Data Protection and Freedom of Information Authority (NAIH) is nominated by the President of the Republic on the proposal of the Prime Minister. He may be reappointed for a second term which only strengthens his political dependency.[9]

[8]§ 38 of Act CXII. of 2011 on the Right to Informational Self-determination and Freedom of Information.

[9]In details see also Polyák and Szőke (2011), pp. 164–165.

2.1.2 Sending Judges into Retirement

Similar reorganisational measures have been adopted in the judiciary: new administrative organs have been established[10] and the Supreme Court has been renamed 'Curia'.[11] At the same time, the president of the Supreme Court was released and the Curia started its work with a new president.[12] The new constitution further prescribed that 'with the exception of the President of the Curia, no judge may serve who is older than the general retirement age.'[13]

The law on the status of judges prescribed that judges had to retire at the age of 62 instead of the former 70. The new rule affected about 10% of the judges.[14] Prosecutors and notaries had to meet the same age-requirements too. The law would have entered into force with a tight *vacatio legis*: half a year before the affected judges would have had to retire.

2.1.3 Labelling Foreign Funded NGOs

Unlike in 2012 and 2013, when the institutional reforms concerned state institutions, the Hungarian government found quite different targets by 2017. These were nongovernmental institutions: civil society organisations on one hand, and a university, on the other—moreover, only a few particular players within these specific categories were affected.

After the government started to systematically undermine the rule of law, to limit the powers of the Hungarian Constitutional Court (HCC) and to amend the constitution routinely in line with its political interests, it had received harsh criticism from civil society, particularly from different NGOs like the Hungarian Civil Liberties

---

[10]The National Judicial Office (NJO) has been established by the new Fundamental Law. It is led by its president who is elected by the parliament: accidentally, she is the wife of a Fidesz-politician and an old friend of the Prime Minister. Her most criticised competence was the transfer of cases between different courts but later this was abrogated by the fifth amendment of the constitution in autumn 2013. For details about the judiciary reform see e.g. Sonnevend et al. (2015), pp. 102–103. Since the beginning of 2017, a conflict has developed between the NJO and the self-administration body of the judiciary, the National Judiciary Council (NJC). Namely, the president of the NJO often declared applications to judicial positions as void in order to avoid the control of the NJC. The controversies in details are discussed by Vadász (2018).

[11]Originally: Art. 25 (1) of the Fundamental Law, due to amendments now Art. 25 (2).

[12]The former Supreme Court president, András Baka made a complaint before the European Court of Human Rights on the issue. The Strasbourg court dismissed Hungary on the grounds of the right to access to court and the freedom of expression. Concerning the latter, the Court found that the reason of 'the early termination of his mandate as President of the Supreme Court was not the result of a justified restructuring of the supreme judicial authority in Hungary, but in fact was set up on account of the views and criticisms that he had publicly expressed in his professional capacity on the legislative reforms concerned'. (ECHR decision no. 20261/12, Baka v. Hungary, paras. 75, 96.).

[13]Art. 26 (2) of the Fundamental Law.

[14]Szente (2017), p. 466.

Union (TASZ), the Hungarian Helsinki Committee, or, the Hungarian division of Amnesty International.

Their activity must have been a thorn in the government's eye for a couple of years but the first concrete legislative step against them was linked to the migration crisis—at least on the rhetorical level. According to the government's narrative, the Hungarian-American billionaire George Soros planned to smuggle millions of migrants into Europe and is financing NGOs to fulfil this plan.[15]

The new law on the transparency of foreign funded NGOs was adopted in June 2017. According to the new rules, NGOs receiving more than 7.2 million HUF (approximately 24,000 Euros) from abroad per year must register themselves as 'organisations supported from abroad'. This label must be used on their website and on their materials. They were also obliged to provide detailed information to the authorities about the funding they receive.[16]

Some affected NGOs declared civil disobedience and refused to register themselves as being financed from abroad, emphasizing at the same time, that their financial background was already transparent.[17] Several NGOs made constitutional complaints before the Constitutional Court based on personality and privacy rights and the freedom of expression.[18] Additionally, opposition MPs issued a norm control procedure before the Constitutional Court, arguing that the law violated the principles of legal certainty and the rule of law and threatened the freedom of association.[19] For now, all cases are pending before the Court.

2.1.4 Targeting the 'Soros University'

The other problematic law applies to an even narrower circle of addressees and has an important overlap with the NGO law: George Soros. The amendment of the Higher Education Law adopted in April 2017 clearly targets the Central European University (CEU) founded by the Hungarian-American billionaire. The amendment has set up new requirements for universities operating from a third country (non-EEA) to continue their activities in Hungary.

The most significant change is that an international agreement between Hungary and the third state is needed. If this is a federal state, a prior agreement with the

[15]The story contains truth in small and fragmented pieces in so far as the abovementioned NGOs get funding from the Soros founded Open Society Foundations and some of them offer legal aid to asylum seekers. However, it is not the only and main focus of their activity and the financing sources (including the OSF) had been published in their financial reports at their website already earlier.

[16]Act LXXVI of 2017 on the transparency of civil organisations financed from abroad.

[17]The boycott declared by HCLU/TASZ, Amnesty International and Hungarian Helsinki Committee was joined later by four further NGOs. By doing so, they are risking a fine between 10,000 and 900,000 HUF (30-3,000 Euros). For now, they have not announced being fined because of that.

[18]AB cases no. IV/01830/2017, IV/01685/2017 and IV/01857/2017.

[19]AB case no. II/01460/2017.

federal government is required. The amendment further prescribes that the affected foreign universities must perform educational activity in their country of origin too.[20] There are 27 third country universities operating in Hungary but most of them have only a few study programs together with other Hungarian universities. Conversely, the entirety of CEU's educational program has been threatened by this law. Further, this is the only university among the addressees having no campus and educational activity in its country of origin (the U.S.) at all. The sum of these special requirements has made one thing clear: the exclusive target was the 'Soros University', the CEU.

The amendment has set a tight *vacatio legis*: originally, the deadline for compliance with the new rules was the 1st of January 2018. However, in October 2017—after an infringement procedure and several constitutional reviews had been initiated[21]—the government suddenly realised that this was not realistic and extended the deadline for one more year.[22] In December 2018 the CEU announced it would move to Vienna because the Hungarian government rejected to sign or ratify the required international agreement.[23]

The decision on the constitutionality of the law still has not been made by the Constitutional Court. The Constitutional Court suspended the procedures of the lex CEU and the NGO law in June 2018 with a very strange reasoning. Namely, referring to the European constitutional dialogue and the obligation of cooperation within the European Union, the Court found it necessary to wait for the closing of the parallel cases pending before the European Court of Justice.[24] The decision illustrates that the HCC did not (want to) acknowledge that the CJEU will decide on grounds of EU law, which is a totally different yardstick than the Hungarian constitution.[25]

---

[20] § 2 of Act XXV of 2017 on the amendment of Act CCIV of 2011 on the national higher education.

[21] The university issued a constitutional complaint and opposition politicians initiated norm control before the Constitutional Court. Both cases are still pending under case numbers II/01036/2017 and IV/01810/2017. Details about the infringement procedures in Sect. 3 below.

[22] Act CXXVII on the amendment of Act CCIV of 2011 on the national higher education and of Act XXV of 2017 *supra* note 20.

[23] The development that started with the lex CEU, continued in the Summer of 2019 the law on the Hungarian Academy of Sciences was amended. The most important point of the amendment is that the Academy would be deprived of its research network (Act. LXVIII of 2019). Opposition MPs initiated a norm control before the Constitutional Court (pending case no. II/01214/2019). The president of the Academy also announced to file a constitutional complaint in the matter. Since the Academy is a public institution and a part of the central budget, the reform itself does not necessarily mean that it was a *lex enemy*. However, such motivations cannot be excluded either, especially taking into account that the government has no visible and constructive plans for a reasonable restructuration of the Academy.

[24] AB orders no. 3198/2018 (VI. 21), 3200/2018 (VI. 21) and 3199/2018 (VI. 21) (ABH 2018, 1050, 1057, 1064, respectively).

[25] This point is however addressed in some parallel reasonings and dissenting opinions. See e.g. the dissenting opinion of István Stumpf and the parallel reasoning of Balázs Schanda and Ildikó Hörcherné Marosi to AB order no. 3200/2018, *supra* note 24.

2.1.5 'Stopping Soros' (and Migration)

The latest package amending several laws related to immigration has been named 'Stop Soros'[26] by the government in order to link the fight against immigration and Soros stronger in their political rhetoric. However, contrary to the name, this is not a typical piece of targeted legislation (unlike the 'lex CEU' that was officially labelled the amendment of the Higher Education Law).

The package was adopted in Summer 2018, after Fidesz won a third two thirds majority in the parliament in the aftermath of the elections held in Spring 2018. The most striking point of the law is the introduction of a new criminal offense called 'facilitating illegal migration.' The offence refers to any 'organisational activity' aimed at enabling a person to file an asylum application in the event that the latter is ineligible for asylum.[27] The police is also empowered to issue injunctions against persons suspected (not even accused or condemned) to facilitate illegal migration or other immigration-related offences from approaching the border closer than 8 km.[28] Therefore, it seems that the ultimate objective is not to condemn but rather to keep away any *persona non grata* from the border.

2.1.6 The System of *Lex Friends* and *Lex Enemies*: The Fundamental Challenge to the Rule of Law in Hungary

The above listed pieces of targeted legislation are by far not unique examples, but they are the ones that have been noticed in Brussels. However, many other targeted legislations have not triggered the EU's attention yet. One of the most striking examples of *lex enemies* is strongly related to the EU-values, especially to the principle of democracy. It is most commonly known as the 'billboard law' and was adopted with a procedural trick. In the summer of 2017—ahead of the 2018 elections—the parliamentary majority adopted an amendment of Act LXXIV of 2016 on the protection of the landscape.[29] On its face, the law has nothing to do with political campaigns. Yet its new § 11/G prohibits parties ('organisations supported from the central budget') to advertise under a certain listed price beyond the period of election campaigns.

The new provisions clearly target opposition parties, especially Jobbik, which was supported at the 2018 elections by an investor owning several billboards. The

---

[26]Officially: Act VI. of 2018 on the amendment of certain law related to the measures against illegal immigration.

[27]§ 353/A of Act C of 2012 on the Criminal Code. It must be noted that according to the general rules of Hungarian criminal law, intentional crimes can only be committed deliberately: See Blaskó (2016). Therefore, it is not that easy to condemn someone according to this provision: it has to be proven before the court that the accused person exactly knew that the migrant he helped was safe in his home country or during his journey.

[28]New § 46/F of Act XXXIV of 1994 on the police.

[29]Act CIV of 2017.

governing Fidesz, however, can easily avoid the scope of this law by labelling its advertising as 'government information' instead of party campaigning.[30] The reason why this provision had to be implemented through the law on landscape protection was the fact that at that time Fidesz did not have the two-thirds majority in parliament. Both the election procedure—including the rules of campaigning—and party financing must be regulated through cardinal laws that require the support of the two-thirds majority of attending MPs.[31] So Fidesz bypassed its 'own' Basic Law by hiding the rules in a piece of ordinary legislation that could be adopted with simple majority.

Besides these examples, several laws have been made to favour 'friends', to make them eligible to certain positions[32] or to benefit them otherwise. The content of such *lex friends* may change according to who the friend is, and which position he holds. For example, the company called MAHIR was owned by an oligarch who had been an old friend of the Prime Minister: MAHIR owned several billboards in the country. A concurrent company, the ESMA owned smaller advertisements on electricity poles along the roads. In order to influence the competition between both companies, the government amended the law on road traffic and prohibited advertising on electricity poles and similar objects.[33] However, the Prime Minister broke with said friend and competition was immediately restored. After another government-friendly oligarch purchased the ESMA, the law was changed again allowing to advertise on objects along the roads with permission.[34] Further, a lex friend has been introduced, that may be applied flexibly to any friendly businesses if needed. A specific exception was added to the law on the prohibition of unfair commercial practices and of restriction of competition in 2013. The general rule prescribed that corporate mergers concerning companies whose annual turnover exceeded 15 billion HUF (47–48 million EUR) in total, were bound to take permission from the Competition Authority. The new exception rule made it possible for the government

[30]See e.g. decision no. 647/2018 of the National Election Office. The Office argued that basically, the 'information campaign of the government' should not be able to be confused with the campaign of the ruling party. However, in the concrete case, the massive anti-immigration 'government information' was not found to be such intervention to the election campaign—even if it happened only 8 days before the day of the election. The law was challenged before the Constitutional Court by opposition parties but the Court found no violation of the constitution. The Constitutional Court argued that the law in question did not regulate a cardinal subject because in fact, it did not change the normative content of the law on the functioning and management of parties. That law (Act XXXIII of 1989) is also cardinal and it sets up the elements of the asset of a party (§ 4). See AB decision no. 3001/2019. (I. 7.), ABH 2019, 35, especially para. 68 et seq.

[31]Art. VIII of the Basic Law, § 354 of Act XXXVI of 2014 on the election procedure.

[32]The news portal Index collected many of them: https://index.hu/belfold/2012/06/04/lexek/. Beyond these examples, the so called 'lex Mocsai' is worth to be added. Namely Act XXXVI. of 2014 on the amendment of certain education laws prescribed (in its § 39) that Olympic medals count to be equal to an academic PhD in the higher education of sport: a month later, ex-trainer of the national water polo team, Lajos Mocsai became the rector of the University of Physical Education.

[33]§ 7 (3b) of Act CXIX of 2012 on amending certain laws related to the traffic.

[34]§ 1 of LXXXVII of 2015 on amending certain laws related to the traffic.

to qualify certain mergers to be of strategical importance: such mergers do not have to be reviewed by the Competition Authority.[35] Since then, this exception has been used several times: for the first time, in the same year, through a two-step privatisation of the biggest savings bank Takarékbank.[36]

In light of these examples, one thing becomes clear: these laws are targeted. Some have a wider, some have a narrower scope but the intention behind them is always the same: to punish the enemies or favour the friends of the government. Legislation designed to target individuals is not a new feature in the Hungarian legal system.[37] A good example for this is the CEU itself which was recognised by a distinct law in 2004 by the then socialist government.[38]

Yet, individually designed legislation is always problematic because the rule of law requires laws to be general, applying to subjects in an undifferentiated manner.[39] Therefore, it is questionable whether laws that genuinely apply only to a distinct scope of individuals, institutions or companies fulfil these essential requirements. Even more dangerous are laws, which pretend to have general effect but are designed in a way that they *de facto* apply only to a circumscribed circle of people. This is the common feature of the recent *lex friends* and *lex enemies* which became everyday practice of Hungarian politics. They became the 'silver bullets' for resolving almost any problem. This is one of the most important systemic rule of law problems in Hungary now—even if it has not been acknowledged by the EU institutions as a general pattern.

2.2 *Unrestrained Constitutional Amendments*

Even more alarming, however, are the developments at the constitutional level. The amendment of the constitution is relatively easy in the Hungarian unicameral parliamentary system: it simply requires the two-thirds majority of all MPs.[40] With regard to the Hungarian mixed election system,[41] however, it was not expected that one single party could obtain such an overwhelming majority. In this sense, the two thirds majority requirement seemed to be a proper guarantee for political

[35]§ 24/A of Act LVII of 1996 on the prohibition of unfair commercial practices and of restriction of competition.

[36]The case was especially delicate because smaller savings banks were forced by law (Act no. CXXXV of 2013) to integrate into that Takarékbank, but their constitutional complaint against that law remained unsuccessful for the most part: see AB decision no. 20/2014 (VII. 3).

[37]In details Erdős (2013), pp. 47–56.

[38]Act LXI. of 2004 on the recognition of the Central European University.

[39]Similarly Erdős (2013), p. 55.

[40]Art. S of the Fundamental Law. The majority requirement has not changed with the new constitution, see § 24 (3) of Act XX of 1949 on the constitution of the Republic of Hungary (in effect until 31. December 2011).

[41]About the half of MPs are elected in constituencies, and the other half from party lists.

compromises. The situation changed in 2010 when—due to the scandalous governance of the socialists—the right-conservative Fidesz gained a two-thirds majority alone. After this victory, the Fidesz party did not feel obliged to prescribe stricter rules for amendments of the constitution.

To the contrary: the governing party used its overwhelming power for amending the constitution with controversial provisions several times. Some of these new provisions had even been annulled by the Constitutional Court previously.[42] The probably most notorious of these amendments, was the Fourth Amendment to the Fundamental Law in April 2013. As a result of this amendment, the government implemented significant parts of the so called 'transitional provisions' to the Fundamental Law. These provisions had formerly been annulled by the Constitutional Court because they would have introduced some 'actually not transitional' provisions into the constitution. The Court had also pointed out that the 'transitional provisions' were neither parts of the constitution nor constitutional amendments: they were in the 'no men's land of public law'.[43]

Further, the Fourth Amendment concerned topics like the possibility of levying taxes to finance obligations stemming from judgments of the Constitutional Court or of international courts, the National Judicial Office's president's right to reallocate cases,[44] the introduction of the concept of 'dignity of communities' as a special limit to the freedom of speech,[45] and the possibility of local governments to penalize homeless people if they live on the streets.[46] Some of these laws had earlier—as ordinary legislation—been declared void by the Constitutional Court[47] or were pending before the Court at that time.[48] Further, point 5 of the closing provisions to the Fourth Amendment states: 'the decisions of the Constitutional Court taken prior to the entry into force of the Fundamental Law are repealed'. The reason for

[42]The first over constitutionalisation of the Fidesz government happened under the old constitution yet. After the Constitutional Court annulled the introduced 98% special tax on redundancy payments in the public sector, the Fidesz-majority amended the old constitution and explicitly allowed that and also limited the competences of the Constitutional Court in financial matters. See AB decision no 184/2010 (X. 28) (ABH 2010, 1161) and §§ 1-2 of Act CXIX of 2010 on the amendment of Act XX of 1949 on the Constitution of the Republic of Hungary. The rate of the tax was decreased to 75% at the end of 2013, and after the third election victory resulting in two third majority, the Fidesz-majority of the parliament silently terminated this extra tax (§§ 41-42 of Act XLI of 2018 on the amendment of certain laws about taxation and on the immigration tax).

[43]AB decision no. 45/2012 (XII. 29.), (Magyar Közlöny [Official Journal] 184/2012, p. 38979).

[44]These two provisions have been later abolished by the Fifth Amendment of the Fundamental Law in September 2013.

[45]Art. IX (5) of the Fundamental Law. Since then, the seventh amendment codified an explicit prohibition.

[46]Art. XXII (3) of the Fundamental Law.

[47]See e.g. AB decision no. 38/2012 (XI. 14.) (ABH 2012, 185) on the unconstitutionality of criminalising homelessness, AB decision no. 6/2013 (III. 1.) (ABH 2013, 194) on the unconstitutionality of the regulation of churches.

[48]See e.g. AB decision no. 36/2013 (XII. 5.) (ABH, 2013, 1045) on the 'case transfer' within the judiciary.

this provision was that the Court often followed its former case law even after the Fundamental Law entered into force, at least in cases when the affected provision of the Fundamental Law and of the old constitution were the same or very similar.[49] However the Court interpreted the newly amended closing provisions very creatively: it pointed out that point 5 of the closing provisions only gave the Court the *opportunity*, not to refer to its former decisions even if the affected rules and the context are the same.[50]

In order to overcome any restrictions and constitutional checks placed upon the government by the Constitutional Court, the Fidesz government established a strategy of 'over-constitutionalisation'. Namely, after the Court declared ordinary laws to be unconstitutional, the two-thirds majority simply 'solved the problem' by amending the respective provision of the constitution. Since the Constitutional Court cannot review the substance of constitutional amendments,[51] constitutional checks and balances are in fact disabled. Further these constitutional amendments concern topics, which would normally be considered to be a matter of ordinary law. As such they lead to an inflated, trivialized constitutional law—to an 'over-constitutionalisation'. The consequences of this development for the Hungarian constitutional architecture are difficult to foresee.

Recently, this practice can be further illustrated with the seventh constitutional amendment. The Hungarian government has been a strict opponent of the EU migration policy and especially of the Council decision no. 2015/1601 on the relocation of 120,000 asylum applicants. While the government challenged this decision before the CJEU, the Hungarian Commissioner for Fundamental Rights initiated proceedings before the Hungarian Constitutional Court, practically requesting an ultra vires- and fundamental rights review. The motion was pending before the HCC when the Hungarian government decided to hold a referendum on the 'EU migrant quota system' (without an explicit legal basis).[52] Since the turnout remained under 50%, the referendum was legally invalid.[53] In order to make it 'valid', the prime minister initiated a constitutional amendment in the autumn of 2016. Alongside the prohibition of settling 'foreign population' in Hungary, the amendment would have introduced an obligation for all state bodies to respect the constitutional identity of Hungary—without, however, defining this concept. This explicit reference to constitutional identity was obviously aimed at challenging the authority of EU law. Further, the constitution's EU-clause was intended to be

[49]See primarily AB decision no. 22/2012 (V. 11) (Magyar Közlöny [Official Journal, 52/2012, p. 9737), para. 40.

[50]AB decision no. 13/2013 (VI. 17) (Magyar Közlöny [Official Journal], 98/2013, p. 54958), para. 31.

[51]See on this under Sect. 2.3.2.

[52]It makes no sense to hold a national referendum on an issue ruled by EU law: neither it is foreseen by the Hungarian constitution as it allows referendums only in questions which belong to the competence of the Hungarian National Assembly. See Art. 8 of the Hungarian Fundamental Law.

[53]According to Art. 8 (4) of the Fundamental Law, a referendum is valid if the number of valid votes exceed 50% of all citizens eligible to vote.

amended so as to make the 'joint exercise of competences' subject to the fundamental rights and freedoms guaranteed by the Hungarian Fundamental Law and without limiting Hungary's sovereign right to command its population, territory and state order.[54] Yet, this amendment failed because by that time the governing party did not hold the needed two-thirds majority anymore. After Fidesz regained a two-thirds majority in spring 2018, the seventh constitutional amendment[55] was placed on the agenda again—this time with success. The amendment did not only provide for the constitutionality of the aforementioned 'Stop Soros' package on facilitating 'illegal migration'.[56] It further concerned the law on the administrative courts,[57] the new law on the freedom of assembly[58] and the criminalisation of homelessness. Concerning the latter it not only established the possibility to ban habitual residence at public spaces by local governments' decrees[59] but generally prohibits it at the constitutional level.[60] In addition, the rules on the EU-clause and the reference to the obligation of all state bodies to respect constitutional identity have been codified at the

[54]Draft legislation no. T/12458. The text is available in Hungarian at the website of the National Assembly.

[55]The consolidated version of the Fundamental Law after the seventh amendment is available in official English translation at: www.njt.hu/translated/doc/TheFundamentalLawofHungary_20181015_FIN.pdf.

[56]The new Art. XIV of the Fundamental Law now stipulates that foreign population cannot be settled in Hungary and the basic rules of granting asylum and asylum procedure must be defined by cardinal law. That means that an eventual future easing on the asylum rules will require a two thirds majority in the parliament. Further, it has been codified on the constitutional level that those who arrived through a safe third country, are not eligible to get asylum (this last point is codified also in the German Basic Law anyway: see Article 16a (2) GG). The 'Stop Soros' anti migration package was published in the official journal on the same day than the seventh constitutional amendment. See Act VI. of 2018 on the amendment of certain laws related to measures against illegal immigration.

[57]The constitutional amendment established the constitutional basis of a distinct system of administrative courts with the Administrative High Court on the top of it (new Article 25 of the Fundamental Law). See also Act CXXX of 2018 on the administrative courts. After the European elections of 2019, the government decided to delay the entering into force of this law for an indefinite period. The reason behind is most probably political: Fidesz still wants to stay in the European People's Party—where its membership has been suspended because of concerns over the rule-of-law-conformity of their governance—and therefore they made a gesture to show some willingness for a compromise.

[58]Art. VI of the Fundamental Law has been amended with a sentence with regard to the collision of privacy rights and of the freedom of expression and assembly. Namely, 'exercising the right to freedom of expression and assembly shall not impair the private and family life and home of others.' less than a month later, on the 20th of July 2018, the parliament adopted the new law on the freedom of assembly. The new law makes it possible to ban an assembly if it is likely to violate others' right to privacy and family, or to human dignity. (§ 13 (4) of Act LV of 2018 on the freedom of assembly.).

[59]As it had been the case since the fourth amendment which overruled AB decision no. 38/2012 (XI. 14.) (MK 2012/25417).

[60]Art. XXII (3) of the Fundamental Law as amended through the seventh amendment. In effect since 15. October 2018.

constitutional level.[61] This latter part of the amendment is especially interesting because it perfectly illustrates how the role and significance of the Constitutional Court has changed. Namely, through implementing these provisions into the constitution, an earlier decision of the Constitutional Court has not been overruled, but on the contrary, confirmed.

2.3 *The Constitutional Court: Still a Counterbalance or, Already an Ally of the Government?*

The significant event between the first attempt for the seventh constitutional amendment and its adoption in its final form was a judgment of the Constitutional Court. A few weeks after the planned constitutional amendment introducing the notion of constitutional identity in the constitution failed in autumn 2016, the Constitutional Court delivered a decision on the aforementioned motion of the Commissioner for Fundamental Rights concerning the Council decision on refugee-quotas.[62] In that judgment, the Court established the possibility of an identity review of EU law (without being asked on such a review competence). Until then, the concept of constitutional identity had no significance in the case law of the Constitutional Court.[63] The Court recycled the German case law on the matter, however in a rather selective way without clearly defining the content of this constitutional identity.[64]

The decision perfectly shows how the attitude of the Constitutional Court towards the government has changed in the last couple of years. Indeed, the case illustrates how the initial relationship between the Court and the government has been reversed: initially, the government tried to circumvent decisions of the court striking down ordinary laws through constitutional amendments. After the governing party lost its constitution-amending majority in the parliament, the Court presented itself as an institution compensating the government's lack of majority by constitutional interpretation. The Court substituted the requirement of two thirds majority through constitutional interpretation.

---

[61] New Art. E and the Preamble of the Fundamental Law as amended.

[62] AB decision no. 22/2016 (XII. 5.) (ABH 2016, 1418).

[63] The concept occurred only once, in the parallel reasoning of (then constitutional judge, now justice minister) László Trócsányi to the Lisbon-decision (AB decision no. 143/2010 (VII. 14.), (ABH 2010, 872). Since then, the concept has only been referred by Fidesz-appointed constitutional judges at the Fide Congress in the spring of 2016—when the motion of the ombudsman was already pending before the Court. See the speeches of András Zs. Varga and Tamás Sulyok at the XXVII. FIDE Congress. See Varga Zs (2016), pp. 9–10; Sulyok (2016), p. 40.

[64] There is only an illustrative list of the elements of constitutional identity in the decision with e.g. rights and freedoms, separation of powers, republican state form, parliamentarism, equality, protection of ethnic minorities. The rule of law is lacking from the list. AB decision no. 22/2016 *supra* note 62, para. 65. For a detailed critical analysis of the judgment see Bakó (2018), pp. 863–902.

The push for the seventh amendment of the Fundamental Law shows, however, that the government still does not regard the Court as a 'trustworthy' ally. A portion of the seventh amendment secured the constitutionality of some reforms in the event that the Court's helpful attitude should change. On the other hand, the amendment, concerning the EU clause and the question of constitutional identity, illustrates the misgivings that the government still harbours regarding the Constitutional Court. Safe is only what is codified in the constitution—that is the general strategy of the Fidesz-government.

The changed relationship between the parliamentary majority and the Constitutional Court is easier to understand by analysing the changed composition and competences of the Court and the new strategies applied by the Court in its everyday practice.

2.3.1 Filling the Court with Fidesz-Loyalist Judges

Constitutional judges are elected with two thirds majority of the parliament. This has not changed since 1990. However, prior to 2010, candidates used to be proposed by a parity-based committee comprising of all parliamentary groups. Therefore, even if a government had a supermajority in the parliament, a compromise with the opposition would have been required concerning the candidates.

In July 2010, Fidesz with their supermajority amended the old constitution to ensure that the composition of the committee represents the power relations in the parliament.[65] Since then, no compromise has been needed—at least as long as the governing parties had a supermajority. In September 2011, the number of the constitutional judges was raised from eleven to fifteen and their mandate was extended from 9 to 12 years.[66] Between 2010 and 2013, eight constitutional judges had been appointed exclusively with the votes of the Fidesz. By spring 2013, Fidesz-appointed judges had a majority in the Court. In autumn 2014, three further judges were elected by the Fidesz-MPs.[67] While Fidesz temporarily lost its two-third majority in February 2015, the term of some judges expired. In order to not jeopardize the Court's pro-Fidesz attitude by electing judges of a different political orientation, the Court was left to operate with 11 judges instead of 15 for months and the election of new constitutional judges was not even put on the agenda of parliament for some time. Finally, in autumn 2016, the parliament elected four

[65] § 32/A (5) of the old constitution as amended on the 5th of July 2010.

[66] Act LXI of 2011 on the amendment to the (old) constitution, § 3; Act LXII. of 2011 on the amendment to the (old) Act on the Constitutional Court (Act XXXII. of 1989), § 1 (2). New Fundamental Law Art. 24 (8) and the new Act on the Constitutional Court (Act CLI of 2011), § 6 (3)—both have been in force since 1. January 2012.

[67] In his empirical analysis focusing on the period between 2010 and 2014, Zoltán Szente pointed out that the level of political adaptation of the majority of the constitutional judges was surprisingly high. In details see Szente (2016), p. 66.

new judges with the support of the green party. However, this could not significantly change the balance and the attitude of the Court.

2.3.2 Limiting Constitutional Review in Important Cases

Concerning the powers of the Court, two problematic points must be emphasized. First, substantive review of constitutional amendments has been explicitly excluded.[68] Neither the old constitution nor the original version of the new Fundamental Law contained any reference to the substantive review of constitutional amendments. Yet the Constitutional Court generally considered itself not competent for such a review.[69] From 2011 on, it has happened several times that constitutional amendments have been introduced to incorporate provisions that had been formerly invalidated by the Constitutional Court. As described above,[70] the government acting through parliamentary supermajority amended the constitution incorporating several provisions that were previously declared invalid. While the Constitutional Court theoretically had the chance to take an activist step by changing its former case law and review constitutional amendments on their substance, the Fourth Amendment erased the Court's discretion in this regard. The Fourth Amendment of the Fundamental Law explicitly prohibits the Constitutional Court to substantially review constitutional amendments by limiting judicial review of constitutional amendments to *procedural* aspects alone.[71] Absent any other constitutional guarantees limiting the amending power of the parliament, these constraints placed on the Constitutional Court raise substantial concerns. Since constitutional amendments are also excluded subjects for referendums,[72] neither the Constitutional Court nor the people have any direct control over how the two thirds majority in parliament amends the constitution.

Second the new Fundamental Law restricted the competence of the Constitutional Court regarding the review of acts concerning public revenue and expenditure. Until the state debt exceeds 50% of the GDP, the Constitutional Court may review the Act

[68]Art. 24 (5) of the constitution stipulates: 'The Constitutional Court may review the Fundamental Law or the amendment of the Fundamental Law *only* in relation to the procedural requirements laid down in the Fundamental Law for making and promulgating it.' (My italics).

[69]For details see e.g. Jakab and Szente (2009), para 117; Bakó (2017), pp. 105–108.

[70]See Sect. 2.2.

[71]See the present Art. 24 (5) of the Fundamental Law. The Commissioner for Fundamental Rights made a motion against the Fourth Amendment, arguing that the amendment caused inner contradictions within the constitution. However, the Court declared its lacking competence for the review of the constitutional amendment, referring to the terms of the constitution as amended through the amendment subject to that review, see AB decision no. 12/2013 (V. 24.) (ABH 2013, 390).

[72]Holding a referendum about constitutional questions is now explicitly excluded by Art. 8 of the Fundamental Law: under the old constitution, it was an unwritten taboo, established and consequently reaffirmed by the Constitutional Court. See primarily AB decisions no. 2/1993 (I. 22.) and 25/1999 (VII. 7.).

on State Budget and other acts related to public finances only if they violate human dignity or other enumerated fundamental rights.[73] Some authors consider this rule to be a 'dishearteningly materialistic reading of constitutionalism' as it practically means the suspension of the rule of law until a certain debt is reached[74] implying that the constitution is not necessarily the highest law anymore.[75] On a theoretical level, such criticism is right and well founded, especially taking into account the circumstances. The taboo of reviewing financial laws has been a part of the strategy of 'over-constitutionalisation', described above. After the Constitutional Court struck down a law that levied a 98% tax on certain severance payments in the public service,[76] the old constitution was amended in order to allow levying special taxes on remunerations 'received against the good morals' *retroactively*.[77] Further, the aforementioned limitation of the Constitutional Court's competences concerning laws related to the central budget, was introduced.[78] Following this new restriction, constitutional complaints in financial and economic matters have mostly been rejected in their entirety or to a large extent.[79] However, these complaints were not necessarily rejected on the grounds of lack of jurisdiction but because the respective limitations of fundamental rights were not unnecessary and disproportional.[80]

2.3.3 New Strategies of the Constitutional Court: Shifting Away from the Control of the Legislative

In light of the changes to the competences and composition of the Court, a crucial question relates to if and how the attitude of the institution has evolved. Although

---

[73] Art. 37 (4) of the Fundamental Law. The state debt was 77.6% of the GDP at the beginning of 2012—as the Fundamental law entered into force. According to the last data of the Hungarian Central Statistical Office, the debt was 73.3% in 2017 (http://www.ksh.hu/docs/hun/xftp/stattukor/edp/edp181024.pdf). So, this restriction probably will remain in place for a while.

[74] Vincze and Varju (2012), p. 451.

[75] Halmai (2012), p. 1082.

[76] AB decision no. 184/2010. (X. 28), ABH 2010, 1161.

[77] § 70/I (2) of the old constitution as amended. At the same time it must be seen, especially in the EU-context, that national constitutional courts and the effectiveness of national constitutional principles are often limited by EU-law and by measures of EU institutions in the field of financial legislation. See the *OMT* case (BVerfG, 2 BvR 2728/13, *OMT* and CJEU, Case C-62/14 *Gauweiler*, ECLI:EU:C:2015:400) and the PSPP case (BVerfG, 2 BvR 859/15, *PSPP* and CJEU, Case C-493/17 *Weiss*, ECLI:EU:C:2018:1000).

[78] In details see e.g. Sonnevend et al. (2015), pp. 94–95.

[79] Gárdos-Orosz (2016), p. 444.

[80] See e.g. AB decision no. 20/2014 (VII. 3.) (MK 91/2014, 10918) regarding the integration of cooperative banks and AB decision no. 3194/2014 (VII. 15.) (ABH 20/2014, 991) regarding the commerce of tobacco products. For an overview of the Constitutional Court's case law on budgetary matters see Tilk (2014).

there are some positive examples in the Court's latest case law related to fundamental rights[81] and the rule of law,[82] two relevant tendencies can be identified.

First, the Court has distanced itself from politically relevant questions. As the abstract norm control has been subsequently displaced by concrete forms of judicial review, primarily by the newly established constitutional complaint, the focus has shifted from the constitutional review of *legislation* towards the constitutional review of the *application* of the law.[83] Thus, the role of the Constitutional Court in the system of checks and balances has changed profoundly.[84] The Court is no real counterweight to the parliament anymore. A recent example is the judgment on the penalisation of homelessness, established by the seventh amendment to the constitution. Finding first that the newly introduced offence was constitutionally valid, the Court established a constitutional requirement for the practical application of the relevant paragraph. In order to comply with the aim of this constitutional prohibition, respectively the integration of homeless people into the social care system, § 178/B of the Act on Offences may only be applied if the affected person can be provided with accommodation at the time the offence was committed.[85] However, the Court did not even discuss the question of whether the penalisation itself was a proportional tool for the implementation of the constitutional prohibition. The Court decided to avoid any conflict with parliament by annulling the law. Instead, it left the law in force and only modified its interpretation in light of constitutional requirements.

Second, even when the Court adjudicates on the validly of a piece of legislation and finds it to be contrary to the constitution, it has been cautious to strike it down and applied a more lenient approach.[86] Instead of annulling a law, it often prescribes constitutional requirements for the law's interpretation by ordinary courts. This happens even in politically significant matters or cases concerning fundamental rights.[87] Further, the timing of the decisions (in relation to politically important events, like referendums or elections) might also have significant impact (see e.g. the constitutional identity decision discussed above).

---

[81] In December 2017, the Court ruled that it is an obligation for the parliament to decide on the status on churches within a reasonable time and ordered the legislator to establish proper guarantees in order to keep the 60 days deadline. See decision no 36/2017. (XII. 29.), ABH 2018, 2. Another recent case concerned media freedom: a CC judgment delivered at the end of 2017 made clear that a medium is not liable for the violation of personality rights if it was covering a press conference. AB decision no. 34/2017. (XII. 11.), ABH 2017, 2058.

[82] The Constitutional Court annulled some parts of an order of the president of the National Judicial Office because it foresaw unconstitutional sanctions against judges, moreover, without the right of appeal. AB decision no. 33/2017. (XII. 6.), ABH 2017, 2031.

[83] For empirical data see Gárdos-Orosz (2016), pp. 448–452.

[84] Orbán (2016), pp. 7–9.

[85] AB decision no. 19/2019 (VI. 18.), ABH 2019, 1052, paras. 105–110.

[86] Gárdos-Orosz (2016), p. 449.

[87] Id. See also Halmai (2015), p. 146.

Finally, many sensitive cases are still pending before the Court—like the NGO law and the 'lex CEU', which are both subject to an infringement procedure and therefore (questionably) suspended by the Constitutional Court with the probable motivation of avoiding any conflict with the government.[88]

3 Why Infringement Procedures Are Ineffective in the Case of Hungary

Currently, the only judicial tool of enforcing EU values compliance is the infringement action. However, this procedure is intended to enforce compliance with EU law concerning rather specific matters, instead of addressing systemic rule of law deficiencies. This problem is also illustrated by the infringement actions launched against Hungary in the past few years related to EU values. Although Hungary did *de facto* not comply with the CJEU's decisions in some of the cases, the respective issues were regarded as solved. In this section, I will briefly discuss the infringement proceedings regarding some of the above-mentioned targeted laws. It is important to recall that 'rule of law' deficiencies in Hungary arise from the whole gamut of constitutional malfunctions on one hand and the system of targeted legislation on the other. Therefore, individual infringement procedures against some selected pieces of targeted legislation cannot solve the problem, even if the Hungarian government fully complies with the decisions of the CJEU.

3.1 CJEU Judgments Being Fully or Partly Ignored

In the case concerning the premature termination of the data protection ombudsman's term of office, the European Commission initiated an infringement procedure based on a violation of the Data Protection Directive (95/46/EC). The Hungarian government argued that the directive required independence in an operational sense[89] which had not been violated by the personal and institutional changes.

The CJEU delivered its decision in April 2014 dismissing Hungary's plea. According to the Court, the threat of a premature termination of the term of office 'could lead it to enter into a form of prior compliance with the political authority, which is incompatible with the requirement of independence'.[90] It stated that merely preserving the operational independence of the president of the new Data Protection

[88]See Sect. 2.1.4 above.

[89]95/46/EC directive, Art. 28 (1).

[90]CJEU, Case C-288/12 *Commission v. Hungary*, ECLI:EU:C:2014:237, para. 54.

Authority was not enough[91] and the reorganisation of the institutional framework was not sufficient ground for the termination of the ombudsman's term without applying proper transitional measures.[92] The status of the Data Protection Authority has not been changed since the judgment.

Regarding the new retirement rules applying to judges, the government has shown some readiness for compromise and recommended raising the retirement age to 65 from the originally intended 62. The Commission did not accept that and initiated an accelerated infringement procedure.

Simultaneously, the Hungarian Constitutional Court also examined the question and ruled in July 2012 that the regulation was violative of judicial independence and thus unconstitutional. The Hungarian Constitutional Court knew that a parallel infringement procedure was in progress. As such, the Constitutional Court could challenge the government without taking any risk[93] and voided the law retroactively.[94]

The decision of the CJEU in the infringement procedure, delivered 4 months later examined the case as pertaining to a question of discrimination under Directive 2000/78. The CJEU ruled that the Hungarian regulation violated the directive[95] without, however, basing its decision on the requirement of judicial independence.[96]

Following these rulings, the laws on the status of judges (and of prosecutors and notaries too) have been amended: affected judges had to choose whether they wanted to retire or continue assuming their office. Such decisions were also motivated by a legal amendment according to which those judges who do not want to return to service were eligible to compensation in the amount of 12 months remuneration.[97]

[91] Id., para. 51.

[92] Id., para. 61.

[93] For a comparative analysis of the judgments of the CJEU and of the Hungarian Constitutional Court, see Vincze (2013), pp. 330–333. Of course, normally, a constitutional court would not have to take any risk in cases like that but in Hungary, the government's recent practice shows that it is likely to amend the constitution with the content of laws which has been just annulled by the Constitutional Court.

[94] AB decision no. 33/2012. (VII. 17) (MK [official journal] 2012, 13918). The meanwhile retired judges did not get back to office automatically, but they had to claim an action before the Labour Court—many of them decided rather not to do that.

[95] CJEU, Case C-286/12 *Commission v. Hungary*, ECLI:EU:C:2012:687. The Court did not take into account that the Hungarian Constitutional Court meanwhile annulled the provisions in question because that happened after the start of the infringement procedure.

[96] Interestingly, the case law of the CJEU had changed significantly within a couple of years. In the very similar case of sending Polish Supreme Court judges into retirement, the CJEU's dismissing judgment, delivered in June 2019, was primarily based on the principle of judicial independence and to Art. 19 (1) TEU. CJEU, C-619/18 *Commission v. Poland*, ECLI:EU:C:2019:531, paras. 96, 124.

[97] § 323/I (6) of Act XX of 2013 on certain legal amendments related to the age limit in certain positions in the justice system.

Thus, many judges were not reinstated into their former, leading positions.[98] Further, they must still retire by reaching the general retirement age of 65 years.[99] To sum up, the initial situation has not fully been restored. Further, other threats to judicial independence, like the controversial appointment practice of the president of the National Judicial Office,[100] have not even been addressed by infringement procedures.[101]

3.2 *Infringement Cases Regarding the NGO Law and the Lex CEU*

In parallel to the procedure before the Hungarian Constitutional Court, the European Commission launched an infringement procedure concerning the NGO law. The ECJ ruled in June 2020 that the law represented unjustified restrictions to the free movement of capital and to the right to privacy, data protection and the freedom of association as guaranteed by the EU Charter of Fundamental Rights.[102]

Further, the 'Stop Soros package' has been subject to an infringement procedure since July 2018. The procedure is based on a twofold argument. First, the Commission criticises the non-compliance with the Asylum Procedures Directive, the Asylum Qualifications Directive and the Reception Conditions Directive by criminalising the support for asylum applications and by introducing a new non-admissibility ground.[103] Second, the Commission challenges the injunction to stay away from the border, arguing that the respective legal provision is contrary to the TFEU, the Charter and the Free Movement Directive because it 'unduly restricts the exercise of free movement rights of EU citizens without due regard for procedural guarantees.' In September 2018, the Hungarian government refused to make any changes to the package.[104]

---

[98]This was also the subject of a complaint of more than 150 judges before the ECtHR. The Strasbourg Court finally dismissed the complaints. In the appendix of the judgment it is apparent that the majority of the applicants accepted the lump-sum compensation for not being reinstated. See *J. B. and others v. Hungary*, ECtHR case no. 45434/12.

[99]See the new § 91 of Act CLXII of 2011 on the Legal Status and Remuneration of Judges (following Act XX of 2013 on amendments regarding the retirement age in certain jurisdictional position).

[100]See Vadász (2018). Meanwhile, the practice of the NJO president has been subject to a preliminary reference, see CJEU, Case C-564/19, *IS*.

[101]The problem, that systemic deficiencies of the independence of the judiciary, are not holistically handled by the CJEU, occurred more clearly in the case of Poland. See e.g. opinion of AG Tanchev in Joined Cases C-585/18, C-624/18 and C-625/18, *A.K.*, para. 147.

[102]Judgment in case no. C-78/18, para 143. ECLI:EU:C:2020:476

[103]See press release no. IP/18/4522.

[104]A kormány válasza az Európai Bizottságnak: marad a Stop Soros [The government's answer to the European Commission: Stop Soros remains].

Concurrently, affected NGOs launched constitutional complaints before the Hungarian Constitutional Court arguing that the introduction of the new offence of 'facilitating illegal migration' unconstitutionally restricted the freedom of association and the freedom of expression. One of these complaints has already been rejected. Nevertheless, the Court seemed to have a rather open attitude towards the case. First, the complaint was not submitted by an affected person (but by an organisation with a more abstract relationship to the contested provision) and without exhausting the ordinary remedies beforehand.[105] Instead of dismissing the case as inadmissible, however, the Court referred to an exceptional rule of the Act on the Constitutional Court[106] and to the HCC's function as a protector of fundamental rights[107] and examined (and eventually rejected the case) on the merits.

Finally, the 'lex CEU' is by far the most problematic case. Generally, education is a Member States' competence. The Commission based its charges on the freedom of establishment and the freedom to provide services with reference to universities from third countries. The applicability of EU law, however, is highly questionable in this case considering that only universities with links to *third countries* are affected.[108] Due to the lack of any *intra-EU* cross-border element, this argument presupposes an extensive interpretation of the freedom of establishment clause: an understanding similar to that adopted in *Ruiz Zambrano.*[109] However, unlike the applicants in the *Zambrano* case, the CEU is a *legal* person and thus could not rely on the 'substance' of Union citizenship under Article 20 TEU. Therefore, the Commission's reference to academic freedom, freedom of education and freedom to conduct a business as guaranteed by the EU Charter of Fundamental Rights raises the question: how can the scope of EU law in the sense of Article 51 (1) of the Charter be triggered? A way to circumvent these problems happened to be WTO law. The CJEU, contrary to its former case law, applied WTO law directly in the case and ruled that Hungary failed to comply with its commitments under the GATS convention and this equals to the failing to fulfil its obligations under EU law. The fact that this convention was an integral part of EU law was found to be enough reason also for the application of the Charter.[110]

---

[105]See §§ 26-27 of Act CLI of 2011 on the Constitutional Court about the requirements of submitting a constitutional complaint.

[106]§ 26 (2) of Act CLI of 2011 on the Constitutional Court regulates the exceptional requirements when constitutional complaints are acceptable also beyond the general conditions. These include cases when the threat of fundamental rights violation is direct and does not require a judicial decision and cases when no remedies are provided. In the case of the amendment of the Criminal Code, neither requirement is fulfilled, so by accepting the complaint, the Constitutional Court obviously made an activist step in the field of individual fundamental rights protection.

[107]AB decision no. 3/2019 (III. 7.), Magyar Közlöny [official journal] 2019, 912, paras. 32–42.

[108]See press release no. IP/17/1952 and MEMO/17/3494.

[109]See e.g. the Zambrano judgment: C-34/09, ECLI:EU:C:2011:124.

[110]Judgment in case no. C-66/18, especially paras 86–93. and 212–215. ECLI:EU:C:2020:792.

The amendment of the Higher Education Law—or, the 'lex CEU' as it is often referred to—is much easier to be challenged under Hungarian constitutional law than under EU law. Unlike the Charter provisions, the academic freedom and freedom of education as guaranteed by the Hungarian constitution undoubtedly apply to the act in question. Further, the legislation arguably violates the principle of the rule of law as guaranteed in Article B) (1) of the Fundamental Law: not only through the tight—although later extended—*vacatio legis*, but also by posing a threat to legal certainty and legitimate expectations. Further, by requiring prior consent of the federal government for agreements with federal states, the law demands the legally impossible.[111] Additionally, if an international agreement is a prerequisite for the further functioning of an accredited university, it practically means that the exercise of academic freedom 'depends on the political discretion of two sovereigns'.[112] This is very problematic regarding both fundamental rights and the rule of law.

Yet the Hungarian Constitutional Court suspended the review of the lex CEU with reference to the pending cases before the CJEU. The strategy of the HCC was probably the following: waiting for the decision of the CJEU and hoping that the lex CEU will get the green light under EU law. That would have been a win-win situation for the HCC: it would have been able to reaffirm the constitutionality of the law and avoid any conflict with the CJEU or the government. The strategy did not work, the CJEU dismissed Hungary. The aforementioned infringement proceedings were directed against specific pieces of targeted legislation, without embedding them in the broader context and evaluating the general practice of personalised legislation. The fact, that 'ordinary' infringement procedures are not suitable to address systemic patterns, has been pointed out by legal scholarship long ago.[113] Yet, the respective proposals have not been implemented in EU legislation or practice.

[111]In detail see the amicus curiae brief of András Jakab, Miklós Lévay, László Sólyom and Zoltán Szente to the Constitutional Court (case no. II/01036/2017). It has to be added that this impossible requirement has already been ignored by the Hungarian Government itself by closing such an agreement with the state of Maryland. See the Agreement between the government of Hungary and the state of Maryland and on cooperation in the field of higher education as promulgated by Act CXIV. of 2017. The agreement provides the further functioning of the McDaniel College in Budapest under the new legal framework. In the agreement, there is no reference to any prior consent of the US federal government.

[112]Uitz (2017).

[113]Scheppele (2013a) and Bárd and Śledzińska-Simon (2019).

4 Making a Try with Article 7: The Sargentini Report on Hungary

As seen above, the infringement procedure as currently operated by the Commission is insufficient for addressing the systemic key issues in Hungary. The following section will analyse whether procedures in the political realm are more apt to challenge the Hungarian rule of law deficiencies.

The first comprehensive political document on the new Hungarian constitutional system and its compatibility with EU values was adopted as early as June 2013: this was the non-binding EP resolution named after its rapporteur Tavares.[114] The report criticised the media situation,[115] the legislation concerning the judiciary and the Constitutional Court,[116] some fundamental rights issues, especially the rules of the recognition of churches,[117] the reform of the election system[118] and not least, the practice of amending the Fundamental Law systematically along political interests, with special regard to its Fourth Amendment.[119] As a reaction to the Tavares report, the Fundamental Law has been amended for the fifth time in September 2013. Some points of criticism have been slightly modified or suspended (like the case transfer within the judiciary or, the possibility of levying special taxes to finance obligations stemming from decisions of the HCC or of international courts). Yet, the main

[114]EP report no. P7_TA(2013)0315.

[115]The most criticised point was the independence of the Media Authority. However, it has been proven in the last years that the media problem is not of an institutional kind. It is rather about the fact that government friendly investors purchase even more formerly independent media platforms and turn them to be loyal to the government or even propagandistic (or they just simply close them, as it happened to the biggest daily newspaper called Népszabadság in October 2016). In detail, see e.g. Bátorfy (2017), pp. 12–13.

[116]See Sects. 2.1.2 and 2.3.2 above on these matters.

[117]The Constitutional Court annulled some earlier versions of the law on churches: AB decisions no 164/2011 (XII. 20) (ABH 2011, 1263) and 6/2013 (II. 26.) (ABH 2013, 334). In its later decisions, it called the government more times for amending the relevant laws, see AB decisions no. 23/2015 (VII. 7.) (ABH 2015, 1043), 36/2017 (XII. 29) (ABH 2018, 2). The ECtHR also dismissed Hungary upon the issue (*Magyar Keresztény Mennonita Egyház and others v. Hungary*, Application Nos. 70945/11 23611/12, 26998/12 et al.). The rules have been changed quite often meanwhile, most recently in November 2018. The basic idea is however the same: there are different categories of churches, and they are recognised by the parliament. Pursuant to the latest amendment, the recognition by the parliament only applies to 'settled churches' while other religious communities will be registered by courts (see Act CXXXII of 2018 on the amendment of Act CCVI of 2011 on the freedom of religion and on the status of churches and other religious communities, especially the new §§ 9/A-9/G).

[118]The new election law (Act CCIII of 2011 on the election of the members of parliament) basically upholds the former mixed system but it has been complemented with a tricky gerrymandering and some unfair rules for the campaign (Section VIII of Act. XXXVI. of 2013 on the election procedure).

[119]More details in Sect. 2.2 above.

problematic points remained in place and the rule of law in Hungary has not improved through this amendment.[120]

4.1 *Getting Lost in Details, Missing the Bigger Picture*

Unfortunately, very little of the deficiencies discussed above were addressed by the Sargentini report adopted in September 2018. This second comprehensive EP resolution on the situation in Hungary triggered an Article 7 TEU procedure[121] and concentrated on 12 issues related mainly to fundamental rights protection[122] and the rule of law.[123] Although the report mentions many relevant deficiencies, it gets lost in irrelevant details and misses the bigger picture.

To name just but a few examples: concerning the Constitutional Court, the Data Protection Authority and judicial independence, mostly the findings of the Tavares report remain repetitive without analysing the recent developments in these fields (points 8–9, 12–18). Related to fundamental rights, the report echoes some partly unfounded criticism concerning the alleged oppression of Roma, Jewish minorities or women (points 59-61, 46).[124] Further issues included in the report relate to media freedom (points 27-30), the secret surveillance for national security purposes without sufficient legal guarantees (points 25–26), the penalization of homelessness (point 73), and violations of the academic freedom, the freedom of assembly and the freedom of expression (points 33–36, 41–45). Furthermore, a new topic took centre stage: corruption. On the one hand, the report correctly mentions cases where OLAF found serious irregularities and possible fraudulent activities related to the spending of EU funds, some of them share links to the family of the prime minister (point 23).[125] On the other hand, the report also discusses irrelevant technical details like MPs asset declarations or the system of campaign financing (points 20–21).

[120]Similarly, Szente (2017), p. 470.

[121]European Parliament resolution of 12 September 2018 on a proposal calling on the Council to determine, pursuant to Article 7(1) of the Treaty on European Union, the existence of a clear risk of a serious breach by Hungary of the values on which the Union is founded (2017/2131(INL)).

[122]Freedom of expression, freedom of association, academic freedom, freedom of religion, privacy and data protection, the right to equal treatment, social rights, rights of asylum seekers.

[123]Functioning of the constitutional system, the independence of the judiciary, corruption.

[124]The most striking false statement is that the Criminal Code does not fully protect women who have been victims of domestic violence (point 46). Actually, a new offense has been introduced already during the governance of the Fidesz, exactly in order to address this problem. See 212/A. § of Act C of 2012 on the Criminal Code.

[125]The company of the son-in-law of the prime minister won public procurement procedures in several towns and villages for the modernisation of street lightings. Many of the procurement tenders were directly designed exactly and exclusively for his company. The Hungarian authorities started an investigation but it was finally cancelled in November 2018. (Hungarian investigative portal Átlátszó wrote about the story in details: https://atlatszo.hu/category/cikkek/eliosaktak/.) It is

Eventually, the report does the Hungarian government a huge favour when dealing exhaustively with Fidesz's old-time campaign topic—migration. Yet even here the report misses the crucial point: the introduction and emphasis by the government on the 'crisis situation caused by mass migration'. This new state of emergency enables the government to apply less guarantees during the asylum application procedures in order to significantly accelerate them.[126] The crisis situation has constantly been prolonged since 2015, even if the legal requirements are clearly not fulfilled.[127] Instead of identifying this obvious and systemic rule of law deficiency, the report rather concentrates on recording statistical data on the detention circumstances and the frequent refusal of appeals (points 62–72). Moreover, by criticising a judgment in a specific criminal case, the report makes the impression of intervening into that case,[128] which is highly questionable with regard to the rule of law itself.

In sum, proper grounds could be found for launching an Article 7 procedure against Hungary, but only a few of them have been identified. And even those elements that have been identified, are not convincingly placed within the system of constitutional malfunctions. The report failed to realise the patterns: neither the tendency of targeted legislation, nor the logic of "over-constitutionalisation" behind some constitutional amendments were identified. Further, relevant arguments are diluted with rather strange and minor, sometimes unfounded allegations:[129] this feeds such counterarguments that portray the report as a purely politically motivated attack. Based on such an ill-founded report, Article 7 will surely remain a tool of political cherry picking, failing to play a serious role in safeguarding the rule of law.

4.2 *Limited Political Relevance*

Despite several shortcomings of the Sargentini report, the Hungarian government decided not to go into a substantial debate on the rule of law or fundamental rights. Instead, the government challenged the report on formal grounds arguing that the

---

worth to recall at this point that the Prosecutor General was elected by the two thirds majority of the parliament and actually, he is an ex-Fidesz member and an old friend of the Prime Minister.

[126]§§ 80/I-J-K of Act LXXX of 2007 on asylum.

[127]Such crisis situation may be announced basically if more than 500 applicants arrive daily in the average of at least a month. This is not the case for a long time according to the statistics, but there is a more flexible rule too- namely, the threatening of the public order in any Hungarian municipality (not necessarily closed to the border). The interpretation and application of this flexible provision belongs to the discretion of the government. See 80/A § of Act LXXX of 2007 on asylum.

[128]That is the case Ahmed H, who has been condemned for 5 years imprisonment because of an 'act of terror' by the Hungarian courts following a riot at the boarder to Serbia. See Article 67 of the report. In January, 2019 he was ordered to be expelled from Hungary.

[129]For example the oppression of LGBT, Jewish or Roma minorities and the lacking protection of women from domestic violence etc.

two thirds majority requirement for the EP voting was not fulfilled because abstentions were not counted as votes cast.[130] After referring to these procedural defects and declaring the Sargentini report as void, there seems to be no place for stepping back and finding compromises. As such, the Sargentini report was an ideal target for the Hungarian government in the campaign before the EP-election of 2019. Fidesz called the Hungarian voters to resist pro-migration EU bureaucrats 'punishing their own border guards': 52.56% of them did so by voting for the Fidesz.

More than two years have passed since the EP adopted the Sargentini report, but the Council still has not made any decision. Only some hearings took place over 2019. This is not a surprise as a similar inertia can be observed with regard to Poland. Nevertheless, rapporteur Sargentini has been eager to keep the issue of Hungary on the agenda of the LIBE committee and to pressure the Romanian Council presidency to table the case during the first half of 2019. In light of the fact that serious concerns have been raised concerning the rule of law in Romania,[131] it is no surprise that the Romanian Council presidency did not hurry up with the Article 7 processes either against Hungary or Poland. It is worth recalling that the Hungarian and Polish governments promised to veto any steps against each-other in the Article 7 procedure.

5 How to Take 'Informed' Measures in Defence of the Union's Values?

Until here, I have tried to illustrate the complexity of the Hungarian developments and also show how insufficient the different processes launched by EU institutions have been. If values are codified normatively—as they are in Article 2 TEU—and rule of law is to be taken seriously, there should be an objective and transparent tool to "measure the unmeasurable".[132] As such, it comes as no surprise that the idea of measuring the rule of law is a matter of increasing importance within the EU institutions nowadays. In this last section, I will briefly outline some recent proposals and point out the difficulties of using indicators to detect systemic rule of law problems.

---

[130]CJEU, Case C-650/18, *Hungary v. Parliament* (pending). The legal situation is not obvious at this point. The Rules of Procedure reads that 'in calculating whether a text has been adopted or rejected, account shall be taken only of votes cast for and against, except in those cases for which the Treaties lay down a specific majority' (Rule 178 (3) RoP). So the question is whether the two thirds majority required by Article 354 (4) TFEU counts as a 'specific majority'.

[131]See EP resolution no. P8_TA(2018)0446.

[132]Cf. Schmitt (1996), p. 3.

5.1 *Measuring, Buying or Monitoring the Rule of Law?*

In October 2016 the European Parliament made a proposal to the Commission[133] to introduce an Interinstitutional Agreement—the European Union Pact on Democracy, the Rule of Law, and Fundamental Rights (DRF Pact). It seemed to be inspired by an earlier academic debate on the 'Copenhagen dilemma' and especially by Jan-Werner Müller's idea of a 'Copenhagen Commission'.[134] The proposal concentrated primarily on two shortcomings of the present system: first, the EP intended to define the Article 2 TEU values by setting up a framework of indicators. Second, it would have provided for the Member States to be assessed regularly by an expert group according to a 'DRF Scoreboard'. A 'DRF policy cycle' was also foreseen to assess the EU institutions.

The draft of the DRF Scoreboard outlined some rather general indicators to measure democracy, rule of law and fundamental rights in the Member States, involving existing expert bodies, civil organisations, EU institutions and not least, national parliaments (Articles 6–8). Depending on the scores of the Member States, the draft proposed initiating different proceedings under the Rule of Law Framework, Article 7 (1) or even 7 (2) TEU. Further, the EP suggested that the Commission launch systemic infringement procedures by bundling several infringement cases together.[135]

Of course there are difficulties: In light of the considerable differences between the systems of the Member States with regard to democracy and rule of law, a comprehensive and detailed list of indicators, which claims validity for *all* Member States, would have been difficult to establish.[136] Further, the proposal mentioned the Charter as the only indicator for fundamental rights: however, that would have meant an extension of the Charter's scope beyond the limits of Article 51 (1).

Yet the proposal had some obvious advantages. Monitoring all Member States (and the EU institutions as well) would certainly be more just and balanced than criticising only some selected 'suspicious' Member States. The DRF proposal would not have changed the current system of EU values enforcement fundamentally in so far as Article 7 TEU would have remained the main and final tool of sanctioning non-compliance with EU values. However, the political process would have been *preceded* by an exhaustive legal analysis: this way, expertise and political considerations could have been better balanced. Unfortunately, the Commission has opted for the usual course and refused to initiate any legislative proposal following the

---

[133]European Parliament resolution of 25 October 2016 with recommendations to the Commission on the establishment of an EU mechanism on democracy, the rule of law and fundamental rights (2015/2254(INL)), 8_TA(2016)0409.[DRF Proposal].

[134]Müller (2016), pp. 206–224.

[135]The systemic infringement action was first advised by Scheppele (2013a).

[136]For details about the methodological questions see e.g. Jakab and Lőrincz (2017).

EP's DRF-proposal.[137] The Commission argued that it had 'serious doubts about the need and feasibility' of setting up such annual reports. Further, the involvement of an expert panel raised 'serious questions of legality, institutional legitimacy and accountability,' and rather, 'best possible use should be made of existing instruments while avoiding duplication', the Commission argued.[138]

These arguments are hypocritical for several reasons. First, the Commission presumes that its own Rule of Law Framework does not pose legality and legitimacy concerns.[139] Second, the Commission is clearly aware of the fact that the existing instruments are not very effective to solve the EU's value crisis, as illustrated by the case of Poland[140] and Hungary.[141] The legality and legitimacy concerns could be allayed exactly if Article 7 would result in *informed* sanctions: and the best way to inform politicians about the legal system of other Member States is a thorough and holistic legal assessment. Further, the judicial dialogue through preliminary proceedings also raised great hopes. Yet, after the LM judgment,[142] it seems that simply triggering an Article 7 procedure against the affected Member State is not enough to generally overcome the present 'horizontal Solange' model[143] operating with exceptions from the mutual trust.

By rejecting the DRF proposal, it seemed that the Commission waived the legal assessment in order to keep inappropriate tools of political threat. This raised the question of whether the Commission's position corresponds to its function as guardian of the Treaties.[144] The proposals on the protection of EU values developed since then, still reflect the need for a thorough legal assessment.

An example for that is the Commission's proposal from 2018 for a regulation to protect 'the Union's budget in case of generalised deficiencies as regards the rule of law in the Member States'.[145] The proposal aims to withhold payments from EU sources in the case of generalised rule of law deficiencies, trying to find the balance

[137]Follow up to the European Parliament resolution on with recommendations to the Commission on the establishment of an EU mechanism on democracy, the rule of law and fundamental rights, adopted by the Commission on 17 January 2017, Ref. no. A8-0283/2016/P8_TA-PROV(2016) 0409.

[138]See the follow up document no. A8-0283/2016, point 6.

[139]See e.g. Skouris (2015), p. 14.

[140]In its third Rule of Law recommendation, the Commission admitted that the situation of a systemic threat to the rule of law in Poland has 'seriously deteriorated' since the start of the process. (Commission recommendation no. C(2017) 5320, point 45). This impression definitely was strengthened after triggering Article 7 TEU against Poland—following that efforts made in the frames of the Rule of Law Framework were useless. (Proposal for a Council decision on the determination of a clear risk of a serious breach by the Republic of Poland of the rule of law (2017/ 0360(APP, especially para. 175).

[141]See Sect. 3.1 above.

[142]Case no. C-216/18 PPU (ECLI:EU:C:2018:586).

[143]Canor (2013), pp. 383–421.

[144]Petra Bárd and Sergio Carrera answer this question obviously for the disadvantage of the Commission. See Bárd and Carrera (2017), pp. 9–10.

[145]A8-0469/2018, procedure no. 2018/0136 (COD).

between the general and systemic rule of law violations and the concrete individual cases of fraud or corruption regarding EU sources. In fact, the proposal of the Commission basically foresees a somewhat similar but much simpler political process than that of the Article 7, to be applied to a narrower circle of problems. The main practical differences are that this process has only one stage, the European Council would not be involved and the required majority in the Council would be much lower. In the first reading of the legislative procedure, the European Parliament suggested that both the consent of the Parliament and of the Council should be needed to approve a transfer proposal for a budgetary reserve.[146]

The problem is that the proposal of the Commission explains only very briefly, what is meant under the 'rule of law' or 'generalised deficiency' of the rule of law, which gives ground to restrict the use of EU funds by the affected Member State. Different aspects of the proper functioning of the judiciary system are set out in the proposal: judicial independence, legal remedies, effective investigation and the implementation of judgments, legal certainty, pluralistic and transparent legislative process, lack of arbitrariness and so on. The proposal defines not only legal acts and measures but also 'widespread and recurrent practices and omissions' as possible sources of a generalised rule of law deficiency (Article 2 b).

However, it was not clear from the original proposal, how the Commission and the Council would find out whether such a practice takes places in a Member State. The European Parliament made an important amendment at this point and suggested setting up an advisory panel composed of independent experts in constitutional law and financial and budgetary matters, appointed by each of the national parliaments and by the European Parliament (new Article 3 a as proposed). The suggestion clearly reflects the idea of the failed DRF proposal[147] but applied only to a narrower field, related to rule of law deficiencies affecting the financial interests of the EU.

Regardless of this ongoing legislative process, the Commission seems to realise that it was a mistake to dismiss the Parliament's DRF Scoreboard. It is hard to find any other reason, why the Commission returned to the basic idea of that scoreboard. Namely, in July 2019, the Commission announced the introduction of a 'Rule of Law Review Cycle' and the publication of an 'Annual rule of law report' in order to prevent 'negative developments' regarding the rule of law in the Member States.[148] Similar to the DRF Scoreboard, all Member States will be subject to this monitoring mechanism, but unlike that scoreboard without a distinct expert panel. Further, the Commission aims at collecting data from existing bodies, also beyond the EU, like the OSCE, the Council of Europe or the EU Fundamental Rights Agency. The reason for that are the Commission's legitimacy and accountability concerns again. In its communication, however, the Commission made clear that 'external expertise cannot take the place of an assessment made by the Commission itself,

---

[146] New Art. 5, paras. 6a-6c as proposed and Art. 5 paras. 7–8 as proposed to be deleted.

[147] See Sect. 5.1 above.

[148] COM(2019) 343 final.

particularly when the Commission's conclusions could be the basis for acts that come with legal and financial consequences'.

The question occurs, why extra-EU expert bodies count automatically as accountable and legitimate in the matter of EU values, and how is it guaranteed that the Commission will make an informed assessment concerning the rule of law in the Member States. The first annual rule of law reports, published in September 2020, unfortunately verified these concerns. In the country report on Hungary, the Commission correctly raised criticism concerning a number of issues, but it failed to point out to the big picture: how the criticised elements will affect the constitutional reality in context.

5.2 *How to Indicate Overlapping Systemic Rule of Law Deficiencies?*

To 'measure' the rule of law, it is clearly not enough to 'simply take the Copenhagen criteria off the legal shelf'.[149] Simple governance checklists do not work either.[150] However, that is not a reason for giving up any attempts to 'measure' the rule of law. Yet, complex indicators should be used instead of checklists. Aggregating the presence or absence of certain institutional structures does not make much sense without taking into account the wider context and the interrelatedness of different aspects within (and beyond) the rule of law.[151]

Several international rule of law indicators exist, which are based on different factors of the rule of law: still, their results usually are almost identical.[152] If the EU wants to set up a rule of law indicator, that will be a ground for sanctions, this must be more than a mere *checklist*. Such a rule of law indicator could only work if it follows a truly holistic approach. The Hungarian example illustrates very well, how many levels of rule of law problems could occur. Particular rule of law problems may affect each other in a way that is extremely difficult to translate into scores and numbers if we work with strictly distinct factors of the rule of law.

For example, targeted legislation seems to be a problem that is relatively easy to detect by assessing to whom a certain law actually applies. Still, the issue becomes more difficult, once the options for constitutional remedies are taken into account. The constitutionality of that targeted law will be reviewed by a Constitutional Court that is composed of judges loyal to the government. Moreover, if the law regulates a financial subject or is part of an 'over-constitutionalisation', it might not be constitutionally reviewed at all. Of course, a weakened Constitutional Court will get lower scores in any system of indicators—but it is questionable whether this lower score

[149]Müller (2017), p. 241.

[150]Scheppele (2013b), p. 562 et seq.

[151]Similarly, Ginsburg (2011), p. 272.

[152]See the empirical analysis of Versteeg and Ginsburg (2017), p. 102 et seq.

properly describes its actual effects on the legal system. Such complex outcomes can hardly be expressed in a score-system based on separate factors.

But there is another side of the coin too: if once a constitutional court gets a lower score because of its restricted competences, to what extent does it make sense to complain further about the method of selecting judges? Namely: if the Court could not decide about anything important, why does it matter that it is composed of government-friendly judges? Of course, the question is simplified in so far that *some* important decisions could surely be made by any constitutional court. Still, if the factors of competence and composition are put in proportion, the final score of a constitutional court will be better balanced.

The correlation and interrelatedness of different factors should not only be measured within the elements of the rule of law (e.g. generality of laws, independence of judges, constitutionalism), but also in the broader context of the state order. For example, it might sound good that two thirds parliamentary majority is needed for appointments for the most important positions and for the amendment of the constitution. But it should also be measured, how easy or how difficult it is to win such a majority in the given election system. By asking this question, we are already beyond the realm of the rule of law, and within the principle of democracy, which is another founding value of the EU. A founding value that seems to be overlooked in the current rule of law debates. And that is a pity for an important reason.

The above-analysed legislative changes are protected by the government always with the same argumentation: they are legitimised by the people to make such reforms and this legitimation does not only establish an opportunity for them, but also an obligation. They must fulfil the people's will by implementing these legislative changes, and anyone who doubts that these reforms comply with the rule of law, actually questions the democratically expressed will of the Hungarian people. As such, they are echoing the idea of 'political constitutionalism' under the slogan of 'illiberal democracy'. However, not only the rule of law, but also the functioning of democracy could convincingly be criticised in Hungary.[153] The difference between the paradigms of legal and political constitutionalism, between the ideas of 'liberal' and 'majoritarian' democracy was perfectly illustrated through the debates on the Hungarian rule of law. EU institutions could be much more successful in these debates if they distanced themselves from the idea of legal constitutionalism and tried to set a trap for Orbán in his own territory by pointing out to some problems of democratic legitimacy beyond (but related to) the strictly understood rule of law concerns.

Such arguments are more effective if they are not echoed (only) by politicians, but they have a solid background. A background that is more than a report made by a MEP who was bound to party bargains, and more than a mere checklist based on scores of *separate* factors. A complex EU-indicator of the rule of law (or more

[153]E.g. the rules of the election procedure and campaigning (see Sect. 2.1.6 and *supra* note 113), restrictions regarding direct democracy (*supra* note 78) and the media situation (*supra* note 110).

broadly, of EU values) can only be set out if it is sensitive to correlations and it is based on legal reality instead of abstract legal possibilities.

Of course, such an indicator will not be a solution for every problem either. It would also be necessary that the Commission repeatedly launches infringement actions if judgments of the CJEU in rule of law related matters are not respected, and it would further be useful if the CJEU would be more eager to systemically scrutinise the rule of law breaches in those processes.[154]

6 Conclusion

As seen above, the Hungarian government works primarily with the instrument of personalised, targeted legislation—this tendency has not been acknowledged in Brussels as one of the main pillars of Hungary's rule of law-deficit. Only some individual pieces of the targeted legal regime reach the thresholds of EU criticism from time to time. The reason for limiting the powers of the Hungarian Constitutional Court was mainly to ensure that the Court does not prevent the introduction of some targeted and politically important laws and constitutional amendments. Ultimately, Hungary has been made subject to an Article 7 procedure. Yet from the Sargentini report it is clear that the rule of law problems of Hungary are only partly captured by the EP: the 'lex CEU' and the 'lex NGO' were the obvious red lines in the eyes of many politicians but they are by far not the most problematic points in the whole constitutional pattern. That pattern could have been identified if EU values would be considered at least worth to be defined—at best, along factors of a scoreboard that takes systemic correlations into account. For Hungary and Poland the purely political Article 7 procedure still awaits—without a minimum of legal certainty provided by clear concepts but with guaranteed political motivations behind the decision. If a final decision comes at all. . .

References

Bakó B (2017) Láthatatlan után inkoherens alkotmány. A korlátlan alkotmánymódosító hatalomról [First invisible, then incoherent constitution. On the unlimited constitution-amending power]. Magyar Jog 2017:2

Bakó B (2018) The Zauberlehrling unchained? The recycling of the German Federal Constitutional Court's case law on identity-, ultra vires- and fundamental rights review in Hungary. ZaöRV 78 (4):863–902

Bárd P, Carrera S (2017) The Commission's decision on 'Less EU' in safeguarding the rule of law: a play in four acts. CEPS Policy Insights 1:8

[154] AG Tanchev already criticised the CJEU's approach followed in the infringement case regarding the Polish Supreme Court. See the opinion of AG Tanchev in Joined Cases C-585/18, C-624/18 and C-625/18, *A.K.*, para 147.

Bárd P, Śledzińska-Simon A (2019) Rule of law infringement procedures A proposal to extend the EU's rule of law toolbox. CEPS Papers in Liberty and Security in Europe, 2019-09

Bátorfy A (2017) Az állam foglyul ejtésétől a piac fogvatartásáig. Orbán Viktor és a kormány médiamodellje 2014 után [From state capture to market capture. The media model of Viktor Orbán and the government]. Médiakutató 2017:1–2

Bellamy R (2007) Political Constitutionalism. A Republican defence of the constitutionality of democracy. Cambridge University Press, Cambridge

Blaskó B (2016) Commentary to § 7 to the Hungarian Criminal Code. In: Polt P (ed) A Büntető Törvénykönyvről szóló 2012. évi C. törvény nagykommentárja [Great Commentary to Act c. of 2012 on the Criminal Code]. Opten, Budapest

Canor I (2013) My brother's keeper? Horizontal Solange: "An ever closer distrust among the peoples of Europe". Common Market Law Rev 50:383. 2

Erdős C (2013) Visszaélés a jogalkotással – avagy egyedi rendelkezések jogszabályba foglalásának alkotmányossági megítélése [Misuse of legislation – assessing the constitutionality of including individual provisions into law]. Diskurzus 2

Gárdos-Orosz F (2016) Alkotmánybíróság 2010-2015 [Constitutional Court 2010-2015]. In: Jakab A, Gajduschek G (eds) A magyar jogrendszer állapota [The state of the Hungarian legal system]. MTA TK, Budapest, p 2016

Ginsburg T (2011) Pitfalls of measuring the rule of law. Hague J Rule Law 3(2):269–280

Glencross A (2014) The absence of political constitutionalism in the EU: three models for enhancing constitutional agency. J Eur Public Policy 21(8):1163–1180

Halmai G (2012) From 'Rule of Law Revolution' to an illiberal democracy in Hungary. In: Sachs M, Siekmann H (eds) Festschrift für Klaus Stern zum. 80. Geburtstag. Duncker & Humblot, Berlin

Halmai G (2015) Pártos alkotmánybíráskodás 2010–2014 [Partisan constitutional jurisdiction 2010–2014]. In: Gárdos-Orosz F, Szente Z (eds) Jog és politika határán. Alkotmánybíráskodás Magyarországon 2010 után [At the border of law and politics. Constitutional jurisdiction in Hungary after 2010]. hvg orac, Budapest

Jakab A, Szente Z (2009) Commentary to paragraph 19 § of the constitution. In: Jakab A (ed) Az Alkotmány kommentárja [Commentary of the Constitution], vol 1. Századvég, Budapest

Jakab A, Lőrincz OV (2017) International indices as models for the rule of law scoreboard of the European Union: methodological issues. Max Planck Institute for Comparative Public Law & International Law (MPIL) Research Paper 21/2017

Kochenov D (2017) Busting the myths nuclear: a commentary on Article 7 TEU. EUI Working Paper Law, 2017/10

Müller J-W (2016) Protecting the rule of law (and Democracy!) in the EU. The idea of a Copenhagen Commission. In: Closa C, Kochenov D (eds) Reinforcing rule of law oversight in the European Union. Cambridge University Press, Cambridge

Müller J-W (2017) A democracy commission of one's own, or what it would take for the EU to safeguard liberal democracy in its member states. In: Jakab A, Kochenov D (eds) The enforcement of EU law and values ensuring member states' compliance. Oxford University Press, Oxford

Orbán E (2016) A bírói döntések ellen benyújtott alkotmányjogi panaszok tapasztalatai [Experiences of constitutional complaints directed against judicial decisions]. Pázmány Law Working Papers, 2016/20

Polyák G, Szőke GL (2011) Elszalasztott lehetőség? Az új adatvédelmi törvény főbb rendelkezései [A missed opportunity? The main provisions of the new data protection law]. In: Drinóczi T (ed) Magyarország új alkotmányossága [The new constitutionality of Hungary]. Pécsi Tudományegyetem Állam- és Jogtudományi Kar, Pécs

Scheppele KL (2013a) What can the European Commission do when member states violate basic principles of the European Union? The case for systemic infringement actions (her proposal is available at the website of the Commission: http://ec.europa.eu/justice/events/assises-justice-2013/files/contributions/45.princetonuniversityscheppelesystemicinfringementaction brusselsversion_en.pdf)

Scheppele KL (2013b) The rule of law and the frankenstate: why governance checklists do not work. Governance 26(4):559–562

Schmitt C (1996) The Tyranny of values. Plutarch Press, Washington DC

Skouris V (2015) Die Rechtsstaatlichkeit in der Europäischen Union [The rule of law in the European Union]. Europarecht Beiheft 2

Sonnevend P, Jakab A, Csink L (2015) The constitution as an instrument of everyday party politics: the basic law of Hungary. In: von Bogdandy A, Sonnevend P (eds) Constitutional crisis in the European constitutional area. Theory, law and politics in Hungary and Romania. Hart Publishing, Oxford

Sulyok T (2016) Erga omnes Effect of Member States' Constitutions and Composite Constitutionality. Fontes Iuris 2016, Special Edition on the FIDE Congress

Szente Z (2016) Die politische Orientierung der Mitglieder des ungarischen Verfassungsgerichts zwischen 2010 und 2014. Jahrbuch für Ostrecht 18(1):45–67

Szente Z (2017) Challenging the basic values – problems in the rule of law in Hungary and the failure of the EU to tackle them. In: Jakab A, Kochenov D (eds) The enforcement of EU law and values. Ensuring member states' compliance. Oxford University Press, Oxford

Tilk P (2014) Az Alkotmánybíróság és a pénzügyi tárgyú törvények vizsgálati lehetősége [The Constitutional Court and its possibility to review financial acts]. Fundamentum 2014:1–2

Uitz R (2017) Academic freedom in an illiberal democracy: From rule of law through rule by law to rule by men in Hungary. Verfassungsblog, 13. October, 2017

Vadász V (2018) Krízis a bírósági igazgatásban? [Crisis in the judiciary administration?]. MTA Law Working Papers 2018/13

Varga Zs A (2016) Final conferral of sovereignty or limited power-transfer?. Fontes Iuris 2016, Special Edition on the FIDE Congress

Versteeg M, Ginsburg T (2017) Measuring the rule of law: a comparison of indicators. Law Soc Inq 42(1):100–137

Vincze A (2013) Der EuGH als Hüter der ungarischen Verfassung – Anmerkung zum Urteil des EuGH 6. 11. 2012, Rs. C-286/12 (Kommission/Ungarn) [The ECJ as the guardian of the Hungarian constitution – A remark to the ruling of the ECJ in case C-276/12 from the 6th of November 2012]. Europarecht 3

Vincze A, Varju M (2012) Hungary: the new fundamental law. Eur Public Law 18:437. 3

von Bogdandy A et al (2012) Reverse Solange – protecting the essence of fundamental rights against EU member states. Common Market Law Rev 49:489. 2

Walker N (2007) Constituent constitutionalism? The case of the European Union. In: Loughlin M, Walker N (eds) The paradox of constitutionalism. Constituent power and constitutional form. Oxford University Press, Oxford

Beáta Bakó is a Max Weber Fellow at the Law Department of the European University Institute, Florence. She is the co-editor-in chief of the Hungarian online newspaper Azonnali.hu.

2

Suspension of EU Funds Paid to Member States Breaching the Rule of Law: Is the Commission's Proposal Legal?

Justyna Łacny

Contents

This chapter is a result of the research project No 2019/35/B/HS5/01024 financed by the National Science Centre, Poland.

J. Łacny (✉)
Department of Administration and Social Sciences, Warsaw University of Technology, Warsaw, Poland
e-mail: justyna.lacny@pw.edu.pl

Abstract The existing scale of violations of the rule of law by some Member States, including capturing judicial independence by their governments, is a relatively new phenomenon for the EU; the one for which the EU based on the EU common values (Article 2 TEU) originally was not prepared to effectively deal with. The EU reacts to current rule of law crisis by using different legal methods and instruments: it *inter alia* applies existing procedures (Article 7 TEU procedure and with more success general infringement procedure under Articles 258-260 TFEU) and struggles to develop new ones. This contribution is focused on the new EU legislative initiative of connecting in the Multiannual Financial Framework (MFF) 2021–2027 transfers of EU funds to Member States with their observance of the rule of law. Or to put it differently, this legislative initiatives would authorize the EU institutions to suspend regular transfers of EU funds to Member States that systematically breach the rule of law.

1 Introduction

Although in many people's views the EU was established to achieve individual and common interests of the Member States, it would be over simplistic to recognise the EU only as the community of interests. The EU is, if not primarily, the community of values such as human dignity, freedom, democracy, equality, the rule of law and respect for human rights (Article 2 TEU). If these values are put at risk or violated and the mutual trust among the Member States is hence infringed, possibilities of identifying and accomplishing common European interests are weakened. This may undermine legitimacy and rationality of the whole 'European project'. Therefore the protection of the common European values (Article 2 TEU) lies at the heart of the EU integration process.

This chapter presents the latest Commission's proposal aimed to ensure the Member States' respect of the rule of law—one of the common values on which the EU is based. The Commission intends to make regular transfers of EU funds to Member States paid from the EU budget for the implementation of different EU policies (mainly the agriculture and the cohesion policies) conditional upon their respect of the rule of law (known as 'the conditionality mechanism'). This contribution comments on the Draft Regulation as first proposed by the Commission (hereinafter: Commission version[1]) and amended during the first reading by the European Parliament (hereinafter: European Parliament version[2]). This mechanism

[1]Proposal for a regulation of the European Parliament and of the Council on the protection of the Union budget in the event of generalized gaps in the rule of law in the Member States (COM(2018) 324 final). See Halmai (2018).

[2]European Parliament legislative resolution of 4 April 2019 on the proposal for a regulation of the European Parliament and of the Council on the protection of the Union's budget in case of generalised deficiencies as regards the rule of law in the Member States (COM(2018) 324 final).

toward Member States and relations between this mechanism and other EU Treaties procedures aimed at stopping breaches of the rule of law (the Article 7 TEU procedure) and the general infringements procedure (Article 258-260 TFEU).

2 Conditionality Mechanism in EU Law

2.1 The Conditionality Mechanism in EU Internal and External Relations

The conditionality mechanism is an EU policy tool which has been in use since the late 1980s.[3] It is based on the assumption that the Member States and third countries are prompted to comply with requirements established under EU law in return for the advantages obtained. Or in other words, they would adhere to EU law due to the risk of losing advantages, particularly financial ones.

Initially, the conditionality mechanism was applied in the EU's external relations, in international agreements in which the EU made the granting of humanitarian aid to third countries conditional upon their respect for human rights.[4] It continues to be so applied at present. To give some examples. If countries participating in the European Neighbourhood Policy[5] implement actions agreed upon with the EU, in return they receive financial assistance and the trade and visa facilitation from the EU.[6] As another example, if candidate countries want to join the EU, they must have institutions which guarantee a stable democracy, the rule of law, respect for human and minority rights as well as market economy allowing the national producers to cope with competitive pressure and market forces within the EU (the so called 'Copenhagen criteria').

Increasingly, the conditionality mechanism is being used in the EU's internal relations as well, in legal acts governing relations between the EU and its Member States. For example, the macroeconomic conditionality mechanism was introduced in 1994 to support the establishment of the European Monetary Union. It conditioned access of the less developed Member States (then Greece, Ireland, Spain and Portugal) to the Cohesion Fund on the adoption by these States of economic convergence plans and their compliance with the EU budgetary deficit rules. It has

[3]For more on the concept of the conditionality see: Vita (2017).

[4]Fierro (2003), Bartels (2005), McKenzie and Meissner (2017) and Cornelius (2016).

[5]Through its European Neighbourhood Policy, the EU works with its southern and eastern neighbours to foster stabilisation, security and prosperity, in line with the Global Strategy for the EU Foreign and Security Policy. See: https://eeas.europa.eu/diplomatic-network/european-neighbourhood-policy-enp/330/european-neighbourhood-policy-enp_en; Joint Communication to the European Parliament, the Council, the European Economic and Social Committee and the Committee of the Regions, *A review of the European Neighborhood Policy* (JOIN (2015) 50 final).

[6]Council Implementing Decision 2012/156/EU of 13 March 2012 suspending commitments from the Cohesion Fund for Hungary with effect from 1 January 2013, OJ L 78/19.

been enforced only once, against Hungary in 2011, albeit without leading to an actual cut-off in funding.[7] As another example, in order to address the 2008 financial crisis in the EU and support those Member States with major budgetary difficulties, the EU made the financial assistance granted to them conditional on their compliance with the macro-economic convergence criteria.[8]

It has been observed that the increasing use of the conditionality mechanism in the EU's internal relations marks a shift towards a generalised 'conditionality culture' in the relationship between the EU and its Member States. The compliance function that the conditionality mechanism was aimed to ensure in the EU's external relations was—in the EU's internal relations—initially supposed to be fulfilled primarily by the principle of sincere cooperation between the EU and the Member States.[9] If a Member State breaches its EU obligation(s), the principle of sincere cooperation does not allow the EU institutions themselves or other Member States to deprive the State in breach of its EU benefits; however the Commission or another Member State can take the case against this State to the CJEU, and as a last resort financial sanctions may be imposed on the breaching State.[10] Based on this principle, the compliant Member States must continue to comply with their EU obligations, even if others do not. It has been observed that the shift from the principle of loyal cooperation to the conditionality mechanism in the EU's internal relations was brought about by the 2004 enlargement, with its attendant concerns that some 'new' Member States might decline to fulfil their EU obligations.[11] Calls for the establishment of the conditionality mechanism, allowing for the suspension of EU funding to Member States breaching the rule of law (discussed further on in this chapter), may be considered as proof that these concerns related with 'new' Member States were correct. That could mean that we are heading toward a new era of conditionality in the EU.

2.2 *The Financial Conditionality Mechanisms in EU Secondary Law on EU Funds*

In the debate on the Draft Regulation introducing a new conditionality mechanism to EU law it is rightly noted that there already exists a legal basis that the Commission could apply to suspend transfers of EU funds to Member States violating the rule of law.[12] It has been claimed that such an opportunity is provided by the Common

[7]Council Implementing Decision 2012/156/EU of 13 March 2012 suspending commitments from the Cohesion Fund for Hungary with effect from 1 January 2013, OJ L 78/19.

[8]Atik (2016) and Louis (2010).

[9]Article 4 (3) TEU.

[10]Article 258-260 TFEU.

[11]Cremona (2005).

[12]Butler (2018), Scheppele et al. (2018) and Kelemen and Scheppele (2018).

Provisions Regulation (hereafter: CP Regulation)[13] containing rules on spending the European Structural and Investment Funds (hereafter: ESIF) which finance implementation of the cohesion policy in the Member States. Similar rules also allow for the suspension of EU funds transferred to Member States for implementation of Common Agricultural Policy (CAP).[14]

Under the CP Regulation, the Member States spending ESIF must establish a management and control system and ensure its effective functioning.[15] This system is comprised of the bodies designated by the Member States (e.g. the managing authorities, audit institutions), tasks they carry out in relation to EU funds (e.g. carrying out controls, making payments, imposing sanctions) and tools allowing for proper management and control of EU funds (e.g. databases, computer systems). This system should guarantee that these funds are spent in the Member States in accordance with EU law and that the risk of their losses is minimised. If the Commission finds a serious deficiency in the effective functioning of the management and control system in the Member State, which has put at risk the EU funds, it is authorised to suspend the payments of these funds transferred to this State.[16] It may also recover them[17] by imposing financial corrections on this State which leads to definitive loss of the amount of the EU funds imposed as corrections. It is claimed in the EU legal doctrine that systemic violations of the rule of law by a Member State, e.g. undermining of judicial independence, can be classified as a serious deficiency in the effective functioning of the management and control system in such State. In such a case, the Commission could suspend the EU funds transferred to this State, or recover them by imposing financial correction on this State. So far, the Commission has not explored either of these possibilities.[18]

Another example provided by the CP Regulation relates to the national system of legal complaints. Under this Regulation, the Member States must ensure they have effective arrangements for the examination of complaints concerning the EU funds.[19] They thus must ensure the access of natural and legal persons to remedies

[13]Articles 23-24 Regulation No 1303/2013 of the European Parliament and of the Council of 17.12.2013 laying down common provisions on the European Regional Development Fund, the European Social Fund, the Cohesion Fund, the European Agricultural Fund for Rural Development and the European Maritime and Fisheries Fund and laying down general provisions on the European Regional Development Fund, the European Social Fund, the Cohesion Fund and the European Maritime and Fisheries Fund and repealing Council Regulation (EC) No 1083/2006 (OJ L 347, 20.12.2013, p. 320).

[14]Article 58 (2) Regulation No 1306/2013 of the European Parliament and of the Council of 17 December 2013 on the financing, management and monitoring of the common agricultural policy and repealing Council Regulations (EEC) No 352/78, (EC) No 165/94, (EC) No 2799/98, (EC) No 814/2000, (EC) No 1290/2005 and (EC) No 485/2008 (OJ L 347, 20.12.2013, p. 549).

[15]Articles 72–74 and Article 122 (1) CP Regulation. The same concerns the agricultural spending, see: Article 58 (2) 2 and Articles 67–73 Regulation No 1306/2013.

[16]Article 142 (a) CP Regulation.

[17]Article 144 (1) (a) CP Regulation.

[18]Kelemen and Scheppele (2018).

[19]Article 74 (3) CP Regulation.

allowing effective legal protection in cases concerning these funds, including access to independent and impartial tribunals.[20] For a Member State with an established record of breaching the rule of law, including capturing an independent prosecution and judiciary, it could be difficult to prove that it fulfils this requirement.

So far the Commission has not applied the possibilities offered by the CP Regulation to try to influence on Member States breaching the rule of law. Therefore, the real problem may be not the lack of adequate legal tools, but the lack of political will on the part of the Commission to use the tools that already exist. Instead, the Commission has proposed the Draft Regulation establishing the conditionality mechanism which is commented on in this chapter.

3 The Conditionality Mechanism Applied for Breaches of the Rule of Law

The EU is a community of law and its values constitute the very basis of its existence. Respect for these values must be ensured throughout all EU policies, including the EU budget.[21] Having this in mind the Commission presented the Draft Regulation to respond to the common diagnosis that the EU lacks effective legal instruments to stop systemic breaches of the rule of law by Member States.[22] It claimed that it cannot be accepted any longer and that these breaches damage the financial interests of the EU.[23] Some authors point out a paradox: that the EU transfers the largest amounts of EU funds to governments of the Member States with a history of long-standing violations of the rule of law,[24] for example to

[20]Article 19(1) TEU and Article 47 of the Charter of Fundamental Rights. See: CJEU, Case C-562/12, *Liivimaa Lihaveis MTÜ*, ECLI:EU:C:2014:2229, paras 67–75.

[21]Communication from the Commission. A new, modern Multiannual Financial Framework for a European Union that delivers efficiently on its priorities post-2020. COM(2018) 98 final.

[22]Closa and Kochenov (2016), Jakab and Kochenov (2017), Schroeder (2016), Hatje (2018), Costa (2017) and Konstadinides (2017).

[23]The Commission based the Draft Regulation on Article 322 (1) (a) TFEU which authorises the European Parliament and the Council to adopt regulations containing financial rules determining *inter alia* procedures for establishing and implementing the EU budget. This Article is commonly applied as a legal basis for adopting Financial Regulations—the main EU secondary budgetary law (presently binding Financial Regulation no 2018/1046). Selection of this legal basis could indicate that the Commission finds the conditionality mechanism as an instrument ensuring sound implementation of the EU budget (Article 317 TFEU). This is, however, in contradiction with the overall assumption expressed in the Draft Regulation that its primary objective is to protect the financial interests of the EU against damages resulting from the breaches of the rule of law by the Member States. Protection of these interests would require that the Draft Regulation would be adopted based on Article 325 (4) TFEU. Under both articles (Article 322 (1) (a) TFEU and Article 325 (4) TFEU) legal acts are adopted by the European Parliament and the Council in accordance with the ordinary legislative procedure after consulting the Court of Auditors.

[24]Kelemen and Scheppele (2018) and Peel et al. (2019).

Poland—the largest overall recipient taking in 86 billion EUR from various ESIF in the Multiannual Financial Framework (MFF) 2014–2020; and Hungary—the largest recipient of EU funds on a *per capita* basis, with more than 95% of all public investment in MFF 2014–2020 having been co-financed by the EU.[25] The conditionality mechanism proposed to be introduced by the Draft Regulation is supposed to remedy this situation. Before discussing this, it is necessary to engage in some terminological explanations.

3.1 The Notion of 'the Rule of Law'

Understandably, the key notion '*the rule of law*' was defined in the Draft Regulation with regard to the Union values enshrined in Article 2 TEU.[26] They include the principles of legality, implying a transparent, accountable, democratic and pluralistic process for enacting laws; legal certainty; a prohibition of arbitrariness of executive powers; effective judicial protection by independent courts, including protection of fundamental rights; separation of powers; and equality before the law. On top of this the European Parliament proposed to include the 'Copenhagen criteria' in this notion, which candidate countries must fulfil in order to accede to the EU. They include, beyond the rule of law, the stability of the institutions guaranteeing democracy, respect for and protection of human rights and minorities, and further a functioning market economy and the capacity to cope with the competition and market forces, as well as the ability to meet the obligations of Union membership.[27]

3.2 The Notion 'Generalised Deficiency As Regards the Rule of Law in a Member State'

A key notion of the Draft Regulation is '*the generalised deficiency as regards the rule of law in a Member State*'.[28] Detection of such a deficiency in a Member State is a necessary premise to apply the conditionality mechanism to this State.

A generalised deficiency as regards the rule of law in a Member State is defined as a widespread or recurrent practice or omission, or a measure by public authorities which violates the rule of law and affects or risks affecting the principle of sound

[25]It has been noted that the situations of Poland and Hungary differ, since there are no well-proven cases that breaches of the rule of law by the Polish authorities have led to the misspending of EU funds (von Brauneck 2019), while such is the case in Hungary (Kelemen and Scheppele 2018) and Romania (Pech et al. 2019).

[26]Article (a) Draft Regulation (Commission proposal).

[27]Article 49 TEU.

[28]On similar notion of 'systemic deficiency as regards the rule of law' see: von Bogdandy (2019).

financial management or the protection of the financial interests of the EU.[29] Some clarification is necessary as regards the principle of sound financial management and the protection of the financial interests of the EU.

3.2.1 The Principle of Sound Financial Management (Article 317 TFEU)

The '*principle of sound financial management*', as set forth in the TFEU,[30] relates to the EU budget and its implementation. The Financial Regulation no 2018/1046[31]—the main EU secondary budgetary law act—provides explanations on the meaning of these terms.

The EU budget forecasts and authorises for each financial year all revenue and expenditures considered necessary for the EU. Implementation of this budget requires the carrying out of activities related to the management, monitoring, control and auditing of EU appropriations, undertaken in accordance with the relevant methods of its implementation.[32] The TFEU entrusts responsibility for the implementation of the EU budget to the Commission.[33] The latter is obliged to implement the EU budget in cooperation with the Member States, on its own responsibility and within the limits of the appropriations, having regard to the principles of sound financial management. Member States must cooperate with the Commission during implementation of the EU budget in order to ensure that the appropriations are used in accordance with this principle.[34] When the European Court of Auditors (the ECA) undertakes its core tasks and examines how the Commission implements the EU budget, it checks, *inter alia*, whether the financial management has been sound.[35]

According to Financial Regulation no 2018/1046,[36] the principle of sound financial management—one of the EU budgetary principles[37]—requires that the EU budget is implemented in accordance with the principles of economy, efficiency,

[29] Article 2 (b) Draft Regulation.

[30] Article 287 (2) 2 TFEU, Article 310 (5) TFEU and Article 317 TFEU.

[31] Regulation (EU, Euratom) 2018/1046 of the European Parliament and of the Council of 18 July 2018 on the financial rules applicable to the general budget of the Union, amending Regulations (EU) No 1296/2013, (EU) No 1301/2013, (EU) No 1303/2013, (EU) No 1304/2013, (EU) No 1309/2013, (EU) No 1316/2013, (EU) No 223/2014, (EU) No 283/2014, and Decision No 541/2014/EU and repealing Regulation (EU, Euratom) No 966/2012, OJ L 193, 30.7.2018, p. 1, hereafter Financial Regulation no 2018/1046.

[32] Article 2 (7) Financial Regulation no 2018/1046.

[33] Article 310 (5) TFEU.

[34] Article 317 TFEU.

[35] Article 287 (2) TFEU.

[36] Article 2 (59), Article 6 and Article 33 Financial Regulation no 2018/1046.

[37] Next to principles of unity, budgetary accuracy, annuality, equilibrium, unit of account, universality, specification, and transparency.

and effectiveness.[38] The CJEU claims that the principle of sound financial management (applied in area of the EU funds) corresponds to the principles of sincere co-operation (applied in general terms of EU law[39]). The CJEU often recalls this principle in the context of EU rules establishing tasks related to the management and spending of EU funds, to underline the necessity to protect them.[40]

3.2.2 Protection of the Financial Interests of the Union (Article 325 TFEU)

The objective of the conditionality mechanism, eventually to be established by the Draft Regulation, is to protect the financial interests of the Union (the EU budget) against damages deriving from breaches of the rule of law by the Member States. This fact is stipulated in the title of this Draft (Regulation on the protection of the Union's budget) and in its provisions.[41] They foresee that this Draft would establish rules necessary for the protection of the Union's budget in the case of generalised deficiencies as regards the rule of law in the Member States.[42] What's more, a generalised deficiency as regards the rule of law in a Member State—a premise necessary to launch the conditionality mechanism—was defined as a common national practice violating the rule of law and affecting or risking to affect the protection of the financial interests of the EU.[43]

---

[38]The principle of economy stipulates that the resources used by the EU institutions concerned in the pursuit of its activities are made available in due time, in appropriate quantity and quality, and at the best price. The principle of efficiency concerns the best relationship between the resources employed, the activities undertaken and the achievement of objectives. The principle of effectiveness concerns the extent to which the objectives pursued are achieved through the activities undertaken.

[39]Article 4 (3) TEU.

[40]CJEU, Cases C-138/03, C-324/03 and C-431/03 *Italy v. Commission*, ECLI:EU:C:2005:714, para. 44; CFI, Case T-345/03 *Evropaïki Dynamiki v. Commission*, ECLI:EU:T:2015:168, para. 77; CFI, Case T-549/08 *Luxemburg v. Commission*, ECLI:EU:T:2010:244, para. 47; Court, Case T-265/08 *Germany v. Commission*, ECLI:EU:T:2012:434, para. 40; CJEU, Case C-500/99 *P Conserve Italia v. Commission*, ECLI:EU:C:2002:45, para. 88; CFI, Case T-308/05, *Italy v. Commission,* ECLI:EU:T:2007:382, para. 109; opinion of AG Trstenjak, Case C-539/09 *Germany v. Commission*, ECLI:EU:C:2011:345, para. 95.

[41]See also paras 9–11, opinion of the Court of Auditors No 1/2018 concerning the proposal of 2 May 2018 for a regulation of the European Parliament and of the Council on the protection of the Union's budget in case of generalised deficiencies as regards the rule of law in the Member States, hereafter: ECA opinion No 1/2018.

[42]Article 1 Draft Regulation.

[43]Article2 (b) Draft Regulation.

The notion '*protection of the financial interests of the Union*', is used in the TFEU,[44] defined in EU secondary law,[45] and clarified by the CJEU.[46] The '*financial interests of the Union*' encompass revenues, expenditures, and assets covered by the EU budgets, the budgets of the EU institutions, bodies, offices and agencies established under the EU Treaties, and budgets directly or indirectly managed and monitored by them. Article 325 TFEU, the main Treaty provision regarding financial interests of the Union, obliges the Member States and the EU institutions to counter fraud and any other illegal activities affecting these interests through deterrent measures that should ensure their effective protection. In turn, the Member State on their side should take the same measures to counter fraud affecting the financial interests of the EU as they take to counter fraud affecting their own financial interests (the assimilation principle).

To sum up, a generalised deficiency as regards the rule of law, the existence of which in a Member State is a necessary premise of launching the conditionality mechanism, indicates (1) a common conduct on the part of public authorities of the Member States that (2) violate the rule of law, which (3) adversely affects or is likely to affect the EU funds (the financial interests of EU, Article 325 TFEU) or its management (the sound financial management of the EU, Article 317 TFEU).

3.2.3 Types of Generalised Deficiency As Regards the Rule of Law

Presented definition of 'a generalised deficiency as regards the rule of law' was formulated broadly-worded. To give some examples of these generalised deficiencies and to limit the scope of interpretation of this notion at the same time, the Commission and the European Parliament established their specific types.

The Commission provided for two lists of generalised deficiency as regards the rule of law. The first list includes, generally speaking, the conduct of national authorities (administrative, investigative, and judicial) related to EU funds. The list is left open. Deficiencies included there do not have to be serious, since they include, e.g., practices on the part of a national authority affecting the effective and timely cooperation with the European Anti-Fraud Office (OLAF) or the European Public Prosecutor's Office.[47] Detection of these types of deficiencies as regards the rule of law in the Member States *leads to*[48] the launching of a conditionality mechanism. In contrast, the second list of generalised deficiencies as regards the rule of law indicates conducts on the part of national administration that *may lead*[49] to the initiation of the conditionality mechanism. In this case the deficiencies are related

[44] Article 310 (5) and Article 325 TFEU.

[45] Article (1) (a) Directive (EU) 2017/1371.

[46] Opinion of AG Jacobs in Case C-11/00 *Commission v. ECB*, ECLI:EU:C:2002:556.

[47] Article 3 (1) (f) Draft Regulation (Commission proposal).

[48] Article 3 (1) Draft Regulation (Commission proposal).

[49] Article 3 (2) Draft Regulation (Commission proposal).

merely to the national judiciary and concern its constitutional determinants (e.g. judicial independence), administration (e.g. lack of relevant financial and human resources), and actions performed (e.g. prosecuting, sanctioning). There is, however, no requirement that these deficiencies must or may affect the financial interest of the Union.

The European Parliament's approach was similar, as it also created two lists of generalised deficiencies as regards the rule of law. The first, also open list, relates to the conduct of national administration and justice and includes, e.g., failing to prevent, correct and sanction arbitrary or unlawful decisions made by public authorities; limiting the availability and effectiveness of legal remedies, including through restrictive procedural rules; lack of implementation of judgments or limiting the effective investigation, prosecution and sanctioning of breaches of law. This list includes *inter alia* 'endangering the administrative capacity of Member States to respect the obligations of Union membership, including the capacity to effectively implement EU law'. Last but not least, measures that weaken the protection of confidentiality of communications between lawyers and clients were also included on this list.[50] The second list includes generalised deficiencies as regards the rule of law that endanger or risk to endanger financial interests of the Union.[51] This list includes general deficiencies included on the Commission's first list,[52] as well as two new breaches, concerning among other Copenhagen criteria[53] and fundamental rights.[54]

To sum up deliberation on the notion of '*a generalised deficiency as regards the rule of law*'—the premises necessary to launch a conditionality mechanism, it can be said that it has been formulated extremely broadly, and its scope is virtually impossible to determine. The general wording leaves the Commission and the Council—the EU institutions that would launch the conditionality mechanism—with a wide margin of discretion, which is undesirable, especially from the point of view of the principles of legal certainty and legality of sanctions. This principle requires that any provision imposing sanctions on entities must be formulated clearly and precisely, so that they can determine with certainty the scope of their rights and

[50]Article 2 (a) Draft Regulation (European Parliament proposal).

[51]Article 3 Draft Regulation (European Parliament proposal).

[52]Article 3 (1) Draft Regulation (Commission proposal).

[53]Distortion or risk of distortion of proper functioning of the market economy and effective implementation of obligations of membership, including adherence to the aim of political, economic and monetary union could constitute generalised deficiencies as regards the rule of law (Article 3 (1) aa Draft Regulation, European Parliament proposal).

[54]This same classification could be given to the shortages in proper implementation of the EU budget following a systemic violation of fundamental rights (Article 3 (1) fa Draft Regulation (European Parliament proposal).

obligations and take appropriate actions.[55] As required by the CJEU, this principle should be rigorously observed, particularly in the case of provisions that have or may have a financial impact. Viewed in this light, it may be stated that the notion of a generalised deficiency as regards the rule of law is neither clear nor precise. Its strict formulation is even more necessary if one takes into account the oppressive nature that the conditionality mechanism may have on the Member State and beneficiaries (see Sect. 5.2). It seems highly undesirable that the EU institutions, in taking actions against Member States for breaching the rule of law, may itself frustrate this rule by applying premises which are formulated (too) broadly. The wide scope of the competences conferred on the EU institutions under the conditionality mechanism has also been criticized by the ECA, which recommended to the EU legislator to establish precise criteria defining the concept of a generalised deficiency as regards the rule of law, and to specify measures to be taken in this framework. The suggested clarifications, sharpening the Draft Regulation, could satisfy the principle of legal certainty and legality of sanctions as well as limit the scope of the EU institutions' discretion.[56]

4 Measures Applied Under the Conditionality Mechanism

The conditionality mechanism is a general term under which specific measures would be imposed on the Member States breaching the rule of law. These measures would depend on which method of implementing the EU budget is used for spending the EU funds. These methods—namely direct, shared, and indirect management—require different entities incurring expenditures financed from the EU budget (EU funds) to comply with related tasks and responsibilities established in EU law, and authorise the Commission to take supervisory actions to ensure their proper spending.[57] These methods vary according to which entity is spending the EU funds. In the case of direct management, the funds are spent by the Commission, through its departments and executive agencies; in the case of shared management—by the Member States; and in the case of indirect management—by third countries, international organizations, and other entities.[58]

[55]CJEU Cases: 70-83, *Kloppenburg*, ECLI:EU:C:1984:71; 325/85, *Ireland v. Commission*, ECLI: EU:C:1987:546, para. 18; C-143/93, *Gebroeders van Es Douane Agenten*, ECLI:EU:C:1996:45, para. 27; C-177/96, *Banque Indosuez*, ECLI:EU:C:1997:494; C-439/01, *Cipra, Kvasnicka*, ECLI: EU:C:2003:31, para. 49; C-110/03, *Belgium v. Commission*, ECLI:EU:C:2005:223, para. 30; C-158/06, *Stichting ROM-projecten*, ECLI:EU:C:2007:370, paras 25–26.

[56]ECA opinion No 1/2018, paras 12-16, 19.

[57]The methods of implementation of the EU budget is determined by Financial Regulation 2018/104, Article 62.

[58]Financial Regulation 2018/1046, Article 62 (1) (c).

Here we focus on shared management,[59] under which the EU funds are spent for the implementation of the CAP and the cohesion policy, altogether constituting about 70% of the EU's budgetary expenditures.[60] If the EU funds are spent under shared management, the following measures can be applied under the conditionality mechanism: suspension of approval of programs or amendments thereof; suspension of commitments; reduction of commitments, including through financial corrections or transfers to other spending programs; reduction of pre-financing; an interruption of payment deadlines; and suspension of payments.[61]

The Draft Regulation does not establish how these measures should operate in practice, nor even provide their general legal characteristics. There is also no guidance as to which types of the above-mentioned measures should be applied in the case of certain generalised deficiencies as regards the rule of law. The Draft Regulation simply refers to the names of particular measures, which may suggest the essence of the activities undertaken. Very general information is given in the preamble, which states that these measures should include the suspension of payments and of commitments, a reduction of funding under existing commitments, and a prohibition on concluding new commitments with recipients.[62]

The application of these measures requires recourse to the EU sectoral Regulations, which provide specific rules for the spending of the EU funds for EU policies, e.g. for the CAP and the cohesion policy. Surprisingly, the Draft Regulation does not mention such a reference. It must also be noted that, at present, a detailed and final assessment of these sectoral Regulations is not possible since they are undergoing legislative processes in the EU institutions heading the new MFF 2021–2027.[63] At this point in time, it can only be stated that these measures can be taken at various stages of the implementation of EU policies: from the stage of approval of national programs by the Commission to the stage of making legal commitments by the Commission, followed by the payments of the EU funds to the Member States. It is clear however that one of these measures consists of suspending the payment of EU funds,[64] and this is what the remainder of this contribution will mainly focus on.

The undefined nature of the measures to be imposed under the conditionality mechanism deserves the same criticism which was already formulated towards the

---

[59]Craig (2012), p. 27; Hofmann et al. (2012); Schöndorf-Haubold (2011).

[60]Communication from the Commission. A new, modern Multiannual Financial Framework for a European Union that delivers efficiently on its priorities post-2020. COM(2018) 98 final.

[61]Article 4 (1) (b) Draft Regulation (Commission proposal).

[62]Recital 13 preamble Draft Regulation (Commission proposal).

[63]Proposal for a Regulation of the European Parliament and of the Council on the financing, management and monitoring of the common agricultural policy and repealing Regulation (EU) No 1306/2013 (COM(2018)393 final) and proposal for a Regulation of the European Parliament and of the Council laying down common provisions on the European Regional Development Fund, the European Social Fund Plus, the Cohesion Fund, and the European Maritime and Fisheries Fund and financial rules for those and for the Asylum and Migration Fund, the Internal Security Fund and the Border Management and Visa Instrument (COM(2018)375 final).

[64]See point 7 ECA opinion No 1/2018.

vagueness of the premise of its application, namely notion of 'a generalised deficiency as regards the rule of law' (see: Sect. 3.2 above). Principles of legal certainty and legality of sanctions must be recalled once again to evoke that any provision imposing sanctions must be formulated clearly and precisely.[65] The CJEU requires that these principle should be rigorously observed, particularly in the case of provisions that have or may have a financial impact. Viewed in this light, it may be stated that neither the premise of launching the conditionality mechanism (the notion of 'a generalised deficiency as regards the rule of law') nor measures imposed under this mechanism are clear nor precise. Its strict formulation is even more necessary if one takes into account the oppressive nature that the conditionality mechanism may have on the Member State and beneficiaries (see Sect. 6).

What's important and deserves credit, the Draft Regulation provides rules which the EU institutions (the Commission or the Council) should take into account when imposing measures under the conditionality mechanism.[66] They would be obliged to ensure that these measures should be proportionate to the nature, gravity, and scope of the generalised deficiency as regards the rule of law. These measures also should, insofar as possible, target the EU actions affected or potentially affected by that deficiency. The requirement of proportionality between the generalised deficiency as regards the rule of law, that is EU law infringement leading to launching of the conditionality mechanism on one side, and measures adopted under this mechanism on the other side signifies that these measures are deemed as sanctions imposed upon the Member State for breaching the rule of law. Under EU law, the principle of proportionality is the *sine qua non* condition of adoption of any sanctions imposed as the result of an infringement of a law.

To sum up this sub-section, the Draft Regulation provides generally-formulated premises for launching the conditionality mechanism together with their very specific examples, which can lead to measures of a really unknown (as yet) character. This extremely broad formulation of provisions defining prohibited infringements of the law and sanctions imposed for their perpetration raises concerns as to their legality. It is because it cannot be claimed that these provisions are clear and or precise, as the principles of legal certainty and legality of sanctions would require. No matter how challenging this may be, respect for the principles of legality and legal certainty would require the premises for launching the conditionality mechanism to be formulated more unequivocally. Provisions of the Draft Regulation should clearly indicate major types and a closed list of examples of systematic breaches of the rule of law that could lead to the activation of this mechanism.

---

[65] CJEU Cases: 70-83, *Kloppenburg*, ECLI:EU:C:1984:71; 325/85, *Ireland v. Commission*, ECLI:EU:C:1987:546, para. 18; C-143/93, *Gebroeders van Es Douane Agenten*, ECLI:EU:C:1996:45, para. 27; C-177/96, *Banque Indosuez*, ECLI:EU:C:1997:494; C-439/01, *Cipra, Kvasnicka*, ECLI:EU:C:2003:31, para. 49; C-110/03, *Belgium v. Commission*, ECLI:EU:C:2005:223, para. 30; C-158/06, *Stichting ROM-projecten*, ECLI:EU:C:2007:370, para. 25–26.

[66] Article 4 (3) Draft Regulation (Commission proposal) and Article 5a Draft Regulation (European Parliament proposal).

These provisions should be formulated taking into account the standards established in the case-law of the CJEU and the ECtHR for the imposition of sanctions.

5 The Procedure for Adoption of a Decision Applying the Conditionality Mechanism

While the proposals lodged by the Commission and the European Parliament concerning premises for launching the conditionality mechanism are generally in line with each other, their proposals for procedural rules to be applied to this end differ considerably. Disparities concern the key issue, namely determining the EU institution that would adopt a decision applying the conditionality mechanism and the procedural steps that would be taken in this regard. While the Commission proposed that this decision should be adopted by the Council, on a request from the Commission, according to the European Parliament this decision should be adopted by the Commission, with a right of the European Parliament and the Council to oppose it or change it. These issues are presented below.

5.1 Initiation of the Procedure

According to the Draft Regulation, initiation of the conditionality mechanism would require a determination that there is at least one generalised deficiency as regards the rule of law in the Member State targeted (see Sect. 3.2).

The Commission proposes that it would conduct an inquiry by itself and that if it found a generalised deficiency, it would indicate it in a written notification submitted to the Member State concerned. The Commission could request additional information from this State, including proposals for remedial measures. The Member State would have to provide the Commission with information within the time-limits set by the Commission, not less than 1 month from the date of the written notification. When assessing the existence of a generalised deficiency as regards the rule of law, the Commission could take into account all information, including judgments of the CJEU, reports of the ECA, and recommendations of international organizations.[67]

The European Parliament has proposed two modifications to this procedure. The first concerned the establishment of an advisory panel of independent experts (hereafter: Panel) that would assist the Commission in assessing the existence of a generalised deficiency as regards the rule of law in a given Member State. The second one concerns obliging the Commission to take into account certain Copenhagen criteria while making such an assessment.

[67] Article 5 Draft Regulation (Commission proposal).

The primary function of the Panel would be to assist the Commission in identifying generalised deficiencies as regards the rule of law in the Member States.[68] This function would be achieved in a twofold manner. Firstly, the Panel would adopt *ad hoc* opinions concerning generalised deficiencies as regards the rule of law as examined by the Commission. Secondly, the Panel would annually assess situations in all Member States as regards their respect for the rule of law and would make a public summary of its findings each year. The Draft Regulation thus would create a new body—the Panel—entrusted with the task of continuous monitoring of the rule of law situation in all the Member States.

As regards the Copenhagen criteria, the European Parliament proposes that the Commission should examine them when assessing the existence of generalised deficiencies as regards the rule of law in a Member State. The criteria should include: chapters of the *aquis* on judiciary and fundamental rights, justice, freedom and security; financial control and taxation; as well as guidelines used in the context of the Cooperation and Verification Mechanism (CVM).[69] The idea to link the compliance with the rule of law with the Copenhagen criteria may raise concerns. It is not evident why and how the compliance of the Member States with the legal principle (the rule of law) could be assessed by evaluation of political criteria, in some cases not even substantially related with the rule of law (e.g. financial control and taxation).

5.2 *Who Adopts the Decision?*

The subsequent action, after the Commission finds a generalised deficiency as regards the rule of law in the Member State, consists of the adoption of a decision launching the conditionality mechanism (see Sect. 4). The Commission's and the European Parliament's proposals considerably differ as to who should adopt this decision.

---

[68]The Panel would be established by the Commission from specialists of constitutional law and financial and budgetary matters. Each national parliament of the Member States would nominate one expert to this Panel and the European Parliament would appoint five experts. Representatives of relevant organisations and networks could be invited to the Panel as observers. Article 3a Draft Regulation (European Parliament proposal).

[69]CVM is a transitional measure established by the Commission to assist Romania and Bulgaria in progress after their accession to the Union in the fields of judicial reform, corruption and organised crime. The Commission assesses progress under CVM based on benchmarks established for each State. The benchmarks for Romania concern effectiveness and transparency of the judicial system and the fight against and prevention of corruption. The benchmarks for Bulgaria deal with the independence, professionalism, and efficiency of the judicial system and the fight against corruption and organised crime. The Commission reports on developments on a regular basis. For more, see: https://ec.europa.eu/info/policies/justice-and-fundamental-rights/upholding-rule-law/rule-law/assistance-bulgaria-and-romania-under-cvm/cooperation-and-verification-mechanism-bulgaria-and-romania_en.

The Commission proposes that if it detects a generalised deficiency as regards the rule of law in a Member State, it would submit to the Council a proposal for a decision imposing measures on this State, e.g. suspending its payments from the EU funds.[70] This decision would be deemed to have been adopted unless the Council rejects it by a QMV within 1 month of the Commission's submission of its decision.[71] The Council may also amend this proposal by a QMV, with no time limits established for amendment.

The European Parliament proposal differs, as it foresees the adoption of two decisions, both by the Commission. In the first decision, addressed to the Member State concerned, the Commission indicates a measure to be imposed on this State under the conditionality mechanism (e.g. suspension of EU funds). In the second decision, addressed to the European Parliament and to the Council (the EU budgetary authorities), the Commission indicates an amount equivalent as a measure adopted in the first decision (e.g. amount of EU funds suspended). Then this amount is classified as a EU budgetary reserve. The idea to adopt the latter decision, regulating the legal and financial status of the amount concerned under the conditionality mechanism, fills the gap in the Commission proposal, which would not determine what would in legal terms happen to these funds. Both decisions are considered to be adopted unless the European Parliament (acting by majority of the votes cast) or the Council (acting by QMV), amend or reject it within 4 weeks of its receipt.[72]

5.3 Voting in the Council by Reverse QMV

The procedure to be followed by the EU institutions to adopt a decision launching the conditionality mechanism is peculiar and therefore deserves attention. This decision is *not* adopted under the standard legislative procedures provided by the EU Treaties (most commonly applied—the ordinary and special legislative procedures[73]), but under a peculiar procedure created by the Draft Regulation. The same concerns the voting cast in the Council. The Council would *not* vote on this decision by the simple majority votes or by the *ordinary* QMV, the latter being the standard cast provided for the Council's voting by the EU Treaties,[74] but by *reverse* QMV—not foreseen by the EU Treaties.

---

[70]Article 5 (6-8) Draft Regulation (Commission proposal).

[71]The Council votes on the Commission's proposal by *reverse* QMV. For more on this, see Sect. 5.3 below.

[72]Article 5 (6 a) (6 b) (6 c) Draft Regulation (European Parliament proposal).

[73]Articles 289 and 294 TFEU.

[74]Qualified majority votes is the 'standard' voting method in the Council used when the Council takes decisions during the ordinary legislative procedure. About 80% of all EU legislation is adopted with this procedure. A qualified majority is reached in the Council if 55% of Member States vote in favour (16 out of 28) and the proposal is supported by the Member States representing at least 65% of the total EU population. The blocking minority includes at least four Council members representing more than 35% of the EU population (Article 238 TFEU).

In general, when the Council votes by the *ordinary* QMV, obtaining this majority leads to the adoption of a legal act. In the case of voting by *reverse* QMV the logic is different—a proposal submitted by an applicant (in our case—the Commission) is adopted unless the legislator (the Council) *rejects* or *amends* it acting by *standard* QMV in a vote held in a given period. Following this period, a decision is considered adopted. Thus, in the case of *reverse* QMV—a failure to obtain the *standard* QMV necessary to block or change a proposal results in its *adoption* (in the wording of the Draft Regulation 'the decision shall be deemed to have been adopted'), while this majority is necessary to reject or amend it. Under *reverse* QMV abstention counts as positive votes, forcing the Member States to take a clear position and obliging them to explicitly vote against the proposal, rather than following a more politically expedient route of abstaining.

It can therefore be concluded that if the Commission sought to suspend EU funds to a Member State for breaching the rule of law, but it was not convinced of the Council's support, it would much easier achieve its intention under the *reverse* QMV then under the *ordinary* QMV. This is because in the case of voting by *reverse* QMV the decision would only require that the Council would not *reject* it by *ordinary* QMV (within 1 month) or otherwise amend it by such QMV. So, if there is no *ordinary* QMV to reject (within 1 month) or amend the decision, it would be adopted. In contrast, if this decision would be voted by ordinary QMV, to be adopted, it would have to be *approved* by *ordinary* QMV.

According to the Commission, the idea that the Council would vote on a decision launching the conditionality mechanism by *reverse* QMV is dictated by the necessity to protect the financial interests of the Union (in short—the EU funds).[75] It seems rather unthinkable to claim that necessity to protect the EU funds requires circumvention of the EU legislative procedure. It is not the first time in history of the EU when voting in the Council by *reverse* QMV is to be introduced as a remedy allowing an effective implementation of the EU policies. Such voting was already established in 2011 when rules aimed to strengthen effective enforcement of the EU fiscal policy were agreed. Under EU fiscal rules (Article 126 TFEU), the euro area Member States must avoid excessive government deficit (3% of GDP), debt (60% of GDP) and maintain sound and sustainable public finance. The Stability and Growth Pact (the SGP) was signed by all Member States based on Articles 121 and 126 TFEU to facilitate and maintain these rules. The SGP provides for fiscal monitoring of the Member States' budgetary situation by the Commission and the Council. It purpose was to ensure that the Member States maintain and enforce EU fiscal rules and do not exceed budgetary deficit and debt limits. Under the SGP ('preventive arm') each year all Member States submit a compliance report presenting expected fiscal development for the current and subsequent 3 years ('stability programmes' for eurozone Member States and 'convergence programmes' for non-eurozone Member States). If a Member State does not comply with the EU fiscal rules, an 'Excessive Deficit Procedure' (EDP) is initiated under the SGP

[75]Recital 15 preamble Draft Regulation. See critics: ECA opinion No 1/2018, para. 12.

('dissuasive arm'). If this situation continues to remain despite multiple warnings, sanctions can be imposed on this Member State. In 2011, in the face of the world financial crisis, enforcement of the SGP was strengthened by the adoption of '*Six Pack*', '*Two Pack*' and '*Fiscal Compact*'. These acts provided for automaticity of sanctions, including interest-bearing deposits, non-interest-bearing deposits and fines to be imposed on the Member States for recurrent breaches of the EU fiscal rules.[76] These sanctions are imposed based on the *reverse* QMV in the Council. The Commission can impose them unless the Council decides by the *reverse* QMV to reject the Commission recommendation within a specified period (usually 10 days). Adoption of these sanctions thus requires a minority of the Member States to agree on the Commission proposal or alternatively an *ordinary* QMV to block or change this proposal.[77] Legality of imposing sanctions on the Member States by voting in the Council by the *reverse* QMV was not contested in action brought before the CJEU. Therefore the position of the CJEU on this issue is unknown.

Coming back to the conditionality mechanism, it can be stated that the logic applied in 2011 in the '*Six Pack*', '*Two Pack*' and '*Fiscal Compact*' in area of sanctions to be imposed for breaching—by the Member States—the EU fiscal rules established under Article 126 TFEU and the SGP was reused in 2018 in the Draft Regulation (the Commission proposal) providing for suspension of EU funds transferred to the Member States systematically breaching the rule of law. In both cases the procedural peculiarities facilitate a procedure of adopting EU secondary acts imposing sanctions on the Member States and strengthen the procedural role of the Commission *vis à vis* a Member State suspected to breach the EU law (the EU fiscal rules or the rule of law). Procedural peculiarities concern both the type of a legislative procedure to be followed to adopt a decision initiating the conditionality mechanism (a special procedure established by the Draft Regulation) and the necessary vote cast in the Council to adopt it (*reverse* QMV). As regards the legislative procedure (adoption of a decision by the Council) the EU Treaties neither provide it as one of the standard legislative procedures that the EU institutions apply to adopt EU secondary law (e.g. legislative, delegated, implementing acts and acts 'without adjective') nor authorise the EU institutions to apply it. So, the Draft Regulation establishes a legislative procedure specially for the sake of the conditionality mechanism, which remains outside of the EU Treaties regime. The same can be said about voting by the Council under the *reverse* QMV to adopt a decision launching the conditionality mechanism. Such a majority is not foreseen under the

[76]Articles 4-6 Regulation No 1173/2011 of the European Parliament and of the Council of 16 November 2011 on the effective enforcement of budgetary surveillance in the euro area (OJ L 306, 23.11.2011, p. 1); Article 3 Regulation No 1174/2011 of the European Parliament and of the Council of 16 November 2011 on enforcement measures to correct excessive macroeconomic imbalances in the euro area (OJ L 306, 23.11.2011, p. 8); Article 10 (4) Regulation No 1176/ 2011 of the European Parliament and of the Council of 16 November 2011 on the prevention and correction of macroeconomic imbalances (OJ L 306, 23.11.2011, p. 25); Article 7 Treaty on Stability, Coordination and Governance in the Economic and Monetary Union (Fiscal Compact).

[77]Van Aken and Artige (2013), p. 131; Chalmers et al. (2015), p. 751.

EU Treaties. Just to remind Article 16 (3) TEU foresees that the Council act by a *standard* QMV except where the Treaties provide otherwise. There is no provision under the Treaties which authorise the Council to vote under *reverse* QMV. These doubts inevitably lead to a question of legality of the Draft Regulation establishing procedural conditions of adopting a decision initiating the conditionality mechanism, not mentioned nor foreseen under EU Treaties.

5.4 Decision Lifting the Measures

The Member State against whom the conditionality mechanism was initiated is authorized at any time to provide the Commission with evidence that it has remedied or eliminated the generalised deficiency as regards the rule of law. On this base the Commission assesses the situation in this State with a view toward adopting a decision lifting the conditionality mechanism.[78] This formula was presented by the Commission, and the European Parliament subsequently added two elements to it. The first is that the Commission should assess the situation in the Member State taking into account the opinion of the Panel (see Sect. 5.1) and second, that the Commission should act within 1 month and in any case within a reasonable timeframe from the date of receipt of the notification from the Member State.[79]

A decision lifting the conditionality mechanism would be issued by the EU institutions that have adopted it—by the Council (as the Commission proposes) or by the Commission (as the European Parliament proposes). The same procedure would apply *mutatis mutandis.*[80]

6 Impact of the Conditionality Mechanism

The key issue related to the conditionality mechanism concerns its real financial impact. In the public debate it is frequently claimed that its essence is a temporary suspension of transfers of EU funds to the Member State breaching the rule of law. However, analysis of the Draft Regulation reveals that this diagnosis seems overly simplistic, and launching of the conditionality mechanism may end up as well in a definitive loss of the EU funds by the Member State in question. What's more, this may also affect individuals. These issues are presented below.

[78]Article 6 (2) Draft Regulation (Commission proposal).

[79]Article 6 (2) Draft Regulation (European Parliament proposal).

[80]Article 6 (2) Draft Regulation (Commission proposal and European Parliament proposal).

6.1 Impact of the Conditionality Mechanism on the Member States

According to the Draft Regulation, if EU funds are suspended under the conditionality mechanism, the amounts corresponding to the suspended commitments are re-entered into the EU budget subject to the Article 7 Draft Multiannual Financial Framework Regulation[81] (the Draft MFF Regulation). Re-entering allows reallocation and future reutilisation of the EU funds in question (see Sect. 5.2). What is important, the Article 7 Draft MFF Regulation proposes that commitments suspended in year 'n' due to a generalised deficiency as regards the rule of law in a Member State may not be re-entered into the EU budget later than in the year 'n'+2.[82] The Draft Regulation contains a similar provision, stipulating that suspended commitments for year 'n' may not be entered into the EU budget beyond year 'n'+2.[83] On the top of this, from year 'n'+3, amounts corresponding to the suspended commitments should be entered in the Union Reserve for Commitments (hereafter: Union Reserve).[84] This Reserve is a new financial instrument which would be financed from, *inter alia*, funds committed to the EU budget but ultimately not spent for the implementation of EU programmes and thus de-committed. Amounts of the Union Reserve would be made available for the Member State in the new MFF 2021–2027.

In should be thus reminded that according to political declarations and its common understanding by the public, the conditionality mechanism is supposed to only lead to a temporary suspension of EU funds of the Member States breaching the rule of law, thus motivating them to eliminate the breaches promptly. If that is the case, the funds should be returned to these States. However, this may not happen because of the 'n+2' rule contained in the Draft Regulation and in the Draft MFF Regulation. Application of the conditionality mechanism may thus relatively easily result not in the suspension, but in the permanent loss of EU funds by the Member States.[85] This is because these Drafts introduce the 'n+2' rule which authorizes the Commission to enter into the EU budget only the amounts corresponding to the amounts suspended under the conditionality mechanism which were lifted within 2 years (year 'n'+2) from the year they were suspended (year 'n'). After the elapse of these 2 years, the Commission will have no legal basis to enter these amounts into the EU budget anymore. From year 'n'+3 these amounts would be entered into the Union Reserve and could be allocated to the Member States—all Member States, not only the one on which the conditionality mechanism was applied and spend in the MFF 2021–2027.

---

[81]Article 6 (3) Draft Regulation (Commission proposal).

[82]Proposal for a Council Regulation laying down the multiannual financial framework for the years 2021 to 2027 (COM(2018) 322 final).

[83]Article 6 (3) Draft Regulation (Commission proposal).

[84]Article 12 Draft MFF Regulation.

[85]Para. 8 ECA opinion No 1/2018.

This indicates that a Member State whose EU funds were suspended under the conditionality mechanism practically has 2 years from the year of suspension (year 'n') to remedy the generalised deficiency as regards the rule of law and to request the EU institutions to lift the suspension and re-enter the amounts corresponding to the suspended commitments to the EU budget.[86] If the Member State fails to undertake these actions during the 2-year period, it loses the possibility to benefit from the suspended EU funds. Conducting all these actions within 2 years can be extremely difficult, taking into account that the elimination of rule of law breaches is usually time-consuming and in addition further time is needed to complete the proceedings in the EU institutions to lift the suspension.

6.2 *Impact of the Conditionality Mechanism on the Beneficiaries of EU Funds*

In principle, the conditionality mechanism should solely affect those Member States breaching the rule of law, and the consequences of the suspension of EU funds should not in any way influence the beneficiaries of these funds (e.g. farmers, entrepreneurs).[87] To achieve this objective, the Commission foresees, in the Draft Regulation, that unless the decision adopting the measures imposed under the conditionality mechanism provides otherwise, its adoption does not affect the obligation of the Member States to implement the programme or fund those affected by the measures, and in particular the obligation to make payments to the beneficiaries of EU funds (hereafter: beneficiaries).[88] In other words, despite the fact that the regular transfer of the EU funds from the EU budget to Member States' budget is suspended under the conditionality mechanism, this State is nevertheless obliged to continue to implement programmes financed from these funds and make payments to beneficiaries. It could be assumed that since the Commission recognized the need to protect the beneficiaries against the possibility that Member States will cease to make payments to them due to the suspension of EU funds under the conditionality mechanism, it should also specify in the Draft Regulation legal measures that beneficiaries could apply against the Member States if this should occur. However, the Commission has not done so.[89]

[86] Article 6 Draft Regulation (Commission proposal).

[87] The European Parliament formulated this assumption in its resolution of 14 March 2018 on the MFF (2017/2052(INI)). The Commission also pointed out that beneficiaries of EU funding must not be affected by breaches of the rule of law by Member States. See page 2 of the Draft Regulation.

[88] Article 4 (2) Draft Regulation (Commission proposal).

[89] See critics: ECA opinion No 1/2018, point 27.

The European Parliament has tried to remedy this deficiency and strengthen the legal protection of beneficiaries against the misconduct of Member States.[90] It proposed that the Commission should provide information and guidance *via* a website or internet portal for beneficiaries on the obligations of Member States to implement the programme, in particular to make payments to them. The Commission should also provide, on the same website or portal, adequate tools allowing beneficiaries to inform it of any breaches of these obligations by the Member States. The information provided by the beneficiaries may only be taken into account by the Commission if it is accompanied by a proof that they have lodged a complaint to the competent national authority. Beneficiaries informing the Commission would be protected under the proposed Directive on whistle-blower protection.[91]

The above-mentioned rules establish communication channels between the Commission and beneficiaries enabling them to exchange information on any eventual negative effects experienced by the latter due to Member States stopping to make the payments of EU funds. It is, however, doubtful whether such communication itself may effectively protect beneficiaries, without being accompanied by any formal legal actions. Three solutions appear to exist. Firstly, beneficiaries could apply legal remedies established under the national law to claim continuation of payments of EU funds from national authorities. This may however be challengeable or even unattainable in Member States in which an illiberal democracy has captured the national administration and independent prosecution and judiciary. Secondly, the beneficiaries could initiate an action for damages against the Member State claiming the State has infringed its obligation under the Draft Regulation to make payments of EU funds (*Francovich* liability). The success of this claim may still however depend on the effectiveness and independence of the national judiciary, which could and is troublesome in the case of some Member States. The Commission's legal position is more meaningful, as it could—as a third solution—initiate a general infringement action (Article 258 TFEU) against a Member State who breaches the Draft Regulation by ceasing to make the payments of EU funds to beneficiaries.

It is important to note that the Draft Regulation has equipped the Commission with competences that may help to ensure that beneficiaries would receive their EU funds if its transfer would be suspended on a national level. These competences depend on the method under which the EU budget is implemented (see Sect. 4). Two possibilities exist in this respect, since these EU funds may be spent under indirect management[92]—by public and private law Member States' organisations—or under shared management[93]—by Member States, mostly for implementation of CAP and the cohesion policy. If EU funds are spent under indirect management (by public and

---

[90]Recital 14 preamble and Article 4 (3) (a) and (3) (b) Draft Regulation (European Parliament proposal).

[91]Proposal for a Directive on the protection of persons reporting on breaches of Union law COM (2018)218 final.

[92]Article 62 (1) (c) of the Financial Regulation no 2018/1046.

[93]Article 62 (1) (b) of the Financial Regulation no 2018/1046.

private law Member State organisations), the Commission may recover the payments directly made to these organisations for an amount equivalent to the amount not paid to beneficiaries.[94] When EU funds are spent under shared management (by the Member States), the Commission may impose a financial correction[95] on them to recover the EU funds from these State. In both cases amounts recovered by the Commission are transferred to the Union Reserve.[96]

These provisions, however, do not change the general rule describe above according to which the Member States are obliged to make payments to beneficiaries despite the transfer of EU funds to these States is suspended under the conditionality mechanism. In other words, suspension of EU funds transferred to a Member State does not change a legal situation of beneficiaries who can claim payments of these funds only from the national administration, not from the Commission.

6.3 Impact of the Conditionality Mechanism on Relations Between the National Authorities

Independently of the financial losses that the conditionality mechanism causes to the Member State (Sect. 6.1) and may cause to beneficiaries (Sect. 6.2), it may also affect internal relations within the national administration. More specifically, it may lead to conflicts between the central government of the Member State (the addressee of the EU decision suspending the EU funds) and public authorities functioning on the lower levels in the structure of this State. This is because the Draft Regulation imposes the obligation to make payments to beneficiaries not only on the central government of the Member States, but also on 'government entities', which, as defined, include all public authorities at all levels of government, i.e. national, regional, and local authorities as well as Member State organizations.[97] It can thus be predicted that if transfers of EU funds would be suspended under the conditionality mechanism, these funds would not be paid to the government of a Member State, whereas the obligation to pay them to beneficiaries would still rest on government entities, e.g. local authorities and national organisations, which are defined broadly. This could easily give rise to internal domestic conflicts.

[94] Article 12 draft MFF Regulation.

[95] Article 98 of CP Regulation, COM(2018) 375 final.

[96] Article 12 (2) (a) draft MFF Regulation.

[97] Article 2 (c) Draft Regulation (Commission proposal).

7 The Conditionality Mechanism and Other Rule-of-Law Mechanisms

The verification of Member States' compliance with the rule of law that would be performed under the conditionality mechanism if the Draft Regulation is adopted may also be checked under other legal procedures established in EU Treaties. The most important are: the Article 7 TEU procedure and the general infringement procedures (Articles 258-260 TFEU). Since the Draft Regulation does not specify the relationship between the proposed conditionality mechanism and these procedures, this may lead to major legal disputes[98] and require some clarifications.

7.1 The Article 7 TEU Procedure

Article 7 TEU allows the EU institutions to examine whether the Member States respect the values on which the EU is based (Article 2 TEU) which include, *inter alia*, the rule of law. Article 7 TEU foresees a procedure to be followed and measures to be adopted if a breach of these values is detected. This procedure has already been launched against Poland (in 2017) and Hungary (in 2018).

The Article 7 TEU procedure consists of two stages: '*the preventive stage*', where decisions are taken by the Council;[99] and *'the sanctioning stage',* which belongs to the European Council and the Council.[100] At '*the preventive stage*' of the Article 7 TEU procedure, the Council hears the Member State, addresses recommendations to it, and determines whether there is a clear risk of a serious breach by this State of the rule of law.[101] At '*the sanctioning stage*' of the Article 7 TEU procedure, the European Council determines the existence of a serious and persistent breach of the rule of law by this State.[102] After that, the Council may decide to suspend certain rights of this State deriving from the application of the Treaties, including the voting rights of the representative of the government of this Member State in the Council.[103] In response to changes in the situation which led to the imposition of the above measures, the Council may decide to alter or revoke them.[104] As regards the judicial control of actions taken based on Article 7 TEU, the CJEU decides only on

[98]Taborowski (2019), pp. 205–207.

[99]Article 7 (1) TEU.

[100]Article 7 (2) and (3) TEU.

[101]The Council acts by a majority of 4/5 of its Members, on a reasoned proposal of 1/3 of the Member States, by the European Parliament or by the Commission, after obtaining the consent of the European Parliament.

[102]In this stage the European Council acts unanimously, on a proposal from 1/3 of the Member States or by the Commission, after obtaining the consent of the European Parliament.

[103]The Council acts by QMV.

[104]The Council acts by QMV.

the legality of the procedural stipulations contained in this Article,[105] with no substantive control of measures (e.g. sanctions) adopted.

Article 7 (3) TEU, which allows the Council to suspend certain rights of the Member States deriving from the application of the Treaties, deserves a closer look inasmuch as actions undertaken on its basis *prima facie* may be similar to actions performed under the Draft Regulation. The legal nature of actions undertaken based on Article 7 (3) TEU is not determined by the Treaties. These provisions simply indicate the essence of such actions (suspension of rights deriving from the application of the Treaties) and provide one example (suspension of the voting right in the Council); otherwise they describe such actions by using the neutral term '*measure*'. The scope of competences conferred on the Council based on Article 7 (3) TEU have given rise to a heated debate, in which it is commonly accepted that the Council's actions constitute political sanctions imposed on Member States for breaching the values on which the EU is founded.[106] It should thus be determined whether, based on Article 7 (3) TEU, the Council is authorized to suspend the EU funds of a Member State found to be in breach of the rule of law. In other words, is it true that the competences to be created under the conditionality mechanism (the Draft Regulation) already exist under Article 7 (3) TEU?

Given that under Article 7 (3) TEU the rights of a Member State deriving from the application of the Treaties may be suspended, it should also be possible to suspend transfers of EU funds to this State on this basis.[107] Undoubtedly, receipt of the EU funds is a right that the Member States benefit from as a result of their EU membership, and the amounts received are set out in the MFF Regulations based on political agreements reached by all Member States. It can therefore be stated that by suspending transfer of the EU funds, the Member State is temporarily deprived of the possibility to enjoy its right deriving from the Treaties.

It thus follows that the suspension of the EU funds of Member States breaching the rule of law is possible both under Article 7 (3) TEU and would be under the conditionality mechanism as well if the Draft Regulation is adopted. It has already been pointed out that the Draft Regulation does not specify the relationship between the Article 7 TEU procedure and the conditionality mechanism. This silence calls for an analysis in which two options should be taken into consideration.

The first option, based on the hierarchy of EU legal norms, is that the Article 7 TEU procedure and the conditionality mechanism are interdependent. The Article 7 TEU procedure (regulated by EU Treaty) has a primary role and the conditionality mechanism (regulated in the Draft Regulation) supplements it. The Article 7 TEU procedure provides a general framework for a suspension of EU funds for breaches of the rule of law, and the Draft Regulation ensures its practical implementation. Based on this reasoning, in legal terms the suspension of EU funds under the conditionality mechanism would constitute a '*measure*' within the meaning of

[105] Article 269 TFEU.

[106] Geiger (2015), Mangiameli and Saputelli (2013), Besselink (2017) and Dumbrovský (2018).

[107] Taborowski (2019), pp. 194–197.

Article 7 (3) TEU. Following this logic, the suspension of EU funds would have to be first imposed under Article 7 (3) TEU and only then under the conditionality mechanism. In this scenario, however, one breach of the rule of law would be double-checked in two different procedures—first under the Article 7 TEU procedure and then under the conditionality mechanism. At a glance, this seems counterproductive. It may not be also excluded that decisions made under the Article 7 TEU procedure and under the conditionality mechanism would differ, depending on the political ambience, not to mention how unpractical and time-consuming this may be. If one recalls that the reasons to create the conditionality mechanism regulated by the EU secondary law was to overcome the political difficulties or even impossibility of conducting the Article 7 procedure, proven by the unsuccessful proceedings launched against Poland and Hungary, the idea to merge the Article 7 TEU procedure and the conditionality mechanism multiplies existing difficulties. Therefore the second option requires scrutiny.

The second option is based on the argument of procedural effectiveness, or the *effet utile* principle. Under this option the Article 7 TEU procedure and the conditionality mechanism are parallel and independent of each other, because their legal nature is different. The Article 7 TEU procedure is a political one, while the conditionality mechanism is a legal proceeding. In the Article 7 TEU procedure decisions are made by a political body (the Council) based on political assessments. Judicial control of the legality of these decisions performed by the CJEU is limited only to reviewing the procedural requirements stipulated in Article 7 TEU. This procedure aims exclusively to eliminate breaches of values on which the EU is based, including the rule of law. In contrast, the objective of the conditionality mechanism is more clear-cut, as it should safeguard the EU funds, or more precisely their sound management[108] and protection[109] against damages resulting from systematic breaches of the rule of law in the Member State. In this procedure decisions are made based on an assessment of the legal (and not political) criteria established under the Draft Regulation, namely the existence of a generalised deficiency as regards the rule of law in the Member State as defined in this Draft (see Sect. 3.2). The key decisions are taken by the Commission,[110] which is the guardian of the EU Treaties,[111] also responsible for the EU budget.[112] The legality of these decisions is fully checked by the CJEU under an action for annulment.[113] This kind of jurisdiction of the CJEU significantly strengthens the legal situations of the Member States in comparison to the purely procedural checks of decisions performed by the CJEU under the Article 7 TEU procedure.[114] In conclusion, it is thus justified to claim the

108 Article 317 TFEU.

109 Article 325 TFEU.

110 The European Parliament proposal.

111 Article 17 TEU.

112 Article 317 TFEU.

113 Article 263 TFEU.

114 Article 269 TFEU.

Article 7 TEU procedure and the conditionality mechanism are parallel and independent of each other.

One could imagine to attack the Draft Regulation as an illegal circumvention of the Article 7 TEU procedures. However, Article 7 TEU does not contain an explicit statement as to whether other Union institutions may defend European values using other instruments. Thus, the general rules apply. It is well established that a specific procedure designed to deal with a certain problem does not exclude developing other instruments,[115] a core doctrine since the *Van Gend en Loos* judgment.[116] Accordingly, it is, in principle, admissible to develop new instruments,[117] such as the Commission's Rule of Law Framework, or to use the budget to defend European values.

7.2 *The General Infringement Procedure (Arts. 258-260 TFEU)*

The general infringement procedure is another legal proceeding that can be initiated against a Member State's breaching the rule of law. Under this procedure, if the Commission considers that a Member State has failed to fulfil its obligation under the Treaties it may bring the matter before the CJEU. If the CJEU finds that the Member State indeed infringed provisions of EU law, it confirms its finding in a judgment.[118] The Member State is then obliged to eliminate the infringement found, and if it does not do so the CJEU may impose financial penalties on this State.[119]

The possibilities offered by the general infringement procedure (Article 258-260 TFEU) in the context of rule of law breaches have already been described by legal scholars.[120] Unlike the Article 7 TEU procedure fruitlessly conducted against Poland and Hungary, the general infringement procedure has already been successfully completed in 2019 in cases against Poland. In case C-192/18 *Commission v. Poland* the CJEU ruled that by establishing a different retirement age for men and women judges and prosecutors in Poland, Poland has failed to fulfil its obligations under Article 157 TFEU and Articles 5(a) and 9(1)(f) of Anti-Discrimination Directive 2006/54/EC. In addition, by granting the Minister for Justice the right to authorise judges to continue to carry out their duties beyond the new retirement age, Poland has failed to fulfil its obligations under Article 19 (1) TEU.[121] In similar cases C-619/18 *Commission v. Poland* the CJEU also ruled that Poland had failed to fulfil

[115]Bast (2006), pp. 60–63.
[116]CJEU, Case C-26/62, *Van Gend en Loos*, ECLI:EU:C:1963:1, para. 26.
[117]Bast (2006), pp. 42–67.
[118]Article 258 TFEU.
[119]Article 260 TFEU.
[120]Wennerås (2017), Gormley (2018), Schmidt and Bogdanowicz (2018) and Taborowski (2019).
[121]CJEU Cases C-192/18, *Commission v. Poland,* ECLI:EU:C:2019:924.

its obligations under Article 19 (1) TEU by lowering the retirement age of the judges of the Supreme Court and by granting the President of Poland the discretion to extend the period of their judicial activity beyond the newly fixed retirement age.[122] In 2019 the Commission brought another case against Poland (C-791/19 *Commission v. Poland)* concerning disciplinary proceedings against judges also with charges of breaching Article 19 (1) TEU. Although the charge of breaching the rule of law was not explicitly raised in that case, it concerned judicial independence, which is a key element of the rule of law.[123]

All in all, the general infringement procedure (Article 258-260 TFEU) and the conditionality mechanism (Draft Regulation) are initiated by the Commission against Member States in cases of possible breaches of the EU law, with a view toward eliminating them. However, these procedures significantly differ.

While the general infringement procedure is regulated by EU primary law (Arts. 258-260 TFEU), the conditionality mechanism will be regulated by EU secondary law (the Draft Regulation). Litigation is also resolved differently. In the case of the general infringement procedure, the dispute between the Commission who brings charges and the accused Member State is resolved by the CJEU. Under the conditionality mechanism, the CJEU is involved only if a Member State—an addressee of a decision launching the conditionality mechanism—challenges its legality in the front of the CJEU under action for annulment (Articles 263 TFEU).

Last but not least, while the general infringement procedure is of a horizontal nature, as it may concern all different kinds of violations of EU law (including breaches of the rule of law), the conditionality mechanism is of a sectoral nature, since its concerns only one specific EU law violation, namely a breach of the rule of law detrimental to EU funds. The relationship between the general infringement procedure (Articles 258-260 TFEU) and the sectoral procedures provided in EU regulations allowing the Commission to protect the EU funds has already been analysed by the CJEU. In cases concerning EU funds, the Member States have claimed that if the Commission finds that expenditures financed by EU funds were incurred in breach of EU law, it should initiate the general infringement procedure against them (Article 258 TFEU), under which the CJEU would assess the charges and legality of EU expenditures. By this approach the Member States opposed the Commission's practice to initiate, in such cases, '*the clearance of accounts procedure'*, regulated in the CAP regulations. In these procedures, now already also conducted in the cohesion policy, if the Commission detects irregular EU expenditures incurred in a Member State, it adopts a decision imposing financial corrections on said State, which obliges it to return the irregularly spent EU funds to the EU budget. The CJEU did not share the Member States' argumentation and ruled that infringements of EU law related to the illegal spending of EU funds should be decided within the framework of sectoral procedures and not under the general

[122]CJEU Cases C-619/18, *Commission v. Poland,* ECLI:EU:C:2019:53, see: Wyrzykowski (2018), Waelbroeck and Oliver (2018), Kmieciak (2019) and Klatt (2019).

[123]Bárd and Ballegooij van (2018).

infringement procedure (Article 258 TFEU).[124] The practice of bringing cases involving the irregular spending of EU funds under sectoral procedures, developed in, e.g., agriculture and cohesion regulations, is currently applied today. In such cases the Commission does not bring general infringement proceedings against the Member States (Arts. 258-260 TFEU) but applies procedures established under EU secondary law regulations. The question that can be asked is whether the above-mentioned case-law of the CJEU would apply to the conditionality mechanism. *Prima facie* there are no legal obstacles excluding such a possibility.

8 Conclusions

Analyses of rule of law instruments established under EU law, analysed in this chapter, lead to the following conclusions.

Practice of conducting the Article 7 TEU procedure—the main EU Treaties procedure aimed to protect the 'European values', including the rule of law (Article 2 TEU) is disappointing. After few years from initiating it against Poland (in 2017) and Hungary (in 2018) there is hardly any real progress made. With more success the general infringement procedure is conducted (Article 258-260 TFEU)—in 2019 two cases were settled by the CJEU (C-192/18 *Commission v. Poland* and C-619/18 *Commission v. Poland)* and one case was brought (C-791/19 *Commission v. Poland*), all concerning capturing judicial independence of Polish courts. For some (unknown) reasons, the possibilities offered by the EU secondary law, namely the CP Regulation on the EU funds, allowing for the suspension and recovery of the EU funds from the Member State infringing EU law, have not been tested yet by the Commission. Instead the Draft Regulation establishing the conditionality mechanism allowing for the suspension of EU funds transferred to the Member State breaching the rule of law (commented on in this chapter) was put on the table. Scrutiny of this Draft lead to the following conclusions. Two most important remarks concern legality of (1) (too) generally formulated premises for applying of the conditionality mechanism and unknown shape of measures to be imposed under this mechanism and (2) launching this mechanism by the Council by the *reverse* QMV.

First of all, premises for applying the conditionality mechanism were set out extremely broadly, to the extent that their exact meaning and scope is extremely difficult to determine (see Sect. 3.2). Their very essence is 'a generalised deficiency as regards the rule of law' defined as widespread or recurrent practice of public authorities which violates the rule of law and affects or risk affecting the EU funds—their sound financial management (Article 317 TFEU) or the protection (Article

[124] CJEU Cases: 15 and 16-76, *France v. Commission*, ECLI:EU:C:1979:29, paras 22-35, C-247/98, *Greece v. Commission*, ECLI:EU:C:2001:4, paras 13-14; C-332/00, *Greece v. Commission*, ECLI:EU:C:2002:235, para. 46.

325 TFEU). To make this abstract notion of a 'generalised deficiency' more pragmatic, the Draft Regulation provided some of their examples. This list contains, on the one hand, such explicit infringements as e.g. ineffective and late cooperation of national authorities with OLAF and EPP; or breaches of confidentiality of communication between lawyers and clients. On the other hand, the list also contains very general breaches, e.g. limiting the effective investigation, prosecution and sanctioning of breaches of EU law; jeopardizing judicial independence; or endangering capacity of the Member State to respect the obligations of EU membership, including the capacity to effectively implement EU law. Instead of legal certainty, this list creates further legal confusion. This lack of precision in formulation of premises to apply the conditionality mechanism is problematic, if one takes into account that the CJEU consequently requires that the principle of legal certainty should be respected particularly rigorously in the case of sanctions and provisions having financial implications. It is clear that the Draft Regulation establishing conditionality mechanism consists of sanctions that would have a financial impact on the Member States breaching the rule of law. This is its essence and *raison d'être*. Therefore, it can be claimed that excessively general phrasing of premises necessary to launch the conditionality mechanism frustrates the principle of legal certainty.

The same can be said about specific measures (e.g. suspension of EU funds, their recovery) to be imposed under the conditionality mechanism (see Sect. 4). These measures are not regulated by the Draft Regulation, but under EU sectoral Regulations that would establish EU spending rules to be applied in MFF 2021–2027 in specific EU policies (e.g. agricultural, cohesion). Since these Regulations are presently under EU legislative processes run independently from legislative works on the Draft Regulation, the final outcome and impact of the conditionality mechanism, depended on this sectoral rules, cannot be presently assessed. Surprisingly, the Draft Regulation does not mention such reference. What's striking, in the legal debate on the conditionality mechanism a legal relation between the EU sectoral Regulations and the Draft Regulation is often missed with the effect that the conditionality mechanism is described as the self-regulatory one. This is an evident omission.

Secondly, serious legal doubts concern peculiar procedure of adoption of a decision launching the conditionality mechanism. This decision is not adopted under the standard procedure and vote cast established by the EU Treaties but under the specific procedures provided by the Draft Regulation in which the Council votes by the *reverse* QMV. A proposal of a decision launching a conditionality mechanism submitted by the Commission is adopted unless the Council *rejects* it within 1 month or otherwise amend it by *ordinary* QMV. This procedure places the Commission in a privileged position and facilitates the adoption of decisions. If the Council is unable to obtain *ordinary* QMV to reject the decision (within a month), the Commission's proposal would become a legally binding decision. After 1 month the decision may be however changed, if the Council votes on it by *ordinary* QMV. At this point in time, it is difficult to definitively assess the legality of this procedure, given the fact that the CJEU has not expressed its view on legality of voting by the Council by *reverse* QMV. Establishing the legislative procedure and vote cast remaining outside the EU Treaties toolbox may, however, raise serious legal concerns. To conclude this part, there is a strong evidence in the above-mentioned parts of the Draft Regulations concerning (1) premises for applying the conditionality mechanism and measures to be imposed under it as well as (2) voting by the Council by the *reverse* QMV to initiate this mechanism violates the EU Treaty. Despite these reservations, other provisions of the Draft Regulation can also be critically assessed.

Despite the common narration that the conditionality mechanism should only lead to suspension of EU funds, it is clearly regulated in the Draft Regulation that a Member State whose EU funds were suspended under the conditionality mechanism can easily lose them forever (see Sect. 6.1). This will happen if, within 2 years from the year of their suspension, this State will not remedy the breach of the rule of law and convince the EU institution to lift (or alter) the suspension. In such a case the Commission would not be authorised to re-enter the suspended amounts in the EU budget. Because of this serious and automatic effect, the conditionality mechanism may turn out to be a far more severe and detrimental financial penalty than perhaps is envisioned. For this reason formulating precise premises for the adoption of the conditionality mechanism, as stated above, is even more important.

The Draft Regulation provides beneficiaries of EU funds with a weak legal protection if the Member States whose EU funds were suspended under the conditionality mechanism stop making payments to them (see Sect. 6.2). The E-communication channel foreseen would rather not suffice. Thus in effect the real financial impact of suspension in some cases may be passed on beneficiaries. Then the most effective legal remedy they could undertake would probably be an action for damages brought against a Member State breaching the EU law (the *Francovich* liability). From its side, the Commission could bring to the CJEU a general infringement action (Article 258-260 TFEU) against this State.

The Draft Regulation does not specify the relationship between the conditionality mechanism and other EU Treaties procedures (the Article 7 TEU procedure and general infringement procedure under Articles 258-260 TFEU) that may be applied in cases of breaching the rule of law by the Member States (see Sect. 7). There are, *prima facie*, no legal obstacles to introduce the conditionality mechanism to EU law, as its legal construction (objectives, premises and procedure) significantly differs from the EU Treaties procedures aimed at safeguarding the rule of law. While the Article 7 TEU procedure is political in nature, the general infringement procedure (Articles 258-260 TFEU) is aimed at any kind of infringement of EU law. In contrast, the conditionality mechanism is a clear-cut procedure, regulated by the EU secondary law, aimed to safeguard the EU funds from damages resulting from systemic infringements of the rule of law by the Member States. It is mainly in the hands of the Commission, as it is the guardian of the EU Treaties (Article 17 TEU) and also responsible for management of the EU budget (Article 317 TFEU). In case of doubts, any legal disputes arising from the application of the conditionality mechanism are to be settled by the CJEU under the action for annulment (Article 263 TFEU).

To conclude the thoughts concerning the Draft Regulation it can be claimed that the important issue to be tackled during coming legislative works on it would be to finding a way to ensure the protection of the rule of law without compromising this rule and other values on which the EU is based.

References

Atik J (2016) From 'no bailout' to the European stability mechanism. Fordham Int Law J 39 (5):1201

Bárd P, Ballegooij van W (2018) The AG Opinion in the Celmer case: why lack of judicial independence should have been framed as a rule of law issue. https://verfassungsblog.de/the-ag-opinion-in-the-celmer-case-why-lack-of-judicial-independence-should-have-been-framed-as-a-rule-of-law-issue/

Bartels L (2005) Human rights conditionality in the EU's international agreements. Oxford University Press, Oxford

Bast J (2006) Grundbegriffe der Handlungsformen der EU. Springer, Heidelberg

Besselink L (2017) The bite, the bark and the howl: Art. 7 TEU and the rule of law initiatives. In: Jakab A, Kochenov D (eds) The enforcement of EU law and values, ensuring member states' compliance. Oxford University Press, Oxford, pp 128–144

Butler I (2018) Two proposals to promote and protect European values through the multiannual financial framework: conditionality of EU funds and a financial instrument to support NGOs. Liberties, 7.03.2018, https://www.liberties.eu/en/news/european-vaues-fund-two-proposals-mff/14471

Chalmers D, Davies G, Monti G (2015) European Union Law: text and materials. Cambridge University Press, Cambridge

Closa C, Kochenov D (2016) Reinforcing rule of law oversight in the European Union. Cambridge University Press, Cambridge

Cornelius J (2016) The European Union development policies are based on European values, democracy, respect for the rule of law and human right. In: Goudappel F, Hirsch B (eds) Democracy and rule of law in the European Union. T.M.C. Asser, The Hague, pp 109–126

Costa M (2017) The accountability gap in EU law. Routledge, London

Craig P (2012) EU administrative law. Oxford University Press, Oxford

Cremona M (2005) EU enlargement: solidarity and conditionality. Eur Law Rev 30(1):19

Dumbrovský T (2018) Beyond voting rights suspension. Tailored sanction as democracy catalyst under Article 7 TEU. In: Hatje A, Tichý L (eds) Liability of member states for the violation of fundamental values of the European Union. Nomos, Baden-Baden, pp 203–228

Fierro E (2003) The EU's approach to human rights conditionality in practice. Martinus Nijhoff Publishers, The Hague

Geiger R (2015) Commentary to Article 7 TEU in: European Union treaties. Commentary. Beck, München

Gormley L (2018) Infringement proceedings. In: Jakab A, Kochenov D (eds) The enforcement of EU law and values, ensuring member states' compliance. Oxford University Press, Oxford, pp 65–78

Halmai G (2018) The possibility and desirability of economic sanction: the rule of law against the EU Member States. 2018/06, EUI Working Paper Law, http://cadmus.eui.eu/handle/1814/51644

Hatje A (2018) Liability of member states for the violation of fundamental values of the European Union. Nomos, Baden-Baden

Hofmann HCH, Rowe GC, Türk AH (2012) Administrative law and policy of the European Union. Oxford University Press, Oxford

Jakab A, Kochenov D (2017) The enforcement of EU law and values: ensuring member states' compliance. Oxford University Press, Oxford

Kelemen D, Scheppele KL (2018) How to stop funding autocracy in the EU. Verfassungsblog, 10.9.2018, https://verfassungsblog.de/how-to-stop-funding-autocracy-in-the-eu/

Klatt MK (2019) Herabsetzung des Ruhestandsalters für Richter in Polen. Neue Zeitschrift für Verwaltungsrecht 2019:1109–1118

Kmieciak Z (2019) Ochrona tymczasowa w sprawie ze skargi Komisji przeciwko Polsce dotyczącej przepisów ustawy obniżającej wiek przejścia w stan spoczynku sędziów SN. Glosa do postanowienia TSUE z 19.10.2018 r., C-619/18 R. Państwo i Prawo 2019:143–150

Konstadinides T (2017) The rule of law in the European Union. Hart Publishing, Oxford

Louis J-F (2010) The no-bailout clause and rescue packages. Common Market Law Rev 47(4):971

Mangiameli S, Saputelli G (2013) Commentary to Article 7 TEU. In: Blanke H-J, Mangiameli S (eds) The treaty on European Union. Springer, Berlin, p 350

McKenzie L, Meissner K (2017) Human rights conditionality in European Union trade negotiations. J Common Market Stud 55(4):832–849

Pech L, Perju V, Platon S (2019) How to address rule of law backsliding in Romania: the case for an infringement action based on Article 325 TFEU. Verfassungsblog, 2019.5.29, https://verfassungsblog.de/how-to-adress-rule-of-law-backsliding-inromania, https://doi.org/10.17176/20190529-121940-0

Peel M, Hopkins V, Shotter J (2019) Finland to push EU budget rule of law clampdown. Financial Times, September 8 2019, https://www.ft.com/content/c3d655fe-cfe7-11e9-99a4-b5ded7a7fe3f

Scheppele KL, Pech L, Kelemen RD (2018) Never missing an opportunity to miss an opportunity: the council legal service opinion on the Commission's EU budget-related rule of law mechanism. Verfassungsblog, 2018.11.12, https://verfassungsblog.de/never-missing-an-opportunity-to-miss-an-opportunity-the-council-legal-service-opinion-on-the-commissions-eu-budget-related-rule-of-law-mechanism, https://doi.org/10.17176/20181115-215538-0

Schmidt M, Bogdanowicz P (2018) The infringement procedure in the rule of law crisis: how to make effective use of Article 258 TFEU. Common Market Law Rev 55:1061–1100

Schöndorf-Haubold B (2011) Common European administration: the European structural funds. In: Jansen O, Schöndorf-Haubold B (eds) The European composite administration. Intersentia, Antwerp, p 25 et seq

Schroeder W (2016) Strengthening the rule of law in Europe. Hart Publishing, Oxford

Taborowski M (2019) Mechanizm ochrony praworządności państw członkowskich w prawie Unii Europejskiej. Studium przebudzenia systemu ponadnarodowego. Wolters Kluwer, Alphen aan den Rijn

Van Aken W, Artige L (2013) Reverse majority voting in comparative perspective: implications for fiscal governance in the EU. In: de Witte B, Héritier A, Trechsel A (eds) The Euro crisis and the state of European democracy. European University Institute, Fiesole, p 129 et seq

Vita V (2017) Revisiting the dominant discourse on conditionality in the EU: the case of EU spending conditionality. Camb Yearb Eur Legal Stud 19:136

von Bogdandy A (2019) Principles and challenges of a European Doctrine of systemic deficiencies. MPIL Research Paper No. 2019-14, https://ssrn.com/abstract=3431303 or https://doi.org/10.2139/ssrn.3431303

von Brauneck J (2019) Gefährdung des EU-Haushalts durch rechtsstaatliche Mängel in den Mitgliedstaaten? Europarecht (EuR) 2019:37–60

Waelbroeck M, Oliver P (2018) Enforcing the rule of law in the EU: what can be done about Hungary and Poland? https://blogdroiteuropeen.com/2018/01/31/enforcing-the-rule-of-law-in-the-eu-what-can-be-done-about-hungary-and-poland-par-michel-waelbroeck-et-peter-oliver/

Wennerås P (2017) Making effective use of Article 260 TFEU. In: Jakab A, Kochenov D (eds) The enforcement of EU law and values, ensuring member states' compliance. Oxford University Press, Oxford, pp 79–98

Wyrzykowski M (2018) Rule of law: European Commission v. Poland. In: Hatje A, Tichý L (eds) Liability of Member States for the violation of fundamental values of the European Union. Nomos, Baden-Baden, pp 169–199

Justyna Łacny is Professor at the Warsaw University of Technology.

3

The Rule of Law and the Roll of the Dice: The Uncertain Future of Investor-State Arbitration in the EU

Wojciech Sadowski

Contents

Abstract Investment treaty law and EU law began to develop in the same era and share some important philosophical and axiological foundations. The pressure on the

---

All opinions expressed herein are personal to the author and should not be attributed to Queritius or its clients.

W. Sadowski (✉)
Queritius, Warsaw, Poland
e-mail: wojciech.sadowski@queritius.com

CEE countries to enter into numerous bilateral investment treaties in late 80s and early 90s, in the context of the EU accession aspirations of the former communist countries, was likely to result, eventually, in a conflict between EU law and investment treaty law. The conflict could have been managed in three different ways, yet the CJEU decided in *Achmea* to declare an undefined volume of intra-EU arbitrations to be incompatible with EU law. This important judgment, which delivered an outcome desired by the European Commission and a number of Member States, is based on questionable legal reasoning that creates high uncertainty in this area of law. The doubts include the scope of application of *Achmea*, which is now a highly debatable issue. The CJEU itself saw it necessary to limit the scope of *Achmea* by declaring in Opinion 1/17 (*CETA*) that the legal reasoning of *Achmea* did not apply to investment protection treaties with third countries. The Member States of the EU remain politically divided in their views as to whether *Achmea* applies to the Energy Charter Treaty. And while the problems with the rule of law and independence of the judiciary in certain Member States continue to grow, *Achmea* has left an important gap for which there is no substitute in the current architecture of the EU legal system.

1 Introduction

Yogi Berra, a baseball player and coach, once famously said it was difficult for him to make predictions, especially about the future. His job should be easier in legal studies, since law is supposed to be a set of rules intended to yield reasonably high predictability of result. A frequent connotation of the rule of law is that legal matters should unfold in an orderly and foreseeable fashion, instilling the sense of certainty in legal subjects. When it comes, however, to the interactions between EU law and investor-state arbitration, predictability of outcome has been rather low lately. Politics clearly trumps technical legal reasoning in this field. This should probably be of little wonder. International investment protection law has always been a highly political issue. In the early 90s, investment protection treaties were used in Europe as a way to foster economic expansion of Western European companies to the former Soviet bloc, without much technical legal thought being given to the long-term consequences of creating this new legal order in Europe and its relation to EU law.

The potential for conflict between EU law and investment treaty law was not identified at that time, though it was eventually unavoidable. When these two worlds finally came to a clash, their confrontation could have been managed in several different ways. Advocate-General Wathelet made an ingenuous proposal in *Achmea*,[1] which could have established harmonious co-existence of both legal systems, and at the same time, surrender intra-EU investment treaty tribunals to

[1]CJEU, Case C-284/16, *Achmea*, ECLI:EU:C:2017:699.

the functional supremacy of the CJEU.[2] The CJEU, however, chose a radically different approach, declaring an undefined volume of intra-EU arbitrations to be incompatible with the EU law.[3] That decision elated certain European Governments, but not necessarily those most adherent to the rule of law. The CJEU then purported to clarify in *Opinion 1/17* that only the investor-state dispute resolution clauses in intra-EU treaties should be deemed incompatible with EU law, and not those in the treaties with third countries.[4] In the latter case, the outcome seems to depend on whether a treaty in question complies with the threshold criteria defined by the CJEU in *Opinion 1/17*. By declaring that the CETA[5] complied with such criteria, the CJEU cleared the path to the ratification and entry into force of that treaty. *Opinion 1/17* reads as if the pendulum swang in the direction opposite to *Achmea*, since the position the CJEU took in it contradicts in many important aspects the legal reasoning underlying the *Achmea* judgment.[6] Nonetheless, the CJEU confirmed in *Opinion 1/17* that *Achmea* applies broadly to intra-EU proceedings, but sought to distinguish it from the case of treaties with third countries.[7] As shall be shown below, however, the distinction between the intra-EU and extra-EU investment treaties is not sufficient to justify the contradictory conclusions reached by the CJEU in these two decisions. A more plausible explanation is that in either case the delivered outcome was conforming to the existing political expectations, which in each case were different. In *Achmea*, the expectation was to do away with investment treaty arbitration in Europe.[8] In *Opinion 1/17*, to confirm the ability of the EU to create a new system of international justice in investment matters, featuring the Investment Court System.[9]

Because of these important decisions, the EU is now facing three important challenges. *Firstly*, the elimination of intra-EU investment arbitrations has left an important gap in the legal protection of individuals in Europe. There is no substitute for it in the current architecture of the EU legal system.[10] At the time when certain illiberal governments pursue systemic actions intended to undermine the

---

[2]See Buczkowska et al. (2017).

[3]CJEU, Case C-284/16, *Achmea*, ECLI:EU:C:2018:158.

[4]CJEU, Opinion 1/17 *Comprehensive Economic and Trade Agreement between Canada, on the one part, and the European Union and its Member States, of the other part*, ECLI:EU:C:2019:341, see dispositive part and paras. 126–129.

[5]See http://trade.ec.europa.eu/doclib/docs/2014/september/tradoc_152806.pdf. Last accessed on 17 July 2019.

[6]Koutrakos (2019), pp. 239–294.

[7]CJEU, Opinion 1/17, *supra* note 4, paras. 126–127.

[8]See Hartley (2019), p. 335: 'It will be clear from the cases discussed that the law in this area is almost entirely based on policy. The Treaty provisions are important, but they are regarded simply as underpinning the wider policies inherent in the EU Treaties.[. . .] it would be futile to search for a narrow formula which encapsulates the law.'

[9]See http://europa.eu/rapid/press-release_IP-19-2334_en.htm. Last accessed on 17 July 2019.

[10]Which is admitted even by the enthusiastic supporters of the *Achmea* judgment, see e.g. Hindelang (2019), p. 383.

independence of the judiciary in certain EU countries, it is also riskier than ever to assume that state courts in these countries can remain capable of providing effective protection of EU rights to individuals.[11] *Secondly*, *Achmea* has created significant uncertainty as to its exact meaning and scope. Its reasoning is far from clear and the judgment itself is based on seemingly mistaken assumptions.[12] Even the EU Member States differ among themselves in their official positions as to the impact of *Achmea* on the Energy Charter Treaty.[13] *Achmea* also creates a conflict between international and EU law. In particular, it puts EU Member States in a delicate situation, since they are obliged to comply with existing arbitral awards in accordance with the investment protection treaties, but *Achmea* prevents them from complying voluntarily. This may create real practical problems especially outside the EU, where local courts seized with requests for enforcement against state assets do not necessarily have to recognize the principles of primacy and autonomy of EU law.[14] Thirdly, *Achmea* creates lingering problems for the ambitious plans of the EU to reform the investor-state dispute resolution system globally, in particular through the creation of a multinational investment court.[15] *Opinion 1/17* resolves this problem only partially and superficially. Future arbitrations under the CETA shall likely lead to the situation in which the CJEU's position taken in *Opinion 1/17* may have to be revisited in light of the views expressed in *Achmea*. Predictability in this area of law has been reduced to a roll of the dice.

---

[11] See Sadowski (2018), pp. 1025–1060.

[12] As the Arbitral Tribunal in ICSID Case No. ARB/15/15, *9REN Holding S.À.R.L. v. Spain*, award of 31 May 2019, para. 150, put it: 'The Tribunal has attempted, with the Parties' assistance, to understand the truncated reasoning in the CJEU's decision in *Achmea*. There is much to understand.'

[13] Compare the Declarations of the Member States of 15 and 16 January 2019 on the legal consequences of the *Achmea* judgment and on investment protection, available at https://ec.europa.eu/info/publications/190117-bilateral-investment-treaties_en, last accessed on 20 June 2019.

[14] The U.S. courts currently seem to be the principal extra-EU destination of EU investors who were awarded damages by investment treaty tribunals against Spain. See, for example, N*extEra Energy Global Holdings B.V. and NextEra Energy Spain Holdings B.V. v. Kingdom of Spain*, Petition to Confirm International Arbitral Award Pursuant to the 1965 ICSID Convention of 3 June 2019, Case no. 1:19-cv-01618, https://www.italaw.com/sites/default/files/case-documents/italaw10570.pdf, last acceded on 17 July 2019.

[15] Lavranos and Singla (2018), p. 351 et seq.

2 From Friends to Foes

2.1 Early Co-existence

Modern investment treaty law and European integration have contemporaneous origins. The 1959 treaty between Germany and Pakistan,[16] regarded as the first bilateral investment treaty worldwide, was adopted just 2 years after the Treaty of Rome was signed. The arbitration between a UK company *AAPL and Sri Lanka* in the late 80s was the first dispute in which an arbitration agreement conferring jurisdiction on an arbitral tribunal, was construed from a combination of a provision in an international treaty and the express or implied will of an investor.[17]

When the CEE countries began the process of their association with the EEC (later the EU) in the 90s, it was the European Commission which requested them, in the so-called Europe Agreements, to enter into bilateral investment treaties with the then Member States.[18] This is the explanation of the high number of bilateral investment treaties between Eastern and Western European countries. The European Union and its Member States also adopted the Energy Charter Treaty, which provides for the settlement of a broad range of investor-state disputes through international arbitration.[19] There does not seem to be evidence that at the time these treaties were signed, serious discussions were held as to whether international investment law and investor-state arbitration were compatible with EU law, or whether candidate Member States from Central and Eastern Europe should renounce these treaties once they are admitted to EU membership.

[16]Treaty for the Promotion and Protection of Investments (with Protocol and exchange of notes), Germany and Pakistan, 25 November 1959, 457 U.N.T.S. 24 (entered into force 28 November 1962), available at http://treaties.un.org/Pages/showDetails.aspx?objid=0800000280132bef, last accessed on 20 June 2019.

[17]Arbitral Tribunal, *Asian Agricultural Products Ltd. v. Republic of Sri Lanka*, ICSID Case No. ARB/87/3, Final Award of 27 June 1990.

[18]See, e.g., Article 72(2) of the Europe Agreement establishing an association between the European Communities and their Member States, of the one part, and the Republic of Hungary, of the other part, signed in Brussels on 16 December 1991, OJ 1993 L 347/2; see also: CJEU, Case C-284/16, *Achmea*, ECLI:EU:C:2017:699, footnote 41 for similar examples concerning Poland, Romania, Slovakia or Croatia.

[19]The text of the Energy Charter Treaty is available at https://energycharter.org/fileadmin/DocumentsMedia/Legal/ECTC-en.pdf, last accessed on 20 June 2019. The (non-exhaustive) list of investment treaty arbitration initiated under the ECT is available here: https://energycharter.org/what-we-do/dispute-settlement/all-investment-dispute-settlement-cases/, last accessed on 20 June 2019.

2.2 *Rise in Intra-EU Arbitrations*

The surge in investor-state arbitrations, which began worldwide in late 90s, did not spare Central and Eastern Europe.[20] In fact, the economic and legal transformation, including massive privatization plans and the process of adaptation of the CEE legal systems to the requirements of the European Union were fruitful grounds for numerous treaty claims related to that part of the world.[21] Following the accessions of 2004 and 2007, new Member States were among the first ones to note the potential conflict between EU law and investment protection treaties. Defending themselves against treaty claims, they started to raise, in various shapes and forms, objections related to the alleged incompatibility of the two legal regimes. The European Commission also stepped in to support these contentions. Arbitral tribunals, often composed of prominent international judges and scholars in public international law, consistently rejected, however, jurisdictional objections based on EU law.[22]

The arguments in favour and against the 'EU objection' were rehearsed so many times and from so many angles that the matter can now be said to have been profoundly examined and discussed by arbitral tribunals. The case law which emerged from those decisions could be regarded as *jurisprudence constante* in investment treaty law. The unequivocal conclusion was that neither the accession of the new Member States to the EU, nor the inherent features of the EU legal system, deprived arbitral tribunals of the jurisdiction conferred upon them by investment protection treaties.

2.3 *Game-Changing Catalysts*

Three catalysts then played a major role in undermining the position of investment treaty arbitration in Europe. The first one was the emergence of cases, which, rightly or wrongly, were considered to threaten the autonomy of the EU legal order. These

[20]See e.g. UNCTAD Fact Sheet on Investor–State Dispute Settlement Cases in 2018, available at https://unctad.org/en/PublicationsLibrary/diaepcbinf2019d4_en.pdf, last accessed on 20 June 2019, p. 1.

[21]See UNCTAD Fact Sheet on Investor–State Dispute Settlement Cases in 2018, p. 2. Czechia and Poland have been among the most frequently sued countries, along Ukraine and Russia.

[22]Among many decisions preceding the CJEU judgment in *Achmea*, see e.g. Arbitral Tribunal, SCC Case No. 088/2004, *Eastern Sugar B.V. v. Czech Republic*, Partial Award of 27 March 2007; *Jan Oostergetel and Theodora Laurentius v. Slovak Republic*, UNCITRAL, Decision on Jurisdiction of 30 April 2010; PCA Case No. 2008-13, *Achmea B.V. (formerly Eureko) v. Slovak Republic*, Award on Jurisdiction, Arbitrability and Suspension of 26 October 2010; ICSID Case no. ARB/07/19, *Electrabel S.A. v. Republic of Hungary*, Decision on Jurisdiction, Applicable Law and Liability of 30 November 2012; ICSID Case No. ARB/05/20, *Ioan Micula, Viorel Micula, S.C. European Food S.A, S.C. Starmill S.R.L. and S.C. Multipack S.R.L. v. Romania*, Final Award of 11 December 2013 et al.

included *Micula v. Romania*, which was often presented as a clear example that investment treaty arbitration could be used to circumvent the EU rules on state aid.[23] Such statement was inaccurate with respect to *Micula*, since the facts of that case concerned the consequences of the benefits, which were withdrawn *before* Romania joined the EU and started to be bound by the *acquis communautaire*. By implication, since the alleged internationally unlawful act occurred before the accession, the alleged liability in damages of the respondent state also arose before that date. These points were correctly identified by the General Court of the EU in its judgment of 18 June 2019, which annulled the decision of the European Commission (EU) 2015/1470 of 30 March 2015 on State aid SA.38517 (2014/C) (ex 2014/NN) implemented by Romania—Arbitral award *Micula v. Romania* of 11 December 2013.[24] Indeed, it should not be a controversial issue that benefits withdrawn 2 years before Romania's accession to the EU should not be regarded as state aid under EU law.[25] However, the perception impact of the *Micula* case had already taken its toll and influenced the development of international investment law.[26] Furthermore, it is not inconceivable that in another case with a different set of facts, a conflict between EU state aid law and an investment protection treaty could actually arise.

The second catalyst was the emergence of high profile disputes related to politically or socially sensitive matters. This includes, for example, the *Vattenfall* arbitration concerning the consequences of the uncompensated phasing out of nuclear power plants in Germany.[27] Along with a small number of other high profile cases, including the *Philip Morris* arbitrations concerning the plain tobacco packaging rules in Australia and Uruguay,[28] *Vattenfall* attracted considerable interest

[23]*Micula, supra* note 22.

[24]GCEU, Cases T-624/15, T-694/15 and T-704/15, *European Food SA and Others v. European Commission, ECLI:EU:T:2019:423*. See also Croisant (2019) and Bakos (2019).

[25]Interestingly, the Arbitral Tribunal in the *Micula* award calculated the amount of damages due to the investors on the basis of hypothetical assumption that the benefits would remain in force also beyond the date of the Romania's accession to the EU. The Court noted that point, but ruled that since the Commission did not draw a distinction, among the amounts to be recovered, between those falling within the period predating accession and those falling within the period subsequent to accession, the decision by which it classified the entirety of the compensation as aid is necessarily unlawful (GCEU, *European Food, supra* note 24, para. 108).

[26]See e.g. Art. 8.9.4 of the CETA: 'nothing in this Section shall be construed as preventing a Party from discontinuing the granting of a subsidy or requesting its reimbursement where such measure is necessary in order to comply with international obligations between the Parties or has been ordered by a competent court, administrative tribunal or other competent authority, or requiring that Party to compensate the investor therefor.' A footnote to that provision explained that with respect to EU, subsidies also embrace state aid. See also e.g. Article 2.2.4 of the Investment Protection Agreement between the European Union and its Member States, of the one part, and the Socialist Republic of Viet Nam, of the other part.

[27]See the official explanation of Vattenfall for the reasons of its action: https://group.vattenfall.com/press-and-media/news%2D%2Dpress-releases/newsroom/2016/why-vattenfall-is-taking-germany-to-court, last accessed on 20 June 2019.

[28]Arbitral Tribunal, ICSID Case No. ARB/10/7, *Philip Morris Brands Sàrl, Philip Morris Products S.A. and Abal Hermanos S.A. v. Oriental Republic of Uruguay* (formerly *FTR Holding SA, Philip*

within the civic societies of Western European states. These cases spurred protests against the then ongoing negotiations of the trade and investment agreements with Canada (CETA) and the US (TTIP).[29]

Thirdly, the global financial crisis required some Member States to intervene on its financial markets or to implement austerity measures, in particular with respect to certain ill-conceived public support schemes for the renewable energy sector. That led to more arbitrations where, for the first time, some of the Western European states found themselves on the receiving end and began to reconsider the risks and benefits of intra-EU investment treaty disputes.[30] These cases, too, have had an impact on the further erosion of the investors' rights in the newest generation of investment protection treaties.[31]

2.4 *Achmea*

Such was the landscape on 6 March 2018, when the CJEU rendered its judgment in *Achmea*. The case concerned an action brought by Slovakia to German courts to set aside a jurisdiction award of an arbitral tribunal, in a relatively low profile and low-value dispute between a Dutch insurance company and Slovakia over regulatory measures in the life insurance sector. The German Supreme Court, which referred the preliminary questions to the CJEU, considered that it essentially had no major doubts that the provisions of the Netherlands-Slovakia bilateral investment agreement conferring jurisdiction on the arbitral tribunal were compatible with EU law, but asked the CJEU to confirm that view. In the proceedings before the CJEU, the intervening Member States formed two opposing camps. The polarization of views

Morris Products S.A. and Abal Hermanos S.A. v. Oriental Republic of Uruguay) and PCA Case No. 2012-12.*Philip Morris Asia Limited v. The Commonwealth of Australia*, UNCITRAL.

[29]The TTIP negotiations were launched in 2013 and ended without conclusion at the end of 2016, see: http://ec.europa.eu/trade/policy/in-focus/ttip/index_en.htm, last accessed on 20 June 2019. This happened due to a wave of civil opposition in various EU countries, including massive street protests. See e.g. https://www.theguardian.com/business/2016/sep/17/ttip-protests-see-crowds-take-to-streets-of-seven-german-cities, last accessed on 20 June 2019.

[30]Spain is by far the most-frequently sued EU Member State and the second most-often sued country in the world with 49 known cases, closed or pending, by the end of 2018. Among other 'old' Member States, Italy follows with 11 cases, followed by Greece (4 cases) and Germany (3 cases), see UNCTAD Fact Sheet on Investor–State Dispute Settlement Cases in 2018, available at https://unctad.org/en/PublicationsLibrary/diaepcbinf2019d4_en.pdf, last accessed on 20 June 2019, pp. 11–13.

[31]See note 23 above. The problem, from the investors' perspective, is that the ability of the states to freely withdraw subsidies incentives states to play the bait-and-switch, i.e. to first lure investors to make heavy capital expenditures in order to create the required infrastructure in exchange for a promise of long-term subsidy scheme, and then cancel the scheme shortly after the investment is completed. This is particularly problematic in sectors such as renewable energy, or water and sewage distribution and collection systems, which require very high initial capex, but then do not generate high operating costs.

in Europe was manifest, and the dividing lines were clearly marked between the capital-exporting, and capital-importing states, the latter category supported by the Member States with a high number of pending investment treaty claims.[32]

Arguably, the CJEU could have dealt with the alleged potential incompatibility between EU law and investment treaty law in three different ways. Firstly, it could have agreed with the *Bundesgerichtshof* and declare investment treaty arbitration to be compatible with EU law. This may have left unresolved the problem of potential future clashes between EU and investment treaty law in some borderline scenarios. Secondly, the CJEU could have created a framework for dialogue between arbitral tribunals and the CJEU on issues related to the application and interpretation of the EU law. To that effect, the CJEU could have recognized investment treaty tribunals as 'courts or tribunals' in the sense of Article 267 TFUE. This was exactly what Advocate General Wathelet was suggesting to the CJEU in his opinion in the *Achmea* case. The third option, and the one chosen by the CJEU, was to declare investment treaty arbitration incompatible with the EU law. In its judgment, the CJEU said it considered intra-EU investment treaty arbitration as threatening the autonomy of the EU legal order. The CJEU considered arbitral tribunals sitting under the intra-EU bilateral investment treaties to be trespassing on its own exclusive jurisdiction and refused to enter into a dialogue with them under the auspices of Article 267 TFUE. As a consequence, it ruled that the EU law 'precludes' the investor-state arbitration provisions such as the one in the treaty between the Netherlands and Slovakia.

2.5 *Reception of Achmea by Arbitral Tribunals*

Contrary perhaps to the CJEU's expectations, its judgment has not brought investment treaty arbitration to a halt, although the number of new claims has dropped considerably. However, arbitral tribunals have so far failed or refused to give broad effects to the *Achmea* judgment.[33] Not a single arbitral tribunal after the 6 March 2018 declined jurisdiction because of *Achmea*, although the *Bundesgerichtshof*

---

[32]This polarization was recorded in paras. 34 and 35 of the Opinion of Advocate General Wathelet in *Achmea*, *supra* note 1.

[33]Among others, see: Arbitral Tribunal, ICSID Case No. ARB/13/31, *Antin Infrastructure Services Luxembourg S.à.r.l. and Antin Energia Termosolar B.V. v. Kingdom of Spain*, Award of 15 June 2018; PCA Case No. 2014-0, *Antaris Solar GmbH and Dr. Michael Göde v. Czech Republic*, Award of 2 May 20181; ICSID Case No. ARB/14/1, *Masdar Solar & Wind Cooperatief U.A. v Kingdom of Spain*, Award of 16 May 2018; ICSID Case No. ARB/13/35, *UP and C.D. v Hungary*, Award of 9 October 2018; SCC Arbitration V 2015/150, *Greentech Energy Systems A/S et al. v Kingdom of Spain*, Award of 23 December 2018; ICSID Case No. ARB/13/30, *RREEF Infrastructure (G.P.) Limited and RREEF Pan-European Infrastructure Two Lux SARL*, Award of 30 November 2018; SCC Case No. 2015/063, *Novenergia II—Energy & Environment (SCA) (Grand Duchy of Luxembourg), SICAR v The Kingdom of Spain*, Award of 15 February 2018; ICSID Case No. ARB/15/15, *9REN Holding S.À.R.L. v. Spain*, *supra* note 12.

eventually annulled the *Achmea* award as a consequence of the CJEU decision.[34] Arbitral tribunals recurred to various legal reasons in order not to give effect to *Achmea*. Most notably, the arbitral tribunal in *Vattenfall* issued a lengthy and thoroughly reasoned decision in which it declared that *Achmea* should not apply to arbitrations based on the Energy Charter Treaty.[35] Given that at least several dozen cases brought under the Energy Charter Treaty are currently pending against various EU Member States, the *Vattenfall* decision is of clear importance to the future of investment-treaty arbitrations in Europe.

In reaction to the *Vattenfall* decision and the general pushback from arbitral tribunals, on 15 and 16 January 2019, all EU Member States adopted three, partially concurring declarations on the *effects* of the *Achmea* judgment.[36] More than anything else, these declarations are strong political statements against investment-treaty arbitration in Europe. However, these declarations also include specific promises, such as an undertaking to deposit their instruments of ratification, approval or acceptance of a plurilateral treaty or of any bilateral treaty terminating bilateral investment treaties between Member States, by 6 December 2019.[37]

In parallel to, and somehow in spite of, its quest against the intra-EU investment protection treaties, the European Commission has launched an ambitious initiative to reform the global investor-state dispute resolution system through the creation of a multilateral investment court.[38] Such court would be intended as a dispute resolution forum, including between the EU or its Member States and investors of the other contracting parties to the investment protection and trade agreements. There are many problems how to conciliate the functioning of such system with *Achmea*. More broadly, the reasons underlying *Achmea* should also be seen as the legal obstacles to investment protection treaties with third countries. This is why Belgium (on behalf of Wallonia) questioned the compatibility of the EU-Canada trade and protection

[34] Order of the *Bundesgerichtshof* of 31 October 2018, file no. I ZB 2/15, available at: http://juris.bundesgerichtshof.de/cgi-bin/rechtsprechung/document.py?Gericht=bgh&Art=en&nr=89393&pos=0&anz=1, last accessed on 20 June 2019.

[35] Arbitral Tribunal, ICSID Case No. ARB/12/12, *Vattenfall AB and others v. Federal Republic of Germany*, Decision on the Achmea Issue of 31 August 2018; *9REN Holding S.À.R.L. v. Spain*, *supra* note 12.

[36] See: https://energycharter.org/what-we-do/dispute-settlement/all-investment-dispute-settlement-cases/, last accessed on 20 June 2019. See also e.g. Power (2019).

[37] See https://ec.europa.eu/info/sites/info/files/business_economy_euro/banking_and_finance/documents/190117-bilateral-investment-treaties_en.pdf, last accessed on 20 June 2019. The Agreement for the termination of Bilateral Investment Treaties between the Member States of the European Union was signed on 5 May 2020 (OJ L 169, 29.5.2020, p. 1–41) by 23 Member States and enterd into force for the first time on 29 August 2020.

[38] The European Commission proposed a new Investment Court System for TTIP and other EU trade and investment negotiations already in September 2015, see: http://europa.eu/rapid/press-release_IP-15-5651_en.htm. This model was initially included in the series of bilateral trade and investment agreements which the EU was negotiating with Singapore, Canada and Vietnam. Subsequently, on 20 March 2018, the Council authorised negotiations for a treaty establishing a multilateral investment court (MIC).

agreement with the TFEU. Notwithstanding, the CJEU followed the opinion of Advocate-General Bot[39] and ruled on 30 April 2019 that the CETA is compatible with EU law.[40] This is a good outcome for the future of investment treaty arbitration in Europe, but it fails to provide legal certainty and bears an inherent risk of being revisited once the actual cases under the CETA (or another similar treaty) are decided one day.

3 Three Question Marks About *Achmea*

The root of all uncertainty is obviously *Achmea.* The judgment provoked diagonally opposite emotions and reactions worldwide. It came as a blessing to the governments of the EU Member States with large numbers of pending arbitrations or unenforced awards, and as a curse to entrepreneurs who had made substantial long-terms investment in Europe. It has already been addressed by multiple articles[41] and arbitral awards.[42] However, even the supporters of *Achmea* recognize its ambiguities, and there are many. This chapter purports to deal with only three of them.

3.1 Scope of Application

Firstly, it is unclear to which investment protection treaties *Achmea* applies. The dispositive part of *Achmea* reads: 'Articles 267 and 344 TFEU must be interpreted as precluding a provision in an international agreement concluded between Member States, such as Article 8 of the Agreement on encouragement and reciprocal protection of investments between the Kingdom of the Netherlands and the Czech and Slovak Federative Republic, under which an investor from one of those Member States may, in the event of a dispute concerning investments in the other Member State, bring proceedings against the latter Member State before an arbitral tribunal whose jurisdiction that Member State has undertaken to accept.' Thus, the interpretation rendered by the CJEU does not seem to be confined to the specific treaty in question, but is likely to extend to other international treaties concluded between Member States which include provisions 'such as' the provision analysed by the CJEU in *Achmea*. Now, at the time of the judgment there were close to 300 bilateral investment treaties between Member States, which significantly differed from each other. Remarkably, the CJEU failed to notice these differences in *Achmea*, and it did

[39]CJEU, Opinion 1/17 *Accord ECG UE-Canada*, ECLI:EU:C:2019:72.

[40]Id.

[41]Among others, see Hess (2018); Lavranos and Singla (2018), pp. 348–357; Berger (2017), pp. 282–291; Hartley (2019), pp. 321–337.

[42]*Supra* note 33.

not explain which criteria should be taken into account to determine whether a dispute resolution clause in a given treaty was 'such as' Article 8 of the Netherlands-Slovakia BIT.

This omission could create significant lack of legal certainty. However, EU Member States have addressed this problem with the subtleness of Alexander the Great approaching the Gordian knot. Their declarations of 15 and 16 January 2019 start from the assumption that *Achmea* applies to *all* bilateral investment treaties between EU Member States, no matter how similar or different they could be from the Netherlands-Slovakia BIT.[43] Moreover, although the CJEU did not pronounce in *Achmea* over the conformity of substantive provisions of the bilateral investment treaties with EU law and confined its decision only to the jurisdictional aspects of the Netherlands-Slovakia treaty, the Member States went further in their declarations. They undertook to terminate all intra-EU investment protection treaties by way of a treaty, they promised to adopt still in 2019. This step was clearly not required by the *Achmea* judgment and should rather be considered a political decision, for which *Achmea* provides a convenient supportive argument. It lead to the adoption of a treaty which shall likely have the effect of immediate termination of all intra-EU bilateral investment treaties, notwithstanding the existence of sunset clauses in many of such treaties.[44] Accordingly, the uncertainty concerning the scope of the *Achmea* judgment in practice may be limited to intra-EU arbitrations, which were pending at the time of its entry into force, and to enforcement of awards rendered to date under intra-EU BITs.

3.2 Energy Charter Treaty

Secondly, it is unclear whether *Achmea* extends onto intra-EU disputes under the Energy Charter Treaty. Here, the positions of EU Member States seem to be divided, although a large majority of them (22 out of 27) thinks that *Achmea* has such effect. Five other Member States, namely Finland, Luxembourg, Malta, Slovenia and Sweden, noted however, that *Achmea* is silent on the Energy Charter Treaty. They referred to the fact that while a number of international arbitration tribunals post the *Achmea* judgment have concluded that the Energy Charter Treaty contains an investor-State arbitration clause applicable between EU Member States, this interpretation was contested before a national court in a Member State. Against this background, those Member States considered that it would be inappropriate, in the absence of a specific judgment on this matter, to express views as regards the compatibility with EU law of the intra EU application of the Energy Charter

[43] *Supra* note 37.

[44] *Supra* note 37.

Treaty.[45] One Member State, i.e. Hungary, went against the wind and declared that in its view, the *Achmea* judgment concerns only the intra-EU bilateral investment treaties and it 'does not concern any pending or prospective arbitration proceedings initiated under the ECT'. Hungary also stated that the ongoing and future applicability of the ECT in intra-EU relations requires further discussion and individual agreement amongst the Member States. Indeed, the revision process of the Energy Charter Treaty has already started[46] and it cannot be excluded that this treaty could prospectively be changed so as to limit or exclude admissibility of intra-EU claims based on its provisions. This, however, should not have an impact on the legal ramifications of the claims brought before any such future change takes place. As of the time present, arbitral tribunals accept ECT claims brought by EU investors against EU Member States and EU national courts have not taken any firm position on this point.

3.3 Commercial Arbitration

The *third* area of ambiguity resulting from *Achmea* concerns commercial arbitration. Namely, although the CJEU made a very clear distinction between commercial and investment state arbitration in *Achmea*, some of the reasons and arguments underlying the approach that the CJEU took with respect to investment treaty arbitration also extend logically to commercial arbitration. Similar to investment treaty tribunals, arbitral tribunals in commercial matters also cannot refer questions to the CJEU pursuant to Article 267 TFEU. The position of the Court in this respect is well settled.[47] Similar to investment treaty arbitration, commercial arbitration also derogates from jurisdiction of national courts of EU Member States, certain matters in which EU law could be interpreted or applied. Awards of arbitral tribunals sitting in commercial matters, and awards of arbitral tribunals sitting in non-ICSID investment treaty matters are subject to the same scope and degree of review from EU national courts in the context of actions for annulment or applications for enforcement. Therefore, although it results from *Achmea* that the same standard of review is

---

[45]Declaration of the Representatives of the Governments of the Member States, of 16 January on the Enforcement of the Judgment of the Court of Justice in Achmea and on Investment Protection in the European Union, available at https://www.regeringen.se/48ee19/contentassets/d759689c0c804a9ea7af6b2de7320128/achmea-declaration.pdf, last accessed on 24 June 2019.

[46]See Modernisation of the Energy Charter Treaty (ECT), TDM 2019(1), https://www.transnational-dispute-management.com/journal-browse-issues-toc.asp?key=83%20; see also https://energycharter.org/fileadmin/DocumentsMedia/CCDECS/2018/CCDEC201818_-_STR_Modernisation_of_the_Energy_Charter_Treaty.pdf and Negotiating directives for the European Commission issued by Council on 2 July 2019, https://data.consilium.europa.eu/doc/document/ST-10745-2019-ADD-1/en/pdf, last acceded on 17 July 2019.

[47]CJEU, Case C-102/81 *Nordsee*, ECLI:EU:C:1982:107 and CJEU, Case C-126/97 *Eco Swiss*, ECLI:EU:C:1999:269.

sufficient to ensure autonomy of EU law in commercial matters and insufficient in investment treaty matters, it is completely unclear why. Some could argue this is because of the reportedly sensitive nature of the matters, which are dealt with in investment treaty matters. But if these matters are sensitive, they are typically sensitive to particular national interests and national policies of EU Member States and not of the EU. On the other hand, EU law expressly approves and endorses commercial arbitration in matters involving EU competition law.[48] There could be hardly anything more sensitive in the entire body of EU law, yet the CJEU is satisfied with the limited purview of national courts in these matters.

Another attempt to justify the distinction of investment treaty arbitration and commercial arbitration under *Achmea* has been to show that in investment treaty arbitration it is a treaty between the EU Member States that is the reported source of the derogation of the jurisdiction of national courts. Accordingly, some authors purported to claim that the existence of such treaty collides with Article 344 TFEU and thus creates the problem. This argument, however, does not justify the distinction with commercial arbitration and is incorrect for a number of reasons. Firstly, in order for jurisdiction of an investment treaty tribunal to arise (and thus to derogate any existing competence of national state courts), also the investor needs to give its consent. Accordingly, an investment treaty is not *per se* the autonomous and enforceable basis for jurisdiction of investment treaty tribunals. Rather, the treaty is a set of mutual undertakings of the contracting states that each of them should respect and honour future decisions of eligible investors to refer disputes to international arbitration (and not to state courts). However, an arbitration agreement is perfected between the state and the investor.[49] Secondly, in commercial arbitration, the derogation of competence of state courts in favour of arbitral tribunals has dual basis. On the one hand, such derogation is governed by national arbitration laws. On the other, the derogation is rooted in Article 2 of the New York Convention on the Recognition and Enforcement of Foreign Arbitral Awards,[50] which obliges the

[48]See e.g. *Eco Swiss*, *supra* note 47, where the CJEU agreed that matters of EU competition law were arbitrable and was satisfied that proper application of EU competition law could be ensured by national courts reviewing arbitral awards as part of the action for enforcement or annulment of award. It is simply illogical and inconsistent on the part of the CJEU, to accept in *Eco Swiss* that annulment proceedings before national courts offer sufficient guarantees of proper application of EU law by commercial arbitral tribunals, and to claim at the same time in *Achmea* that they do not. Commercial arbitration is also widely used and promoted in the EU as legal remedy for parties injured by anti-competitive behaviour of parties abusing dominant position. See e.g. Commission Decision of 24.5.2018 relating to a proceeding under Article 102 of the Treaty on the Functioning of the European Union (TFEU) and Article 54 of the EEA Agreement Case AT.39816—Upstream Gas Supplies in Central and Eastern Europe. See also e.g. recital (48) of the Directive 2014/104/EU of the European Parliament and of the Council of 26 November 2014 on certain rules governing actions for damages under national law for infringements of the competition law provisions of the Member States and of the European Union, OJ L 349, 5.12.2014, 1–19, which expressly admits private enforcement of infringements of EU competition law through arbitration.

[49]See e.g. Wychera and Mimnagh (2019), pp. 395-419.

[50]https://www.uncitral.org/uncitral/en/uncitral_texts/arbitration/NYConvention.html.

contracting parties to honour and give effect to the arbitration agreements in derogation of national courts. The question following *Achmea* therefore is whether the New York Convention, insofar as it was made between the EU Member States, also should be reviewed in the light of Article 344 TFEU.[51]

In addition, the logic of *Achmea* may likewise apply to the individual applications to the European Court of Human Rights, which are based on a similar mechanism that intra-EU bilateral investment treaties. Member States have agreed among themselves to authorize individuals to refer issues which may involve the application or interpretation of EU law, to an international court. Moreover, the CJEU has already precluded the possibility of the EU's accession to the European Convention of Human Rights in *Opinion 2/13*. It also held there that inter-state applications under Article 33 of the Convention would not be compatible with Article 344 TFEU.[52] It may now be an open, but still unaddressed question whether and to which extend *Achmea* takes the conclusions of *Opinion 2/13* another step further, to individual applications under Article 34.

4 Investor, Mind the Gap

4.1 How EU Law Purports to Replace Intra-EU BITs...

Assuming for a moment that *Achmea* could indeed achieve its political objective, which is to eradicate investment treaty arbitration from within the EU, the judgment would create a gap in the system of judicial protection in Europe.[53] This would be its natural consequence. For so long, investment treaty arbitration and EU law have co-existed and provided complementary protection to the beneficiaries of the four fundamental freedoms in Europe that there were no demands for an extension of EU law onto guarantees similar to those offered under investment treaties. Then in the aftermath of *Achmea*, a sudden realization came that the judgment of the CJEU could deprive a large number of EU investors of important substantive rights they required in order to maintain and develop their cross-border investments. The pressure was such that within 4 months after *Achmea*, the European Commission prepared and submitted to the European Parliament and Council, the Communication on Protection of intra-EU investment.[54]

The document opened with a bold statement that the 'European Union's single market is a unique area of investment opportunities'. The European Commission

[51] See also further Paschalidis (2019), pp. 219–236.

[52] CJEU, Opinion 2/13 *Accession of the EU to the ECHR*, ECLI:EU:C:2014:2454, see para. 213.

[53] See e.g. Balthasar (2018), pp. 227–233.

[54] European Commission, Communication on Protection of intra-EU investment, 19.7.2018 COM (2018) 547 final.

then went to declare it 'is committed to preserving and improving both a predictable, stable and clear regulatory environment and the effective enforcement of investors' rights.' It failed to mention that at the time of the communication, EU Member States were respondents in over 100 investment treaty disputes,[55] the majority of which related to allegations of unpredictability, instability or lack of clarity of the regulatory framework in the energy,[56] financial[57] or mining sectors.[58]

The European Commission was presumably mindful of those claims, but it nonetheless declared in the Communication that 'EU laws allows for markets to be regulated to pursue legitimate public interests such as public security, public health, social rights, consumer protection or the preservation of the environment, which may have consequences also for investments. Public authorities of the EU and of the Member States have a duty and a responsibility both to protect investment and to regulate markets. Therefore, the EU and Member States may legitimately take measures to protect those interests, which may have a negative impact on investments.'[59] This statement, again, did not take into account that in many cases the EU Member States were declared to be in breach of their international law obligations and obliged to pay damages.

The European Commission went on to recognize that 'In the aftermath of the Achmea judgment, the unlawfulness of intra-EU investor-State arbitration may result in the perception that EU law does not provide for adequate substantive and procedural safeguards for intra-EU investors. However, the EU legal system protects cross-border investors in the single market, while ensuring that other legitimate interests are duly taken into account. When investors exercise one of the fundamental freedoms, they benefit from the protection granted by: (1) the Treaty rules establishing those freedoms; (2) the Charter of Fundamental Rights of the European Union ("Charter"); (3) the general principles of Union law; and iv) extensive sector-specific legislation covering areas.'[60]

The Communication went on to demonstrate with examples that EU protects intra-EU investors with respect to the acts of investing in, acquiring and setting up companies; the right to acquire, use or dispose of immovable property; the repurchase of shares and bonds dealt in and quoted on a stock exchange; the receipt

---

[55]According to UNCTAD, there are currently 105 known pending investment treaty arbitrations against EU Member States (https://investmentpolicy.unctad.org/investment-dispute-settlement/advanced-search, acceded on 16 July 2019). This does not take into account unreported arbitrations.

[56]E.g. see cases *The PV Investors v. Spain, Vattenfall v. Germany, CSP Equity Investment v. Spain, Europa Nova v. The Czech Republic, EVN v. Bulgaria, I.C.W. v. The Czech Republic, MOL v. Croatia, Natland and others v. Czech Republic, Photovoltaik Knopf Betriebs-GmbH v. The Czech Republic, RREEF v. Spain, Voltaic Network v. The Czech Republic, InfraRed and others v. Spain* or *NextEra v. Spain.*

[57]E.g. cases *Cyprus Popular Bank v. Greece, Adamakopoulos and others v. Cyprus, UniCredit Bank and Zagrebačka Banka v. Croatia* or *Addiko Bank v. Croatia.*

[58]E.g. case *Gabriel Resources v. Romania, Lumina Copper v. Poland* or *Corcoesto v. Spain.*

[59]European Commission, *supra* note 54, p. 1.

[60]European Commission, *supra* note 54, p. 3.

of dividends and interest; the commercial grant of credits (including consumer credits); the acquisition of units of an investment fund; mortgages, legacies and loans, etc. and the acquisition of patents, trademarks and other intellectual property rights.

4.2 . . . And Why It Fails

The point is, however, in what the Communication did not show. Notably, it did not show that the EU protects investors against unfair or unfavourable treatment at the hands of the Member State, that it protects them against breach of legitimate expectations, instability, arbitrariness, or polititcally charged measures. That EU procedural law offered a one-stop-court in the event of a concerted action of various state organs targeting a single investor. It also failed to show that EU national courts could effectively protect the investors' rights including by way of award of damages commessurate with the loss suffered.

The point is, EU law—including the specific instances featured by the European Commission in the Communication—protects intra-EU investors from a different angle and at a different level than bilateral investment treaties. To use an example invoked in the Communication, the taxation which was found by the CJEU to be incompatible with EU law in C-493/09 *Commission v. Portugal*[61] would not need to be declared incompatible with a bilateral protection treaty.[62] On the other hand, investment treaty law could protect an investor against an oppressive and harassing tax enforcement proceedings or unjustified freezing of assets in the course of tax proceedings related to the collection of that tax, while EU law would not.

The differences in the protection of investors between EU law and bilateral investment agreements can also be shown on the example of the joined cases C-52/16 and C-113/16 *SEGRO and Horváth,*[63] which are being regarded by the European Commission as a reportedly apposite example of the ability of EU law instruments to protect investors in the EU.[64] In that matter, amendments to the relevant Hungarian law in 2013 extinguished all usufructuary rights on arable land, unless it could be proven that they were created between members of the same family. Consequently, the rights of the EU foreigners concerned were

[61]ECLI:EU:C:2011:635.

[62]In that matter, the CJEU dealt with discriminatory taxation which exempted Portuguese-based pension funds from corporate income tax which was applied on dividends, when this tax was applied to pension funds from other EU Member States. If that matter had been referred to an investment treaty tribunal under a bilateral investment treaty, the questions for the tribunal to consider would include e.g. whether the foreign-seated fund could demonstrate to have an investment in Portugal and whether the tribunal's jurisdiction was not excluded or restricted in tax-related matters.

[63]ECLI:EU:C:2018:157.

[64]European Commission, *supra* note 54, p. 14.

cancelled from the property register. The CJEU, responding to the preliminary question of Hungarian courts, declared that the legislation infringed the provisions on the free movement of capital. In a subsequent judgment of 21 May 2019, the CJEU also confirmed that by adopting the contested legislation, Hungary was in breach of its obligations under the TFEU.[65]

The outcome of *SEGRO* can be, in many respects, more favourable for investors than the outcome of a theoretical investment treaty claim in a parallel case. First of all, the claimants could eventually receive restitution, i.e. its rights should be returned to it. This would not be possible in investment treaty arbitration, where damages would be the principal remedy.[66] Proceedings before Hungarian courts, even including the reference to the CJEU, would be cheaper, and not necessarily longer than an investment treaty arbitration. On the other hand, claimants in the SEGRO-type scenario *depend* on the willingness of national courts to refer matters to the CJEU, and sometimes national courts can bend over backwards to arrive at an interpretation that would deny the claimants their relief in spite of the CJEU decision.[67] Also, because of the sectoral and limited jurisdiction of national courts, as well as the limited scope of application of EU law, the SEGRO-type scenario is not apposite for complex factual patters, where claimant is affected by various measures taken by different state organs. Thus, despite the attempts of the European Commission to prove the contrary, the EU law cannot effectively make up for the legal vacuum that shall be created when the system of intra-EU investment treaty protection is terminated.

5 Triumph of Hope Over Experience

5.1 Risk of Conflicting Decisions

Another risk created by *Achmea* is that in the future, this judgment may undermine the attempts of the EU to create a new mechanism of resolution of investor-state disputed, involving a multilateral investment court and, more broadly, call into question the trade and investment agreements which are now being negotiated by the EU. This may be the situation e.g. when an arbitral tribunal established under one of these treaties comes to conclusion that conflicts with the interpretation of EU law

---

[65]CJEU, Case C-235/17 *Commission v. Hungary* (Usufruct of agricultural land), ECLI:EU: C:2019:432.

[66]But see Arbitral Tribunal, ICSID Case No. ARB/11/23, *Mr. Franck Charles Arif v. Republic of Moldova*, Award of 8 April 2013.

[67]See e.g. CJEU, Cases C-213/11, C-214/11 and C-217/11 *Forta, Fortuna and Grand*, ECLI:EU: C:2012:495 and the subsequent case law of the Polish courts, such as the judgment of the Constitutional Court of 11 March 2015, file no P 4/14 (accessible at www.trybunal.gov.pl) and resolution of the Supreme Administrative Court of 16 May 2016, II GPS 1/16 (accessible at http://orzeczenia.nsa.gov.pl/doc/98C5206CE9).

provided by the CJEU. So far, and for some unexplained reason, the European Commission and the CJEU seem to believe that the EU or its Member States would never lose a dispute under such treaties and that in any event, no friction between such treaties and the TFEU could arise.[68] In the light of *Micula*, *Achmea* and the numerous cases confirming the breach of international law standards by EU Member States, this optimism is difficult to understand.[69]

The core of the *Achmea* reasoning is that an arbitral tribunal could misinterpret or misapply EU law and therefore affect its autonomy. Accordingly, it is—according to *Achmea*—wrong to derogate investor-state disputes from national courts (who can ask questions by virtue of Article 267 TFEU) and to refer these disputes to arbitral tribunals (who cannot ask such questions). But if so, would not the same concerns arise if a matter is referred to an arbitral tribunal (or a multilateral investment court) established to resolve investment treaty dispute on the basis of a treaty between the EU and a third country?

5.2 Application of EU Law As Facts?

An arbitral tribunal, or a multilateral investment court seized with a dispute under the investment treaty between the EU and a third country shall likely have to apply or interpret provisions of EU law just to the same extent as the arbitral tribunal would under the Netherlands-Slovakia bilateral investment treaty. In *Opinion 1/17*, the CJEU purported to distinguish the arbitral tribunal under the CETA from investment tribunals sitting under intra-EU bilateral investment treaties by pointing to the explicit provision of the CETA (Article 8.31.2) pursuant to which a CETA tribunal would have to evaluate EU law merely as a fact. Whereas, in the view of the CJEU expressed in *Achmea*, bilateral investment tribunals *could* apply EU law *qua* law and not *qua* facts. The distinction is not persuasive for many reasons. Firstly, not all bilateral investment treaties have had similar choice of law clauses, and in many instances domestic and EU law of the EU Member States would be regarded as facts.

---

[68] See in particular CJEU, Opinion 1/17, *supra* note 4, paras. 152 and 153. The CJEU has focused on the fact that according to its provisions, the CETA 'cannot be interpreted in such a way as to prevent a Party from adopting and applying measures necessary to protect public security or public morals or to maintain public order or to protect human, animal or plant life or health, subject only to the requirement that such measures are not applied in a manner that would constitute a means of arbitrary or unjustifiable discrimination between the Parties'. On that basis, the CJEU declares in para. 153 of Opinion 1/17 that the CETA Tribunal 'has no jurisdiction to declare incompatible with the CETA the level of protection of a public interest established by the EU measures specified in paragraph 152'. This conclusion not only confuses the question of jurisdiction with the decision on merits, but more importantly it overlooks that it will be for the CETA tribunal to decide what was necessary for the Member States to pursue a public interest and whether its actions were not arbitrary, disproportionate or abusive.

[69] On Opinion 1/17 see e.g. Koutrakos (2019), p. 294 who refers to the approach of the CJEU in Opinion 1/17 as to a leap of faith.

Secondly, even if an arbitral tribunal under a BIT were to interpret EU law *qua* law, it would not differ in such operation from an arbitral tribunal resolving a commercial dispute under national law of an EU Member State. Thirdly, such interpretation would not in any event be binding on the CJEU.

The point is, regardless of whether EU law is applied as law or as facts, it does always require certain interpretation on the part of the arbitral tribunal, whether under the CETA or not. It is not possible to assume that a future CETA tribunal would not have to review the conduct of an investor, or state authorities, against the yardstick defined in an act of EU law. Nor that in view of conflicting submissions of the parties as to whether each side could reasonably rely on its own interpretation of that act, assess that conduct. Such assessment could then be contrary to an anterior or posterior interpretation given to that act by the CJEU. Alternatively, it could well happen that a CETA tribunal would find that an interpretation given by the CJEU to a particular provision of the EU law constitutes a breach (or part of a breach) of the CETA provision.

Two other arguments have been used to distinguish between intra and extra EU situations. They are the principle of mutual trust and involvement of the EU as the contracting party to the treaty. Starting with the latter argument, it goes only as far as Article 344 TFEU is concerned. However, the fact that the involvement of the EU as a party may do away with the issue of an Article 344 violation is irrelevant for the principal problem, which is the risk of incompatibility of the award with the principle of autonomy of EU law. As far as the problem concerns the autonomy of EU law, it is immaterial who the parties to the treaty are. The point is, even the EU cannot enter into an international treaty that would be incompatible with the TFEU.

5.3 Role of Mutual Trust

Turning to mutual trust, this principle merely means that a court of a Member State should assume that courts of another Member State can be trusted to comply with a minimum (*nota bene*, vague and undefined) standard of due process. The argument to be built on the principle of mutual trust is that in an intra-EU context, it is not necessary to take a dispute out of the purview of the courts of a Member State because it is supposed that those courts would ensure due process of law. But in relation with third countries, the principle of mutual trust simply implies that courts of *all* Member States seen as one, are deemed to offer the same type of due process guarantees and be subject to the supervision of the CJEU. Accordingly, a provision in an investment protection treaty with a third country conferring jurisdiction onto an arbitral tribunal operating outside the judicial structures of the Member States, logically implies that the EU would agree to waive these guarantees which are presumed to exist (pursuant to the mutual trust principle) in the entire EU. Such provision also implies the waiver of the power of the CJEU to ensure that an arbitral tribunal properly applies and/or interprets EU law.

The justification given in *Opinion 1/17* for these concessions was that respect for the rule of law could not be presumed in the third countries with whom such treaties are made.[70] Accordingly, it seems following *Achmea* and *Opinion 1/17* that the CJEU is prepared to sacrifice the autonomy of EU law and limit the jurisdiction of national courts because certain third countries may have inadequate judicial systems, but is not prepared to accept investment treaty arbitration in a purely intra-EU context, where the risk of an actual conflict between a decision of an arbitral tribunal with EU law would be much lower. The reasoning here is plainly incoherent and the issue would have to be revisited by the CJEU at some point in the future.

In summary, the derogation of a dispute from Member State courts in favour of an international court or tribunal (one of the key reasons why the CJEU declared intra-EU arbitration to be incompatible with EU law in *Achmea*), could create similar legal issues in an intra-EU as in an extra-EU dispute.[71] Moreover, an international investment court could even declare that the CJEU acted in violation of the respective investment protection treaty through the adoption of a particular judgment on the interpretation or application of EU law. All these points, adopting the logic of *Achmea*, would strongly advocate against alleged conformity of extra-EU investment protection treaties with EU law. One would therefore think that following the decided stance taken in *Achmea*, the CJEU should take the next logical path and decide in *Opinion 1/17* that investment treaty arbitration is likewise prone to undermine the effectiveness of EU law in the non-intra EU context. As we have seen, this did not happen. But this does not mean that the issue will not be revisited one day.

6 Simply Bad Outcome for Europe

6.1 Imprudence of Trusting National Courts Only

Putting aside the technical legal flaws in the reasoning of *Achmea*, it is submitted that the judgment was also imprudent from the perspective of protection of the rule of law in Europe. At the time when independence of the judiciary is under attack from illiberal governments, promoting judicial monopolism is not the best strategy. Thus, while *Achmea* strengthens the position of the CJEU and national courts, a better route to defend the rule of law precisely in those Member States where it most needs to be protected would be to allow for a multiplicity of legal remedies at the choice of

[70] Expressed clearly in para. 82 of the opinion of AG Bot, supra 40, and implied in paras. 128–129 of Opinion 1/17, *supra* note 4.

[71] Admittedly, the conferral of jurisdiction would take place pursuant to an agreement entered into not by and between EU Member States, but pursuant to a treaty entered into by the EU and the Member States with a third country. This, however, only addresses the concerns raised by the CJEU in *Achmea* in relations to Article 344 TFEU, but not these related to Article 267 TFEU nor these related to Article 19 TEU and the principle of autonomy of EU law.

the aggrieved party. A useful analogy is the engineering concept of redundancy. In a technical context, redundancy is understood as duplication of critical components or functions of a system with the intention of increasing reliability of the system in the event of a failure or break-down.[72] Thanks to redundancy, for example, passenger airplanes may safely continue a flight even in the case of the breakdown of one (or more) engines. Similarly, multiple safeguards are routinely put in place to ensure safety in air traffic. In law, redundancy is intuitively regarded as unwelcome as it entails the risk of multiplicity of proceedings and conflicting judgments. As a result, duplications in legal systems are eliminated. This, however, exposes the critical components of the legal infrastructure designed to protect the rule of law to the risk of a single successful attack from an illiberal or autocratic political power.

The existing system of investment treaty arbitration in Europe not only offered a choice but was importantly different from proceedings before state courts and more immune to current threats. International investment law enforces the rule of law principally through non-state, apolitical *quasi*-judicial bodies, notably international arbitral tribunals, which are constituted on an *ad hoc* basis for the limited purpose of determining the outcome of a single case. The decentralized, dispersed system of arbitration results more resilient to the potential attacks to which national courts may be exposed from illiberal governments. Additionally, investment treaty arbitration enables individuals to bypass national courts and assert their claims directly before supra-national *quasi*-judicial bodies, which they cannot do under EU law.

6.2 *Three Salient Advantages of Investment Treaty Arbitration*

Three specific features of international investment arbitration make it more attractive for investors than any remedy available under EU law. Firstly, international arbitration under investment protection treaties typically allows creating a level playing field for the individual and the government with respect to the composition of the arbitral tribunal. From the perspective of an individual claimant, this is a remarkable advantage, which is simply not available elsewhere. In national courts, judges are appointed exclusively by the competent organs of the executive power.[73] Individuals

---

[72]Adams (2017), p. 77.

[73]The perceived bias of domestic courts is typically indicated as one of the reasons that investors prefer international arbitration to litigation before domestic courts, see e.g. Brower and Steven (2001), p. 196. This phenomenon was also recognized by the European Commission in the 2013 Factsheet Investor-State Dispute Settlement, http://trade.ec.europa.eu/doclib/docs/2013/october/tradoc_151791.pdf (last visited on 18 July 2019), in which it stated at p. 2: 'Firstly, the investor may not want to bring an action against the host country in that country's courts because it might think they are biased or lack independence. Secondly, investors might not be able to access the local courts in the host country. There are examples of cases where countries have expropriated foreign investors, not paid compensation and denied them access to local courts. In such situations,

are similarly disadvantaged in proceedings before permanent international courts, to which judicial candidates are often nominated by states. In international arbitration, however, an individual and a state are on a par regardless of whether each party appoints a co-arbitrator (and the president of the tribunal is appointed by those two or by an arbitral institution) or the entire arbitral panel is chosen from among neutrals by an arbitral institution.

Secondly, investment arbitral tribunal can be harsher to respondent states with respect to damages. Domestic courts often feel constrained from ruling against states with respect to the consequences of measures taken in pursuit of their sovereign powers. Therefore, even in high value disputes, high damages are rare. In proceedings before the European Court of Human Rights, settled case law regarding a taking in breach of Article 1 of Protocol No. 1 confirms that the compensation need not be full.[74] Confronted with such benchmarks, the prevailing approach in investment treaty arbitration favoring the full compensation model[75] is attractive to investors. It allows to assume that owners of a business project frustrated by unlawful acts of a state could receive compensation calculated on the basis of expected future streams of revenue that were missed because of the contested measures.

Thirdly, enforcement of investment arbitral awards need not take place in the territory of the Member State concerned. Arbitral awards are enforced either pursuant to the Washington Convention[76] or the New York Convention,[77] which implies that the grounds for refusal of enforcement on the leading international financial markets is very limited. This poses an important risk to the states that refuse to settle the awards voluntarily. The existence of a number of unsettled awards may create problems for a state when seeking to gain access to international funding. It can also increase the perceived political risk of doing business within that state, thus affecting the inflow of foreign investments and augmenting the cost of service of sovereign debt. Furthermore, the very prospect of being engaged in costly arbitration proceedings is a nuisance to the states.[78] In the end, the disadvantages of investment treaty arbitration proved in the past to have a chilling effect on the attempts of various states to take measures inconsistent with the rule of law.

---

investors have nowhere to bring a claim, unless there is an ISDS provision in the investment agreement.'

[74]ECtHR, *Lithgow and others v. United Kingdoms,* Judgment of 8 July 198, *Applications nos. no. 9006/80; 9262/81; 9263/81; 9265/81; 9266/81; 9313/81; 9405/81.*

[75]PCIJ, the *Chorzów Factory* case (*Germany v. Poland*), Judgment of 13 September 1928, P.C.I.J., Series A, No. 17, p. 47.

[76]Convention on the Settlement of Investment Disputes Between States and Nationals of Other States, Washington D.C., 18 March 1965, 575 UNTS 159.

[77]Convention on the Recognition and Enforcement of Foreign Arbitral Awards, New York, 10 June 1958, 330 UNTS 38.

[78]Pelc (2017), p. 567 estimates the average defence cost for a state per case at approximately USD 5.5 million.

For aforementioned reasons, investment treaty arbitrations played an important role in the European Union as a tool of fostering and enforcing the rule of law. Member States of the EU, particularly in Central and Eastern Europe, felt there was real risk of facing adverse financial consequences if they would adopt measures that are incompatible with the rules laid down in the investment protection treaties. Investors could assume that if they did not trust local courts in that part of the world,[79] they had recourse before an international forum. Following *Achmea*, the accuracy of that assumption was undermined. Following *Opinion 1/17*, it has been partially restored, as it seems that the CJEU shall tolerate—at least for some time—recourse to arbitration by investors from Canada (and possibly also other jurisdictions) or their EU subsidiaries,[80] against EU Member States.

7 Conclusions

The decisions in *Achmea* and *Opinion 1/17* have critical importance for the future of cross-border investment protection in Europe. Their political manifesto is clear. Protection of cross-border investments within the EU should not take place pursuant to current investment protection treaties, and should not involve international arbitration as it has been known to date. With respect to investments involving third countries, the EU has green light to engage in trade and investment protection treaties, provided that investor-state dispute resolution provisions in such treaties comply with certain conditions believed to preserve the autonomy of EU law. However, the technical legal analysis used by the CJEU to justify these conclusions is wanting in many important aspects and it is internally incoherent. Therefore, it undermines legal certainty and meets with considerable pushback from international arbitral tribunals and international business community.

The source of these problems is clearly *Achmea*. The principal issue with this judgment is that it purports to deliver a simplified political message that all investor-state arbitrations based on intra-EU BITs are reportedly unlawful. By doing so, *Achmea* overlooks not only the legal and factual niceties concerning almost 300 potentially affected international treaties which were formally in force at the time when the judgment was issued, but also the potential collateral effect which the legal reasoning employed in that judgment may have e.g. for commercial arbitration or the European Convention of Human Rights.

[79]The situation in national judicial systems in many EU Member States if far from ideal, which is being admitted even by the European Commission. See e.g. the 2018 EU Justice Scoreboard, https://ec.europa.eu/info/sites/info/files/justice_scoreboard_2019_en.pdf.

[80]See Article 8.23.1. (b) of the CETA.

The timing of *Achmea* could not be worse as it coincided with the systemic actions taken in countries such as Poland to undermine the independence and efficiency of the national judicial system and to subjugate it to the political will of the executive branch.[81] It is of course most desirable that the CJEU intervenes to protect the rule of law by supporting the independence of the judicial systems of the Member States. However, the contested legislative acts in Poland, and earlier in Hungary, were not a result of innocent errors of the national legislator. They were undertaken in wilful disregard of due process of law and they were intentional. As of today, the jury on the future of judiciary in Poland is still out. It also seems that the procedure under Article 7 TEU has encountered serious difficulties and it is uncertain whether it can be completed at all.[82] Given the continuing rise of populism and extremism in Europe is may be that also other political powers are watching the space closely. In these circumstances, cutting the intra-EU investors off from an alternative way of pursuing their legal claims and referring them before the mandatory jurisdiction of national courts was not a prudent move.

The same arguments which served to justify the decision in *Achmea* can also turn in the future against the trade and investment agreements which have been entered into, or are currently being negotiated by the EU. As long as these treaties provide for access of investors to international arbitration, they will incentivize EU investors to bypass *Achmea* by setting up subsidiaries in such third countries parties to these treaties. Clearly, there is a tendency in the current international investment and tax law to deprive post-box (or conduit) companies of the benefits of preferential tax treatment[83] and investment protection. This, however, makes it only harder—but not impossible—to engage in jurisdiction shopping and treaty planning.

Finally, *Achmea* puts EU Member States into a position of conflicting obligations. On the one hand, the intra-EU treaties remain in force and create certain obligations for these Member States under public international law, which may benefit third parties (investors). On the other, under the interpretation of *Achmea* as the Member States adopted on 15 and 16 January 2019, they are constrained from complying with these obligations voluntarily. What results is an increasing mass of

[81]See e.g. CJEU, Case C-619/18 *Commission v. Poland (retirement of Supreme Court judges)*, judgment of 24 June 2019, ECLI:EU:C:2019:531; CJEU, Case C-192/18 *Commission v. Poland (retirement rules for Polish judges)*, AG Opinion of 20 June 2019, ECLI:EU:C:2019:529; CIEU, Joined Cases C-585/18, C-624/18 and C-625/18 *Krajowa Rada Sądownictwa and Others*, AG Opinion of 27 June 2019, ECLI:EU:C:2019:551.

[82]The process was brought to a stall in 2018. Moreover, senior EU officials admit the procedure has had limited impact on Poland's behaviour, see https://www.reuters.com/article/us-poland-katainen-eu/eus-katainen-says-article-7-procedure-against-poland-has-had-little-impact-idUSKCN1S73C6; last acceded on 17 July 2019.

[83]See e.g. CJEU, Joined Cases C-116/16 and C-117/16, *Skatteministeriet v. T Danmark and Y Denmark Aps*, ECLI:EU:C:2019:135.

unpaid awards rendered against EU Member States that one day shall reach the gravitas required for the problem to be resolved at a political, and not legal level. How and when can this may happen remains to be seen.

References

Adams H (2017) Systemic decision making: fundamentals for addressing problems and messes. Springer, Heidelberg

Bakos A (2019) Schrödinger's investment: the EU's General Court considers that the compensation ordered by the Micula tribunal is not a form of state aid (Although it Might as Well Have Been). EFILA Blog, https://efilablog.org/2019/06/26/schrodingers-investment-the-eus-general-court-considers-that-the-compensation-ordered-by-the-micula-tribunal-is-not-a-form-of-state-aid-although-it-might-as-well-have-been/. Last acceded on 17 July 2019

Balthasar S (2018) Investment protection in Europe: international investment treaties, the European Convention on Human Rights and the need for reform at EU level. SchiedsVZ 4:227–233

Berger J (2017) Intra-EU investor-state arbitration: the uncertainty continues – unpacking the advocate general's opinion in Case C-284/16 (Achmea). SchiedsVZ 15:282–291

Brower C, Steven LA (2001) Who then should judge? Developing the international rule of law under NAFTA Chapter 11. Chicago J Int Law 2:193–202

Buczkowska E, Treder P, Sadowski W (2017) The house always wins remarks on AG Wathelet's opinion in the C-284/16 Achmea case. Kluwer Arbitration Blog, 22 November 2017, http://arbitrationblog.kluwerarbitration.com/2017/11/22/house-always-wins-remarks-ag-wathelets-opinion-c-28416-achmea-case/. Last accessed on 17 July 2019

Croisant G (2019) Micula Case: the general Court Quashes the Commission's decision and rules that the award is not state aid. Kluwer Arbitration Blog, 19 June 2019, http://arbitrationblog.kluwerarbitration.com/2019/06/19/micula-case-the-general-court-quashes-the-commissions-decision-and-rules-that-the-award-is-not-state-aid

Hartley TC (2019) The European Court, the rule of law and the reach of judicial power in the European Union. Law Q Rev 135:321–337

Hess B (2018) The fate of investment dispute resolution after the Achmea decision of the European Court of Justice. MPILux Research Paper 2018/3. Available at https://doi.org/10.2139/ssrn.3152972

Hindelang S (2019) Conceptualisation and application of the principle of autonomy of EU law – the CJEU's Judgement in Achmea put in perspective. Eur Law Rev 3:383–400

Koutrakos P (2019) More on autonomy – opinion 1/17 (CETA). Eur Law Rev 3:293–294

Lavranos N, Singla T (2018) Achmea: groundbreaking or overrated. SchiedsVZ 17:348–357

Paschalidis P (2019) Chapter 14: challenges under EU law to the enforcement of arbitral awards under the New York Convention. In: Fach Gomez K, Lopez-Rodriguez AM (eds) 60 years of the New York convention: key issues and future challenges. Kluwer, Alphen aan den Rijn, pp 219–236

Pelc K (2017) What explains the low success rate of investor-state disputes. Int Organ 71:559–583

Power R (2019) The (Final?) death of intra-EU investor-state arbitration. Kluwer Arbitration Blog of 28 January 2019, http://arbitrationblog.kluwerarbitration.com/2019/01/28/the-final-death-of-intra-eu-investor-state-arbitration/. Last acceded on 17 July 2019

Sadowski W (2018) Protection of the rule of law in the European Union through investment treaty arbitration: is judicial monopolism the right response to illiberal tendencies in Europe. Common Market Law Rev 55:1025–1060

Wychera B, Mimnagh W (2019) Chapter IV: investment arbitration, the nature of state consent expressed in BITs. Austrian Yearb Int Arbitr:395–419

4

The Rule of Law as a Value in the Sense of Article 2 TEU: What does it Mean and Imply?

Werner Schroeder

Contents

Abstract The rule of law is a value on which the European Union is founded, and which shall be respected and observed by its Member States. This value is not merely an ethical standard but a binding legal principle that is applicable to legal disputes under Union law. The treaties, however, do not provide a definition of this principle. From a Union law perspective, it is therefore indispensable to determine the rule of law more precisely; not only is it referred to in treaty law (Article 2 TEU), but understood by Union courts as a constitutional meta-principle that informs other constitutional norms and may justify review proceedings and sanctions against Member States. The Commission Framework to strengthen the Rule of Law of 2014 does not suffice to shape a 'Union rule of law'. It relies primarily on the case

---

W. Schroeder (✉)
Department of European Law and Public International Law, University of Innsbruck, Innsbruck, Austria
e-mail: werner.schroeder@uibk.ac.at

law of the Court of Justice of the European Union. Yet, this judicial concept of the rule of law is somehow restricted as it focuses almost exclusively on the role of the judicial branch in the Union's constitutional system. Common European constitutional traditions, however, show that the core concern of the rule of law is the containment of public authority by institutional arrangements. In view of these traditions and the practice of the Union institutions, including the CJEU, consensus at the Union level might be achieved on the fact that the rule of law comprises not only strictly formal standards, but also material criteria of justice related to the juridical shaping of decision-making processes. These elements of the rule of law are intrinsically linked to fundamental rights and shall ensure that within the scope of Union law any public power is exercised in a non-arbitrary and legitimate way. To this end, the Union rule of law may not only be understood as a formal set of objective norms, but as ensuring the protection of individual rights as well.

1 Dangers for the Rule of Law in the Union

According to the first sentence of Article 2 of the Treaty on European Union (TEU), the European Union is founded on values among which figure the respect for human dignity, freedom, democracy, equality, the rule of law and the respect for human rights, including the rights of persons belonging to minorities. The second sentence of this provision assumes that the Member States respect and observe these values. In the last years, however, the political situation in some Member States has made manifest that these values are in part jeopardised to a considerable degree; this notably holds true for the principle of the rule of law[1] which, as a common principle of the EU Member States, restricts the majority rule in the State through institutions such as separation of powers, independence of the courts and which guarantees the liberty of individuals.[2] Since the Union draws a great part of its legitimacy from the fact that its organs and Member States respect the rule of law, the indicated dangers for the rule have meanwhile grown into a significant problem for European integration.[3]

It is problematic, however, to operationalise the rule of law in the Union's constitutional system and, in particular, to use it as an argument for sanctioning certain Member States without having clarified its normative character, its meaning and scope. In this contribution the issue of 'content' shall be addressed: What does the principle of the rule of law, as mentioned in Article 2 TEU, actually mean and imply?

---

[1]Scheppele (2015), p. 112.

[2]For the genesis of Art 2 TEU, see Mangiameli (2013), para. 2 note 6.

[3]Kochenov (2013); von Bogdandy and Ioannidis (2014), p. 60; Hillion (2016), pp. 59 et seq.; von Bogdandy et al. (2018), pp. 983 et seq.

2 Origins As a Principle of Union Constitutional Law

Already at the beginning of the 1960s, Walter Hallstein coined, in regard to the then European Economic Community (EEC), the concept of a 'community based on law'.[4] This term has made a remarkable career since then and represents an essential element of Union law doctrine nowadays.[5] Interestingly, however, Hallstein's remark did not refer to the Member States of the then Community as all being States governed by the rule of law. He did not primarily seek to illustrate that the Community has institutions such as fundamental rights, separation of powers, legal protection and so on, and is therefore endowed with all insignia of a State based on the rule of law. He rather aimed at emphasising that the Community 'solely' disposed of legal power, not of means of coercion. Hence, the Union's power is exclusively based on the respect for the law.[6] The Union's legal concept for the handling of borderline situations[7] that involve a threat of the rule of law in and by Member States does not provide for the use of force, but—as it is common in other modern federal systems—relies on cooperation[8] and consideration. The sanctioning procedure for massive violations of rule of law principles, as enshrined in Article 7 TEU, does little to change this, precisely because it does not allow for the use of force against a Member State.

As is commonly known, the Court of Justice endorsed the notion of a 'community based on law' in its famous *Les Verts v. Parliament*-Ruling in 1986, linking it to the constitutional character of the Treaties. According to the Court, the then EEC is 'a Community based on the rule of law, inasmuch as neither its Member States nor its institutions can avoid a review of the question whether the measures adopted by them are in conformity with the basic constitutional charter, the Treaty'.[9] Methodologically, this jurisprudence draws on the fact that the rule of law stems from a common European heritage. It can be conceived of as an element of the common constitutional traditions of the Member States and as an element of the European Convention for the Protection of Human Rights and, therefore, as a general principle of Union Constitutional law.[10] The Court of Justice made the *topos* of the rule of law

[4]Hallstein (1979), p. 109. See also Fuß (1968), pp. 16 et seq.

[5]Critically von Bogdandy (2017), p. 487.

[6]Hallstein (1969), p. 33.

[7]For the state of emergency as a test case of jurisdiction, see Schmitt (1985), p. 11. Critically with regard to the application of Schmitt's theory to the Union system, see Pernice (1995), pp. 109 et seq.; Schroeder (2002), p. 220.

[8]Scharpf (1985), pp. 323 et seq.

[9]CJEU, Case C-294/83 *Les Verts v. Parliament*, ECLI:EU:C:1986:166, para. 23; Joined Cases C-402/05 P and C-415/05 P *Kadi and Al Barakaat International Foundation v. Council and Commission*, ECLI:EU:C:2008:461, para. 281. But see CJEU, Case C-362/14 *Schrems v. Data Protection Commissioner*, ECLI:EU:C:2015:650, para. 60: the European Union is a 'union based on the rule of law'.

[10]von Bogdandy (2009), pp. 23, 28 et seq.; Pech (2010), pp. 361 et seq., 367. On the general principle see Tridimas (2013).

part and parcel of its own constitutionalisation strategy.[11] It perfectly lends itself to support the proposition that the Union is not an intergovernmental organisation as the others, but a public authority *sui generis* endowed with a supranational constitution.[12] The Court of Justice also applies such 'constitutional' and 'rule of law' terminology to the effect of securing the substantial legitimacy of the law of the Union, particularly by underscoring that the rule of law constitutes an element of the Union's particular identity on the international plane.[13]

It has, however, taken several decades for the rule of law to acquire the status of and establish itself as a principle pertaining to the constitutional law profile of the Union (Article 2, second sentence and Article 7 TEU), i.e. to be understood as a 'constitutional principle'.[14] This is understandable, given the fact that the objectives and means of operation originally agreed upon by the Member States of the Community were primarily of an economic and social-policy character, with the 'Common Market' and 'market freedoms' forming the heart of this economic order. Therefore, the Treaties of Rome did not contain, with the exception of legal protection, any elements testifying an explicit rule of law terminology.[15]

With the advent of the interpretation of the Treaties as a constitution which organises and legitimises supranational public authority not only in economic, but also in highly political fields, the Member States became increasingly interested in giving an explicit status to 'constitutional principles' governing the Union's public authority. The rule of law principle, as one of these constitutional principles, is first mentioned in a Union law context in the Conclusions of the European Council of Copenhagen in 1993 committing the candidate countries for EU membership to 'stability of institutions guaranteeing democracy, the rule of law, human rights, respect for and protection of minorities'.[16] The Amsterdam Treaty of 1997 adopts this approach inasmuch as in Article 6 paragraph 1 TEU it states that the Union is founded on the principles of liberty, democracy, the respect for human rights and fundamental freedoms; these principles are common to all Member States. In Article I-2 of the 2004 Treaty establishing a Constitution for Europe which has not entered into force, these principles were re-baptised as 'values'. This very term, by the way, is also used by the identical provision of Article 2 TEU.

[11]See Weiler (1981), p. 274; Mancini (1989), pp. 595 et seq.; Lenaerts (1990), pp. 205 et seq. See also Fuß (1968), pp. 16 et seq.; Hallstein (1969), pp. 41, 48 et seq.

[12]CJEU, Opinion 1/91 *EEA I,* ECLI:EU:C:1991:490, para. 108; Opinion 2/13 *Accession of the EU to the ECHR II*, ECLI:EU:C:2014:2454, paras. 156 et seq., 163 et seq.

[13]In contrast to the UN system, see CJEU, *Kadi*, *supra* note 9, paras. 281 et seq. See further Hilf and Schorkopf (2015), paras. 12–54.

[14]See von Bogdandy (2009), pp. 13, 22.

[15]Calliess (2011), para. 1. On the impact of the deepening of European integration for the meaning of the rule of law see Lenaerts (2017a), p. 640.

[16](1993) 26 (6) EC Bull, para. I.13.

3 No Homogeneity as Regards the Rule of Law in the Union

Article 2 TEU is sometimes referred to as a 'homogeneity clause'. It is derived from Article 2, first and second sentence TEU as well as from Article 7 TEU that a similar rule of law standard applies both vertically between the Union level and the Member States' level and horizontally among the Member States themselves. Every exercise of public authority, irrespective of whether it has its origin on the Union or national level, is subject to a set of legal limitations and shall be assessed according to this standard.[17]

Such claims for congruence of constitutional principles in federal systems are often based on federal ideas or models.[18] When applied to the law of the Union, they imply the existence of a supremacy of the Union vis-à-vis its Member States and suggest supervisory powers in the relationship between the both. But can a claim for constitutional homogeneity and for similar rule of law standards on Union and national level be sustained under these conditions in the first place? Such a claim is in need of critical reflection. First of all, it is problematic to reconstruct the Union's constitution in the light of federal state models since the institutional situation of the Union follows its own rules.[19] Even though the Union exercises and organises public authority,[20] only limited conclusions for the understanding of the Union's constitution can be drawn from theories that take national federal systems as their point of reference. In view of the different nature of the Union as a community of integration, its constitutional structures and principles differ from those of the Member States.[21] The claim for constitutional homogeneity between Union and Member States must thus be rejected.[22]

Furthermore, it is difficult to assume that there exists a form of rule of law homogeneity in the relationship among the Member States (horizontally). No Union law fiction is available in this regard since, concerning essential constitutional

---

[17]Hilf and Schorkopf (2015), paras. 9 et seq.; Pech (2010), p. 364; Mangiameli (2013), paras. 42 et seq.; von Bogdandy et al. (2012), pp. 509 et seq.

[18]For a homogeneity requirement with respect to federalism and the principle of democracy, Schmitt (2008), p. 388. With respect to positive constitutional law see Art. 28 para. 1 German Basic Law, which is calling for constitutional homogeneity between the German Basic Law and the federal states. The German Constitutional Court handles the claim strictly, see BVerfG, 1 BvL 30/88, *Rundfunkentscheidung*, Judgment of 22 February 1994, paras. 84–88. See also Art. 99 para. 1 B-VG, which states that the state constitutions in Austria may not contradict the federal constitution. This does also apply for the principle of the rule of law.

[19]See CJEU, Case C-359/92 *Germany v. Council*, ECLI:EU:C:1994:306, para. 38. Against constitutional analogies, see also ECtHR [GC], *Matthews v. United Kingdom*, Judgment of 18 February 1999, Application No. 24833/94, para. 48.

[20]CJEU, Opinion 1/78 *International Agreement on Natural Rubber*, ECLI:EU:C:1979:224, para. 7.

[21]BVerfG, Judgment of 31 May 1995, 2 BvR 635/95. See previously BVerfG, 1 BvR 1474/92, *Maastricht*, Judgment of 17 August 993, para. 182; BVerfG, 2 BvE 2/08, *Lissabon*, Judgment of 30 June 2009, para. 370.

[22]But see von Bogdandy et al. (2012), p. 489.

principles such as the content of human dignity, there is no respective 'common conception' of the Member States, as the CJEU has acknowledged.[23] Also with respect to the other elements of the rule of law such as legal protection, separation of powers and so on, as regards the details a common conception of the Member States cannot be found.[24]

The claim for the rule of law should therefore not be understood as a claim for homogeneity. This would do justice neither to the European constitutional reality nor to the Treaties. Article 4 paragraph 2 TEU acknowledges that the 'national identity' of the Member States, which the Union shall respect, is based on their 'fundamental structures, political and constitutional'. Thus, it is the law of the Union itself recognising that, in spite of the common constitutional values of Article 2 TEU, there exist differences between the Union's constitution and the constitutions of the Member States. Individual national approaches as to the legal classification of the rule of law confirm such an understanding.[25] In areas where Union law may not ensure a uniform level of legal protection, it leaves room for 'rule of law diversity', provided that the 'primacy, unity and effectiveness of EU law are not thereby compromised'.[26] The idea that Article 2 TEU orders and supervises a federal state-type constitutional homogeneity—vertically as well as horizontally—is not compatible with such a model of constitutional pluralism[27] as it is after all laid down explicitly in the Treaty.

The claim for the rule of law of the Union and the Member States does therefore not seek the existence of uniform principles and rules, but solely the observance of a European minimum standard in terms of the rule of law.[28] To define this minimum standard, however, is not an easy task (see Sect. 5 below).

4 Normative Character of the Union Rule of Law

4.1 Rule of Law As Value and Principle

It has already been mentioned that the rule of law was first referred to as a 'principle' in the Amsterdam Treaty and has only been modified into a 'value' with the Lisbon

---

[23]CJEU, Case C-36/02 *Omega*, ECLI:EU:C:2004:614, para. 37.

[24]Regarding the difference of the rule of law in common law and continental legal systems, see Dicey (1961), pp. 189 et seq., 267 et seq.; Konstantinides (2017), pp. 30 et seq., 39; Krygier (2012), p. 233; Classen (2013), pp. 56 et seq.

[25]On the constitutional identity control, see BVerfG, *Lissabon*, *supra* note 21, para. 343, according to which the 'inviolable core content of the constitutional identity of the Basic Law' has to be respected within the framework of the Union.

[26]CJEU, Case C-399/11 *Melloni*, EU:C:2013:107, para. 60.

[27]On constitutional pluralism in the EU, see MacCormick (1995), p. 259; Baquero Cruz (2008), p. 389.

[28]Lenaerts (2017a), p. 640.

Treaty. Although terminology issues should not be overrated in Union law, the question arises what normative consequences this renaming may have. Most scholars take the position that nothing has changed from a legal point of view. They continue to use the term 'principles' as it represents a common category of legal hermeneutics.[29] They interpret the 'linguistic turn' as merely indicating the theoretical uncertainties of the law of the Union in the dealing with constitutional principles. In addition, they refer to the case law of the CJEU, Article 21 TEU and the Preamble of the FRC which, in the context of the rule of law and fundamental rights, continue speaking of 'constitutional principles'[30] and 'principles'.[31]

It is indeed problematic to use the term 'values' in Article 2 TEU because it is a meta-legal term. Values shall, beyond the realm of legal norms, guide the individual in decision-making situations to ethically 'right' conduct. They articulate general considerations on the basis of which one state of affairs is declared preferable in relation to another state of affairs.[32] As moral strategies, values only function on the basis of a consensus on their respective set and content which cannot, however, be assumed and realised at any given time.

However, the distinction between principles and values can be normatively reconstructed on the basis of Union law itself. First of all, values, insofar as they are laid down in black-letter legal texts, such as Article 2 TEU, refer to doctrinal principles which shall guide decision-makers in the Union in their structuring of the legal order. In this context, principles are understood in a pragmatic manner.[33] They are understood as legal norms which do not state specific rights or duties, but which are of a general nature and are in need of being concretised by the legislative, the executive and the judiciary. They can be made operable in the Union legal system by means of adopting more specific legal rules, in particular, by the courts that—by drawing on principles, values, interests and goods which, thus, become an element of a balancing decision—identify them as legally relevant. In so doing, the CJEU has, for instance, derived the principle of legal certainty from the rule of law principle.[34] In such a case, a principle can even turn into a self-standing standard of legality.

Secondly, in the Union legal system, values as being ethical, supra-positive norms have an orientation and ordering function. They are therefore of an identity-building and legitimacy-creating character.[35] This is also the function of the rule of

---

[29]See von Bogdandy (2009), pp. 22 et seq.; Pech (2010), pp. 366 et seq.; Hilf and Schorkopf (2015), para. 21.

[30]CJEU, *Kadi, supra* note 9, paras. 281, 285; Case C-355/04 *Segi*, ECLI:EU:C:2007:116, para. 51.

[31]CJEU, *Accession of the EU to the ECHR II, supra* note 12, para. 167.

[32]Luhmann (1987), p. 433.

[33]On different interpretations of the function of principles in the law of the Union, see von Bogdandy (2009), p. 20; Bengoetxea (1993), pp. 183 et seq.; Schroeder (2002), pp. 262 et seq.

[34]See CJEU, Case C-234/04 *Kapferer v. Schlank & Schick GmbH*, ECLI:EU:C:2006:178, paras. 20 et seq.

[35]Calliess (2004), p. 1034.

law and of the other values mentioned in Article 2 TEU which shall endow the Union with a particular identity,[36] especially on the international level (see Article 3 paragraphs 1 and 5 TEU, Article 8 TEU in Article 21 paragraph 2, Article 32 and Article 42 paragraph 5 TEU), but also vis-à-vis the Union citizens inasmuch as they can form the basis of a common political conscience.[37] The value of the rule of law, in particular, is that of a reference standard for the common self-assurance of the Union and its Member States.[38]

In view of the foregoing, the third point is that values have therefore a legal and ethical double-nature. Legal norms concretise values and transform them from the societal system into the legal system. This double-nature of the rule of law as a value of the Union and a principle of Union law also becomes manifest in the structure of Article 2 TEU. In Article 2, second sentence TEU values such as pluralism, tolerance, solidarity are characterised as contents of the European societal model that have no legal character. The Union is not 'founded' on these values but presupposes them as societal values. This distinction is taken further in the provision on the sanctioning procedure in Article 7 paragraph 1 TEU which solely refers to the 'legally relevant values' in the meaning of Article 2 paragraph 1 TEU. It has also left terminological traces in the CJEU's case law. In the context of human dignity, the Court of Justice, on the one hand, speaks of it as a 'fundamental value' laid down in the national constitutions, but on the other hand also as a 'general principle of [Union] law'.[39] And in its opinion on the accession of the Union to the ECHR, the Court of Justice declares that the legal structure of the Union is based on the fundamental premise that each Member State shares with all the other Member States [. . .] a set of common values on which the EU is founded, as stated in Article 2 TEU.[40]

4.2 *Binding Legal Norm*

If a norm is referred to as a value, this means to shift it to a political or ethical level. In terms of legal doctrine, this creates problems. It notably gives rise to the question of how the values which are laid down in the Union's constitution should be interpreted and applied. Are they subject to judicial control or a standard for such a control?

---

[36]See Commission 'Communication on Article 7 of the Treaty on European Union: Respect for and promotion of the values on which the Union is based' COM (2003) 606 final, 3.

[37]von Bogdandy (2009), p. 14.

[38]Lenaerts (2017a), p. 640.

[39]CJEU, *Omega*, *supra* note 23, paras. 23, 32, 34.

[40]CJEU, *Accession of the EU to the ECHR II*, *supra* note 12, para. 168.

First of all, one must refer to the fact that the rule of law is enshrined in Article 2 TEU, i.e. in a legal text, and has therefore normative character.[41] This proposition is emphasised by the wording and system of the Treaty, namely by pointing out that the rule of law is 'common' to the Member States and that the Union is 'founded' on it, amongst others (Article 2 TEU). The normative character of the rule of law also becomes manifest in Article 3 paragraph 1 TEU which makes it the Union's primary goal to promote its values, as well as in Article 13 paragraph 1 TEU which makes the promotion of values the reference point of the 'institutional framework' of the Union. Both the Union's institutions and the Member States are legally bound by the treaty objectives of the Union, as also follows from Article 4 paragraph 3 TEU. The normative character of the rule of law is further confirmed by the references in the sanctioning procedure pursuant to Article 7 TEU[42] and the accession procedure pursuant to Article 49 TEU.[43] In these cases, specific legal consequences are tied to the respect for and the promotion of the rule of law. This presupposes that the rule of law itself is of legally binding nature.

Moreover, Article 2 TEU only constitutes the black-letter law manifestation of principles which have already been developed by the CJEU in the 1980s as unwritten general principles of law.[44] Against this background, the reference in Article 2 TEU to such principles and their denomination as values is of solely declaratory nature. They do not change their already existing normative character. Their codification is above all relevant as a reference point for the sanctioning procedure against the Member States pursuant to Article 7 TEU as well as for reasons of legal certainty.

In addition, the rule of law has, together with the other values referred to in Article 2 TEU, a programmatic function. Their respect by the Member States is evoked in Article 2, second sentence TEU, and for the Union itself this provision serves as characterisation of the classical structural features of the liberal constitutional model.[45] Due to the systematic position at the beginning of the Treaties, its profound character, its open wording as well as its significance similar to goal and value clauses in the constitutions of some Member States, Article 2 TEU constitutes the fundament of a membership in the Union.[46] Besides, the promotion of the rule of law is, according to Article 3 paragraph 1 TEU, one of the overarching objectives of the Union and its institutional framework (Article 13 paragraph 1 TEU). The realisation of the principle of the rule of law, therefore, pertains to the decision-making programme for the Union's institutions which determines the handling of their

[41]This can be illustrated in the light of the CJEU's case law on Articles 2 and 3 EEC Treaty, which were regarded as legally binding norms, see CJEU, Case C-126/86 *Giménez Zaera*, ECLI:EU:C:1987:395, para. 14; Case C-339/89 *Alsthom Atlantique*, ECLI:EU:C:1991:28, paras. 8 et seq.

[42]See Commission 'Reasoned proposal under Article 7 para. 1 TEU regarding the rule of law in Poland' COM (2017) 835 final, para. 1.

[43]Ohler (2015), para. 15; Cremona (2005), p. 3.

[44]CJEU, Case C-138/79 *Roquette Frères*, ECLI:EU:C:1980:249, para. 33; *Les Verts*, *supra* note 9, paras. 23 et seq. See also Lenaerts (2017a), p. 640.

[45]Hilf and Schorkopf (2015), para. 9; von Bogdandy (2009), p. 22.

[46]Pech (2010), pp. 361 et seq.; Calliess (2004), p. 1036.

discretionary powers[47] and constitutes a guideline for the interpretation of Union law provisions.[48] By virtue of Article 4 paragraph 3 TEU, this objective entails legal effect vis-à-vis the Member States which must refrain from any measures that could jeopardise the attainment of the Union's objectives and shall, *vice versa*, do everything to facilitate the achievement of the Union's tasks.[49]

4.3 Operational Legal Norm

Although it is now undisputed that the rule of law is a legally binding norm, the question arises whether it is also applicable in a legal dispute. The vagueness of the concept of the rule of law—more on this later—raises the question of whether this norm has any self-standing value in legal procedures.[50]

In fact, the Court of Justice has emphasized the normative character of the rule of law principle very early by deriving concrete legal rules from this principle, for example, the duty of the Union to provide legal protection mechanisms.[51] Later, the Court has operationalised the rule of law. Specifically, by referring to the rule of law it called on the Member States to ensure judicial independence and the full judicial protection of the rights of individuals.[52] By now, the rule of law is well established as an operational principle and as a basis for legally assessing the Member States.[53]

The premise that each Member State respects the rule of law, as stated in Article 2 TEU, also entails legal consequences as far as it forms the basis of the principle of mutual recognition. The legal concept of mutual recognition, which is based upon mutual trust among the Member States that Union law will be respected,[54] draws on the idea that in areas which have not been fully harmonised by the Union, the authorities of a Member State have to accept the legal acts of another Member State in regard to certain factual circumstances as binding, thus treating them as if they had been decided upon by the Member State's own legal order.[55] Important fields of application of this principle are the Union citizenship, where the Member States must recognise the grant of citizenship by another Member State,[56] or legal acts in

---

[47]CJEU, Case C-14/68 *Wilhelm and Others v. Bundeskartellamt*, ECLI:EU:C:1969:4, para. 5.

[48]See Case C-6/72 *Europemballage Corporation and Continental Can Company v. Commission*, ECLI:EU:C:1973:22, para 24; *EEA I*, *supra* note 12, para. 18.

[49]CJEU, *Wilhelm and Others v. Bundeskartellamt*, *supra* note 47, paras. 6 et seq.

[50]Kochenov (2015), p. 88.

[51]CJEU, *Les Verts*, *supra* note 9, para. 23.

[52]CJEU, Case C-619/18, *Commission v. Poland*, ECLI:EU:C:2018:910, para. 21; Case C-216/18 PPU, *Minister for Justice and Equality (LM)*, ECLI:EU:C:2018:586, paras. 48 et seq.

[53]von Bogdandy et al. (2018), p. 986.

[54]CJEU, *EEA I*, *supra* note 12, para. 168.

[55]Möstl (2010), p. 405.

[56]CJEU, Case C-200/02 *Zhu and Chen*, ECLI:EU:C:2004:639, para. 37.

the Area of Freedom, Security and Justice (AFSJ) such as the European Arrest Warrant on the basis of Framework Decision 2002/584/JHA.[57]

It becomes clearer and clearer, however, that in some Member States the legislative, administrative and judicial procedures do not satisfy the rule of law minimum standards which are presupposed by the principle of mutual recognition. In such a case, there is no basis in Union law for the recognition of such procedures and decisions by other Member States[58] since 'mutual recognition' must be performed in conformity with primary law, i.e. in conformity with Article 2 TEU. Hence, the CJEU has expressly obliged the Member States, in particular, national courts and administrative bodies to suspend their legal cooperation with such Member States that massively violated rule of law minimum standards.[59] More recent legal acts demonstrate that the Union legislator has become aware of this problem, too. For instance, according to Article 11 paragraph 1 lit f) of the Directive 2014/41/EU regarding the European Investigation Order in criminal matters[60] the recognition or execution of a European Investigation Order on gathering evidence for criminal proceedings issued by the authorities of one Member State may be rejected by the authorities of other Member States where there are substantial grounds to believe this could be incompatible with Article 6 TEU and the FRC. Besides, Article 3 paragraph 2 sub-paragraph 2 of the Regulation (EU) 604/2013[61] (Dublin III Regulation) obliges the Member States, when determining which Member State is responsible for the examining of an application for international protection, to also check whether 'there are substantial grounds for believing that there are systemic flaws in the asylum procedure and in the reception conditions for applicants in [another] Member State, resulting in a risk of inhuman or degrading treatment'. In such case, the determining Member State must not transfer the applicants in that other Member State.[62]

[57]See CJEU, Case C-303/05 *Advocaten voor de Wereld*, ECLI:EU:C:2007:261, paras. 28 et seq.

[58]See CJEU, Case C-135/08 *Rottmann*, ECLI:EU:C:2010:104, paras. 48 et seq. for the limits of recognition of granting citizenship by a Member State by the others in arbitrary decisions.

[59]See CJEU, Joined Cases C-411/10 and C-493/10 *N.S. and Others*, ECLI:EU:C:2011:865, para. 86, regarding Council Regulation (EC) 343/2003 establishing criteria and mechanisms for determining the Member State responsible for examining an asylum application lodged in one of the Member States by a third-country nation (Dublin II Regulation) (2003) OJ L 50/1. With regard to the European Arrest Warrant, see CJEU, Joined Cases C-404/15 and C-659/15 PPU *Aranyosi and Căldăraru*, ECLI: EU:C:2016:198, paras. 77 et seq.; Case C-452/16 PPU *Poltorak*, ECLI:EU: C:2016:858, paras. 44 et seq.; *LM*, *supra* note 52, para. 59. See further Lenaerts (2017b), pp. 810 et seq.

[60](2014) OJ L130/1.

[61]Regulation (EU) 604/2013 of the European Parliament and of the Council establishing the criteria and mechanisms for determining the Member State responsible for examining an application for international protection lodged in one of the Member States by a third-country national or a stateless person (Dublin III Regulation) (2013) OJ L 180/31.

[62]See CJEU, Case C-578/16 PPU *C.K.*, ECLI:EU:C:2017:127, paras. 92 et seq.

These examples demonstrate that the systematic disregard by a Member State of rule of law minimum standards in the scope of application of EU law also can have directs effects on the legal cooperation with other Member States.[63]

5 The Rule of Law As a Legal Concept

It is problematic, however, to operationalise the rule of law without having clarified its content before.

5.1 *Determining the Content of the Rule of Law*

In fact, it is often questioned whether the rule of law, despite its importance being undisputed, is able to perform a valuable function for the Union's legal order as it is too vague and undetermined.[64] Ambiguities as to the content of the Union rule of law can be explained, first of all, by the fact that the Treaties do not contain explicit statements on rule of law issues. To be sure, Articles 7 and 49 TEU refer to the rule of law via Article 2 TEU. Yet, the Treaties do not define what is to be understood by this concept.

The Commission and the courts when enforcing the rule of law vis-à-vis a certain Member State, however, cannot simply refer to Article 2 TEU and content themselves to an 'I know it when I see it'-approach.[65] A concretisation of the rule of law beyond the mere reference in Article 2 TEU is, however, needed from the point of view of the rule of law itself. The principle of legal determinateness requires that legal provisions which impose a certain code of conduct on legal subjects are sufficiently specific, so that the persons affected by them can align their conduct with these provisions.[66] In addition, the policies adopted by some Member States have shown that a lack of consensus on the content of the Union rule of law might be understood as an invitation to test the limits of Article 2 and 7 TEU.

---

[63]von Bogdandy et al. (2018), pp. 992 et seq.

[64]Kochenov (2015), p. 79; Claes and Bonelli (2016), pp. 267 et seq.; Barnett (2018), p. 24.

[65]This famous phrase on the difficulties of legal decision-making appears in U.S. Supreme Court, *Jacobellis v. Ohio*, 378 U.S. 184 (1964) p. 197 (Stewart, J, concurring).

[66]CJEU, Joined cases 212 to 217/80 *Amministrazione delle finanze dello Stato v. Meridionale Industria Salumi and Others*, ECLI:EU:C:1981:270, para. 10; Barnett (2018), p. 26.

5.2 *The European Tradition of the Rule of Law*

There might be a number of reasons why the conceptions as to the content and significance of the rule of law in Europe are unclear, even though the preamble of the TEU refers to the rule of law as a 'universal value'.[67] One of these reasons is certainly that the concept of the rule of law has a more limited European tradition than, for example, the concept of democracy which is meanwhile extensively described in Articles 9 et seq. TEU.

To be sure, the concept of rule of law can be long traced back, at least in the English history of law. The concepts of rule of law in the UK, of 'Rechtsstaatlichkeit' in Germany and of 'État de droit' in France have, however, developed a particular impact only after the nineteenth century and flourished in the era of European constitutionalism.[68] Even more, most EU Member States' constitutions are familiar with the concept of the rule of law only since the 1970s. Ultimately, there is a considerable range of legal concepts in Europe which are gathered under the notion of the rule of law.

5.3 *Formal and Material Aspects of the Rule of Law*

Regardless of different approaches and rule of law traditions most would agree that a basic meaning of the rule of law comes down to the idea that all public power must act within certain constraints by law, i.e. that it is bound by legal norms which are outside of its control.[69] The rule of law is a legal principle organising the relationship between a community and its governing institutions, reducing the discretion of public power by subjecting it to means of effective legal and judicial control.[70]

Sometimes doubts are expressed concerning the usefulness of this broad definition.[71] It reveals that the rule of law does not constitute a straightforward concept, but rather an aggregate notion for a set of subprinciples which are themselves in need of concretisation depending on the respective context.[72] It is correct that constitutional law problems are primarily to be solved on the basis of constitutional subprinciples that form part of the meta-concept of the rule of law but are closer to the problem, for example, principles such as legal certainty or separation of powers; the concept of rule of law should be drawn upon only subsidiarily. At the same time,

---

[67] Cruz Villalón (2007), para. 60.

[68] For a comparative analysis, see Loughlin (2010), pp. 312 et seq., especially 314 et seq.; Heuschling (2002), pp. 384 et seq.; Holterhus (2017), pp. 453 et seq.

[69] Kochenov (2015), p. 81; Crabit and Bael (2016), p. 198.

[70] Holterhus (2017), p. 432; Konstantinides (2017), pp. 29 et seq.; Sobotta (1997), pp. 21 et seq.

[71] See Kunig (1986), pp. 89 et seq., 457 et seq.

[72] Waldron (2008), p. 3; Holterhus (2017), p. 432. See the case law of the German Constitutional Court, e.g. BVerfG, 2 BvL 25/81, Judgment of 22 November 1983 (BVerfGE 65, 283, 290).

the rule of law is far from being a mere ideological formula without any normative self-reliance. It has an autonomous role where the challenge is to link these various elements in systematic fashion in order to thereby obtain functional insights.[73]

Against this background, it may not come as a surprise that there is a discourse in Europe on which subprinciples may be attributed to the rule of law and form part of it. At the heart of the struggle for conceptualising the rule of law lies the choice between a formal ('thin') or on a material ('thick') concept.[74] Behind this discourse lies the question of whether the rule of law principle is identical to claims regarding 'process and form' or whether it also contains demands concerning the content of legal norms in terms of fairness. Formal interpretations of the rule of law as mere obligation to respect the law were for a long time not only common in the UK.[75] The principle of legality and other aspects associated with formal rule of law qualities like the hierarchy of norms also constitute the core elements of the formal 'Rechtsstaatlichkeit' in Germany, Austria and France.[76] In fact, representatives of a 'negative' or 'thin' concept of the rule of law caution even today against overburdening the concept with diverse social objectives, so that it does not become devoid of content and practically irrelevant. They assert that the core of the rule of law rather consists of a set of requirements such as that the legal norms of a given legal order should be general, public, prospective and certain.[77]

There is some truth to this warning, but it is also true that according to most constitutional provisions in Europe, legal norms must satisfy elementary requirements of justice in regard to an obligation of fairness and prohibition of arbitrariness. This claim for a just creation, application and interpretation of legal norms is secured by virtue of binding the legislator to the constitution and material constitutional principles such as fairness, equality and certainty of law.[78] This conception of the rule of law which is based on a combination of both formal and material aspects has become the most accepted one in many Member States.[79] This approach has also found favour on the Union level as will be shown below.

[73]Schmidt-Aßmann (2004), § 26 paras. 8 et seq. See also BVerfG, 2 BvR 215/81, Judgment of 26 March 1981 (BVerfGE 57, 250, 276) where the principle of the rule of law 'selbst' (itself) is used as a systematically relevant anchor for requirements of procedures.

[74]Magen (2016), p. 1052; Wennerström (2007), pp. 76 et seq.

[75]See especially Dicey (1961), p. 188. Critically, Craig (1997), pp. 470 et seq.; Krygier (2012), pp. 236 et seq.

[76]Classen (2013), pp. 63 et seq.; Loughlin (2010), pp. 315 et seq.

[77]See e.g. Raz (1977), pp. 210 et seq.

[78]See e.g. Dworkin (1985), pp. 335 et seq. Regarding Germany, see von Simson (1982), p. 109.

[79]Bingham (2010), p. 37.

6 The Rule of Law in the Union's Practice

6.1 Rule of Law As Described in the Commission Framework

The Commission has sought such clarification in its Communication of 11 March 2014 on a 'New framework to strengthen the rule of law'.[80] The text represents some principles meant to be common to the constitutional traditions in Europe. It relies, however, on the case law of the CJEU when identifying the elements of the rule of law.[81] The CJEU judgments cited in the Communication refer to the principles of legality, legal certainty, effective legal protection as well as prohibition of arbitrariness, but only in regard to the conduct of the Union's institutions and mostly in the field of European competition law. These judgements of the Court of Justice do, however, not deal with the legal situation in the Member States, i.e. whether the conduct of the national powers meets the rule of law standard of the Union.

This does not suffice to give shape to a Union rule of law in the meaning of Article 2 TEU. The reference of the framework to the CJEU's jurisprudence may serve as an indicator when determining the rule of law, but it should be taken into account that the exercise of public authority by Union institutions and national authorities cannot be equally treated in legal terms[82] and that the national constitutional traditions regarding the rule of law in Europe may differ from the concept pursued by the CJEU. Moreover, the framework itself has the character of a checklist that has been created in an inductive way. Like other rule of law checklists, it does not claim to be exhaustive nor of absolute character.[83]

The added value of the new rule of law framework of the Commission particularly lies in the fact that on the basis of a dialogue between the Commission and Member States, the Member States' obligations deriving from the rule of law can be specified. Accordingly, the biggest shortcoming of the Union rule of law, i.e. the indeterminacy as regards its content, can be overcome. The Commission has sought to strengthen the normative relevance of its rule of law definition by reiterating the framework in legal documents relating to the rule of law situation in certain Member States.[84] In addition, it has relied on the framework's rule of law interpretation in its proposal for a regulation on the protection of the Union's budget in case of generalised deficiencies as regards the rule of law in the Member States. However,

---

[80]Commission 'Communication from the Commission to the European Parliament and the Council: a new EU Framework to strengthen the Rule of Law' COM (2014)158 final, 4 and Annex 1; see Crabit and Bael (2016), p. 197; von Bogdandy et al. (2018), pp. 985 et seq.

[81]See Lenaerts (2017a), p. 641.

[82]See CJEU, *Germany v. Council*, *supra* note 19, para 38. Against constitutional analogies also ECtHR, *Matthews v. United Kingdom*, *supra* note 19, para. 48.

[83]See Fuchs (2018), pp. 239, 243 with regard to the 'Rule of Law Checklist' of the Venice Commission for Democracy through Law (Study No. 711/2013, CDL-AD(2016)007 Strasbourg 18 March 2016).

[84]See COM (2017) 835 final, *supra* note 42, para. 1 and other documents relating to the situation in Poland (SWD/2018/219 final).

these measures have contributed little to the establishment of a specific Union rule of law definition because the Commission's definition merely consists of a list of legal subprinciples.[85]

6.2 *Rule of Law in the Case Law of the CJEU*

It has already been outlined that the Court of Justice uses a rule of law terminology reminiscent of national constitutional law and has located the source of the rule of law in the general legal principles of Union law. However, questions arise as to which substantive changes are associated with the conceptual extension and application of the rule of law to the Union level. What are the attributes of a 'Union based on the rule of law'?[86]

The case law of the Court of Justice is based on a twofold concept reflecting formal as well as substantive aspects of the rule of law. The formal binding of the public authority to the law and the requirement that any intervention by public authorities in the sphere of private activities of any person must have a legal basis is—in line with prominent constitutional traditions of the Member States—the nucleus of the rule of law of the Union.[87] Another typical formal aspect of the rule of law, which can also be found in Union law, is the principle on the hierarchical relationship of norms[88] which helps the structuring of the legal order.

Article 19 paragraph 1, second sentence TEU manifests, however, that the Union law contains also material aspects of the rule of law. The Union's public authority must be exercised by respecting supra-positive elements of justice ('the law').[89] This notion of the 'law' itself as mentioned in Article 19 paragraph 1, second sentence TEU served in the jurisprudence as the starting point for the developing of the Union rule of law as a general principle of law. Yet, this judicial concept of the rule of law is somehow restricted. It refers, due to the systematic place of Article 19 TEU within the Treaty, mainly to the role of the judicial branch in the constitutional system of the

---

[85]See Article 2 lit a) of the proposed regulation of the European Parliament and of the Council on the protection of the Union's budget in case of generalised deficiencies as regards the rule of law in the Member States, COM (2018) 324 final defining the rule of law as 'the Union value enshrined in Article 2 of the Treaty on European Union which includes the principles of legality, implying a transparent, accountable, democratic and pluralistic process for enacting laws; legal certainty; prohibition of arbitrariness of the executive powers; effective judicial protection by independent courts, including of fundamental rights; separation of powers and equality before the law'.

[86]See CJEU, *Schrems*, *supra* note 9, para. 60.

[87]CJEU, Case C-496/99 P *Commission v. CAS Succhi di Frutta*, ECLI:EU:C:2004:236, para. 63. See also CJEU, Joined Cases C-46/87 and 227/88 *Hoechst v. Commission*, ECLI:EU:C:1989:337, para. 19. But see Kochenov (2015), pp. 81 et seq.

[88]See CFI, Case T-51/89 *Tetra Pak v. Commission*, ECLI:EU:T:1990:41, para. 25. See Merli (2016), p. 37.

[89]See Rodríguez Iglesias (1996), pp. 125, 128.

Union.[90] This becomes particularly clear when the Court emphasises the relevance of judicial independence to the Union rule of law.[91]

First of all, the Community of law defines itself in view of the obligation of comprehensive and effective legal protection.[92] The CJEU's major reference point for the development of the rule of law was therefore for a long time Article 6 ECHR. Further elements of the rule of law, as emphasised by the Court, such as the right to a fair trial and independent courts, which ensure the respect for rules and rights established by Union law,[93] and even the principle of separation of powers[94] are also interpreted to serve legal protection before the European Courts.

To be sure, one can derive from the case law further propositions on legal principles such as fundamental rights which are inseparably linked to a material perception of the rule of law.[95] Without doubt, also the principles of legal certainty and the protection of legitimate expectations[96] as well as the principle of proportionality pertain to the material concept of 'law', as enshrined in Article 19 TEU, which guarantees 'protection against arbitrary and disproportionate intervention'.[97] The Court of Justice has, however, always placed these material principles in the context of the legal protection in the Union. It regards the respect for these principles as a requirement for the legality of acts 'which it is for the Court to review in the framework of the complete system of legal remedies established by the Treaty'.[98] The Court has repeatedly pointed out that the material elements of the rule of law must integrate themselves into the system of legal protection in the Union.[99]

---

[90]E.g. CFI, Case T-411/06 *Sogelma v. AER*, ECLI:EU:T:2008:419, para. 37. See also Rodríguez Iglesias (1996), p. 125; Lenaerts (2007), p. 1625.

[91]See CJEU, Case C-619/18 *Commission v. Poland*, ECLI:EU:C:2018:1021, paras. 41 et seq.; *Commission v. Poland*, *supra* note 52, paras. 21 et seq. See von Danwitz (2016), p. 155.

[92]This principle is specified in: CJEU, *Les Verts*, *supra* note 9, para. 23. With respect to Community actions and Member States, see respectively CJEU, Case C-222/84 *Johnston v. Chief Constable of the Royal Ulster Constabulary*, ECLI:EU:C:1986:206, paras. 18 et seq.; *Kadi*, *supra* note 9, paras. 281, 316. See von Bogdandy (2017), p. 497 who perceives judicial control as the core of the 'Rechtsidee' (i.e. legal idea) of the Union.

[93]CJEU, Joined Cases C-174/98 P and C-189/98 P *Netherlands and Van der Wal v. Commission*, ECLI:EU:C:2000:1, para. 17. See Badó and Bóka (2016), p. 46.

[94]CJEU, *Poltorak*, *supra* note 59, paras. 44–45; Case C-477/16 *Kovalkovas*, ECLI:EU:C:2016:861, paras. 43–44.

[95]CJEU, *Kadi*, *supra* note 9, para. 285.

[96]CJEU, Case C-10/69 *Portelange v. Smith Corona Marchant International*, ECLI:EU:C:1969:36, para. 15/16; Joined Cases 205 to 215/82 *Deutsche Milchkontor GmbH v. Germany*, ECLI:EU:C:1983:233, paras. 27 et seq. See Gamper (2016), p. 80.

[97]This norm is understood to be a general principle of (EU) law, see CJEU, Case C-4/73 *Nold KG v. Commission*, ECLI:EU:C:1974:51, para. 13; *Hoechst v. Commission*, *supra* note 87, para. 19. See Huber (2016), p. 98.

[98]CJEU, *Kadi*, *supra* note 9, para. 285.

[99]CJEU, *Accession of the EU to the ECHR II*, *supra* note 12, para. 177. See Jaeger (2018), pp. 626 et seq.

The motive of the Court's quest for legal protection is not only a demand for the safeguarding of individual rights, but also a demand for the full and effective application of Union law in the Member States. The legal requirement that all courts and tribunals in the Union have 'to ensure the full application of EU law in all Member States and judicial protection of the rights of individuals under that law', is, in the words of the CJEU, an 'expression (of) the value of the rule of law affirmed in Article 2 TEU'.[100] By this token, the rule of law may be regarded also as an instrument safeguarding the autonomy of the Union legal order and to protect it against internal and external challenges.[101]

7 Essence of the Union Rule of Law

What remains is the insight that the rule of law constitutes a 'conceptual puzzle' in the Union legal order since there exist different conceptions of its significance and its content beyond its basic meaning that any form of public power must be subordinated to some kind of primary, unchangeable norms. This principle cannot be defined conclusively and it may evolve over time.

At the same time, from the point of view of Union law, it is indispensable to determine the rule of law more precisely; not only is it referred to in black-letter treaty law (Article 2 TEU), but understood by Union courts as a constitutional meta-principle that provides a justification for review proceedings and informs other constitutional norms.[102] Moreover, its respect, or not, entails legal consequences. Inasmuch as the rule of law constitutes a general principle of law, it is necessary to draw on both the pertinent case law of the European courts as well as the common constitutional traditions of the Member States (Article 6 paragraph 3 TEU).

Due to the above-explained common European constitutional tradition it is well established that the European rule of law does not only have a formal, but also a material side and includes substantive claims for justice and the prohibition of arbitrariness. At the same time, the vehement warning that the rule of law might be overstretched shows that the containment of public authority by institutional arrangements is still one of the core concerns of the rule of law. This also corresponds to the jurisprudence of the European courts which underscores the procedural safeguarding of justice. Among these principles figure the principle of hierarchy of norms and of legality, i.e. the binding of the legislator to the constitution and of the administrative and judicial powers to the law, the transparency and perceptibility of

---

[100]CJEU, *LM*, *supra* note 52, para. 50. Similar CJEU, Case C-64/16 *Associação Sindical dos Juízes Portugueses v. Tribunal de Contas*, ECLI:EU:C:2018:117, para. 32; Case C-284/16 *Achmea*, ECLI:EU:C:2018:158, para. 36.

[101]This does, however, not imply that in the case law of the CJEU the rule of law is 'pre-empted' by considerations of Union autonomy as Kochenov (2015), pp. 78, 93 et seq. suggests.

[102]Pech (2010), pp. 376 et seq.; Holterhus (2017), p. 460; Barnett (2018), p. 34.

norms. In addition, also the principles of separation of powers and of effective legal protection by independent courts are counted among the formal institutional guarantees of the rule of law. As far as the implementation and understanding of these principles in a more detailed fashion are concerned, there exist significant differences among the Member States' constitutions.

In view of the strong tradition of a formal approach to the rule of law in Europe, consensus at the Union level might be achieved on the fact that the rule of law comprises not only strictly formal standards but also material criteria of justice that are related to the juridical shaping of decision-making processes. Characteristic examples are principles such as legal certainty, protection of legitimate expectations and proportionality.

All these subprinciples of the rule of law shall ensure that any public power is exercised in a non-arbitrary and legitimate way. To this end, they may not only be understood as objective norms but also ensure the protection of individual rights. As Article 52 paragraph 1 of the FRC makes clear in relation to the principle of proportionality, these material standards are intrinsically linked to fundamental rights.[103] To the extent that a restriction of fundamental rights is effected without a legal basis within the meaning of Article 52 paragraph 1, first sentence FRC,[104] that this restriction is disproportionate given certain common interests, that it does not satisfy the claims of legal certainty or that it does not provide for an appropriate legal protection mechanism, one may not only assume that human rights have been violated but also that a violation of the rule of law has occurred, which may be challenged by any individual before a Union court of law.[105]

Fundamental rights and rule of law principles are, in the Union constitutional system, mutually dependent and reinforce each other.[106] The Union rule of law aims at protecting individual fundamental rights and, conversely, fundamental rights are a material prerequisite of such a rule of law. At most, one can say that the guarantee of the institution of fundamental rights is an essential component of a Union under the rule of law. Individual fundamental rights are, however, not necessarily part of the rule of law,[107] as is also made clear by Article 2 TEU which conceives the rule of law and fundamental rights as different principles. Moreover, there is no constitutional law surplus value in qualifying single human rights additionally as an element of the rule of law as they are sufficiently assured by the Article 6 TEU and the European Charter of Fundamental Rights which is legally binding.

---

[103]Venice Commission for Democracy through Law, Study No. 711/2013, *supra* note 83, para. 31.

[104]CJEU, *Hoechst v. Commission*, *supra* note 87, para. 19.

[105]CJEU, *Kadi*, *supra* note 9, para. 316; *Commission v. Poland*, *supra* note 52, para. 21; *LM*, *supra* note 52, para. 48 et seq.

[106]This applies in particular to the principle of effective judicial protection which forms part of the rule of law but finds also expression in Article 47 FRC, see Konstantinides (2017), p. 83.

[107]Lenaerts (2017a), p. 641.

References

Badó A, Bóka J (2016) Access to justice and judicial independence. In: Schroeder W (ed) Strengthening the rule of law in Europe. Hart, Oxford, pp 46–60

Baquero Cruz J (2008) The legacy of the Maastricht-Urteil and the pluralist movement. Eur Law J 14:389–422

Barnett G (2018) Reflections on what the rule of law means and its significance at EU level. In: Hatje A, Tichý L (eds) Liability of member states for the violation of fundamental values of the European Union. Nomos Verlagsgesellschaft mbH & Co. KG, Baden-Baden, pp 23–38. EuR Beiheft 1

Bengoetxea J (1993) The legal reasoning of the European court of justice: towards a European jurisprudence. Clarendon Press, Oxford

Bingham T (2010) The rule of law. Allen Lane, London

Calliess C (2004) Europa als Wertegemeinschaft – Integration und Identität durch europäisches Verfassungsrecht? Juristenzeitung 59:1033–1084

Calliess C (2011) EUV Art 2. In: Calliess C, Ruffert M (eds) EUV/AEUV: Kommentar, 4th edn. CH Beck, Munich

Claes M, Bonelli M (2016) The rule of law and the constitutionalisation of the European Union. In: Schroeder W (ed) Strengthening the rule of law in Europe. Hart, Oxford, pp 265–289

Classen CD (2013) Nationales Verfassungsrecht in der Europäischen Union: eine integrierte Darstellung der 27 Verfassungsordnungen. Nomos, Baden-Baden

Crabit E, Bael N (2016) The EU rule of law framework. In: Schroeder W (ed) Strengthening the rule of law in Europe. Hart, Oxford, pp 197–206

Craig PP (1997) Formal and substantive conceptions of the rule of law: an analytical framework. Public Law 467:1–15

Cremona M (2005) EU enlargement: solidarity and conditionality. Eur Law Rev 30:3–22

Cruz Villalón P (2007) Vergleich. In: von Bogdandy A, Huber PM, Cruz Villalón P (eds) Handbuch Ius Publicum Europaeum, Band I: Grundlagen und Grundzüge staatlichen Verfassungsrechts. CF Müller, Heidelberg, pp 729–778, § 13

Dicey AV (1961) Introduction to the study of the law of the constitution, 10th edn. Palgrave Macmillan, London

Dworkin R (1985) A matter of principle. Oxford University Press, Oxford

Fuchs M (2018) Die Vermessung der Rechtsstaatlichkeit – Die ‘Rule of Law Checklist’ der Venedig-Kommission des Europarates. EuGRZ 45:237–243

Fuß EW (1968) Die Europäischen Gemeinschaften und der Rechtsstaatsgedanke. UGA, Heule

Gamper A (2016) Legal certainty. In: Schroeder W (ed) Strengthening the rule of law in Europe. Hart, Oxford, pp 80–97

Hallstein W (1969) Der unvollendete Bundesstaat: europäische Erfahrungen und Erkenntnisse. Econ-Verlag, Düsseldorf

Hallstein W (1979) Die EWG als Schritt zur Europäischen Einheit. In: Oppermann T (ed) Walter Hallstein — Europäische Reden. Deutsche Verlags-Anstalt, Stuttgart, pp 103–112

Heuschling L (2002) État de Droit: Rechtsstaat: rule of law. Dalloz, Paris

Hilf M, Schorkopf F (2015) EUV Art 2. In: Grabitz E, Hilf M, Nettesheim M (eds) Das Recht der Europäischen Union: EUV/AEUV, 57th edn. CH Beck, Munich

Hillion C (2016) Overseeing the rule of law in the EU: legal mandate and means. In: Closa C, Kochenev D (eds) Reinforcing rule of law oversight in the EU. Cambridge University Press, Cambridge, pp 59–81

Holterhus T (2017) The history of the rule of law. Max Planck Yearb United Nations Law 21:430–466

Huber PM (2016) The principle of proportionality. In: Schroeder W (ed) Strengthening the rule of law in Europe. Hart, Oxford, pp 98–112

Jaeger T (2018) Gerichtsorganisation und EU-Recht: Eine Standortbestimmung. Europarecht 53:611–652

Kochenov D (2013) The EU in its most serious crisis ever (and that's not the Euro crisis). http://verfassungsblog.de/en/the-eu-in-its-most-serious-crisis-ever-and-thats-not-the-euro-crisis-2. Accessed 15 Mar 2019

Kochenov D (2015) EU law without the rule of law: is the veneration of autonomy worth it? Yearb Eur Law 34:74–96

Konstantinides T (2017) The rule of law in the European Union – the internal dimension. Hart, Oxford

Krygier M (2012) Rule of law. In: Rosenfeld M, Sajó A (eds) The Oxford handbook of comparative constitutional law. Oxford University Press, Oxford, pp 233–249

Kunig P (1986) Das Rechtsstaatsprinzip: Überlegungen zu seiner Bedeutung für das Verfassungsrecht der Bundesrepublik Deutschland. Mohr Siebeck, Tübingen

Lenaerts K (1990) Constitutionalism and many faces of federalism. Am J Comp Law 38:205–263

Lenaerts K (2007) The rule of law and the coherence of the judicial system of the European Union. Common Market Law Rev 44:1625–1659

Lenaerts K (2017a) Die Werte der Europäischen Union in der Rechtsprechung des Gerichtshofs der Europäischen Union: eine Annäherung. EuGRZ 21:639–642

Lenaerts K (2017b) La vie après l'avis: exploring the principle of mutual (yet not blind) trust. Common Market Law Rev 54:805–840

Loughlin M (2010) Foundations of public law. Oxford University Press, Oxford

Luhmann N (1987) Soziale Systeme: Grundriß einer allgemeinen Theorie. Suhrkamp, Frankfurt am Main

MacCormick N (1995) The Maastricht-Urteil: sovereignity now. Eur Law J 1:259–266

Magen A (2016) Cracks in the foundation: understanding the great rule of law debate in the EU. J Common Market Stud 54:1050–1061

Mancini GF (1989) The making of a constitution for Europe. Common Market Law Rev 26:595–614

Mangiameli S (2013) Article 2: the homogeneity clause. In: Blanke H-J, Mangiameli S (eds) The treaty on European Union (TEU). A commentary. Springer, Heidelberg, pp 109–155

Merli F (2016) Principle of legality and the hierarchy of norms. In: Schroeder W (ed) Strengthening the rule of law in Europe. Hart, Oxford, pp 37–45

Möstl M (2010) Preconditions and limits of mutual recognition. Common Market Law Rev 47:405–436

Ohler C (2015) EUV Art 49. In: Grabitz E, Hilf M, Nettesheim M (eds) Das Recht der Europäischen Union: EUV/AEUV, 57th edn. CH Beck, Munich

Pech L (2010) 'A union founded on the rule of law': meaning and reality of the rule of law as a constitutional principle of EU law. Eur Const Law Rev 6:359–396

Pernice I (1995) Carl Schmitt, Rudolf Smend und die europäische Integration. Archiv des öffentlichen Rechts 120:100–120

Raz J (1977) The rule of law and its virtue. Law Q Rev 93:195–211

Rodríguez Iglesias GC (1996) Zur 'Verfassung' der Europäischen Gemeinschaft. EuGRZ 23:125–131

Scharpf FW (1985) Die Politikverflechtungsfalle: Europäische Integration und deutscher Föderalismus im Vergleich. Politische Vierteljahresschrift 26:323–356

Scheppele KL (2015) Understanding Hungary's constitutional revolution. In: von Bogdandy A, Sonnevend P (eds) Constitutional crisis in the European constitutional area: theory, law and politics in Hungary and Romania. Hart, Oxford, pp 111–124

Schmidt-Aßmann E (2004) Der Rechtsstaat. In: Isensee J, Kirchhof P (eds) Handbuch des Staatsrechts der Republik Deutschland, Band II: Verfassungsstaat. C.F. Müller, Heidelberg, pp 541–612, § 26

Schmitt C (1985) Politische Theologie - Vier Kapitel zur Lehre von der Souveränität, 4th edn. Duncker & Humblot, reprint, Berlin

Schmitt C (2008) Constitutional theory. Duke University Press, Durham

Schroeder W (2002) Das Gemeinschaftsrechtssystem: eine Untersuchung zu den rechtsdogmatischen, rechtstheoretischen und verfassungsrechtlichen Grundlagen des Systemdenkens im Europäischen Gemeinschaftsrecht. Mohr Siebeck, Tübingen

Sobotta K (1997) Das Prinzip Rechtsstaat: Verfassungs- und verwaltungsrechtliche Aspekte. Mohr Siebeck, Tübingen

Tridimas T (2013) The general principles of EU law, 3rd edn. Oxford University Press, Oxford

von Bogdandy A (2009) Founding principles. In: von Bogdandy A, Bast J (eds) Principles of European constitutional law, 2nd edn. Hart, Portland, pp 11–54

von Bogdandy A (2017) Jenseits der Rechtsgemeinschaft – Begriffsarbeit in der europäischen Sinn- und Rechtsstaatlichkeitskrise. EuR 52:487–511

von Bogdandy A, Ioannidis M (2014) Systemic deficiency in the rule of law: what it is, what has been done, what can be done. Common Market Law Rev 51:59–96

von Bogdandy A et al (2012) Reverse Solange – protecting the essence of fundamental rights against member states. Common Market Law Rev 49:489–520

von Bogdandy A et al (2018) A potential constitutional moment for the European rule of law – the importance of red lines. Common Market Law Rev 55:983–996

von Danwitz T (2016) The rule of law in the recent jurisprudence of the ECJ. In: Schroeder W (ed) Strengthening the rule of law in Europe. Hart, Oxford, pp 155–169

von Simson W (1982) Die Deutschen und ihr Rechtsstaat. Der Staat 21:97–112

Waldron J (2008) The concept and the rule of law. Georgia Law Rev 43:1–61

Weiler JHH (1981) The community system: the dual character of supranationalism. Yearb Eur Law 1:267–306

Wennerström EO (2007) The rule of law and the European Union. Lustu Forlag, Uppsala

Werner Schroeder is Full Professor at the Department of European Law and Public International Law, University of Innsbruck, Austria.

5

The Assessment of Judicial Independence Following the CJEU Ruling in C-216/18 LM

Stanisław Biernat and Paweł Filipek

Contents

Abstract In the *LM* ruling, the Court of Justice developed the *Aranyosi and Căldăraru* test and indicated it as the one to be applied for the assessment of judicial independence and fair trial guarantees in the context of executing European Arrest Warrants. Although serious threats to the rule of law and judicial independence in some EU countries, like Poland, have been documented over recent years, no warrant has so far been definitely rejected as a consequence of the application of the *LM* test, although there are cases in which the execution of warrants to Poland has been suspended. This naturally raises questions as to whether the mechanism proposed by the Court responds to the need of protecting the right to a fair trial and

S. Biernat (✉)
Jagiellonian University, Krakow, Poland
e-mail: stanislaw.biernat@uj.edu.pl

P. Filipek
University of Economics, Krakow, Poland

safeguarding judicial independence. In this contribution we evaluate the mechanism devised by the Court, taking into account the available judicial practice after the *LM* ruling. We point out that the almost automatic transfer of a mechanism proposed to evaluate the functioning of a prison system to that evaluating a fair trial and judicial independence has not been fully successful. The mechanism proposed by the Court reveals a number of problematic issues and proves to be insufficient and not entirely adequate to assess judicial independence and guarantees of a fair trial.

1 Introduction

Immediately after its publication, the judgment in Case C-216/18 *LM*[1] generated different reactions in Poland and abroad.[2] Some commentators treated the judgment as a general vote of no confidence in the Polish judiciary and especially with regard to the changes made into it in the recent years. Others, including the Minister of Justice, found it to be a defeat of the Irish court which referred the case to the CJEU, as the latter did not share all the suggestions made by the referring court. The *LM* case and the Court's judgment have been used as an argument in the current political debate. Because of the CJEU approach to certain significant issues, the judgment received equivocal interpretation, and its full consequences may become apparent only after a certain period of time and in the light of the post-*LM* judicial practice of domestic courts.

The wish of some political actors for the Court of Justice to provide an explicit negative assessment of the rule of law in Poland did not come true. Such anticipations did not take account of the specific nature of the preliminary ruling procedure. The *LM* judgment essentially maintained the standard division of roles between the CJEU and national courts. CJEU is to provide interpretation of EU law and give guidance to national courts.[3] In turn, the national courts are to pass judgments in the domestic proceedings, yet having regard to this guidance. A separate question is, whether the result of this division of roles and the actual instructions issued in the *LM* ruling can prove satisfactory in practice.

There is no doubt that the judgment is of a certain significance for the development of EU case law and the arguments set forth therein may potentially apply to various situations and proceedings. Because of that, some of the findings of the

[1]CJEU, Case C-216/18 PPU, *Minister for Justice and Equality (Deficiencies in the system of justice)*, ECLI:EU:C:2018:586. The case is regularly referred to, in an abridged form, as the *'LM case'*. The text builds on previous publications of the authors: Biernat (2018), Filipek (2018), Filipek (2019).

[2]See. *i.a.* the debate on Verfassungsblog: https://verfassungsblog.de/category/debates/after-celmer/ (Accessed 20 Jul 2019); Bogdanowicz and Taborowski (2018a), Grabowska-Moroz (2018a).

[3]See e.g. CJEU, Recommendations to national courts and tribunals in relation to the initiation of preliminary ruling proceedings (2019) C380/1, especially paras. 1, 5 and 11.

CJEU were formulated in a more general manner, especially in respect of two major perspectives. First, the Court developed and supplemented the arguments invoked in the Case C-64/16 *Associação Sindical dos Juízes Portugueses*,[4] concerning the notion and meaning of independence of national courts in the light of EU law. Secondly, the Court continued to set the limits of mutual trust and exceptions to the principle of mutual recognition of court decisions on account of the denial of fundamental rights in the context of executing a European Arrest Warrant.[5] In doing so, the CJEU developed its earlier ruling in cases C-404/15 and C-659/15 PPU *Aranyosi and Căldăraru* on a number of issues.[6] In this chapter we focus on some points of the *LM* judgment from the first of the aforementioned perspectives taking account of the domestic judicial practice that has followed the CJEU ruling.

2 The CJEU Concept of Judicial Independence

A central notion in the *LM* ruling is the independence of the judiciary. In the Court's view, the requirement of judicial independence forms part of the essence of the fundamental right to a fair trial. The right is of cardinal importance as a guarantee that all the rights which individuals derive from EU law will be protected and that the values common to Member States set out in Article 2 TEU, in particular the value of the rule of law, will be safeguarded. (para. 48). It is clear, the independence of the judiciary forms the essence of a fair trial and the right to effective judicial protection. At the same time, it lies in the very heart of the rule of law.[7] Without judicial independence, the state legal system can only provide an illusion of the rule of law.

In recent years, however, in some EU Member States, we have been witnessing the undermining of the role of independent judiciary. Without it, the protection of all human rights is impaired, including the right to a fair trial. Yet, respect for the right to effective judicial protection is a necessary and inalienable prerequisite for the protection of all other fundamental rights.[8] From the perspective of threats to the protection of judicial independence and thus to the rule of law and to fundamental rights, the *LM* ruling marks a further step towards building and consolidating the defense of the EU legal order and Union values against states that seem to be

---

[4]CJEU, Case C-64/16 *Associação Sindical dos Juízes Portugueses v. Tribunal de Contas*, ECLI: EU:C:2018:117.

[5]In this regard, see *i.a.* Grzelak (2018), especially pp. 51–54, 57–63; Xanthopoulou (2018), Lenaerts (2017), Anagnostaras (2016).

[6]CJEU, Case C-404/15 and C-659/15 PPU, *Pál Aranyosi and Robert Căldăraru v. Generalstaatsanwaltschaft Bremen*, ECLI: EU:C:2016:198.

[7] '*The very existence of effective judicial review designed to ensure compliance with EU law is of the essence of the rule of law.*', CJEU, *Associação Sindical, supra* note 4, para. 36.

[8]See e.g. Górski (2016), p. 37; Safjan (2018), pp. 559–560; Safjan (2019), pp. 5 and 10.

abandoning them and threaten the entire European project.[9] A new, specific point which was made by the CJEU is the following: if the national court executing the European Arrest Warrant finds that there are substantial grounds for believing that the person in respect of whom that warrant has been issued, will—following his surrender to the issuing judicial authority—run a real risk of breach of his fundamental right to an independent tribunal and, therefore, of the essence of his fundamental right to a fair trial, it may ultimately refrain to give effect to the warrant (para. 73).

In developing the understanding of judicial independence, the CJEU relied on the concept worked out in its previous case law and voiced i.a. in the *Associação Sindical* judgment. In the *LM* ruling, the Court broadened its view on the elements that make up and substantiate judicial independence (para. 63–67). This is one of the most important aspects of the judgment whose relevance goes beyond the specific case brought by the Irish High Court.

The notion of 'court' was elaborated in CJEU jurisprudence in the context of the preliminary reference procedure.[10] The CJEU enjoys the power to verify whether a request for a ruling comes from an authorised body, i.e. a 'court or tribunal'. It is empowered to do so both on party's request or of its own motion, when deciding the admissibility of the preliminary ruling request. The Treaty does not determine which body is to be considered a court, yet the Court of Justice has consistently pointed to a number of criteria which it takes into account when assessing if a body is in fact a 'court or tribunal'. The traditional Court's formula reads as follows:

> the factors to be taken into account in assessing whether a body is a 'court or tribunal' include, inter alia, whether the body is established by law, whether it is permanent, whether its jurisdiction is compulsory, whether its procedure is *inter partes*, whether it applies rules of law and whether it is independent.[11]

It is thus not the formal denomination as a 'court' that is decisive for the actual classification of the body admitted under Article 267 TFEU. What matters most of all is whether it carries out the function of adjudicating; if it acts as a *judicial* body. This entails a number of elements. The court proceedings are initiated by action of a party that wants to have a dispute settled. Bringing the case to the court results in the *lis pendens*, and precludes autonomous action in another ordinary court.[12] In most

---

[9] *'The collapse of the rule of law in any member state is tantamount to the rupture of a legal space in the entire European Union.'*, Safjan (2019), p. 7.

[10] See e.g. Lenaerts et al. (2014), p. 52 et seq.; Dashwood et al. (2011), pp. 214–216; Schütze (2018), pp. 389–391; Schwarze (2012), pp. 2234–2235. On the legitimacy of a uniform understanding of the term 'court' both in Article 267 TFEU and Article 47 Charter, see *i.a.*: Pech (2014), p. 1251; Górski (2016), p. 39; Bogdanowicz and Taborowski (2018a), p. 9. For an in-depth discussion of the differences in the concept of a 'court' under both articles see Grzeszczak and Krajewski (2014), pp. 5–11.

[11] CJEU, *Associação Sindical, supra* note 4, para. 38; almost identical with the original formula CJEU, Case C-54/96 *Dorsch Consult Ingenieurgesellschaft mbH*, ECLI:EU:C:1997:413, para. 23.

[12] CJEU, Case C-503/15 *Ramón Margarit Panicello v. Pilar Hernández Martínez*, ECLI:EU:C:2017:126, para. 34.

cases, judicial proceedings are by nature adversarial, and are characterised by opposing positions of the parties. The proceedings eventually lead to a binding ruling.[13] Furthermore, the court cannot refrain from taking a position on the case; it is entitled and, at the same time, called upon to consider and decide the case.[14] The final ruling of the court has the effect of *res judicata*.[15]

It is clear that the independence of the body belongs to the constitutive elements of a 'court' and is intrinsic to the very basic idea of adjudication. This is why it forms an essential requirement of the right to an effective remedy provided for by Article 19 TEU and Article 47 EU Charter of Fundamental Rights. As such it must be guaranteed both at the EU level, within the CJEU, but equally by the Member States at the national level with respect to domestic courts.[16] The Court of Justice in the *Associação Sindical* case proclaimed a general obligation of EU members to guarantee and respect independence of their judiciaries.[17] Domestic courts once they are qualified as a 'court or tribunal' under EU law and are empowered to rule on EU legal issues, have become 'European courts' ('Union courts') whose independence is now protected by the Union, its institutions and the Union's legal system.[18]

The guarantees of judicial independence are intended to protect both the courts and judges as well as those whose cases they handle. Firstly, they create an environment for the judge that enables him[19] to carry out the judicial function being confident about professional and personal safety. The judge must not fear that another public authority will not appreciate the court's decision and that he may suffer some negative consequences for that reason. Secondly, the guarantees of judicial independence provide the parties with a sense of confidence and certitude that the court will keep equal distance from the parties.[20] The facts of the case and the

---

[13]See also Lenaerts et al. (2014), p. 53.

[14]*'It is called upon to give judgment in proceedings intended to lead to a decision of a judicial nature'*, CJEU, *Panicello*, *supra* note 12, para. 28.

[15]Id., at 34; see also Górski (2016), pp. 39–40; Wachowiec (2019), pp. 568–571; for a critical review of these criteria see Grzeszczak and Krajewski (2014), pp. 7–9.

[16]See CJEU, *Associação Sindical, supra* note 4, para 42.

[17]See Pech and Platon (2018), p. 1828.

[18]See also Lenaerts (2018), p. 8.

[19]We use the pronoun 'he' throughout the text, and not the longer formula 'he or she', only for the reasons of readability.

[20]*'Guarantees of independence and impartiality require rules (...) in order to dismiss any reasonable doubt in the minds of individuals as to the imperviousness of that body to external factors and its neutrality with respect to the interests before it'*, CJEU, Case C-506/04 *Graham J. Wilson v. Ordre des avocats du barreau de Luxembourg*, ECLI:EU:C:2006:587, para. 53; see also recent CJEU rulings related to Polish courts: CJEU, Case C-619/18, *Commission v. Poland (Independence of the Supreme Court)*, ECLI: EU:C:2019:531, paras. 74, 111; CJEU, Case C-92/18 *Commission v. Poland (Independence of ordinary courts)*, ECLI:EU:C:2019:924, paras. 111, 124; CJEU, Case C-585/18, C-624/18 and C-625/18 *A.K. and Others v. National Council of Judiciary and Supreme Court (Independence of the Disciplinary Chamber of the Supreme Court)*, ECLI:EU: C:2019:982, paras. 128, 153.

applicable law are of sole relevance to the court, and it shall not take into account other considerations. When, in the end, the court delivers a judgment, it is indeed the very law that speaks.[21]

2.1 Autonomy of Courts

Unquestionably, there is a need to assess the independence of the national judiciary on the basis of a common EU standard. In its case law, the Court of Justice identified external (objective) and internal (subjective) aspects of independence, that to a large extent remain in line with the set of criteria indicated by the European Court of Human Rights.[22] They consist in guaranteeing, on the one hand—the autonomy of the court and, on the other—the objectivity and impartiality of the judge. In a similar way, judicial independence is understood in the jurisprudence of the Polish Constitutional Tribunal.[23]

Judicial independence sets the limits of political influence on the judiciary.[24] When considering a case, the court must remain autonomous. It must be free from outside influence, is protected *'against external intervention or pressure liable to jeopardise the independent judgment of its members as regards proceedings before them'*.[25] It is presumed that *'the court exercises its functions wholly autonomously, without being subject to any hierarchical constraint or subordinated to any other body and without taking orders or instructions from any source whatsoever'*.[26]

These preconditions are ensured by the principle of separation of powers, organizational and functional autonomy of courts which are entrusted with the task of

---

[21]Only in exceptional cases accepted the Court of Justice as a *'court or tribunal'* a body that was not fully independent. It occurred in some cases of administrative bodies which were also acting in a judicial capacity. In such situations the Court required the separation of functions between the departments responsible for administrative tasks and the departments vested with judicial functions. The judicial activities by the latter should be carried out without receiving any instruction from the former. See e.g. CJEU, Case C-110/98 *Gabalfrisa SL and Others v. Agencia Estatal de Administración Tributaria (AEAT)*, ECLI:EU:C:2000:145, para. 39.

[22]For an in-depth analysis of ECHR case law on judicial independence, see *i.a.* Hofmański and Wróbel (2010), pp. 314–325; Lawson (2018), Sillen (2019).

[23]*'Legislative and executive powers cannot exercise judicial power or interfere in areas in which judges are independent'*, Constitutional Tribunal (Judgment), Case Kp 1/15, Law on the Organization of Ordinary Courts, OTK ZU 147/9A/2015, para. III.2.4; *'Independence comprises many elements, namely: (1) impartiality vis-à-vis the parties to the proceedings; (2) independence from non-judicial bodies (institutions); (3) autonomy of the judge in relation to the authorities and other judicial organs; (4) independence from political factors; (5) internal independence of the judge. The independence of a judge is not only the right of a judge but also his constitutional duty, as is the constitutional duty of the legislature and judicial administration bodies to protect the independence of a judge'*, id., para. III.2.5; see also Constitutional Tribunal (Judgment), Case K 47/15 *Novelization of the Act on the Constitutional Tribunal*, OTK ZU 31/A/2018, para. III.6.1.7.

[24]See Lenaerts (2018), p. 5.

[25]CJEU, *Wilson*, *supra* note 20, para. 51; CJEU, *LM, supra* note 1, para. 63.

[26]CEU, *Panicello*, *supra* note 12, para. 37; CJEU, *LM, supra* note 1, para. 63.

administering justice. Other public bodies should be deprived of instruments by which they could exert pressure on courts to comply with their instructions or expectations.

In *Commission v. Hungary* the Court of Justice addressed the issue of political influence. It held that the mere risk that political influence could be exercised is enough to hinder the body in the independent performance of its tasks.[27] It continued by indicating a particular example of such influence: a threat of a premature termination of the body's term of office. This could lead to 'prior compliance' that would be incompatible with the requirement of independence.[28] In this case, the Court of Justice was not referring to a national court, but to a supervisory authority for the protection of personal data, which in accordance with Directive 95/46[29] was required to exercise its functions 'with complete independence'. There is no good reason why the protection of the independence of judicial bodies should deserve anything less.[30]

The current lack of effective separation of powers and the undermining of judicial independence, especially in the absence of guarantees of constitutional review, jeopardises the protection of human rights and disrupts the balance of powers. The consequences of the above deficiencies may be severe and far-reaching, beginning with a *de facto* change of a state's political and legal system. As the conduct of the parliamentary majority over the last few years in Poland demonstrates, the Constitution may be ignored or interpreted in a hostile manner.[31]

2.2 *Objectivity and Impartiality of Judges*

The second aspect of judicial independence embraces the impartiality and objectivity of the members of the court. As the CJEU pointed out, it *'seeks to ensure a level playing field for the parties to the proceedings and their respective interests with regard to the subject-matter of those proceedings. (...)* [it] *requires (...) the absence of any interest in the outcome of the proceedings apart from the strict application of the rule of law.'*[32]

In its previous case law the Court recognised a number of personal and institutional guarantees of independence and impartiality, in particular with respect to: court composition; appointment of judges; length of their service; grounds for

[27] CJEU, Case C-288/12 *Commission v. Hungary*, ECLI:EU:C:2014:237, para. 53.

[28] Id., para. 54.

[29] Directive (EC) 95/46 on the protection of individuals with regard to the processing of personal data and on the free movement of such data (1995) OJ L281/31.

[30] Likewise, Bogdanowicz and Taborowski (2018a), pp. 9–10.

[31] See also i.a. Łętowska (2018), p. 614 et seq.; Wyrzykowski (2017), p. 831 et seq.; Sadurski (2018, 2019).

[32] CJEU, *Wilson*, *supra* note 20, para. 52.

abstention, rejection and dismissal; protection against removal from office[33] (in particular, the dismissals of members of that body should be determined by express legislative provisions);[34] or remuneration of judges which should correspond to their function.[35]

A new accent in the *LM* judgment that expands the Court's perception of guarantees of judicial independence is the incorporation of some qualitative features of disciplinary proceedings against judges. It can be presumed that this is related to the Polish context. The Court pointed out that the system of disciplinary measures should be regulated in such a way that it cannot be used for political control of the content of court rulings. In this context, the Court stressed the need for a normative definition of: the conduct constituting disciplinary offences; the disciplinary penalties; the defendant's right to defence; and the right to appeal against a disciplinary ruling. This point of the *LM* judgment can be seen as a response to the reasoned proposal made by the European Commission under Article 7(1) TEU.[36] It is worth noting that, in addition to the legislative dimension, the actual application of the disciplinary regime to individual judges should equally be taken into account. Even if the disciplinary system met the criteria provided in the *LM* ruling at a normative level, its application in individual cases should be also taken into consideration. It is apparent that the situations, the manner and the context in which disciplinary proceedings against judges are instituted, or even the very incidents where judges are threatened with disciplinary responsibility, may intentionally lead to an oppressive effect and interfere with judicial independence. It is expected that the standards of disciplinary regime for judges will be further developed in the course of the infringement action brought in October 2019 by the European Commission against Poland under Article 258 TFEU. The Commission made an evaluation of disciplinary investigations in Poland and concluded that they may be triggered by the content of judicial decisions. This clearly undermines judicial independence and puts judges at risk of political control. The Commission claimed breach of Article 19 (1) TEU—effective judicial protection, and Article 267 TFEU—the right of a domestic court to refer questions for a preliminary ruling, because of the possibility of the initiation of a disciplinary proceeding if the court exercises that right.[37]

A further contribution to the development of the European concept of judicial independence was made by the CJEU in two recent infringement cases on the independence of the Polish Supreme Court[38] and the independence of ordinary courts[39] initiated by the European Commission on the basis of Art. 258 TFEU. In

[33]Id., paras. 51 and 53.

[34]CJEU (order), Case C-109/07 *Jonathan Pilato v. Jean-Claude Bourgault*, ECLI:EU:C:2008:274, para. 24.

[35]CJEU, *Associação Sindical, supra* note 4, para. 45.

[36]Taborowski (2019), p. 397.

[37]CJEU, Case C-791/19 *Commission v. Poland*, ECLI:EU:C:2020:277.

[38]CJEU, *Independence of the Supreme Court, supra* note 20.

[39]CJEU, *Independence of ordinary courts, supra* note 20.

both of them the Court of Justice found that Poland failed to fulfil its obligations to ensure effective judicial protection. In the course of time, there will be more and more CJEU rulings concerning the effects of changes in the Polish judiciary, as a number of Polish courts have referred questions to the Court for a preliminary ruling. The Court has recently responded to first of these questions (the case *A.K. and Others*).[40]

In both infringements rulings the CJEU underlined the protection of the judges against removal from office, and analysed the mechanism to extend judge's mandate after reaching the retirement age. The Court of Justice emphasised that the principle of irremovability requires that judges may remain in post provided that they have not reached the obligatory retirement age or until the expiry of their mandate, where that mandate is for a fixed term.[41] Though the CJEU admitted that the protection against the removal is not absolute, it nonetheless stressed that the interference with the principle can only be justified on *'legitimate and compelling grounds'* and must satisfy the proportionality test.[42] Whether these substantive and formal conditions are met may now clearly be subject to European scrutiny.

The Court examined in detail the mechanism for extending the active service of a judge. The mechanism is acceptable and it is the exclusive competence of the Member State to decide whether to make use of it in the domestic system. However, EU members are not free to impose arbitrary conditions and rules of such prolongations; their competence is limited by the requirement to ensure that the procedure does not undermine judicial independence. Indeed, neither the rule of law nor the principle of judicial independence prohibits the use of such a procedure, even if the non-judicial (e.g. executive) bodies are involved in its application. Yet, it is prohibited to shape the procedure in such a way that it may interfere with the independence of a judge by tempting him or her, even potentially, to give in to external intervention or pressure.[43] A judge who considers himself to be fit to continue in active service may be inclined to rule in conformity with the expectations of those who will examine the request and/or decide on the prolongation. Recognising the deficiencies of the procedures to extend the mandate of the Supreme Court judges by the President of the Republic and the judicial activity of ordinary courts judges by the Minister of Justice, the CJEU pointed to the discretionary nature of the President's and Ministerial powers, the lack of objective and verifiable criteria for their decisions, no obligation to state reasons for the decision and the lack of a judicial remedy against a possible refusal.[44]

---

[40]CJEU, *A.K. and Others*, *supra* note 20.

[41]Id., para. 76; CJEU, *Independence of ordinary courts*, *supra* note 20, para. 113.

[42]Id.

[43]See CJEU, *Independence of the Supreme Court*, *supra* note 20, paras. 110–112; CJEU, *Independence of ordinary courts*, *supra* note 20, paras. 118–120.

[44]CJEU, *Independence of the Supreme Court*, *supra* note 20, para. 114; CJEU, *Independence of ordinary courts*, *supra* note 20, para. 122. It was a paradox that a judge could have appealed from a preparatory, non-binding opinion of the National Council of the Judiciary which was to advise the President on whether to prolong the judge's mandate; while he could not have appealed against a final negative decision.

Another aspect of the *Independence of the Supreme Court* ruling which deserves special emphasis is that the examination whether judicial independence is preserved in a Member State, may also include checking what were the true aims of judicial reforms.[45] This is the case when serious doubts arise as to whether the aims declared by the government (e.g. standardizing the retirement age; improving the age balance of judges) justify the implementation of the specific measures, e.g. lowering the retirement age of judges, or granting a discretionary power to the political body to extend the active service of a judge. After all, a premature dismissal of judges appears not to be a very subtle means by the government to fill the 'vacated' judicial posts with their own appointees.[46] The examination of the actual aims focuses on the justification and the proportionality of the measures adopted. It covers not only the grounds for their application and the degree of discretion conferred on state bodies, but equally, other modalities of their implementation, e.g. compulsory nature, discriminatory effect, or retro-active application, as well as the results they may lead to (i.e. the removal of judges from the office).

In the most recent judgment *A.K. and Others*, delivered in the preliminary ruling procedure, the CJEU developed a method for assessing the independence of a judicial body.[47] Referring to the functioning of the newly established Disciplinary Chamber of the Supreme Court, but also to the National Council of the Judiciary, which participated in its staffing, the CJEU indicated the criteria for assessing, whether the body preserves its independence, ergo, whether it is in fact a court in the meaning of EU law.[48] In keeping with the terms of the judicial dialogue based on Article 267 TFEU, the CJEU left it up to the national court to carry out the assessment and draw conclusions.[49] The consequences of the CJEU ruling and the subsequent domestic judgments will be of major importance for both national and European administration of justice.

---

[45]CJEU, *Independence of the Supreme Court*, *supra* note 20 paras. 82 et seq. Twenty years ago, in *Köllensperger and Atzwanger*, the CJEU declared a request for a preliminary ruling from the *Tiroler Landesvergabeamt* admissible despite the fact that the provisions on the removal of its members were vague; the Court applied a general presumption that public authorities act in compliance with the national constitution and the rule of law; Case C-103/97 *Josef Köllensperger GmbH & Co. KG and Atzwanger AG v. Gemeindeverband Bezirkskrankenhaus Schwaz*, ECLI:EU: C:1999:52, para. 21 and 24.

[46]See also Kuijer (2018), pp. 532–533.

[47]CJEU, *A.K. and Others*, *supra* note 20.

[48]These criteria include the circumstances in which the body was set up, its characteristics and nature, the manner in which it operates and the public perception of its work; see CJEU, *A.K. and Others*, *supra* note 20, paras. 143–153.

[49]The domestic court made such an assessment in a judgment of 5 December 2019. The three-person panel of the Polish Supreme Court (Chamber of Labour and Social Security) ruled that the National Council of the Judiciary is not an impartial and independent body, and the Disciplinary Chamber of the Supreme Court is not a court within the meaning of EU law (case ref. no. III PO 7/18).

3 The LM Test

The general views of the CJEU on judicial independence set out above have been concretised in the *LM* case with regard to the EAW mechanism. The concretisation concerns the extent of obligations incumbent on judicial authorities which decide to execute the EAW at the request of judicial authorities of Member States with regard to which allegations of breach of the rule of law have been made, including interference with judicial independence. These obligations then consist in carrying out an independence test and ensuring that the fundamental right of the requested person to a fair trial is not at risk.

In the *LM* ruling the Court of Justice confirmed, in a different context, the essential application of the *Aranyosi and Căldăraru* mechanism to assess the risk of a breach of a fundamental right.[50] Ergo, the test applies also when the doubts are raised with respect to judicial independence and the fairness of a court trial.

In the operative part of the *LM* judgment, the Court reiterated the two tests introduced in *Aranyosi and Căldăraru*: the general test and the individual one (paras. 68, 79, and the conclusion). It is a *prima facie* conclusion when reading literally the wording of the judgment itself. This is also how most of the literature commented on this ruling. Yet, a more profound analysis brings us to the point that we may distinguish indeed, not a two- but a three-step test, which more accurately reflects the process of verifying the conditions for the execution of the EAW. The CJEU adapted the original test, by introducing an intermediate stage between a general and the individual risk assessment (para. 74). That stage comprises the assessment of judicial independence of the very courts which are competent to hear the individual case of the requested person. The Court thus indicated that the fair trial guarantees should be considered at three levels: general, intermediate and individual, accordingly making a distinction of: (1) a general risk assessment; (2) the assessment of particular courts competent to deal with proceedings concerning the person covered by the EAW; and (3) the individual risk assessment.

(1) The general test of *Aranyosi and Căldăraru* was left unchanged. It is used to determine whether there is a real risk that the fundamental right to a fair trial may be breached on account of systemic or generalised deficiencies concerning the judiciary, such as to compromise judicial independence in the Member State that issued the arrest warrant (para. 68).
(2) The next is the test of particular courts, i.e. the courts which have jurisdiction over the proceedings for which the individual person was requested by the warrant. At this stage, the executing court should determine to what extent systemic or generalised deficiencies in judicial independence (that were identified under the general test) may affect these courts (para. 74). The introduction of

[50] See also Taborowski (2019), p. 394 et seq.; Taborowski (2018), p. 73 et seq.; Bogdanowicz and Taborowski (2018b), Lewandowski (2019), p. 10; Frąckowiak-Adamska (2018b), p. 98 et seq.; Krajewski (2018), p. 796; Grabowska-Moroz (2018b), p. 21; Nita-Światłowska (2018), p. 8.

the intermediate stage is justified by the subject-matter of the assessment which is different from the other tests and, consequently, by the nature of questions that the executing court needs to consider. Only if the existence of such an impact is confirmed, the judicial authority can take the final test.

(3) The third test in the CJEU mechanism is the individualised test in relations to the specific case and the individual person being prosecuted. It aims to answer the ultimate question, whether there is a real risk of a breach of the fundamental right to a fair trial of the person subject to the arrest warrant. In making this assessment, the executing court should take into account the specific concerns of the person prosecuted and his personal situation, the nature of the offence, the circumstances in which it was committed and the context in which the EAW was issued (para. 75).

The evolution of the two-step *Aranyosi and Căldăraru* test into the three-step *LM* test has already been explicitly reflected in national court decisions taking into account the *LM* judgment. Indeed, the Irish High Court followed the three-stage pattern in its ruling to surrender the suspect.[51] Then, the Supreme Court of Ireland which considered the appeal from the High Court's ruling applied the three-step approach as well and concluded that *'although there was clear evidence of breach of Poland's Charter and Treaty obligations (...) and further evidence leading the trial judge to conclude that a breach of the principle of independence did operate at the level of the courts involved, the available evidence did not, on its own, satisfy the third stage of the test set out by the C.J.E.U. (...)'*.[52]

The consecutive steps of the *LM* test require further analysis and more detailed commentary, which will be made in the following section.

4 Implementation of the LM Test

Judicial independence is an undisputed legal standard of the European Union. Member States have the primary responsibility for ensuring it.[53] The verification of whether Member States fulfil this responsibility can be centralised, *i.e.* carried out by the EU institutions in the framework of political procedures (e.g. the protection of the rule of law, Art. 7 TEU) or judicial proceedings (e.g. an infringement action, Art. 258 TFEU).

Since the *LM* ruling, it has become apparent that the courts in other Member States also have the right and the duty to play an active role in safeguarding the

[51] High Court (Judgment of 19 November 2018), *The Minister for Justice and Equality v. Artur Celmer (No. 5)*, [2018] IEHC 639, paras. 92-98 and 117.

[52] Supreme Court (Judgment of 12 November 2019, *The Minister for Justice and Equality v. Artur Celmer*, S:AP:IE:2018:000181, para. 85.

[53] See CJEU, *LM, supra* note 1, paras. 52–57; CJEU, *Independence of the Supreme Court, supra* note 20, para. 71.

proper standard of judicial independence in the European legal area. The competence of domestic courts in this area is deemed to be a 'safety valve'[54] and a means to protect the EU legal order against the destructive influence of action of certain Member States which are not compliant with the rule of law.[55] The Court of Justice has therefore recognised that this responsibility is also decentralised and lies with all 'Union' courts, including national judiciaries.

4.1 General Risk Assessment

Concerns can be raised in relation to each of the steps of the above test. The mechanism established by the Court of Justice is complex and multilevel. It also appears to be difficult to implement in practice and the degree of difficulty increases with passing to the subsequent levels. From a methodological perspective, the easiest stage to carry out seems the first level: the general test. It may require a considerable amount of work on the part of the executing authority, as it consists in gathering and assessing the information on the general situation in the judiciary of the issuing state.

In this context, the question may be asked: what is the significance of the reasoned proposal of the European Commission opening the proceedings pursuant to Article 7 (1) TEU?[56] Would a similar document, if prepared by the European Parliament, e.g. a resolution on Hungary,[57] or filed by Member States, have a role to play? The Court held in the *LM* ruling that the information provided by the Commission in the proposal is 'particularly relevant' for the purposes of the general risk assessment (para. 61). Thus, the national court is to take account of the information contained in the Commission document.[58]

Nonetheless, it is to be noted that such a document will not be issued in future in each case of suspicion of the risks discussed. After all, in the history of the Union to date, it has only happened once (or twice, if the EP resolution on Hungary is to be counted). In the specific situation in which the Irish High Court was to take the decision, there were no obstacles to relying on the findings and conclusions of the Commission. In particular, no obstacle stemmed from the fact that the Commission proposal was adopted under a different procedure of a political rather than judicial nature; or from the fact that the decision of the Council under Article 7 (1) TEU had

[54]Taborowski (2019), p. 49, 375 et seq.

[55]See Barcz (2019), pp. 4, 12–13.

[56]European Commission, Reasoned proposal in accordance with Article 7 (1) of the Treaty on European Union regarding the rule of law in Poland, 20 December 2017, COM(2017) 835 final.

[57]European Parliament, Resolution on a proposal calling on the Council to determine, pursuant to Article 7(1) of the Treaty on European Union, the existence of a clear risk of a serious breach by Hungary of the values on which the Union is founded, 12 Sep 2018, P8_TA(2018)0340.

[58]See also Taborowski (2019), p. 399.

not been taken before the national court reached its decision on the execution of the warrant.

However, may the national court fully rely on the information presented in the Commission's proposal or perhaps it should verify or supplement it? The CJEU judgment is vague in this regard (cf. para. 61, 69, 73, 79). Yet, it seems justified that the national court may rely on the proposal of the Commission bearing in mind its detailed nature and extensive documentation. It should not, however, be confined to the Commission's document only. It should verify whether this document is up to date and, if necessary, gather further material.

The reference by the Court to the Commission's reasoned proposal should be seen as a recognition of the document as a source of information ensuring a high standard of reliability. Nonetheless, it is left to the executing authority to choose and evaluate the sources of information. The CJEU indicated the qualitative criteria of the information on which the executing authority should base its evaluation: the information should be objective, reliable, specific and properly updated (para. 61). In principle, any sources which provide information helpful for the general risk assessment can be used by the national court. The executing court should examine them, so that its determination is based on accurate, complete and exhaustive information that gives a true representation of the situation.

4.2 Assessment of Particular Courts

Further doubts arise in relation to the next levels of the assessment procedure, i.e. the determination whether there are serious and proven grounds to conclude, in the circumstances of the given case, that the prosecuted person will be exposed to the risk of a breach of the right to a fair trial as a result of being surrendered to the issuing state. The doubts concern both the procedural and the substantive aspects of the mechanism devised by the CJEU.

The executing judicial authority is required to assess whether the general or systemic deficiencies in judicial independence indeed affect the courts which have jurisdiction in criminal cases against the persons requested by the EAW. In the first place, it needs to identify the courts in the issuing state which have jurisdiction to rule on the matters in question. This will require to apply the rules of criminal procedure of that state, either by the executing court itself or with the assistance of other authorities, including the issuing court, e.g. through the judicial dialogue (Art. 15 (2) EAW Framework Decision). In principle, the courts' jurisdiction can be established before the person is transferred to the issuing state. In situations specified by the law in force, it may nevertheless be subject to change after the person's transfer. The risk of the potential change of jurisdiction after the surrender of the person prosecuted creates the danger that the assessment made by the executing authority will not be correct. It is equally difficult for the executing authority to predict later developments in the case. Assessment of the independence of the specific courts competent to carry out proceedings against the person wanted, is therefore only of limited usefulness to safeguard the fair trial guarantees to the individual person.

The example of the manner in which the *Oberlandesgericht* in Karlsruhe dealt with a EAW case (Ausl 301 AR 95/18), provide an interesting illustration of the difficulties that the executing courts may encounter when assessing the guarantee of the independence of judges by whom the requested persons would supposedly be tried after the transfer. Initially, the German court held a dialogue with the Polish court to clarify the doubts that had arisen and to gather additional information with regard to judicial independence in Poland. In doing so, it followed the formula indicated by the CJEU (see *infra*). The correspondence with the Polish counterpart did not allow to clarify all doubts of the German court. In the course of the dialogue, the *Oberlandesgericht* asked specifically for a binding assurance under international law that no disciplinary proceedings will be instituted against judges with regard to the content of their decisions taken during the trial of the requested person.[59] After having received a reply that such an assurance is not possible, the court then decided to make the consent for the surrender of the requested Latvian citizen subject to the assurances that the German ambassador or a person authorised by him will be entitled to be present at the trial conducted with respect to that person and, in the event of a conviction, to visit him in custody.[60] By proceeding in that way, the *Oberlandesgericht* apparently went beyond the formula outlined by the Court of Justice.

4.3 Individual Risk Assessment

The Court of Justice's test as proposed in the *LM* ruling, raises the most serious concerns as regards the final test: the examination of the individual risk. At this stage, the executing judicial authority is to make a final determination as to whether the requested person's fundamental right to a fair trial is at risk. The executing judicial authority ought to take into consideration: the specific concerns expressed by the person prosecuted as well as his personal situation, e.g. the political pressure to prosecute or punish him; possible negative statements by state officials about the person wanted; his possible membership of political opposition, social or ethnic minority; or media activities critical of political power, etc. In addition, the judicial authority should take account of the nature of the offence, the circumstances in which it was committed as well as the context in which the arrest warrant was issued,

[59]Oberlandesgericht Karlsruhe (Decision of 31 October 2018), Ausl 301 AR 95/18, para. 33.

[60]Oberlandesgericht Karlsruhe (Decision of 7 January 2019), Ausl 301 AR 95/18, para. 70.

e.g. the political nature of the act; or the fact that the act was committed in connection with the exercise of the freedom of expression or the freedom of assembly, etc.[61]

Taking the individual test means that the foreign national court has already carried out the two previous stages. It must have then established that judicial independence is endangered in the Member State which requested the surrender of the person, and it must have further recognised that this danger exists also in relation to the particular courts that are to try the person requested. At this stage, there should be therefore no doubt that the Member State whose judicial system is subject to such an examination does not respect the values of the Union, in particular the principle of the rule of law and its fundamental element: judicial independence. Some legal scholars suggested that refusal to execute EAWs should take place after general or systemic deficiencies in judicial independence in the given Member State had been identified.[62] However, this was not enough for the CJEU to complete the test. This is where the Court of Justice came to the rescue of the principle of mutual trust and the mutual recognition of judicial decisions. By protecting the EAW cooperation mechanism by requiring all three levels of the *LM* test to be carried out, the CJEU *de facto* accepted that judicial independence was threatened in the Member State which issued the warrant. This is perhaps the most controversial outcome of the *LM* ruling.[63]

The Court of Justice assumed that the actual realisation of the standard of judicial independence in a given Member State may vary. Moreover, this variation may occur at different levels, corresponding to the levels of the *LM* test. The existence of systemic or generalised deficiencies in the judiciary (the general test) may affect national courts to a differing degree: some courts may be affected, while some others not (the intermediate test). Furthermore, the determination that these deficiencies do have an impact on a particular court still does not preclude, in the Court's view, that in such a court a certain person in a specific criminal proceedings may be tried in accordance with the European standard of judicial independence (the individual test).[64] Therefore,

---

[61]CJEU, *LM, supra* note 1, para. 75. See also written observations in the *LM* case of the European Commission of 30 April 2018, paras. 23-24; CJEU, Case C-216/18, *LM*, Opinion of Advocate General E. Tanchev, ECLI:EU:C:2018:517, para. 103.

[62]E.g. Bárd and van Ballegooij (2018a) Judicial Independence; von Bogdandy (2018), Krajewski (2018), p. 805; Pech and Wachowiec (2019).

[63]See also *i.a.* von Bogdandy (2018), Frąckowiak-Adamska (2018a), Scheppele (2018), Grabowska-Moroz (2019), p. 427; Pech and Wachowiec (2019). It is suggested that in addition to preserving the mutual recognition mechanism, the CJEU intended to distinguish its responsibility (to protect the right to a fair trial in individual cases, based on Art. 19 (1) TEU and Art. 47 Charter), from that of the Council and the European Council (to oversee the systemic compliance of domestic judicial systems with the rule of law, stemming from Art. 7 TEU); see CJEU, *LM*, *supra* note 1, paras. 70–72; CJEU (opinion), *LM*, *supra* note 63, paras. 40, 42 and 44; Frąckowiak-Adamska (2018a), Krajewski (2018), p. 797.

[64]The Court clearly followed the line suggested by the European Commission and supported by the Advocate General; see European Commission (Written observations of 30 April 2018), para. 19; CJEU (opinion), *LM*, *supra* note 63, para. 108. See also Bárd and van Ballegooij (2018b) The AG Opinion, para. 2.2; Taborowski (2019), pp. 400–401.

the third stage of the *LM* test is indeed decisive. It makes the test highly rigorous and extreme, to the point that it becomes rather challenging to justify a refusal to execute a European Arrest Warrant.

The Court will soon re-examine the methodology indicated in the LM ruling following two new preliminary references brought by the Amsterdam Court (C-354 and 412/20). The Court in Amsterdam has asked how to deal with Polish warrants, once it has concluded that the independence of every court in Poland is at risk due to systemic deficiencies caused by changes introduced in recent years, including the possibility of initiating disciplinary proceedings for the content of judicial decisions.

There is another crucial aspect of the *LM* ruling that will definitely have far-reaching consequences for the EAW mechanism. It is the obligation of the executing court to request the issuing authority to provide additional information that it considers necessary for assessing whether there is a risk to a fair trial (the Q&A mechanism). The CJEU stated so in both *Aranyosi and Căldăraru* (para. 95), and *LM* (para. 76) cases. The Court of Justice applied the modal verb 'must' in the context of requesting additional information, which suggests that this horizontal judicial dialogue is of a compulsory nature and national courts cannot derogate from this duty. Such interpretation has been expressly accepted by some executing authorities.[65] Indeed, especially the second and third stages of the procedure developed by the CJEU will generally require launching of a Q&A mechanism. The detailed information that would be needed to carry out the assessment of particular courts as well as the specific case and individual situation of the suspect, usually, will not be fully known to the executing court. However, it should be left to the discretion of the executing authority to decide whether the information in its possession is sufficient for taking a decision about the execution of a EAW, or whether any supplementary information is needed.

The horizontal judicial dialogue is based on Article 15 (2) of the EAW Framework Decision[66] and is intended to allow the collection of 'necessary supplementary information', in particular as regards the grounds for non-execution of the warrant, the guarantees to be provided for its execution or the warrant's content or form. The issuing judicial authority may provide the executing court with any objective material in relation to any changes concerning the conditions for protecting the guarantee of judicial independence in the issuing Member State, which may rule out the existence of that risk for the individual concerned (para. 77). The issuing body may as well seek assistance, if need be, from the central authority or one of the central authorities of the issuing Member State (para. 78). Yet, both the CJEU approach to the formula of judicial dialogue and a relatively short practice of its use reveal a number of issues concerning the way in which it is actually carried out.

[65] See e.g. Rechtbank Amsterdam (Decision of 16 April 2019), ECLI:NL:RBAMS:2019:2721, section 4.4.

[66] Council Framework Decision 2002/584/JHA on the European arrest warrant and the surrender procedures between Member States, OJ L190/1.

5 Judicial Dialogue of National Courts

This part of the contribution presents the experience gained so far in the dialogue between the executing judicial authorities of different Member States and the issuing judicial authorities in Poland. It covers the dialogue not only of the particular courts which were competent in the case which led to the *LM* judgment, but also of other courts which applied the mechanism prescribed by the Court of Justice in other EAW cases. Most of the documents were obtained via the access to public information mechanism;[67] occasionally, some answers of Polish courts to the questions asked by the executing authorities were also made available on the respective courts' websites. The information obtained can be regarded as representative of other cases of judicial dialogue inspired by the *LM* judgment. They follow a similar pattern and show fairly common deficiencies. It should be noted, however, that this mechanism is still at its debut and may be subject to further evolution.

Following the CJEU ruling in the *LM* case, the Irish High Court complied with the requirements set out by the Court of Justice. It twice requested the supplementary information from Polish courts that issued the arrest warrants. In the end, the court in Dublin decided to execute all three warrants and ordered the surrender of the person wanted to Poland.[68] The Irish court confirmed its earlier assessment of the existence of a general risk of breach of the right to a fair trial due to systemic or general deficiencies in judicial independence in Poland.[69] It also concluded that these deficiencies will affect the courts before which the person wanted will be tried.[70] Ergo, it did determine that two out of the three tests of the *LM* ruling were met. Nonetheless, with respect to the last one: the final assessment of the existence of an individualised risk for the prosecuted person, the Court held that this risk was not proven.[71] The prosecuted person filed an appeal from the High Court's judgment which was examined by the Supreme Court of Ireland. The Supreme Court shared the assessment of the lower instance and eventually ruled in November 2019 to dismiss the appeal.[72]

The dialogue carried out in the *LM* case illustrated some problems of the Q&A mechanism established by the CJEU, which will be addressed below. The analogous judicial dialogue initiated in other EAW cases, e.g. by the courts of Madrid,

[67] The courts were asked for information twice: in November 2018 and in June/July 2019. While in the first round only about half of the courts replied, in the second round the success rate of the requests increased to some 80%. Perhaps this should be linked to the paper, which was the result of the first series of inquiries and was published in a legal periodical regularly consulted by judges; see Filipek (2019).

[68] *Celmer No. 5*, *supra* note 53, para. 123.

[69] Id., para. 93.

[70] Id., para. 97.

[71] Id., para. 117.

[72] Supreme Court, *supra* note 54, para. 88.

Amsterdam or Karlsruhe, also shows that the mechanism is deficient and the 'Union courts' are not fully capable to make use of it.

The questions posed by different courts varied greatly in terms of the content and the level of detail: from the most general questions from the Spanish court to inquisitive, detailed sets of questions from the Dutch and German courts. The most frequent questions concerned systemic, structural issues of the Polish judiciary, including the autonomy of courts in performing their tasks, the irremovability of judges, the composition of adjudicating panels, the available legal remedies, the dismissal of presidents and vice-presidents of courts, disciplinary proceedings, etc.[73] Questions referring directly to particular courts that have jurisdiction to hear the case of the person wanted were less frequent. Questions of this kind were raised primarily by the courts of Amsterdam and Karlsruhe (including: indication of competent bodies, changes in court's staff, recent retirement or transfer of judges in the competent courts, allocation of cases, rules on case resolution, disciplinary proceedings, or measures to protect the right to an independent court).[74] Some of the questions on particular courts were indeed of a general nature. In fact, there were only occasional questions related to the last stage of the *LM* test: the personal situation and concerns of the person prosecuted, or the nature of the offence and the circumstances in which it was committed. The latter category included questions about statements made by the deputy minister of justice referring to the person prosecuted as a dangerous offender, which the Irish court interpreted as likely to undermine the presumption of innocence of the person prosecuted.[75]

The analysis of the responses of Polish courts indicates that they may assist the executing authority in taking a decision to surrender a person prosecuted only to a limited extent. Many replies consisted mainly in a brief presentation of general legal rules concerning the judiciary: provisions of the Constitution/statutes and the submission of some basic data requested by the foreign court. In fact, this kind of replies prevailed. Occasionally, they were supplemented with some superficial conclusions, e.g.: *'In Poland, legal norms exclude threats to the independence of judges'*.[76] Only a few answers of the courts (judges) were explicitly critical, and negatively assessed the existing situation and expressed doubts about the independence of judges. In this context, in particular, disciplinary proceedings against judges were mentioned regularly. Other issues raised by the responding courts included: the non-transparent allocation of cases by a classified algorithm, the excessive influence of the Minister of Justice on the functioning of courts through administrative supervision, as well as

---

[73] *Celmer No. 5*, *supra* note 53, para. 3; High Court (letter of 8 August 2018); Juzgado Central de Instrucción (letter of 24 September 2018).

[74] Rechtbank Amsterdam (Decision of 4 October 2018), ECLI:NL:RBAMS:2018:7032, para. 4.4.3; Oberlandesgericht Karlsruhe (Decision of 31 October 2018), Ausl 301 AR 95/18, paras. 21–33.

[75] High Court (Judgment of 1 August 2018), *The Minister for Justice and Equality v. Artur Celmer (No. 4)*, [2018] IEHC 484, paras. 37, 40–41, 47.

[76] Regional Court in Warsaw (Letter of 26 September 2018). http://bip.warszawa.so.gov.pl/attachments/download/7511. Accessed 20 July 2019, p. 9.

the premature, arbitrary dismissal and appointment of (vice-)presidents of courts or the politicised composition of the National Council of the Judiciary. In turn, some replies were limited to expressing views in line with the official stance of the government (e.g. *'the National Council of the Judiciary is the independent body responsible for guaranteeing [judge's] rights'*).[77] or individual, hopeful opinions of the responding judge *('I would like to express my conviction that the majority of judges in the Republic of Poland stand up for their independence')*.[78]

Some of the answers were laconic or evasive and, in the opinion of the requesting court, contributed very little to the understanding of the general situation in Poland.[79] Some courts invoked the lack of a formal competence to provide answers in the required material scope (e.g. concerning the general situation of the rule of law in Poland, disciplinary proceedings against judges, the dismissal of presidents and vice-presidents of ordinary courts, the use of the extraordinary appeal, the evaluation of politicians' statements, the position of the Minister of Justice towards statements of his deputy etc.) or the lack of knowledge (e.g. about the disciplinary proceedings, the employment of assessors or judges' assistants, the extraordinary appeal, the statements of the deputy minister etc.). Sometimes both the lack of competence and the lack of knowledge were invoked simultaneously. In situations where the court is not capable of responding to some questions raised by the executing authority, it should perhaps approach the authority (or person) that has such knowledge or competence rather than ignore the questions or leave them unanswered. Excessive brevity or the lack of answer may make the requesting authority repeat or reformulate the questions, which will generate unnecessary additional communication and negatively affect the length of the proceedings. In ten very similar decisions of early 2019, the court in Amsterdam held that the answers of the Polish courts were insufficient to decide on the surrender of the persons wanted, and resolved to continue the dialogue.[80] This mainly consisted in urging the requested court to provide or supplement the answers to the previously transmitted questions.[81]

Over time, the judicial dialogue began to involve other bodies in Poland, apart from the regional courts (*sądy okręgowe*), as the ones entitled to issue European arrest warrants. The communication also included district courts (*sądy rejonowe*, e.g. in questions about assessors), courts of appeal, the Supreme Court (e.g. with

[77]Regional Court in Świdnica (Letter of 8 October 2010), p. 2.

[78]Regional Court in Rzeszów (Letter of 8 October 2010), p. 5.

[79]*Celmer No. 5*, *supra* note 53, para. 90.

[80]Rechtbank Amsterdam (Decisions of 4 January 2019), ECLI:NL:RBAMS:2019:33, 2019:42–2019:44, 2019:46–2019:51.

[81]In some cases, the second round of Polish courts' replies also left the EAW executing court unsatisfied; in a series of decisions it requested once again that the replies be supplemented; see Rechtbank Amsterdam (Decisions of 16 April 2019), ECLI:NL:RBAMS:2019:2750, 2019:2760, 2019:2792, 2019:2793, 2019:2801.

regard to extraordinary appeals) and the disciplinary bodies (e.g. the scope of disciplinary proceedings with regard to individual judges).[82]

In April 2019, in some cases, after a second round of dialogue, the court of Amsterdam decided to surrender the persons requested. Similarly to the Irish court, the *Rechtbank* Amsterdam acknowledged the general concerns in respect of the impact of the changes in Poland on the rule of law as well as the concerns with regard to the right to a fair trial before the courts in which the transferred person will be tried.[83] That means that, again, two out of three tests were met. It considered, however, that the risk of breaching the right of the individual person to a fair trial was not demonstrated. It held that neither the personal circumstances of the suspect nor the nature of the offences for which he would be tried justifies a negative decision. The court concluded that the charges related to common criminal offences, so the suspect as well as the type of offences were not in any way in the special attention of the ruling politicians in Poland so as to give rise to inappropriate influence on the judges.[84]

6 Evaluation of the CJEU Mechanism for the Assessment of Judicial Independence

6.1 Nemo Iudex in Causa Sua

In the *Aranyosi and Căldăraru* cases, the answers to be given by national courts within the judicial dialogue mechanism were intended to refer to the conditions under which a custodial sentence was to be served. Thus they related to the area for which a separate branch of public administration was responsible: the prison authorities that remain outside the judiciary. In contrast, in the *LM* case while it concerned a fair trial and judicial independence, national courts were requested to comment on themselves. A domestic judicial authority may be asked to assess particular courts of its own country (the ones having jurisdiction to try the case of the person being prosecuted) or the judiciary in general. Ergo, the court is being asked about a branch of the state structure of which it forms a part, within which it is established. This

[82]The survey of correspondence between courts shows that, occasionally, the understanding (translation) of the correspondence between courts could be a problem. Misunderstandings concerned some issues of importance, e.g.: which court will have jurisdiction to rule on the transferred person's case? Which court is actually giving the answer? (district or regional); Were the individual courts' presidents dismissed or they left due to the expiry of their term of office? Does the question relate to assessors or court assistants?

[83]See e.g. Rechtbank Amsterdam (Judgments of 16 April 2019), ECLI:NL:RBAMS:2019:2722, para. 5.4.1; 2019:2751, para. 5.4.1; 2019:2794, para. 6.4.2; 2019:2795, para. 4.4.1; 2019:2799, para. 4.4.1.

[84]ECLI:NL:RBAMS:2019:2722, *supra* note 85, para. 5.4.2; 2019:2751, para. 5.4.2; 2019:2794, para. 6.4.3; 2019:2795, para. 4.4.2; 2019:2799, para. 4.4.2.

gives rise to potential conflicts unknown to the previously examined cases relating to prison conditions.[85] In this context some difficult questions arise. Will such information meet the standard set by the Court of Justice? Will such information be objective and adequate? Will the assessment be fully reliable? Does a judge (court) who does not recognise any threats to the independence of the judiciary, contrary to the widely expressed and well-documented concerns, remain fully independent? How about a judge whose answers comply with to the expectations of political decision-makers, bearing in mind that their voice could have an impact on the judge's career? Would a judge admit receiving explicit or implicit instructions, suggestions or perhaps 'friendly advice' from the executive or other political actors? Answers to these questions can be challenging. On the other hand, how about a judge who provides critical comments on fair trial guarantees? Could he be afraid of condemnation, intimidation, legal harassment or threats of disciplinary proceedings on account of the answers he has given? These are legitimate concerns.

6.2 *Who Shall Answer?*

It is not clear who should answer the questions raised by the executing authority: the judge issuing the arrest warrant, the head of the court's department or the president of the court. The *LM* ruling indicates, in general, that the issuing judicial authority should be addressed. The EAW Framework Decision only in general specifies as the addressee of the questions: the court issuing the EAW. It may seem a minor issue, yet in practice, the actual respondent may be of crucial significance to the content of the answers. It actually did happen that competing answers were provided to the same questions by different judges of the same court: the court's president and the judge who issued the warrant.[86] An additional issue in the specific perspective of the *LM* case was that the warrants to surrender the person were issued by three different Polish courts. The cooperation of the executing court with several issuing authorities, with regard to a single wanted person, may lead the former court to ambiguous conclusions.

In practice, questions from a foreign court are generally answered either by court presidents or heads of court departments or sometimes individual judges indicated by them. Occasionally, questions from the foreign court have been answered by the individual judges who actually issued the arrest warrant; this happened when expressly requested by the court executing the EAW. A review of the current practice of judicial dialogue suggests that when answers are given by court presidents or heads of departments, they are more often abbreviated and kept to a minimum. Their actual usefulness for the executing authority may therefore be limited. On the other hand, in the rare cases where answers are given by the

[85] See also *i.a.* Pech and Wachowiec (2019).

[86] For details see Filipek (2019), p. 29.

individual judge who issued the warrant, these are usually more comprehensive, straightforward, and critical. It should be kept in mind that a number of courts' presidents were appointed by the Minister of Justice during a six-month period, when he enjoyed a fully discretionary power to replace presidents and vice-presidents of courts, or who were appointed by him following the expiry of their predecessor's term of office. The Minister, who is responsible for the changes in the Polish judiciary, is inclined to appoint persons who share his point of view.

6.3 Material Scope of Judicial Dialogue

Further concerns arise with regard to the scope of the questions asked by the judicial authorities executing arrest warrants and the stage at which the Q&A mechanism should be employed.[87] Could these be general questions, which concern systemic issues and therefore serve to perform a general assessment, the first stage of the tests pointed to by the Court of Justice? Or should these questions relate to the individualised courts which are competent to deal with the case of the person prosecuted after his transfer to the requesting country? Or, should they perhaps be limited mostly to the specific case and the person being prosecuted, and therefore serve the purpose of the ultimate individualised risk assessment?

The executing authority may indeed like to obtain information from the issuing court concerning a general or systemic situation in the Member State. This may be the case in particular with regard to the updating of existing information and cover recent legislative amendments, the development of case law or the administrative practice or any incidents that may be relevant to the assessment of threats to judicial independence. However, this possibility should be considered an exception. The executing authority should not make an initial effort to find and verify information simply by addressing, in the first place, the issuing judicial authority. The assessment of the fair trial guarantees and judicial independence by the executing court is also intended to apply to the responding court. The responding body is therefore in a difficult situation, as it speaks *pro domo suo*.

The judicial dialogue indicated by the Court of Justice should primarily serve the purpose of an individualised test carried out by the court executing the warrant, in which it assesses whether the particular person to whom the warrant refers, will be at risk of a breach of the right to a fair trial. A review of the existing practice indicates, however, that the executing courts do not refrain from asking general questions.[88] In

[87]Doubts about the absence of a more precise indication by the CJEU of what the supplementary information should concern were already raised after the *Aranyosi and Căldăraru* judgment, see *i.a.* Kamiński (2019), p. 59.

[88]It would be advisable for judicial authorities from other Member States to use for the first and second stage of the *LM* test, the available, general and up-to-date information from reliable sources, instead of referring to the Polish courts in the first place. Such sources include reports, analyses, opinions or recommendations from the international expert bodies: the Venice Commission, the UN

fact, they are much more frequent than questions about the person prosecuted and his individual case. Nonetheless, there are also such courts, e.g. the London Court, according to which the requests for further information are appropriate only in relation to particular circumstances affecting the person requested by the EAW.[89]

7 Final Remarks

The mechanism of horizontal judicial dialogue between executing and issuing authorities has some potential to permit the gathering and verification of information on the Member State which issued the EAW, and to clarify doubts related to fair trial guarantees in that State. However, it is a deficient instrument which is not fully capable of examining judicial independence and threats to the rule of law. Its functioning so far raises a number of issues: is it mandatory or optional? What should be its material scope? Who should respond to the questions of the foreign court? Is it appropriate and credible to ask the judge to evaluate his own independence and the attitude of fellow judges?

The above considerations illustrate inherent limitations and substantial inadequacy of the model of supplementary questions to assess judicial independence and decide on the execution of the EAW in relation to fair trial standards. This mechanism assumes that judicial authorities will carry out a self-assessment of their independence and share it with foreign authorities. The adequacy and credibility of such an exercise may be disputed. Despite detailed guidance from the Court (or perhaps: due to them), such a procedure does not seem to be able to lead to a satisfactory result in many or perhaps in most cases.

In view of emerging difficulties, a question may arise whether it would not be a better idea to stick exclusively to the general test: i.e. the examination of the systemic risk of breach of independence of the courts following the formula set in the context of asylum law in the judgment in Case C-411/10 and C-493/10 *N.S.*[90] This could lead to a quasi-automatic refusal to execute arrest warrants issued by Polish courts, and *de facto* result in the full exclusion of Poland's participation in the EAW mechanism. Such a solution would be questionable though. Its consequences could prove too far-reaching and hard to accept as it would not allow a more nuanced response to different specific circumstances of EAW cases.

In Poland's current situation, a general exclusion of all courts from judicial cooperation within the EU would result in a vote of no confidence against the

---

Special Rapporteur on the independence of judges and lawyers; the judges' associations: 'Iustitita', 'Themis'; or the civil society organisations: the Helsinki Foundation, the Batory Foundation, etc.

[89]London High Court of Justice (Judgment of 31 October 2018), *Pawel Lis and others*, [2018] EWHC 2848, postscript.

[90]CJEU, Case C-411/10 and C-493/10, *N.S. v. Secretary of State for the Home Department and M. E. and Others*, ECLI:EU:C:2011:865. See also *i.a.* von Bogdandy (2018), Frąckowiak-Adamska (2018a), Pech and Wachowiec (2019).

entirety of the Polish judiciary. However, a prevailing majority of the total of more than 10,000 judges maintain their independence in difficult conditions, both legal and psychological, which they face in their daily work.

Another observation comes to mind relating to the extensive reach of the Court's arguments going beyond the framework of the case presented by the Irish Court, but being of relevance for the scope of judicial cooperation. The independence of national courts is also required when they refer questions for a preliminary ruling. Such a position was emphasized by the CJEU in its judgment in the *Associação Sindical* case,[91] and repeated in the *LM* judgment discussed here (para. 54). It means that in the case of each reference for a preliminary ruling from Poland (or from another Member State in which there are corresponding doubts as to the respect of the fundamental right to a fair trial) it will be necessary for the Court of Justice to begin with a full test of independence of the referring court in the manner specified in the *LM* case. Did the Court in Luxembourg realise that its judgment might have such consequences?

In the context of a new category of questions referred for a preliminary ruling to the Court of Justice, in which national courts ask for an evaluation of their own independence, we may be soon witnessing new developments. Such questions have recently been referred to the CJEU by the courts in Germany (*Verwaltungsgericht Wiesbaden*)[92] and Hungary (*Central District Court in Pest*).[93] A new element is that the CJEU's reply and its appraisal is to apply to the very courts submitting the questions on judicial independence. This situation poses new challenges. First, if the Court of Justice were to answer the questions in the negative, i.e. if it considered that there is, indeed, a lack of a proper standard of judicial independence in the cases referred, the national court would then in fact not be entitled to ask a question for a preliminary ruling at all. In such cases, the answer on the substance of the question simultaneously becomes the answer on its admissibility. Would the Court of Justice therefore make an exception and admit the question on judicial independence from a non-independent court?, or would it rather declare the question inadmissible, yet pointing to the lack of independence of the requesting court?

Secondly, would the CJEU evaluate the independence of those courts by adapting the *LM* test? Not likely. In both cases of the German and Hungarian courts, the questions were asked in the context of individual cases pending before the national court. However, the questions referred to Luxembourg did not directly concern the private party's right to a fair trial, that is, the individual fundamental right. Instead, they dealt with a more general, constitutional issue: the independence of the court. The latter does not have to be linked to the specific case of a particular person. In

---

[91] CJEU, *Associação Sindical, supra* note 4, para. 43.

[92] CJEU, Case C-272/19, *Land Hessen*. The Wiesbaden Court's self-evaluation of its independence from the viewpoint of EU standards was negative: *'Nach alledem dürfte das vorlegende Gericht die europarechtlichen Vorgaben nach Art. 47 Abs. 2 GrCH eines unabhängigen und unparteiischen Gerichts nicht in diesem Sinne erfüllen.'*, Verwaltungsgericht Wiesbaden (Decision of 28 March 2019), 6 K 1016/15. https://openjur.de/u/2169849.html. Accessed 20 July 2019.

[93] Biró (2019) and Szabó (2019).

principle, therefore, there would be no need for a final (third) *LM* test: the individual assessment of the specific case and the risks related to the party of the national proceeding. The Court of Justice could make a ruling after carrying out: (1) the general assessment of the existence of systemic or generalised deficiencies in the Member State's judiciary, and (2) the impact of these deficiencies on the particular courts, namely those which submitted the questions.

If such a scenario were to materialise, it could also be followed by the courts of the Member States deciding on the execution of the EAW. They could start asking questions not just about the protection of the individual's right of the requested person to a fair trial, but at a more general level about the independence of the court that is supposed to hear the case, after the person were transferred. Such an approach would safeguard the individual right to a fair trial while guaranteeing the independence of national courts and protecting the rule of law more effectively than in the *LM* ruling.

References

Anagnostaras G (2016) Mutual confidence is not blind trust! Fundamental rights protection and the execution of the European arrest warrant: Aranyosi and Căldăraru. Common Mark Law Rev 6:1675–1704

Barcz J (2019) Unia Europejska wobec niepraworządnego państwa członkowskiego. Państwo i Prawo 1:3–23

Bárd P, van Ballegooij W (2018a) Judicial independence as a precondition for mutual trust. Verfassungsblog. https://doi.org/10.17176/20180410-104826

Bárd P, van Ballegooij W (2018b) The AG opinion in the Celmer case: why lack of judicial independence should have been framed as a rule of law issue. Verfassungsblog. https://doi.org/10.17176/20180702-173606-0

Biernat S (2018) How to assess the independence of Member State Courts? Verfassungsblog. https://doi.org/10.17176/20180730-100627-0

Biró M (2019) Hungarian judge requests European Court of Justice to examine his own independence. Index.hu. index.hu/english/2019/07/17/hungary_judicial_independence_european_court_of_justice_suspended_case. Accessed 20 July 2019

Bogdanowicz P, Taborowski M (2018a) Brak niezależności sądów krajowych jako uchybienie zobowiązaniu w rozumieniu art. 258 TFUE (cz. I). Europejski Przegląd Sądowy 1:4–11

Bogdanowicz P, Taborowski M (2018b) Wyrok Trybunału Sprawiedliwości w sprawie 'Celmer'. Analiza w 10 punktach. https://archiwumosiatynskiego.pl/wpis-w-debacie/wyrok-trybunalu-sprawiedliwosci-w-sprawie-celmer-analiza-w-10-punktach. Accessed 20 July 2019

Dashwood A, Dougan M, Rodger B, Spaventa E, Wyatt D (2011) Wyatt and Dashwood's European Union law, 6th edn. Hart, Oxford

Filipek P (2018) Challenges to the rule of law in the European Union: the distressing case of Poland. Revista do Instituto Brasileiro de Direitos Humanos 17(18):221–248

Filipek P (2019) Rozproszona europejska kontrola przestrzegania prawa do rzetelnego procesu sądowego w świetle zasady wzajemnego zaufania i wyroku C-216/18 PPU, LM. Europejski Przegląd Sądowy 2:14–31

Frąckowiak-Adamska A (2018a) Drawing red lines with no (significant) bite – why an individual test is not appropriate in the LM case. Verfassungsblog. https://doi.org/10.17176/20180730-104735-0

Frąckowiak-Adamska A (2018b) Następstwa wyroku w sprawie LM (Celmer) i postępowania na podstawie art. 7 TUE dla funkcjonowania sądów polskich w ramach wspólnoty prawnej UE. In: Barcz J, Zawidzka-Łojek A (eds) Sądowe mechanizmy ochrony praworządności w Polsce w świetle najnowszego orzecznictwa Trybunału Sprawiedliwości UE. Warszawa, pp 89–105

Górski M (2016) Prawo do skutecznego środka prawnego w art. 47 Karty Praw Podstawowych UE – znaczenie i deficyty. Europejski Przegląd Sądowy 8:37–44

Grabowska-Moroz B (2018a) Co orzekł Trybunał Sprawiedliwości w sprawie Celmer? https://archiwumosiatynskiego.pl/wpis-w-debacie/co-orzekl-trybunal-sprawiedliwosci-w-sprawie-celmer. Accessed 20 July 2019

Grabowska-Moroz B (2018b) Zaufanie bez wzajemności – czyli europejski nakaz aresztowania w czasach kryzysu praworządności. Refleksje na kanwie sprawy Celmer. Kwartalnik o Prawach Człowieka 1–2:16–26

Grabowska-Moroz B (2019) Sądowa kontrola Trybunału Sprawiedliwości UE w zakresie zmian dotyczących niezależności sądownictwa w państwie członkowskim UE – uwagi na tle Polski i Węgier. In: Bojarski Ł et al (eds) Konstytucja. Praworządność. Władza sądownicza. Aktualne problemy trzeciej władzy w Polsce, Warszawa, pp 403–430

Grzelak A (2018) Wzajemne zaufanie jako podstawa współpracy sądów państw członkowskich UE w sprawach karnych (uwagi na marginesie odesłania prejudycjalnego w sprawie C-216/18 PPU Celmer). Państwo i Prawo 10:50–66

Grzeszczak R, Krajewski M (2014) 'Sąd' w świetle przepisów art. 47 KPP oraz art. 267 TFUE. Europejski Przegląd Sądowy 6:4–14

Hofmański P, Wróbel A (2010) Komentarz do art. 6 EKPC. In: Garlicki L (ed) Konwencja o Ochronie Praw Człowieka i Podstawowych Wolności. Tom I. Komentarz do artykułów 1–18. Warszawa, pp 241–461

Kamiński IC (2019) Unijna zasada praworządności (państwa prawa) i uprawnienia sądów. In: Bojarski Ł et al (eds) Konstytucja. Praworządność. Władza sądownicza. Aktualne problemy trzeciej władzy w Polsce, Warszawa, pp 35–64

Krajewski M (2018) Who is afraid of the European Council? The Court of Justice's Cautious approach to the independence of domestic judges. Eur Const Law Rev 4:792–813

Kuijer M (2018) The rule of law in crisis? – some observations from the perspective of the Venice commission. Osteuropa Recht 4:530–551

Lawson R (2018) Protecting the independence of the judiciary: possibilities and limits of the European Convention on Human Rights. Revista do Instituto Brasileiro de Direitos Humanos 17(18):249–264

Lenaerts K (2017) La vie après l'avis: exploring the principle of mutual (yet not blind) trust. Common Mark Law Rev 3:805–840

Lenaerts K (2018) The Court of Justice and national courts: a dialogue based on mutual trust and judicial independence. http://www.nsa.gov.pl/download.php?id=753. Accessed 20 July 2019

Lenaerts K, Maselis I, Gutman K (2014) EU procedural law. Oxford University Press, Oxford

Łętowska E (2018) Convulsions in the rule of law. Osteuropa Recht 4:607–623

Lewandowski W (2019) Pomiędzy Scyllą zawieszenia wzajemnego zaufania i Charybdą fragmentaryzacji standardu ochrony prawa podstawowego – dylematy Trybunału Sprawiedliwości w wyroku C-216/18 PPU, LM. Europejski Przegląd Sądowy 2:4–13

Nita-Światłowska B (2018) Europejski nakaz aresztowania – ograniczona zasada wzajemnego zaufania. Kwartalnik o Prawach Człowieka 1–2:5–16

Pech L (2014) Commentary to Art. 47. In: Peers S et al (eds) The EU Charter of fundamental rights. A commentary. Hart, Oxford

Pech L, Platon S (2018) Judicial independence under threat: the Court of Justice to the rescue in the ASJP case. Common Mark Law Rev 6:1827–1854

Pech L, Wachowiec P (2019) 1095 Days later: from bad to worse regarding the rule of law in Poland (Part II). Verfassungsblog. https://doi.org/10.17176/20190211-221846-0

Sadurski W (2018) Anti-constitutional transformation in Poland: dimensions, sources, and prospects. Osteuropa Recht 4:624–636

Sadurski W (2019) Poland's constitutional breakdown. Oxford University Press, Oxford
Safjan M (2018) Domestic infringements of the rule of law as a European Union problem. Osteuropa Recht 4:552–560
Safjan M (2019) Rządy prawa a przyszłość Europy. Europejski Przegląd Sądowy 8:4–11
Scheppele KL (2018) Rule of law retail and rule of law wholesale: the ECJ's (Alarming) 'Celmer' decision. Verfassungsblog. https://doi.org/10.17176/20180730-095958-0
Schütze R (2018) European Union law, 2nd edn. Cambridge University Press, Cambridge
Schwarze J (2012) Kommentar zu Art. 267. In: Schwarze J (ed) EU-Kommentar, 3rd edn. Nomos, Baden-Baden
Sillen J (2019) The concept of 'internal judicial independence' in the case law of the European Court of Human Rights. Eur Const Law Rev 1:104–133
Szabó DG (2019) A Hungarian Judge Seeks Protection from the CJEU – Part I. Verfassungsblog. https://verfassungsblog.de/a-hungarian-judge-seeks-protection-from-the-cjeu-part-i. Accessed 20 July 2019
Taborowski M (2018) Naruszenie elementów zasady państwa prawa (art. 2 TUE) jako ograniczenie zasady wzajemnego zaufania w prawie Unii Europejskiej (w świetle wyroku LM (Celmer). In: Barcz J, Zawidzka-Łojek A (eds) Sądowe mechanizmy ochrony praworządności w Polsce w świetle najnowszego orzecznictwa Trybunału Sprawiedliwości UE, Warszawa, pp 73–88
Taborowski M (2019) Mechanizmy ochrony praworządności państw członkowskich w prawie Unii Europejskiej. Studium przebudzenia systemu ponadnarodowego, Warszawa
von Bogdandy A et al (2018) Drawing red lines and giving (some) bite – the CJEU's deficiencies Judgment on the European rule of law. Verfassungsblog. https://doi.org/10.17176/20180730-102416-0
Wachowiec P (2019) Pojęcie na gruncie traktatów unijnych. Polski wkład do redefinicji? In: Bojarski Ł et al (eds) Konstytucja. Praworządność. Władza sądownicza. Aktualne problemy trzeciej władzy w Polsce, Warszawa, pp 565–579
Wyrzykowski M (2017) 'Wrogie przejęcie' porządku konstytucyjnego. In: Bernatt M et al (eds) Wyzwania dla ochrony konkurencji i regulacji rynku, Warszawa, pp 831–853
Xanthopoulou E (2018) Mutual trust and rights in EU criminal and asylum law: three phases of evolution and the uncharted territory beyond blind trust. Common Mark Law Rev 2:489–510

Stanisław Biernat is a Professor of European law at the Jagiellonian University, Krakow.

Paweł Filipek is an Associate Professor at the University of Economics, Krakow.

6

Constitutional Crisis in Poland 2015–2016 in the Light of the Rule of Law Principle

Marcin Wiącek

Contents

Abstract This chapter concerns the constitutional crisis in Poland that began in 2015. It was triggered by appointing judges of the Constitutional Tribunal, by the outgoing Parliament, and then by re-appointing new judges for the same vacancies. Thus, the status of three judges elected by the previous Parliament and three judges elected by the current Parliament remains disputable.

One of the crucial elements of the rule of law is the principle of legality. There are two aspects of this principle: the presumption of legality that covers all acts of state bodies; the revoking of this presumption may be performed only within procedures prescribed by the law. The law should indicate a state body competent to revoke the presumption of legality and define the legal effects of such revoking. If the law is incomplete, incoherent or imprecise in that scope—that may lead to legal and political crisis. Polish legislation and Constitution fail to comply with the said standard. This is one of the causes of the constitutional crisis in Poland.

In a state governed by the rule of law state bodies should mutually respect their acts. State bodies should not treat acts or decisions issued by other state bodies as invalid or non-existent, unless it is declared within a procedure prescribed by the law. Otherwise, a legal chaos may occur. Courts are not empowered to evaluate the

M. Wiącek (✉)
Faculty of Law and Administration, University of Warsaw, Warszawa, Poland

lawfulness of the Tribunal's judgments. One of the crucial elements of the rule of law principle is the certainty of law.

1 Introduction

This contribution concerns the crisis that was caused by the election of five judges of the Polish Constitutional Tribunal (CT) in October and December 2015. The events that took place at that time led to the greatest constitutional dispute in the modern history of Poland and to the so-called 'rule of law crisis' in Poland that was subject to numerous procedures, in particular, before the organs of the European Union and the Council of Europe.[1] The principal aim of this contribution is to explain and evaluate *sine studio et ira* the sequence of actions that led to the crisis and to identify its root causes from the perspective of the rule of law principle.

It should be emphasised that the precise analysis of the aforementioned question is crucial, since the whole rule of law crisis in Poland began with the Constitutional Tribunal-related problem.[2]

2 Facts and Law

The constitutional crisis in Poland began in October 2015. It was triggered by appointing, by the outgoing Parliament (elected for the 2011–2015 term of office), five new judges of the CT. Subsequently, in December 2015, after parliamentary elections, the newly-elected Sejm re-appointed constitutional judges for the same vacancies.[3]

According to Art. 194 para. 1 of the Polish Constitution:[4] 'The Constitutional Tribunal shall be composed of 15 judges chosen individually by the Sejm for a term

[1]See, in particular, Opinion no. 833/2015 of the Venice Commission on Amendments to the Act of 25 June 2015 on the Constitutional Tribunal of Poland; Opinion no. 860/2016 of the Venice Commission on the Act on the Constitutional Tribunal; Commission Recommendation (EU) 2016/1374 of 27 July 2016 regarding the rule of law in Poland; Commission Recommendation (EU) 2017/146 of 21 December 2016 regarding the rule of law in Poland complementary to Commission Recommendation (EU) 2016/1374.

[2]Cf. Sadurski (2019), pp. 15–16.

[3]Detailed information, concerning subsequent stages of the constitutional crisis in Poland 2015–2016, is presented, in particular, in the following publications: Kustra (2016), Szuleka et al. (2016), Krzywoń (2018) and Sadurski (2019).

[4]Constitution of the Republic of Poland, adopted by the National Assembly on 2 April 1997.

of office of 9 years from amongst persons distinguished by their knowledge of the law. No person may be chosen for more than one term of office.'[5] On the basis of this constitutional provision, in 2006, five constitutional judges were appointed. Their terms of office began on 6 November (three judges), on 2 December (one judge) and on 8 December 2006 (one judge). Thus, five vacancies opened 9 years later, accordingly, on 7 November, on 3 December and on 9 December 2015.

On 25 June 2015, a few months prior to parliamentary elections, the Parliament adopted the new CT Act (2015 Act) which repealed the hitherto binding CT Act 1997.[6] The principal aim of the new Act was to simplify the procedure for the constitutional review, to accelerate this procedure and to explain certain procedural doubts that had arisen in the past.

The Sejm decided, however, that the 2015 Act should comprise also some transitional provisions which would concern the election procedure for the vacancies that would open on November and December 2015. According to Art. 137 of the 2015 Act: 'With regard to judges of the Tribunal whose terms of office end in 2015, the time-limit for submitting the proposal referred to in Art. 19 para. 2 shall be 30 days from the date of entry into force of the Act.'[7]

On 21 July 2015, the then Polish President signed the new CT Act. On 30 July 2015 it was published in the Journal of Laws and it entered into force after the expiry of a 1-month *vacatio legis* period.[8] In the meantime, i.e. on 17 July 2015, the President summoned the parliamentary elections. The day of elections was set for 25 October 2015.

During the last session of the outgoing Sejm, the Deputies decided to elect five new constitutional judges. Five Sejm's resolutions on appointing judges were adopted on 8 October 2015, i.e. 17 days before the parliamentary elections. Each resolution indicated the exact date when the term of office of a newly-elected judge would commence. Three of them indicated 7 November (R. Hauser, A. Jakubecki, K. Ślebzak), one—3 December (B. Sitek) and one—9 December 2015 (A. Sokala).

According to Art. 21 para. 1 of the 2015 Act, a person elected by the Sejm to assume the office of a constitutional judge was subsequently obliged to take the oath of office in the presence of the Polish President.[9] As regards persons elected on 8 October 2015, the President did not, however, organize the swearing-in ceremony.

[5] Sejm is the first chamber of the Polish Parliament.

[6] English translations of the 1997 Act and the 2015 Act: www.trybunal.gov.pl/en/about-the-tribunal/legal-basis/the-constitutional-tribunal-act/archive/ (accessed 19 August 2019).

[7] Art. 19 para. 2 of the 2015 Act: 'A proposal of a candidate for the judgeship at the Tribunal shall be lodged with the Marshal of the Sejm no later than 3 months prior to the end of the term of office of a judge of the Tribunal.'

[8] See Art. 139 of the 2015 Act.

[9] According to Art. 21 para. 2 of the 2015 Act: 'Refusal to take the oath of office shall be tantamount to resignation from the office of a judge of the Tribunal.'

Parliamentary elections were held on 25 October 2015. The term of office of the newly-elected Sejm began on 12 November 2015, according to the order of the Polish President, issued on 5 November 2015.[10]

Immediately after the inauguration of the new Sejm's term of office, on 17 November 2015, a group of Sejm Deputies lodged with the CT a motion to review the constitutionality of Art. 137 and some other provisions of the 2015 Act, in particular provisions concerning the swearing-in stage of a constitutional judge nomination procedure. Two days after having received the motion, the CT announced that the hearing of the case would be carried out 2 weeks later, i.e. on 3 December 2015.

A few days before the hearing, on 25 November 2015, the Sejm adopted five resolutions declaring that the elections of constitutional judges, performed by the previous Sejm on 8 October 2015, had been null and void due to procedural irregularities. In the reasoning for these resolutions their authors (a group of Sejm Deputies) acknowledged that the Sejm was not empowered to dismiss a constitutional judge from office, once he/she had been lawfully elected. The Sejm was, however, authorized to proclaim—merely in the form of a declaration, as opposed to a law-making decision—that a resolution on appointing a constitutional judge had been adopted in breach of law and thus it had been invalid from the very beginning. The authors of the November 2015 resolutions argued that, notwithstanding the transitional provisions of the 2015 Act, the resolutions of 8 October 2015 had contravened the Sejm's Rules of Procedure (Standing Orders).[11] For that reason, the majority of the Deputies expressed the opinion that the said resolutions had not brought about any legal effects and, consequently, there were still five judicial vacancies opened at the CT.

Three days before hearing the case, on 30 November 2015, the CT issued a decision on temporary (interim) injunction. The Tribunal called upon the Sejm not to appoint new judges until pronouncing a judgment on constitutionality of the 2015 Act (i.e. until 3 December 2015). It should be pointed out that the temporary injunction was not directly based on the 2015 Act, since this Act did not explicitly empower the Tribunal to issue such injunctions, unless the procedure was initiated by an individual's constitutional complaint (referred to in Art. 79 of the Constitution). The Tribunal explained, however, that legal bases for the injunction have been

---

[10]According to Art. 98 para. 1 of the Constitution: 'The Sejm and the Senate shall be chosen each for a 4-year term of office. The term of office of the Sejm and Senate shall begin on the day on which the Sejm assembles for its first sitting and shall continue until the day preceding the assembly of the Sejm of the succeeding term of office.' According to Art. 109 para. 2 of the Constitution: 'The first sitting of the Sejm and Senate shall be summoned by the President of the Republic to be held on a day within 30 days following the day of the elections (. . .).'

[11]The Deputies argued that, on the day of the elections of constitutional judges by the previous Sejm, Art. 137 of the 2015 Act had been contrary to Art. 30 para. 3(1) of the Sejm's Rules of Procedure according to which a candidature for the office of a constitutional judge shall be presented to the Marshall of the Sejm 30 days before the expiry of a constitutional judge mandate. That lack of coherence between Art. 137 of the 2015 Act and Art. 30 para. 3 subpara. 1 of the Sejm's Rules of Procedure led to the invalidity of the resolutions of 8 October 2015.

found in the Civil Procedure Code 1964 which was applicable, *mutatis mutandis*, to the procedure before the Tribunal in matters not regulated within the 2015 Act.[12]

The Sejm decided not to follow the temporary injunction. On 2 December 2015 (a day before the CT judgment) the Sejm elected five persons for the offices of constitutional judges (H. Cioch, L. Morawski, M. Muszyński, J. Przyłębska, P. Pszczółkowski). They have been forthwith sworn by the Polish President.[13]

Next day, on 3 December 2015, the Tribunal issued the judgment (ref. no. K 34/15).[14] In the operative part of the judgment the Tribunal ruled, *inter alia*, that Art. 137 of the 2015 Act, insofar as it concerned three judges whose terms of office ended on 6 November 2015, was consistent with the Constitution and, insofar as it concerned two judges whose terms of office either ended on 2 December 2015 or would end on 8 December 2015, violated the Constitution. Furthermore, the Tribunal ruled that the Polish President was, in general, devoid of the power to deny giving the oath of office to a person elected by the Sejm for the office of a constitutional judge. In the reasoning part of its judgment, the CT expressed the viewpoint that three judges had been lawfully elected by the previous Sejm and, therefore, the President was still under obligation to give them the oath of office. The Tribunal was of the opinion that the appointment of two other judges lay within the scope of competence of the newly-elected Sejm and, therefore, the previous Sejm had not been constitutionally empowered to fill in these two vacancies 'in advance.'[15]

One day after the Tribunal had delivered the aforementioned judgment, a group of Sejm Deputies lodged with the Tribunal a motion to review five Sejm's resolutions of 25 November 2015 (declaring that the appointments performed by the previous Sejm had been invalid) and five resolutions of 2 December 2015 (on appointing new constitutional judges). These motions were not, however, adjudicated to their merits. On 7 January 2016, the CT discontinued proceedings (ref. no. U 8/15), since according to the majority of judges the Tribunal was not constitutionally authorized to review the aforementioned resolutions.

Subsequently, the then CT President A. Rzepliński expressed an opinion that, as a result of the K 34/15 judgment, three judges elected by the previous Sejm for the

---

[12]See Art. 74 of the 2015 Act. In its hitherto jurisprudence the CT had always rejected motions to issue temporary injunctions in proceedings initiated by a group of Sejm Deputies, due to the lack of legal basis to issue such injunctions (see e.g. the decision of 11 May 2004, ref. no. K 15/04; English summary: www.trybunal.gov.pl/fileadmin/content/omowienia/K_15_04_pp_GB.pdf [accessed 19 August 2019]).

[13]Four judges were sworn on 3 December 2015, prior to the opening of the hearing before the CT. Judge J. Przyłębska was sworn on 9 December 2015, since she had been appointed for the term of office which would inaugurate on this day.

[14]English translation: www.trybunal.gov.pl/en/hearings/judgments/art/8748-ustawa-o-trybunale-konstytucyjnym (accessed 19 August 2019).

[15]See also the similar judgment of 9 December 2015, ref. no. K 35/15 (English translation: www.trybunal.gov.pl/en/hearings/judgments/art/8792-nowelizacja-ustawy-o-trybunale-konstytucyjnym [accessed 19 August 2019]).

terms of office beginning on 7 November 2015 (R. Hauser, A. Jakubecki, K. Ślebzak) were still expecting to be sworn by the Polish President. In consequence, the CT President allowed only two judges, from amongst five persons elected by the new Sejm and sworn by the Polish President, to perform their judicial duties, i.e. judges elected for the terms of office beginning on 3 December and 9 December 2015 (P. Pszczółkowski, J. Przyłębska). The CT President denied assigning cases to three other judges elected by the new Sejm (H. Cioch, L. Morawski, M. Muszyński). The CT President did, however, make it possible for these persons to work at the Tribunal, as its employees. They obtained their own office rooms and their judicial salary has been paid every month.

As a result of the aforementioned facts, the CT was composed of 12 judges allowed by the CT President to perform their judicial duties. Three remaining judgeships have become disputable, since, on one hand, the Polish President did not give the oath of office to three persons elected by the previous Sejm and, on the other hand, the CT President did not allow three persons elected by the new Sejm to perform their judicial duties.

In the meantime, on 22 December 2015, the Parliament adopted the Amendment Act, modifying the 2015 Act (Amendment Act). It envisaged, *inter alia*, that the CT should have adjudicated most of the cases sitting in a plenary session composed of at least 13 judges. It also imposed upon the CT the obligation to adjudicate cases in accordance with the order in which the motions were received by the Tribunal. Furthermore, the Tribunal's judgments, issued by the full bench, were to be adopted by the qualified majority of 2/3 votes. The Amendment Act entered into force upon the day of its publication (on 28 November 2015), without any *vacatio legis* period.

After its entry into force, the Amendment Act was immediately challenged before the Tribunal by two groups of Sejm Deputies, the First President of the Supreme Court, the National Council of the Judiciary and by the Ombudsman. The Tribunal decided to bypass some of the Amendment Act's provisions and to rule upon its conformity with the Constitution sitting in a panel composed of 12 judges, i.e. ten judges appointed prior to parliamentary elections and two judges appointed by the new Sejm, who had been allowed to perform their judicial duties by the CT President. The judgment was issued on 9 March 2016 (ref. no. K 47/15).[16] The Tribunal ruled that the whole Amendment Act was unconstitutional and the Act failed to bring about any legal consequences, in particular it did not effectively modify the original version of the 2015 Act. The majority of judges decided to proceed the case directly on the basis of the Constitution. These judges were of the opinion that Art. 8 para. 2 and Art. 195 para. 1 of the Constitution[17] empowered the Tribunal to deny applying provisions of the Act of Parliament. Hence, the CT

[16]English translation: www.konstytucja.wpia.uw.edu.pl/wp-content/uploads/2017/05/Judgment-of-the-Polish-Constitutional-Tribunal_ref.-no.-K_47_15_en.pdf (accessed 19 August 2019).

[17]Art. 8 para. 2 of the Constitution: 'The provisions of the Constitution shall apply directly, unless the Constitution provides otherwise.' Art. 195 para. 1 of the Constitution: 'Judges of the Constitutional Tribunal, in the exercise of their office, shall be independent and subject only to the Constitution.'

disregarded, *inter alia*, the provision pursuant to which the full bench of the CT should have been composed of at least 13 judges.

On 9 March 2016, the K 47/15 judgment was verbally announced in the courtroom and, subsequently, its operative part, signed by 12 judges,[18] was delivered to the Chancellery of the Prime Minister for official publication in the Journal of Laws. It should be pointed out that according to Art. 190 para. 2 of the Constitution: 'Judgments of the Constitutional Tribunal (. . .) shall be required to be immediately published in the official publication in which the original normative act was promulgated (. . .).' Art. 190 para. 3 of the Constitution stipulates that 'A judgment of the Constitutional Tribunal shall take effect from the day of its publication (. . .).' The duty to publish the Journal of Laws is vested in the Chancellery of the Prime Minister.

The Prime Minister's Chancellery expressed the opinion that the K 47/15 judgment was null and void, since it had been delivered by the 12-judge panel, as opposed to the panel composed of at least 13 judges, as it had been required by the Amendment Act which, during the Tribunal's session, had been in force and had enjoyed the presumption of constitutionality. Therefore, the judgment was not perceived by the Prime Minister as a CT's decision, but rather as a non-binding opinion of the majority of constitutional judges. For this reason, the Prime Minister's Chancellery denied publishing the judgment. However, according to the majority of the constitutional judges, the act delivered on 9 March 2016 was indeed the CT's judgment, its verbal announcement resulted in the revoking of the Amendment Act's presumption of constitutionality and, therefore, this Act may not be applied in the future.

From that moment, the Tribunal continued its routine adjudicating work, but the Prime Minister's Chancellery refused to publish its judgments in the Journal of Laws. It stemmed from the fact that the Tribunal respected the K 47/15 judgment and went on proceeding on the basis of the 2015 Act in its original wording. The Prime Minister's Chancellery was of the opinion that the K 47/15 judgment had not brought about any legal effects. Therefore, in the Chancellery's opinion, the Amendment Act was still in force and decisions issued in breach thereof may not be treated as CT's judgments.

On 22 July 2016, the Parliament adopted the new CT Act, repealing the 2015 Act. The new Act obliged the Prime Minister to publish all CT's judgments issued 'in breach of the 2015 Act,' except for the K 47/15 judgment. The situation became more complex after the Tribunal, several days before the Act of 22 July 2016 entered into force, had ruled that some of this Act's provisions had been unconstitutional (judgment of 11 August 2016, ref. no. K 39/16). That judgment has not been published either, since the procedure within which it was issued ignored the

[18]Two newly-elected judges (J. Przyłębska, P. Pszczółkowski) presented dissenting opinions. They expressed the viewpoint that the CT was not empowered to bypass the Amendment Act, even when reviewing its conformity with the Constitution, and that three remaining persons, who had been elected to be the CT judges in December 2015 (H. Cioch, L. Morawski, M. Muszyński), should have been allowed by the CT President to participate in the adjudication of the K 47/15 case.

Amendment Act of 22 December 2015. Therefore, not only the K 39/16 judgment, but also other CT's decisions pronounced after that judgment were denied being published.[19]

On 30 November and 13 December 2016, three new Acts concerning the CT, the status of its judges and transitional provisions were issued by the Parliament, signed by the President and entered into force.[20] On 19 December 2016, the term of office of the hitherto CT President expired. Two days later the Polish President nominated a new CT President (judge J. Przyłębska).[21]

The newly-appointed CT President allowed the three judges elected on 2 December 2015, who had not been hitherto assigned cases by the previous Tribunal's President (H. Cioch, L. Morawski, M. Muszyński), to perform their judicial duties. Furthermore, the CT President ordered the publication of the hitherto unpublished judgments (except for the K 47/15, K 39/16 and K 44/16 judgments).[22] These CT President's orders were based on transitional provisions contained within the Act of 13 December 2016.[23] The aforementioned three judgments were also removed from the official collection of the CT's rulings.[24] Eventually, the aforementioned three judgments were officially published in 2018.[25]

---

[19]For more details, see Sadurski (2019), pp. 75 et seq.

[20]English translations: www.trybunal.gov.pl/en/about-the-tribunal/legal-basis/the-constitutional-tribunal-act (accessed 1 March 2018).

[21]According to Art. 194 para. 2 of the Constitution: 'The President and Vice-President of the Constitutional Tribunal shall be appointed by the President of the Republic from amongst candidates proposed by the General Assembly of the Judges of the Constitutional Tribunal.' The procedure of proposing candidates for the position of new CT President provoked certain legal doubts as to whether the General Assembly lawfully presented candidatures to the President. These doubts stemmed from the fact that, on 20 December 2016, during the sitting of the General Assembly, only six judges did cast their votes, eight judges denied voting and one judge was on leave. The procedure was based on a special transitional provision (Art. 21 of the Act of 13 December 2016). On one hand, this provision envisaged that candidatures should have been presented 'by resolution' of the General Assembly. On the other hand, it did not require any particular quorum that should have been reached in order to adopt resolutions. That problem has been presented before the Supreme Court by the Warsaw Court of Appeal's referral. The Supreme Court, however, refused to rule the case to its merits (decision of 12 September 2017, ref. no. III SZP 2/17).

[22]The judgment K 44/16, issued on 7 November 2016, concerned the procedure for electing candidates for the positions of the President and the Vice-President of the Tribunal.

[23]According to Art. 18 para. 2 of the Act of 13 December 2016 (containing the transitional provisions), a person performing the duties of the CT President 'shall (. . .) assign cases to the judges of the Tribunal who have taken the oath of office before the President of the Republic of Poland and create conditions that make it possible for the judges of the Tribunal to perform their judicial duties.' The special basis for publishing judgments which had been issued 'in breach of' CT Acts of 2015 or 2016 had been created in Art. 19 of the said Act.

[24]It is published in the electronic form by the CT (see Art. 115 of the Act of 30 November 2016 on the Organization of the CT and the Mode of Proceedings before the CT).

[25]The specific legal basis for these publications was created by the Amendment Act of 12 April 2018. For more details, see Sadurski (2019), p. 78.

3 Controversies Concerning Three Constitutional Judges

From the moment when the new CT President assumed her office, the Tribunal started to continue its routine adjudicating work being composed of 15 judges. However, some constitutional judges, participants to procedures, scholars and publicists express the opinion that the Tribunal's composition is contrary to law, since three mandates at the Tribunal are not exercised by legally-appointed persons. Judges holding these mandates are sometimes even called 'anti-judges' or 'body doubles'.

Some argue that judgments issued with the participation of at least one of the aforementioned three persons are illegal and invalid. For instance, in his dissenting opinion attached to the CT judgment of 4 April 2017 (ref. no. P 56/14), judge S. Rymar stated that one of judges of the adjudicating panel (H. Cioch) was not a constitutional judge, since he had been elected by the Sejm for the judgeship that had been already occupied by a person appointed by the previous Sejm. Therefore, in judge Rymar's opinion, the P 56/14 judgment has been invalid, since it was delivered with the participation of a person who was not legally capable to perform his judicial duties.[26]

On the other hand, arguments are being raised that, currently, the Tribunal is lawfully-composed, since due to the law violations committed by the previous Parliament, the new Sejm was empowered to fill in all five vacancies at the Tribunal. For instance, in the reasoning for one of its latest decisions, i.e. the judgment of 24 October 2017, ref. no. K 10/17, the CT, sitting as a 5-judge panel, expressed the opinion that it was a misunderstanding to argue that the legal status of three constitutional judges had been determined by hitherto-delivered CT's judgments. In particular, the K 34/15 judgment concerned merely the constitutionality of Art. 137 of the 2015 Act which regulated nothing more than time-limits for submitting candidatures for the offices of a constitutional judge. As regards the Sejm's resolutions on appointing constitutional judges, the Tribunal declared, in the U 8/15 decision, that it was not constitutionally authorized to perform the review of such acts. In conclusion of the K 10/17 judgment, the Tribunal stated that the K 34/15 judgment's entry into force did not affect the legality of any of five appointments performed by the new Sejm on 2 December 2015.[27] The detailed analysis of this complicated constitutional problem will be performed hereinafter (in point 6 below).

[26]See also dissenting opinions attached to the following CT's decisions: judgment of 16 March 2017, ref. no. Kp 1/17 (judges L. Kieres, M. Pyziak-Szafnicka, S. Wronkowska-Jaśkiewicz); procedural decisions of 20 April 2017, ref. no. K 23/15, of 16 May 2017, ref. no. P 115/15, and of 11 October 2017, ref. no. K 14/16 (judge P. Tuleja); judgment of 24 October 2017, ref. no. K 1/17 (judge L. Kieres).

[27]See also: CT's procedural decisions of 15 February 2017, ref. no. K 2/15, and of 19 April 2017, ref. no. K 10/15; Muszyński (2017), pp. 127 et seq.

4 The Rule of Law and the Principle of Legality

The rule of law principle, enshrined in Art. 2 of the Constitution and in Art. 2 of the Treaty on the European Union, is a very broad concept and the source of several detailed principles.[28] One of the crucial elements of the rule of law is the principle of legality which, in general, means that all state bodies should act on the basis and within the limits of the law (see also Art. 7 of the Constitution). The discussion on the constitutional crisis in Poland should take into account the fact that there are two specific aspects of the principle of legality:

Firstly, it is the presumption of legality that covers all acts of public power, namely Acts of Parliament, courts judgments, administrative decisions, acts of the President etc. In general, all acts of public powers should be presumed legal and valid.[29]

Secondly, the presumption of legality may be challenged and then revoked. It is obvious that, on one hand, the violation of law by state bodies, or the abuse of powers, should not take place, but, on the other hand, it is not *per se* anything unusual in a state governed by the rule of law that such situations may occur. In the light of the rule of law principle, the revoking of the presumption of legality may, however, be performed only within procedures prescribed by the law. The law should, in particular, precisely indicate a state body competent to revoke the presumption of legality and define the legal effects of such revoking. Should the law be incomplete, incoherent or imprecise in that scope—that may lead to legal and political crisis.

Against that background, I express an opinion that Polish legislation and Constitution fail to comply with the aforementioned standard. The legality of state bodies' activity, which is the element of the rule of law principle, is not sufficiently safeguarded by appropriate procedural provisions of Polish law. That is one of the root causes of the crisis concerning the Polish CT. The Constitution and legislation fail to provide for exhaustive and sufficiently precise procedures within which certain essential legal disputes might be resolved. Therefore, as regards certain legal acts (e.g. constitutional judges' appointments, judgments of the CT), there is no procedural way to finally revoke or confirm their presumption of legality in case of a dispute.

---

[28] See, on the conceptual vagueness of the rule of law principle, e.g. Bárd (2016), pp. 190 et seq. See also Taborowski (2019), pp. 59 et seq.

[29] The concept of the presumption of legality may be found, in particular, in the ECJ case-law, cf. ECJ, Case 101/78 ECR 1979, 38 paras. 4–5; see also General Court Case T 471/11 ECLI EU T 2014, 739 para 117.

5 Constitutional Tribunal's Scope of Competence

The main source of the constitutional crisis were controversies concerning the legality of the Sejm's resolutions, issued on 8 October 2015, on electing new constitutional judges. They have not been sworn by the President, and, after the parliamentary elections, the Sejm declared aforementioned resolutions to be legally-ineffective (resolutions of 25 November 2015) and, consequently, appointed five new constitutional judges (resolutions of 2 December 2015).

One may pose a question whether there is an independent state body which would be legally capable to review the legality and constitutionality of the aforementioned Sejm's resolutions. The answer is 'no', since the Polish Constitution empowers neither the CT, nor any other judicial body, with the competence to examine the legality of the Sejm's individual resolutions, i.e. resolutions on personal nominations. In general, the CT may examine only statutes (Acts of Parliament), international agreements and legal provisions issued by central state bodies.[30] In consequence, certain Sejm's resolutions are reviewable in the proceedings before the Tribunal, but that refers only to so-called 'normative' resolutions, i.e. resolutions that are the source of general and abstract legal norms.[31] For that reason, in the aforementioned procedural decision of 7 January 2016 (ref. no. U 8/15), the Tribunal ruled that it was deprived of the power to review the Sejm's resolutions on appointing constitutional judges.

The Polish Constitution failed to introduce any systemic mechanism enabling constitutional review of state bodies' acts of applying the law, in particular acts issued by the Parliamentary Chambers.[32] Perhaps the situation would be different, should the Polish Constitution expressly empower the Tribunal to review all acts enacted by the Parliament, notwithstanding their contents, like it is, for instance, in Lithuania.[33] In particular, in 2005 the Lithuanian Constitutional Court ruled that the parliamentary resolution on the appointment of a constitutional judge was consistent with the Constitution.[34] Another good example is Spain. The Spanish Constitutional Court is explicitly authorized to control the appointments of constitutional judges.[35] Possibly, should the Polish CT have a similar scope of competence, the

[30]See Art. 188 para. 1–3 of the Constitution.

[31]E.g. the CT found itself to be authorized to examine some provisions of the Sejm's resolution on appointing an investigative committee (see the judgment of 22 September 2006, ref. no. U 4/06; English translation: www.trybunal.gov.pl/en/case-list/judicial-decisions/art/5888-zakres-dzialania-tzw-bankowej-komisji-sledczej [accessed 19 August 2019]; see also Wiącek (2007), pp. 193 et seq.

[32]Cf. Brzozowski (2017), p. 20.

[33]See Art. 102 of the Lithuanian Constitution 1992.

[34]Judgment of 2 June 2005, ref. no. 10/05 (English translation: www.lrkt.lt/en/court-acts/search/170/ta924/content [accessed 19 August 2019]).

[35]See Art. 2 para. 1 lit. (g) of the Organic Law 2/1979 on the Constitutional Court of 3 October 1979 (English translation: www.tribunalconstitucional.es/es/tribunal/normativa/Normativa/LOTC-en.pdf [accessed 19 August 2019]).

constitutional crisis could have been avoided or, at least, it would not have so escalated as it proved to be.

6 Legal Effects of the K 34/15 Judgment

During the debate on the constitutional crisis in Poland the argument was frequently raised that, as a result of the CT judgment of 3 December 2015 (ref. no. K 34/15), the Polish President became obliged to give the oath of office to three judges appointed by the previous Sejm. This judgment was also referred to as the justification of the CT President's refusal to assign cases to three judges elected by the new Parliament. In general, the aforementioned judgment is often understood as declaring the lawfulness of elections of three judges appointed by the previous Sejm.[36] Some important questions should be, however, explained in a more detailed manner.

First of all, it should be explained that the K 34/15 judgment was announced already after the new Sejm had appointed five constitutional judges and the President had sworn four of them. Furthermore, the judgment concerned merely some legal provisions of the CT Act 2015. The Tribunal did not directly examine the Sejm's resolutions adopted within the constitutional judges' appointment procedure, since (as it was explained herein before) it was not constitutionally authorized to review such resolutions. Nonetheless, in the reasoning of the K 34/15 judgment, the Tribunal expressed a viewpoint that the previous Sejm had been empowered to elect, and actually had effectively elected, three judges who should have been sworn by the President, despite the fact that, a few hours before, the President had sworn judges elected by the new Parliament.[37]

It is undisputable that, under the rule of law principle, all state bodies should respect and implement the CT's judgments. Simultaneously, there are many doubts concerning the legal effects of these judgments. Pursuant to the Constitution, the CT's judgments are, in general, prospective and they do not automatically exert influence upon acts or decisions issued before a judgment's entry into force.[38] For

[36]Cf., *inter alia*, the Venice Commission's Opinion no. 833/2015 (referred to in footnote 1), margin numbers 26, 124; the Commission Recommendation (EU) 2016/1374 (referred to in footnote 1), 8.

[37]In the Tribunal's opinion: 'In the case of the two judges of the Tribunal whose terms of office either ended on 2.12 or will end on 8.12.2015, the legal basis of the significant stage of the judicial election process was challenged by the Tribunal as unconstitutional. (. . .) the derogation of the relevant scope of Art. 137 of the CT Act should result in the discontinuance and closure of the procedure (. . .). The completion of the aforementioned procedure is inadmissible (. . .). (. . .) what does not raise constitutional doubts is the legal basis of the election of the three judges of the Tribunal who were to take office after the judges whose terms of office had ended on 6.11.2015. The derogation of Art. 137 of the CT Act within the indicated scope does not affect the election of those judges. (. . .) the judicial election carried out on that basis was valid and there are no obstacles to complete the procedure by the oath of office taken, before the President of Poland, by the persons elected to the judicial offices in the Tribunal.'

[38]See Art. 190 para. 2–4 of the Constitution.

that reason, it is debatable whether, and in what manner, the K 34/15 judgment affected the Sejm's resolutions of 8 October and 2 December 2015 on electing constitutional judges. It would be an oversimplification to argue that the said judgment nullified three out of five resolutions of the new Sejm (adopted on 2 December 2015) and definitively confirmed the legality of three out of five resolutions of the previous Sejm (adopted on 8 October 2015). The constitutional judges have been appointed directly on the basis of Art. 194 para. 1 of the Constitution, as opposed to the 2015 Act which only provided for certain procedural components of the appointment process.

According to the legal doctrine and courts' jurisprudence, including the jurisprudence of the CT, only the operative part of a CT judgment is legally binding within the meaning of Art. 190 para. 1 of the Constitution.[39] Arguments or opinions expressed by the CT in the reasoning parts of its judgments are, on one hand, frequently respected and applied by courts and other state bodies but, on the other hand, they are not universally binding since the Constitution did not introduce such an obligation. Consequently, state bodies are not legally compelled to obey such directives in their activity.[40] It is not unusual that a state body, e.g. a court, refuses to follow the CT's instructions contained within the reasoning part of a CT's judgment, in particular the instructions concerning the legal effects produced by the judgment. Therefore, ignoring certain considerations contained in the reasoning of a CT's judgment, including considerations concerning the legal effects of a judgment, may not be, in general, tantamount to the law violation.

It should also be noted that, as regards the participation of the Polish President in the appointment procedure (the swearing-in stage), the Tribunal issued a so-called interpretative judgment.[41] Yet, the Tribunal's power to issue such judgments remains disputable and, for many years, it has been questioned in some courts' jurisprudence. In particular, in 2009, the Polish Supreme Court adopted a resolution in which it expressed an opinion that the Tribunal was not constitutionally empowered to declare, in a universally binding manner, which interpretation of a legal provision is constitutional and which violates the Constitution.[42]

The legal problem concerning the swearing-in stage is pivotal, since the Constitution fails to envisage any form of the Polish President's participation in the procedure of appointing constitutional judges. One may, therefore, pose a question why the Tribunal decided to resolve the aforementioned problem in the controversial form of an interpretative judgment. Should the Tribunal have quashed the whole

---

[39]'Judgments of the Constitutional Tribunal shall be of universally binding application and shall be final.'

[40]See, in particular, the resolution of the Supreme Administrative Court of 10 January 2011, ref. no. I OPS 3/10.

[41]See point 5 of the K 34/15 judgment's operative part: 'Art. 21 para. 1 of the Act (. . .), interpreted other than that the President of the Republic of Poland is obliged to give the oath of office forthwith to a judge of the CT who has been elected by the Sejm, is inconsistent with Art. 194 para. 1 of the Constitution.'

[42]See the resolution of the Supreme Court of 17 December 2009, ref. no. III PZP 2/09.

provision concerning the swearing-in procedure, the legal effects of its judgment would have been, to that extent, less ambiguous.[43]

In consequence, the legal effects of the K 34/15 judgment remain vague. Perhaps the situation would have been different, should the law have expressly empowered the Tribunal to define the legal effects produced by its judgments and the way they should be implemented, like it is, for instance, in Germany.[44] Maybe it would be also worthy of searching for some ideas in the Amendment of the Spanish Constitutional Court Act, concerning the enforcement of the Court's judgments.[45]

7 May the Constitutional Tribunal Bypass an Act of Parliament?

One of the most important stages of the constitutional crisis occurred when, on 9 March 2016, the majority of the Tribunal's judges decided to bypass some provisions of the Amendment Act of 22 December 2015, which entered into force on the day of its official publication, and to declare this Act's unconstitutionality (the K 47/15 judgment). As it was explained herein before, the judgment was passed by the 12-judge panel, despite the fact that, according to the Amendment Act which had already been in force, the plenary session of the Tribunal should have been composed of at least 13 judges. For that reason, the Prime Minister's Chancellery denied the official publishing of the judgment.

Some arguments that justified the constitutional judges' decision to bypass certain provisions of the binding Act of Parliament might have been found in Art. 195 para. 1 of the Constitution, according to which constitutional judges are subject only to the Constitution.[46] A similar provision is contained in Article 178 para. 1 of the Constitution which stipulates that 'regular' judges (in particular, judges of common and administrative courts) are subject only to the Constitution and statutes (Acts of Parliament). The aforementioned provision is commonly understood in Polish legal doctrine and jurisprudence as empowering judges to bypass sub-statutory acts (*inter alia*, governmental regulations, referred to in Article 92 of the Constitution) which are, in a court's opinion, inconsistent with an Act of Parliament or with the Constitution. Accordingly, Article 195 para. 1 of the Constitution may be interpreted as granting judges of the CT the power to deny applying a sub-constitutional act, in

[43] See Wiącek (2016), pp. 125 et seq.

[44] See Art. 35 of the Act on the Federal Constitutional Court 1951.

[45] See Organic Law 15/2015 of 16 October 2015 on the reform of Organic Law 2/1979 of the Constitutional Court concerning the execution of decisions of the Constitutional Court as a guarantee of the rule of law (English translation: www.venice.coe.int/webforms/documents/default.aspx?pdffile=CDL-REF(2016)035-e [accessed 19 August 2019]).

[46] Cf. Radziewicz (2017), pp. 23 et seq.; Safjan (2016), pp. 35 et seq.

particular an Act of Parliament, in the situation where according to the CT an act in question is unconstitutional.

There are, however, scholars and constitutional judges who express the opinion that the Tribunal should obey even constitutionally questionable procedural norms, since—until ruling upon their inconformity with the Constitution—these norms enjoy the presumption of constitutionality. Furthermore, on one hand, pursuant to Article 195 para. 1 of the Constitution, constitutional judges are bound only by the Constitution but, on the other hand, the Constitution itself, in Art. 197, stipulates that the mode of proceedings before the Tribunal shall be regulated by the Act of Parliament.[47]

Perhaps the situation would be different, if acts concerning the mode of proceedings before the Tribunal were under obligatory constitutional review prior to their entry into force, like it is, for instance, in France.[48] Such a provision would make it possible to avoid the paradox situation where the Tribunal would be obliged to proceed on the basis of an Act which already came into force and, at the same time, is under constitutional review.

Furthermore, the constitutional crisis in Poland could have proved to be less escalated, if the law explicitly stated that the Tribunal may refuse to apply provisions that it deems unconstitutional, like it is in Lithuania. Art. 17 sentence 2 of the Lithuanian Constitutional Court Act 1993 stipulates that the Constitutional Court shall obey the Constitution and only such laws that are not inconsistent with the Constitution.

8 Presumption of Legality of Acts Issued by State Bodies

In the debate concerning the constitutional crisis in Poland, another fundamental question arose, namely whether a Tribunal's judgment may be found, by another organ of public power—e.g. by the Prime Minister (whose duty is to officially publish the Tribunal's judgments) or by a court (whose duty is to apply the Tribunal's judgments in individual cases)—illegal and non-existent due to controversies concerning the composition of a Tribunal's panel that adjudicated a particular case.

In my opinion, the answer to that question is 'no'. Neither the Constitution nor the legislation vest any state body with the power to evaluate the lawfulness of the Tribunal's judgments—in particular, with the power to declare that a judgment was delivered by the unlawfully-composed panel and thus was illegal or non-existent. From the moment when a judgment is ordered to be published by the CT President and referred to the Prime Minister's Chancellery, it should be presumed legal, then

[47]See, in particular, the dissenting opinions of judges J. Przyłębska and P. Pszczółkowski attached to the K 47/15 judgment (referred to in footnote 18). Cf. Zubik (2011), p. 116.

[48]It stems from Art. 61, read in conjunction with Art. 63, of the French Constitution 1958.

officially published and respected by individuals and all state bodies, in particular courts. It is the CT President's legal responsibility that an act sent for publication is indeed a legally-delivered Tribunal's judgment. That act enjoys the presumption of legality.

Nonetheless, I am of the opinion that the Parliament would be empowered to introduce a procedure under which, in certain exceptional circumstances, the Tribunal's judgments might be challenged. In particular, the current Polish legislation makes it possible to nullify a final court judgment issued by the wrongfully-composed judicial panel.[49] There are no constitutional obstacles against introducing such an extraordinary procedure when it comes to the Tribunal's judgments. Not only a final court decision but also a judgment delivered by the CT may be, hypothetically, burdened with such procedural defects that may justify the nullification of a judgment and re-considering a particular case.[50] It should be emphasized that there are some states in Europe where the proceedings before constitutional courts may be, in certain circumstances, re-opened what, in consequence, may lead to the re-examination of a case which was already settled by a final judgment.[51]

9 Closing Remarks. The Crisis of Procedures

The constitutional crisis in Poland is, to some extent, the crisis of procedures. There are some crucial constitutional issues which are not reviewable and, therefore, some pivotal constitutional disputes may remain unsettled by the judiciary. In particular, the authors of the Constitution failed to anticipate that the appointment of a constitutional judge may be subject to legal controversies and they failed to provide for procedures that could lead to the definite resolving of such controversies by an impartial organ of the judiciary. A constitution of a state governed by the rule of law should provide for, one may call it, 'fail-safe procedures', guaranteeing the respect for the principle of legality. The constitutional crisis proved that the Polish Constitution is not sufficiently consistent with this standard. As it turned out, the political will of the majority of Parliament was capable to break the hitherto established

---

[49]See, in particular, Art. 401 para. 1 of the Civil Procedure Code 1964; Art. 542 para. 3, read in conjunction with Art. 439 para. 1 subpara. 1–2, of the Criminal Procedure Code 1997; Art. 271 para. 1 of the Act on the Proceedings before Administrative Courts 2002.

[50]For instance, one of the judges sitting in the Tribunal's panel which pronounced the judgment of 2 April 2003 (ref. no. K 13/02) had been previously a Senator and had voted on the provision that was under review in this case. The Tribunal, however, decided that there was no basis for the re-opening of procedure (see the decision of 17 July 2003, ref. no. K 13/02, English summary: www.trybunal.gov.pl/fileadmin/content/omowienia/K_13_02_GB.pdf [accessed 19 August 2019]; see also Tuleja (2014), pp. 62 et seq.

[51]See, in particular, Art. 119–119b of the Czech Republic Constitutional Court Act 1993; Art. 75–75b of the Slovakian Constitutional Court Act 1993; Art. 62 of the Lithuanian Constitutional Court Act 1993.

practice in electing the CT judges and there was no legal remedy to be filed directly against these decisions.

In particular, the question of legality of electing three judges by the previous Sejm remains controversial and debatable, since no organ of judicial power is vested with the power to finally adjudicate upon that question in a binding manner. As it was explained herein before, the legal effects of the K 34/15 judgment are unclear. Simultaneously, the Sejm's resolutions on electing judges may not be reviewed by the Tribunal, what was confirmed by the Tribunal in the U 8/15 decision. Hence, on one hand, one may raise arguments, based on the CT's stance, expressed in the reasoning parts of judgments delivered in 2015 and 2016, that the previous Sejm was empowered to appoint three constitutional judges who, subsequently, should have been sworn by the Polish President. On the other hand, it should be noticed that the thesis that the previous Sejm was authorized to elect three judges is founded on the assumption that three vacancies at the CT undoubtedly opened in the course of the previous Sejm's term of office (i.e. on 7 November 2015). Such an assumption has basis in facts, the calendar of these facts was, however, unknown on the day when the previous Sejm appointed judges. In other words, on 8 October 2015 it was uncertain whether the previous Sejm's term of office would encompass the day when three vacancies at the Tribunal would open.[52] A question whether this argument, overlooked in the CT's judgments, influenced—in the light of the *tempus regit actum* principle—upon the legality of elections, performed by the previous Sejm, remains open.

Under the rule of law principle, all state bodies should mutually respect their acts and decisions. It means that, except for certain extraordinary and evident situations, a state body should not treat acts or decisions issued by another state body as invalid or non-existent, unless it is declared within a procedure prescribed by the law. Otherwise, a legal chaos may occur, what would be *per se* contrary to the rule of law principle. In particular, in the current system of law the Prime Minister's Chancellery is not vested with the power to deny publishing a CT's judgment in the situation where it was properly sent for publication on the basis of the CT President's order. For the same reasons, Polish courts are not empowered to evaluate the lawfulness of CT's judgments, including the situation where a court raises doubts as regards the composition of a particular Tribunal's adjudicating panel. Such a conclusion flows from the fact that one of the crucial elements of the rule of law principle is the certainty of law. Notwithstanding the legal controversies concerning the current composition of the Tribunal, its judgments should be published, respected and

[52]In the light of Art. 98 para. 1 and Art. 109 para. 2 of the Constitution (see footnote 10) the Sejm's term of office is, to some extent, flexible. The exact date of the inauguration of new Sejm's term of office had been unknown until 5 November 2015, when the President summoned the first sitting of the new Sejm and set its date for 12 November 2015. Theoretically, the new Sejm could have inaugurated its term of office even one day after parliamentary elections, on 26 October 2015. It was, therefore, conditional upon the decision of the Polish President. Cf. Brzozowski (2016), p. 149.

applied by courts and other state bodies. The protection of the principle of legality may not lead to the negation of the principle of law certainty.

References

Bárd P (2016) Scrutiny over the rule of law in the European Union. Polish Yearb Int Law 36:187–208

Brzozowski W (2016) Niezależność konstytucyjnego organu państwa i jej ochrona [Independence of a constitutional state body and its protection]. Wydawnictwo Sejmowe, Warsaw

Brzozowski W (2017) O potrzebie reformy konstytucyjnej [On the need for a constitutional reform]. Państwo i Prawo 12:3–22

Krzywoń A (2018) La crisis constitucional en Polonia (2015–2017): cómo cuestionar el sistema del equilibrio constitucional en dos años. Teoría y Realidad Constitucional 41:359–379

Kustra A (2016) Poland's constitutional crisis. From court-packing agenda to denial of Constitutional Court's judgments. Toruńskie Studia Polsko-Włoskie – Studi Polacco-Italiani di Toruń XII:343–366

Muszyński M (2017) Legal analysis of the election process of the judges of the Polish Constitutional Tribunal in the autumn of 2015. Iustum Aequum Salutare XIII(1):127–143

Radziewicz P (2017) Refusal of the Polish Constitutional tribunal to apply the act stipulating the constitutional review procedure. Rev Comp Law 1(28):23–40

Sadurski W (2019) Poland's constitutional breakdown. Oxford University Press, Oxford

Safjan M (2016) Politics and the constitutional tribunal. The constitution – the last instrument of defence against politics. Ruch Prawniczy, Ekonomiczny i Socjologiczny 1(78):35–42

Szuleka M, Wolny M, Szwed M (2016) The constitutional crisis in Poland 2015–2016. https://www.hfhr.pl/wp-content/uploads/2016/09/HFHR_The-constitutional-crisis-in-Poland-2015-2016.pdf. Accessed 19 Aug 2019

Taborowski M (2019) Mechanizmy ochrony praworządności państw członkowskich w prawie Unii Europejskiej. Studium przebudzenia systemu ponadnarodowego [The European Union law's mechanisms for protecting the rule of law in the Member States: a study on the awakening of the supranational systemta]. Wolters Kluwer, Warsaw

Tuleja P (2014) Proceedings before the Constitutional Court in relation to the Hierarchical Review of Norms. Sejm Rev:47–64. Fifth Special Edition

Wiącek M (2007) A review of the principal reasons for selected judicial decisions issued by the Constitutional Tribunal in the years 1997–2006. Sejm Rev:165–199. Third Special Edition

Wiącek M (2016) Commentary to the judgment of the Constitutional Tribunal of 3.12.2015 (ref. no. K 34/15). Przegląd Sejmowy 2(133):124–132

Zubik M (2011) Status prawny sędziego Trybunału Konstytucyjnego [The legal status of the judge of the constitutional tribunal]. Wydawnictwo Sejmowe, Warsaw

Marcin Wiącek is a professor of the Faculty of Law and Administration at the University of Warsaw; the Head of the Human Rights Division.

7

The Rule of Law Framework in the European Union: Its Rationale, Origins, Role and International Ramifications

Artur Nowak-Far

Contents

Abstract At present, the European rule of law enforcement framework under Article 7 TEU (RLF) is vulnerable to unguaranteed, discretionary influences of the Member States. This vulnerability arises from its procedural format which requires high thresholds in decision-making with the effect that this procedure is prone to be terminated by the EU Member States likely to be scrutinized under it, if only they collude. Yet, the Framework may prove effective to correct serious breaches against human rights (in the context of ineffective rule of law standards). The European Commission is bound to pursue the RLF effectiveness for the sake of achieving relative uniformity of application of EU law (at large), and making the European Union a credible actor and co-creator of international legal order. The RLF is an

A. Nowak-Far (✉)
Institute of Law, SGH-Warsaw School of Economics, Warsaw, Poland
e-mail: artur.nowak-far@sgh.waw.pl

important tool for the maintenance of relative stability of human rights and the rule of law in the EU despite natural divergence propensity resulting from the procedural autonomy of the EU Member States. By achieving this stability, the EU achieves significant political weight in international dialogue concerning human rights and the rule of law and preserves a high level of its global credibility in this context. Thus, RLF increases the EU's effectiveness in promoting the European model of their identification and enforcement.

1 Introduction

The Rule of Law Framework (here referred to as 'RLF' or 'the Framework') is a contingency procedure adopted to reflect on these processes of political (and legal constitutional) developments in the European Union Member States which give rise to significant enough doubts of whether these developments are in line with the fundamental standards set forth in the EU Treaties, i.e. the Treaty on the European Union (TEU) and the Treaty on the functioning of the European Union (TFEU). In the context of the RLF, the most important provisions of these two legal instruments are those which specify the constitutional standard values of the European Union as an international organisation and those which provide for a legal basis of the RLF.

For the sake of analysis, two distinctive forms of RLF are distinguished:

(a) RLF *sensu largo*—which should be construed under Articles 2 and 7 TEU and which includes all other legal vehicles adopted to enforce these two provisions;
(b) RLF *sensu stricto*—which, for analytical purposes, can be considered the mechanism of enforcement of Article 7 TEU designed by the European Commission and adopted pursuant to its communication of 19 March 2014 (further referred to as 'the RLF communication').[1]

The objective of this Chapter is to verify the following hypotheses:

1. In the RLF, the political element dominates over the legal one as much of the Framework is owned by the EU Member States rather than by an independent judiciary; in consequence, the very rationale of the RLF is contradictory: at the material level, it is to protect the rule of law where the role of independent judiciary is enshrined, whereas at the procedural level, its fundamental mechanisms rely upon the political will of the EU Member States to protect them; this makes the RLF a relatively easy prey for at least two European Union Member States prone to collude in the situation where, at the same time, they may find themselves within remit of the Framework because of their defiance of the EU Treaty values.

[1]Communication from the Commission to the European Parliament and the Council: A New EU Framework to Strengthen the Rule of Law, 10 March 2014, document COM (2014) 158 final/2.

2. Despite this vulnerability, the RLF has significant systemic value as it is able to put on a check all EU Member States' practices which manifestly contravene the values enshrined in the Treaties, including the rule of law; moreover, the RLF is not a final format and is very likely to be further developed into a more stringent, and legally certain construct—which is the area where the European Commission evidently sees its significant role in the future, and where it nurtures its powers *vis-à-vis* other EU institutions and the Member States.
3. The Commission is bound to pursue its active and, in terms of competences, rather expansionary policy in order to ensure uniformity of EU law enforcement internally and to preserve a high level of EU credibility as a globally significant promotor of human rights.

2 Rule of Law Framework *sensu largo*: Articles 2 and 7 TEU

2.1 *The Benchmark: Article 2 TEU*

The RLF is meant to assure enforcement of EU values enshrined in Article 2 TEU. Article 2 provides that:

> The Union is founded on the values of respect for human dignity, freedom, democracy, equality, the rule of law and respect for human rights, including the rights of persons belonging to minorities. These values are common to the Member States in a society in which pluralism, non-discrimination, tolerance, justice, solidarity and quality between women and men prevail.

The provision was adopted originally in the Treaty of Amsterdam in 1997. It was intended to provide for the axiological foundations of the European Union. In the post-Lisbon setting (i.e. after 2008) this provision was meant to create—together with the Charter of Fundamental Rights (which in the Treaty of Lisbon was given binding force) and other, already existing, provisions of EU law (pertaining especially to EU citizenship)—a set of overarching systemic reference for any other EU law provision, if only it concerned rights of individuals.

Article 2 TEU has its direct equivalent in Article I-2 of the Treaty establishing the Constitution for Europe, i.e. the EU treaty of 2004 which had been intended to replace the then present EU Treaty framework but had failed as a result of lack of ratifications in all the EU Member States.

In the EUCJ's jurisprudence of recent years, the question of the interpretation of Article 2 TEU has been deliberated quite frequently especially in the context of mutual trust of judicial systems. Thus, in its opinion 2/13[2] (EU accession to the

---

[2]CJEU, Opinion 2/13 of 18 December 2014, *Accession of the European Union to the European Convention for the Protection of Human Rights and Fundamental Freedoms*, ECLI:EU:C:2014:2454.

European Convention of Human Rights), the Court suggested that this mutual trust required that fundamental to the EU legal system values would be recognized in each and every EU member states as a precondition to the proper implementation of EU law;[3] this requirement was construed as a straightforward product of the very fabric of EU law which represents 'a structured network of principles, rules and mutually independent legal relations linking the EU and its Member States'.[4] In the judgment of 27 February 2018 in case C-64/16 *Associaçao Sindicos dos Juízes Portugueses (ASJP),*[5] the Court held that Article 2 was a pivotal provision for the mutual trust of national judiciaries in the EU jurisdictional system construed pursuant to Article 19 (1) TEU to consist also of national courts.[6] Thus, guarantees of judicial independence are required also at the national level.[7] The Court also upheld that the interpretation of art. 19(1) TEU could be rendered independently of whether, in a given situation, Article 51(1) CFR applies.[8] The issue has also been quite extensively discussed in a series of illustrious opinions presented by Advocate General Evgeni Tanchev.[9] AG Tanchev adopted a broader, systemic view of respective elements of judiciary reform in Poland (such as, especially, setting forth a lowered cap on the retirement age of judges during their tenure or subjecting the access to judicial positions or advancement in it to a scheme *de facto* controlled by the executive). In his opinions, he assessed them as contributing to an extensive systemic overhaul of the judiciary defying the relevant EU standards enshrined in the EU Treaty, thus undermining mutual trust principle. All these recent developments has proved to be a departure from a narrower analytical concept which had been adopted by the EU Court of Justice in the case C-286/12 *Commission v. Hungary,*[10] where the question of judiciary-concerned regulation on judges' age of retirement had been assessed in terms of its compliance with the EU principle of proportionality.

No doubt, the systemic position of Article 2 TEU and the exact content of values it enshrines has also been extensively debated in rule of law-concerned publications. Many of them considered *ASJP* judgment to have 'conceptional' importance for the whole rule of law discourse in the context of modifications of judiciary systems in some EU member states.[11] It has been argued in literature that the existing

---

[3]Id., para. 168.

[4]Id., para. 167.

[5]ECLI:EU:C:2018:117.

[6]Id., para. 30.

[7]Id., para. 42.

[8]Id., para. 29.

[9]Opinions in cases C-619/18 *Independence of the Polish Supreme Court* of 11 April 2018, ECLI:EU:C:2019:325; C-192/18 (retirement age of judges) of 20 June 2019, ECLI:EU:C:2019:529; C-585/18, C-524/28, C-625/18 *Polish National Judiciary Council, Disciplinary Chamber of the Supreme Court* of 27 June 2019, ECLI:EU:C:2019:551.

[10]Judgment of 6 November 2012, ECLI:EUI:C:2012:687.

[11]Pech and Platon (2018), pp. 1827–1854; Krajewski (2018), pp. 395–405; Bonelli and Claes (2018), pp. 622–643.

infringement procedures proved to be badly needed to defend basic principles of EU law and that they are paramount for the development of the underlying legal concept.[12] Some authors argued that the rule of law procedures were important to maintain the EU axiological system intact despite possible or existing stresses arising from the ever-changing political strains in the EU member states.[13] The TEU arrangements for the protection of rule of law were interpreted as unique as they were meant to provide for cooperation and axiological consensus instrumental for the EU to maintain its character as a polity of constitutional quality able to effectively protect its citizens whenever whey happen to enjoy EU law rights.[14]

Systemic approach and adequate institutional arrangements were considered to be of acute importance for the effectiveness of the existing EU rules meant to promote and/or protect EU values.[15] It has been argued that a causal model of infringement of values enshrined in Article 2 TEU was needed to make liability of the Member State possible under art. 7 TEU.[16]

2.2 *Two-Stage Procedure Under Article 7 TEU*

A rough equivalent of Article 7 appeared in the EU legal system in 1997, with the successful ratification of the Treaty of Amsterdam. Now it is one of the provisions of the Treaty of Lisbon. Article 7 can be applied in two distinctive situations emerging in the EU Member States:

(a) in a situation of a 'clear risk of a serious breach (. . .) of the values referred to in Article 2';
(b) in a situation of a 'serious and persistent breach (. . .) of the values referred to in Article 2'.

These two situations are addressed upon in two distinctive provisions of Article 7: its paragraph 1 and 2, respectively. Depending on specific circumstances, these provisions can be applied one after another, or—if the gravity of the situation commends it—just paragraph 2 can apply even from the very outset. In the former case, the two paragraphs concerned represent a two-stage description of the situation in which the breach of the values referred to in Article 2 has persisted over sufficiently long time or even aggravated.

For each of the so distinguished stages, different modes of situation identification and application of corrective measures apply. In each of these models a fairly

[12]Prete (2017), pp. 6–10, 301–304.

[13]Kochenov (2017), pp. 9–27.

[14]Tichý (2018), pp. 85–108.

[15]Itzcovich (2017), pp. 28–43; Schmidt and Bogdanowicz (2017), pp. 1069–1073.

[16]Bagińska and Majkowska-Szulc (2018), pp. 125–144.

complex and subtle interplay of the European Commission, the European Parliament, the Council, the European Council and the Member States is granted.

The procedure of Article 7(1) is initiated by $^1/_3$ of the EU Member States, or the European Parliament of the European Commission; under Article 7(2) the mode of the initiation is the same, with the exception that the European Parliament cannot trigger the procedure. The core institution making the pivotal decision for each procedure is different for paragraph 1 and 2. In Article 7(1) procedure, the decision is made by the Council (in its General Council formation, i.e. in the format made up of the European affairs ministers from all EU Member States) acting with a very challenging $^4/_5$ majority of votes. In contrast, in Article 7(2) procedure, the decision on the existence of 'a serious and persistent breach (. . .) of values referred to in Article 2' is to be made by the European Council. Only within the procedure under Article 7(1), the Council may address to the Member State (under the preliminary RLF scrutiny) its corrective recommendations prior to the determination that this Member State experiences a situation of 'a clear risk of a serious breach of the values referred to in Article 2'. The European Council is not empowered to take a similar step under Article 7(2).

The procedures of Article 7(1) and Article 7(2) can be distinguished also by their different outcomes. Under Article 7(1), the Council is invested with the right to regularly verify whether the grounds on which the Member State considered was determined to experience 'a clear risk of a serious breach (. . .) of values referred to in Article 2'. In contrast, in the aggravated situation falling within the ambit of Article 7 (2), the outcome of the procedure is that the Council would now be empowered (pursuant to Article 7(3)) to decide (by a qualified majority) 'to suspend certain of the rights deriving from the application of the Treaties to the Member States in question'. This coercive suspension may take the form of excluding the Member State's representative from voting in the Council; the suspension can as well involve any negative deformation of the regular rights of the Member State under the TEU and TFEU. The only limitations applicable to the power of the Council in this context is that—under Article 7(3) TEU—it should 'take into account the possible consequence of such a suspension on the rights and obligations of natural and legal persons'. Because of a high position of general principles of law in the EU legal system, the Council should also make its measures applied under Article 7(3) in line with these principles, especially with the principle of proportionality. Yet, as any overview of the Court of Justice jurisprudence may indicate, only serious, 'manifest' errors in this principle application are most likely to make the measures so adopted subject to annulment by the Court of Justice.[17] Moreover, these measures may escape any EU Court of Justice's scrutiny initiated by natural and legal persons, as under the well-established *Plaumann* doctrine they are required to substantiate that the contested measures are uniquely applicable to the person challenging them—which is a difficult task. In other words, the decisions adopted under Article 7(3) are

[17]See the judgment in the case 25-62 *Plaumann & Co. v. Commission*, ECR [1963] 95. See also: Arnull (2006), pp. 41–49.

bound to be quite enduring in the EU legal system.[18] The RLF Treaty procedures specified in Article 7 is graphically depicted in Fig. 1.

The Treaty does not offer any further or more detailed elaboration of the system of Article 7 enforcement. This implies that neither does it give any guidelines which may apply to the systematic monitoring of the situation in respective Member States prior to the application of Article 7. This shortage is quite striking when the system of Article 7 TEU is compared with the EU system of enforcement of rules of economic governance set forth in Articles 121 and 126 TFEU as the latter system is elaborated in a significant number of secondary legal acts which set forth detailed rules on the evaluation of relevant criteria and procedural aspects of their application.

The Treaty model of RLF, as it is, is quite vulnerable to the Member States' collective will to trigger its respective stages even in a rather hypothetical situation of serious infringements of any of them against the values enshrined in Article 2 TEU. This vulnerability arises from the very demanding unanimity threshold for the decision made under Article 7(2), i.e. the one which would determine 'serious and persistent breach of the values referred to in Article 2' by one of the EU Member States. It is therefore enough that two EU countries will simultaneously be subject to the RLF procedure to make it manifestly ineffective as each of these countries would be able to vote on the case of another. Such a voting 'complot' is not a novelty in the EU: e.g. exactly this type of cooperative behavior prevented the Council from making its decision effective in the seemingly much less vulnerable system of economic governance.[19]

2.3 *Rule of Law Framework sensu stricto in the Preparatory Stage: Its Origins and Formula*

European Union statutory law does not contain any specific provisions concerning the evaluation of the situation in any Member States with regard to Article 7 TEU. In other words, the initiation criteria for the RLF or the procedure applicable to the initiation of Article 7 application have not been detailed in the Treaties or any legislative legal acts. The fact that the EU law falls short of expectations with regard to the enforcement mechanisms of Article 7 (in connection with Article 2) TEU has not gone unnoticed to many actors of the EU legal system. The most pronounced political initiative to improve this situation was undertaken by a group of Northern EU Member States: Denmark, Finland, Germany, and the Netherlands which advocated for the development of an instrument which would make it possible to monitor the internal rule of law in EU Member States on a permanent basis. In the programming document of this initiative, a 2013 report titled 'Respect and Justice for All',

[18]Tridimas (2000), pp. 89–123.

[19]See the judgment in the case C-27/04 *Commission v. Council*, ECR [2004] I-6649. See also e.g. Andersen (2012), p. 27.

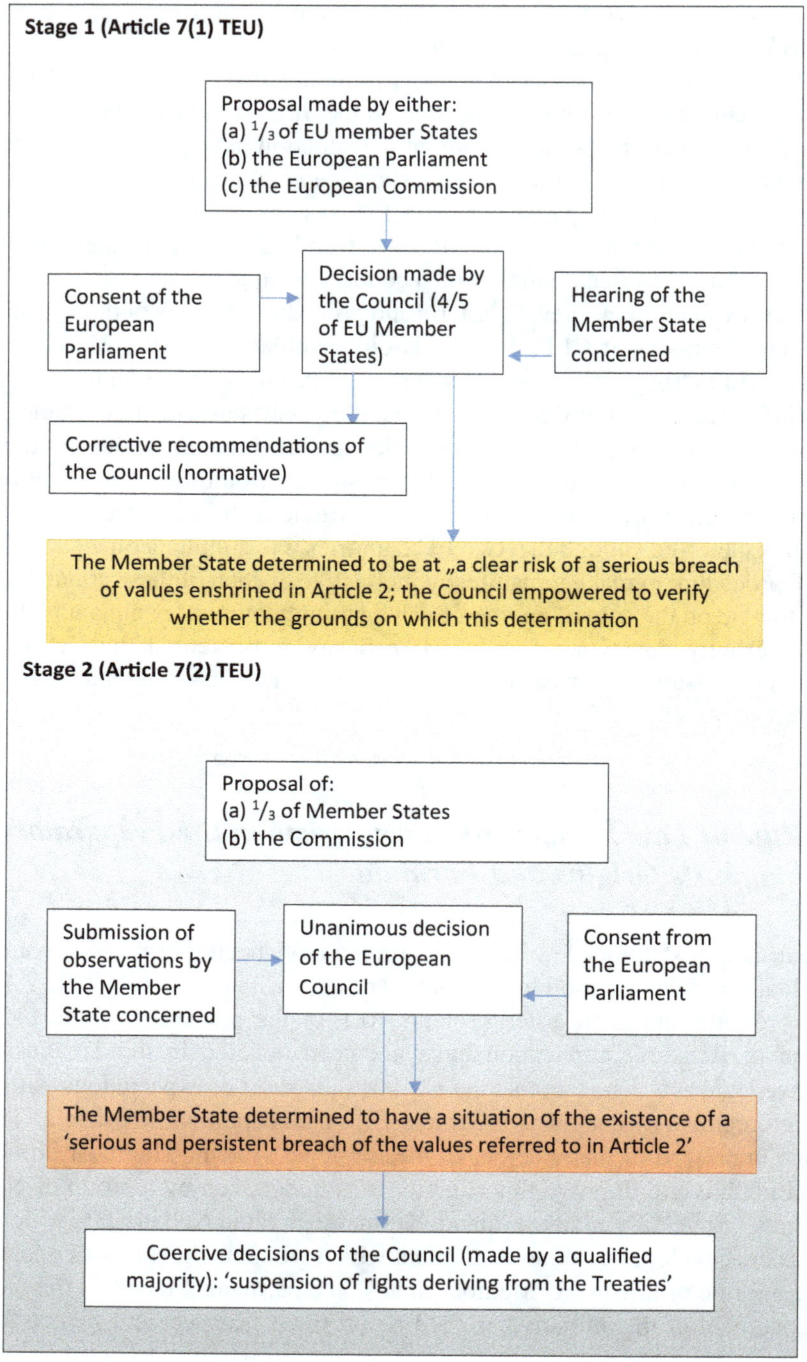

Fig. 1 Procedure of Article 7 paragraphs 1–2 TEU (Treaty of Lisbon). Source: Artur Nowak-Far

the Dutch Ministry of Foreign Affairs explained the rationale of the initiative in the following way:

> . . .the rule of law does not always function sufficiently well, even within EU member states. To strengthen the rule of law within Europe, the government seeks to promote transparent governance, independent judiciaries, respect for human rights, antidiscrimination policy and legislation to curb corruption and conflicts of interest (. . .) Countries wanting to join the EU must comply with strict accession criteria in the realm of the rule of law and human rights (the Copenhagen criteria[20]) (. . .) At the moment, there are still too few resources to call member states to account after their accession to the EU. Ideally, there should be a mechanism within the EU enabling member states to remind each other of their obligations on the basis of equality. There is already a system of this kind in the framework of the United Nations, but the EU also has a responsibility to tackle problems in its own house on a political level.[21]

The initiative coincided with some actions undertaken in the EU institutions: In June 2013 the Justice and Home Affairs Council and the European Parliament, respectively. The former called on the Commission 'to take forward the debate in line with the Treaties on the possible need for and shape of a collaborative and systematic method' to monitor the observance of EU values in respective EU Member States and address detected departures from the generally accepted standards.[22] The European Parliament requested that 'Member States be regularly assessed on their continued compliance with the fundamental values of the Union and the requirement of democracy and the rule of law.'[23]

The said RLF initiative did not earn any firm enough support from other Member States which remained neither neutral or negative to it. The Hungarian government already feared that the procedure would be used against it; some governments (like the Polish one, at least for some time) perceived it as an 'elitist' procedure which would be used by the 'better' states (most likely the 'old' EU members) to scrutinize political practices of the 'worse' countries (most likely to be the 'new' EU Member States, i.e. the ones which acceded past 2004 and which, indeed, had to meet the Copenhagen criteria). Some other Member States perceived the RLF as a tool to expand the European Commission's realm of authority—something they were reluctant to easily accept.

Regardless of these hurdles, in response to these initiatives, the European Commission came up with its own communication concerning the procedure which could be used for activating the mechanisms foreseen in Article 7 TEU.[24] According to the Commission's own statement, the proposed rules were to 'precede and complement

[20]For the explanation of this point refer to the next section of this chapter.

[21]Ministry of Foreign Affairs of the Netherlands (2013), p. 20.

[22]Press release 3244th Council Meeting – Justice and Home Affairs, Luxembourg 6–7 June 2013, document 10461/13 (OR.en).

[23]European Parliament, Committee on Civil Liberties, Justice and Home Affairs, Report of 17 February 2014 on evaluation of justice in relations to criminal justice and the rule of law, rapporteur Kinga Göncz, document A7-0122/2014.

[24]See *supra* Fig. 1.

Article 7 TEU mechanisms'; their application was to be 'without prejudice to the Commission's powers to address specific situations falling within the scope of EU law by means of infringement procedures under Article 258 TFEU' (i.e. its powers to start up an EU law infringement procedure before the European Union Court of Justice). Where there are clear indications of a systemic threat to the rule of law in a Member State, the Commission can launch a 'pre-Article 7 Procedure' by initiating a dialogue with that Member State through the Rule of Law Framework.

According to the Commission communication, the RLF procedure has three stages:

(a) the assessment stage—where the Commission collects and examines all the relevant information and assesses whether there are clear indications of a systemic threat to the rule of law; at this stage, if the Commission's concerns have been substantiated, it would initiate a dialogue with the Member State concerned by sending its 'Rule of Law Opinion' to that state;
(b) the recommendation stage—where the Commission would address its 'Rule of Law Recommendation' to the Member State concerned, in which this EU institution would make public expected actions and their applicable time-frame-work—all meant to improve the situation in the Member State concerned,
(c) the follow-up stage—where the Commission would monitor the Member State's action and, if it found the State's performance unsatisfactory, it would trigger Article 7 procedure—either on its own, or by prompting $^1/_3$ of the Member States or the European Parliament to do so.

The RLF (*sensu stricto*) can thus be interpreted also as a system of structured discourse as it involves a continuous dialogue and exchange or views between the Commission and the Member State concerned and between the European Parliament and the Member States (represented within the Council).

3 Exposition of EU Axiological Basis in the Treaties and Its Procedural Ramifications

3.1 Driving Forces

The idea to expose the EU axiological basis in a EU treaty has been on the agenda for a long time prior to the entry into force of the Treaty of Lisbon (in December 2009). The sense of urgency with regard to this exposition emerged as a result of the following two phenomena:

(a) the EU enlargement negotiations which started in 1998 and were successfully concluded in 2004 and resulted in accepting a group of Central and Eastern European countries as new Member States of the EU,
(b) the emergence of the authoritarian right-wing coalition in Austria (in the period of 2000–2002).

One of the challenges of the EU enlargement negotiations which involved a group of Central and Eastern European countries (i.e. Czech Republic, Estonia, Latvia, Lithuania, Hungary, Poland, Slovakia, Slovenia) was their authoritarian heritage (in fact, a little bit less extensive for the Czech Republic, as prior to WWII, it had been a fully-feathered liberal democracy). All these 8 countries had a Communist past, the Baltic States (i.e. Estonia, Latvia, and Lithuania) were even the component republic of the USSR until 1991. For this reason, the rule of law and other EU democratic values were included in the EU membership criteria negotiation package, most importantly in the form of the so called 'Copenhagen Criteria'. These were set forth by the European Council in its summit Conclusions of June 21–22 1993. The most relevant requirement was formulated in the following way:

> Membership requires that the candidate country has achieved stability of institutions guaranteeing democracy, the rule of law, human rights and respect for and protection of minorities, the existence of a functioning market economy as well as the capacity to cope with competitive pressure and market forces within the Union. Membership presupposes the candidate's ability to take on the obligations of membership including adherence to the aims of political, economic and monetary union.[25]

Thus, throughout the negotiations, the incumbent States were required to modify their institutional and legal systems in a way which could guarantee that the Copenhagen Criteria were met. Interestingly, the question of meeting the Copenhagen Criteria had not been an issue in the 1995 EU enlargement which included Austria, Finland, and Sweden, but had again been quite important in the 2007 EU enlargement onto Bulgaria and Rumania and in 2013 when they were again applied to Croatia. The problem with the sheer application of the Copenhagen Criteria was, however, that—from the perspective of the EU legal order—these criteria represent non-binding set of rules (which does not mean that they cannot be considered to form contractual obligations-reference under international law). This means that they could effectively be applied whenever, in the context of EU membership negotiations, there was enough conditionality to enforce adequate standards in the EU membership-aspiring countries; yet this element was lost whenever they entered the EU as the European Council's presidency conclusions of 1993 were not even their own original political commitment but rather something imposed 'from outside'. Thus, in order to avoid departures from the negotiated standards, an adequate amendment of the Treaty appeared to be badly needed.

As it has already been said, the other phenomenon which prompted the process of adoption of adequate Treaty standards of democracy, the rule of law, human rights, and the protection of minorities was that of the political rise of right, authoritarian parties in Austria. The phenomenon found its pivotal moment after the 1999 parliamentary elections in Austria when the radical right party, Freedom Party of Austria (*Freiheitliche Partei Österreichs, FPÖ*), was able to create a coalition with the mainstream Social Democrats (*Sozialdemokratische Partei Österreichs, SPÖ*).

[25] European Council in Copenhagen. Conclusions of the Presidency, June 21–22, 1993, document SN 180/1/93 REV 1, p. 14.

What now (unfortunately) appears not so unusual anymore, had in 2000 come as a surprise because of a controversial, nationalistic, anti-immigration, and authoritarian penchant of the controversial FPÖ's leader Jörg Haider. The resulting situation made it visible, that the only pressure other EU Member States could exert on the EU country whose policy might not be completely in line with the EU values was the political pressure (in fact, intra-EU cooperation with the Austrian government then was limited), but no firm legal tool could be used.

The first ever legislative reaction to the threat of rightist populists was the amendment of the Treaty introduced by the Treaty of Amsterdam (1997), often referred to as '*Lex Austria*'. Namely, in Article F.1, the Treaty was given a new provision which provided that:

> The Union is founded on the principles of liberty, democracy, respect for human rights and fundamental freedoms and the rule of law, principles which are common to the Member States.

It is quite striking that, when compared to Article 2 of the present TUE, Article F (1) TUE (the Amsterdam version) made its reference to a narrower catalogue of values. Moreover, it made a reference to liberty which is not made any more in the present Treaty. Its reference to human rights goes together with the reference to fundamental freedoms—whereas the present Treaty does not contain a reference to the latter value. Most importantly, Article F(1) TUE does not contain any specific catalogue of values which pertain to the societies of the Member States (such as pluralism, non-discrimination, tolerance, justice, solidarity, and equality between women and men); rather, it points out an axiological network which should be 'common the Member States' but which apparently 'stem from the fundamental EU legal order'.

In Article F.1., the Amsterdam Treaty set forth, for the first time, a RLF procedure, yet it was quite distinctive from the present one. The most important difference is that the Amsterdam RLF was a single-stage procedure with the pivotal role of the Council, acting in a very special format (not used anymore in the EU institutional order) of the heads of states or governments (i.e. with no participation of the President of the Council nor any of its own President, as this position had never existed for this very special type of the Council). The Council was to act by unanimity on a proposal by 1/3 of the Member States or by the Commission and after obtaining the assent of the European Parliament—which is the same arrangement as the one used now (also with respect to the majority requirements). Article F.1 provided also that the Council's decision should be made only after inviting the Member State concerned to submit its observations. The procedure was to be concluded with the determination by the Council of 'the existence of a serious and persistent breach by a Member State of principles mentioned in Article F(1)'. When such a conclusion had been adopted in the decision, the Council, acting by a qualified majority, might decide to suspend certain of the rights deriving from the application of this Treaty to the Member State in question, including the voting rights of the representative of the government of that Member State in the Council. The Amsterdam RLF procedure is depicted in Fig. 2.

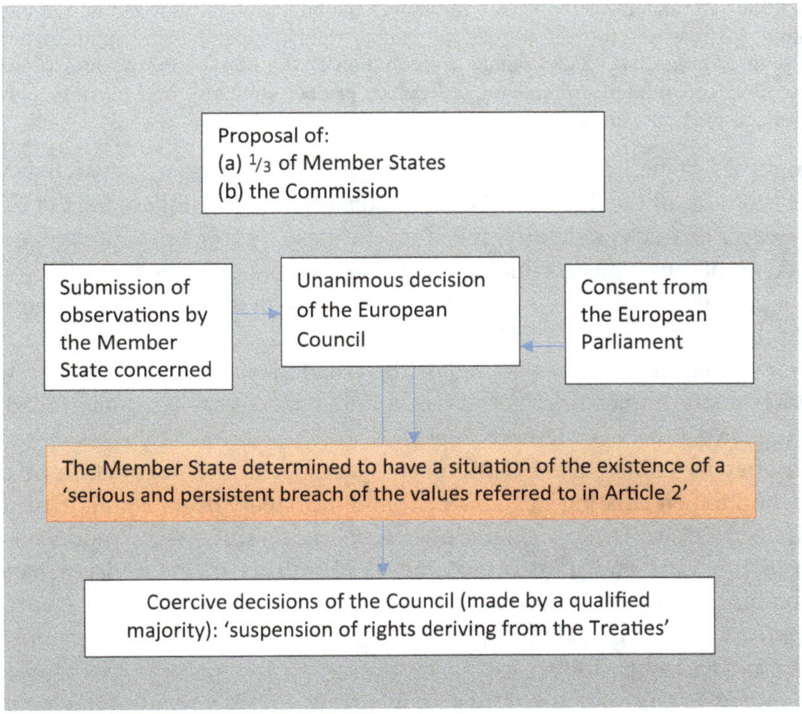

Fig. 2 Single stage RLF procedure of Article 7 TEU (Article F.1. of the Treaty of Amsterdam). Source: Artur Nowak-Far

Article F.1. TEU contained the same modalities as the present Article 7(2). Namely, the Council decision on the suspension of rights of the Member State put under the RLF scrutiny had to take into account 'the possible consequences of such a suspension on the rights and obligations of natural and legal persons'. It could also, acting by a qualified majority, decide to vary or revoke measures originally adopted with respect to that Member States—reflecting on changes in the underlying situation.

The RLF procedure specified in the Amsterdam Treaty was quickly considered too rigid and inflexible as it did not allow for any preliminary stage where the Member State concerned could be involved in a dialogue on its practices. Thus, Article 7 TUE was amended in the subsequent revision of the TEU, now in the Treaty of Nice (2000).

The rule of law became an important element of the agenda within the negotiation of the EU Constitutional Treaty, which, in Article I-2 enshrined it together with other values deemed inextricably interwoven with it: democracy and the human rights. Moreover, it contained a clause not only stating that the EU-specific values listed in it are 'common' to the EU Member States, but also formulating requirements concerning the axiological fabric of their societies—all in the format which was later adopted in the Treaty of Lisbon as well. Thus, the wording of Article I-2 of the Constitutional Treaty was as follows:

> The Union is founded on the values of respect for human dignity, freedom, democracy, equality, the rule of law and respect for human rights, including the rights of persons belonging to minorities. These values are common to the Member States in a society in which pluralism, non-discrimination, tolerance, justice, solidarity and equality between women and men prevail.

With regard to the RLF procedure, the Constitutional Treaty, in Article I-59, took over the wording of the Treaty of Nice. Interestingly and uniquely for the Constitutional Treaty, this act made also reference to these values in its preamble. It also contained numerous clauses which provided significant guidelines for interpretation of the values enshrined in its Article I-2. Interestingly, it also extended the requirements of the rule of law onto EU institutions, as well.

The Constitutional Treaty, adopted in 2004, had been intended to replace the then present EU treaty framework. Yet, it was a failed endeavor—as it had failed to win ratifications in all the EU Member States.

Soon after its failure, the EU Member States began the negotiation of a major revision of the then existing treaties (TEU and the Treaty establishing the European Community, TEC). These negotiations were successful. They produced a new version of the TEU and transformed the TEC into its major revision named the Treaty on functioning of the European Union. The new treaties (technically speaking resulting from the accord called the Treaty of Lisbon), were duly ratified and entered into force in December 2009.

This, however, has not solved the problems of an effective enforcement of the rule of law in the EU. A possibility for the EU venue to achieve a high enough standard in this area would be to accede to the European Convention of Human Rights and Fundamental Freedoms (ECHR). Yet, the EU failed to do it. The EU failure to make an accession to the European Convention of Human Rights and Fundamental Freedoms (ECHR) occurred despite the fact that the Convention is referred to in Article 6 TEU which

(a) in its paragraph 2 provides that the Union shall accede to the ECHR, yet that 'such accession shall not affect the Union's competences as defined in the Treaties',
(b) in its paragraph 3, provides that fundamental rights, as guaranteed by the Convention shall (together with the fundamental rights resulting from constitutional traditions common to the Member States) constitute general principles of the EU law.

The former provision was intended to defy the Court of Justice's negative opinion issued in 1994 (i.e. the opinion 2/94[26]) which upheld that with no express legal Treaty basis, the Community was not entitled to accede to the ECHR. This 'defying' effect seemed to be even reinforced by a modification of the ECHR itself, by the introduction of the Protocol No. 14, which in Article 17 provided for a change in Article 59(2) ECHR with the effect that it now expressly foresaw the EU accession to

[26]CJEU, Opinion 2/94, ECLI:EU:C:1996:140.

the Convention. The process of accession seemed to be reinforced by the fact that, by virtue of the Lisbon Treaty, the EU Chapter of Fundamental Rights (CFR) had been included into the EU legal system as a binding instrument.[27] As such, it required that the rights enshrined in it be identical with the rights arising from the ECHR (Article 52(3) CFR), yet with an important reservation that these rights be not interpreted in departure from the established EU law, international public law (at large) and international conventions to which the Union or all its Member States were counterparties (Article 53 CFR).

The specific conditions on which the EU was to accede to the ECHR were set forth in the Protocol No. 8 attached to the Treaty of Lisbon. This Protocol set forth the following principles applicable to the accession:

(a) the principle of inter-semiotic retention (set forth in Article 1), i.e. the requirement that the accession should make it possible to retain specific features of the EU and the EU legal system (especially with regard to the participation of the EU in controlling mechanisms of the ECHR);
(b) the principle of non-modification of external and internal powers of the EU (Article 2, first sentence),
(c) the principle of non-modification of the status of the EU Member States in the ECHF legal order (Article 3, second sentence);
(d) the principle of exclusive competence of the EU Court of Justice with regard to disputes concerning the interpretation and application of EU Treaties (Article 3 of the Protocol in connection with Article 344 TFEU).

In its opinion 2/13,[28] the EU Court of Justice upheld that the already negotiated agreement on the EU accession to the ECHR should not be signed. One of the most significant arguments which prompted the Court to conclude negatively was that the accession to the ECHR would result in a deformation of the principle of mutual trust inherent in the EU legal system. This principle implies that the Member States should not double-check, in any legal action context, whether other Member States observe fundamental rights guaranteed by the Union.[29] Nevertheless, such rights should be interpreted 'within the framework of the structures and objectives of the Union'[30] which are determined by EU substantive law. In the case of doubt, national courts can refer to the Court of Justice within the preliminary questions procedure

[27]The Chapter of Fundamental Rights had been considered to have just a 'declaratory' value before.

[28]CJEU, Opinion 2/13 of 18 December 2014, *Accession of the European Union to the European Convention for the Protection of Human Rights and Fundamental Freedoms*, ECLI:EU:C:2014:2454.

[29]Id, para. 191 of the Opinion 2/13, *supra* note 2. See also the CJEU's judgment of 25 June 2018 in the case C-216/18 PPU *LM*, ECLI:EU:C:2018:586 in which the Court upheld that such a double-checking should guarantee rights conferred to EU citizens under Article 47 CFR; the CJ emphasized that the check should be based on specific and detailed analysis of the underlying situation and should take into account the specific situation of an individual concerned as well as the information provided for by the Member State whose legal system is to be trusted.

[30]Id, para. 170.

under Article 267 TFEU. This important legal arrangement cannot be reconciled with the mechanisms of application of ECHR, as—among others—any interpretation offered by the EU Court of Justice could not be binding to the separate Court of Justice operating under the Convention. Instead, judiciary decisions of that latter court would be binding onto the EU Court of Justice which could undermine the principles set forth in Protocol No. 8.

Interestingly, this does not mean that the EU Treaties and the ECHR represent two legal systems immune from each other. In practice, they are in a constant intersemiotic dialogue (i.e. the dialogue in which two separate, yet interlegible 'institutional languages' are employed) as the judgments under the ECHR are often treated as a type of preliminary rulings by the EU Court of Justice.[31] In turn, the ECHR Court sometimes invokes the EU preliminary questions procedure under Article 267 TFEU considering denial of its application a breach of the ECHR (i.e. its Article 6(2) which prohibits denial of justice).[32] However, regardless of this dialogue, the linkage between the ECHR and the EU legal order proved to be insufficient to provide for a stronger enforcement mechanism of the EU values, especially those enshrined in the Charter of Fundamental Rights and in Article 2 TEU.

3.2 Legal Interpretation of the RLF sensu stricto

The legal meaning of the procedure set forth in Article 7 TEU does not yield any specific concerns as to its legal binding force. In contrast, the RLF *sensu stricto* does give rise to some concerns about its legal force which would likely be raised by the Member States subject to any form of the European Commission's scrutiny in the context of Article 7.

Admittedly, the RLF *sensu stricto* was set forth in the European Commission communication (i.e. the RLF communication). The communication is not included in the list of binding legal acts specified in the Treaties; most importantly, it is not covered by Article 288 TFUE, which provides that regulations, directives and decisions have binding force in the EU legal system. Thus, the RLF communication can be considered an act of soft law.

The European Commission was empowered to make the RLF communication as it was meant to 'precede and complement Article 7 TEU mechanisms' and provide transparency in the Commission's own actions—as such a specification can be

---

[31]See e.g. the judgment in the case C-404/15 and C/659/15 *Criminal Proceeding against Pál Aranyosi and Robert Căldăraru,* ECLI:EU:C:2016:198 (where the Court upheld that the European Arrest Warrant can be denied effect with respect to the Member State being persistently in contravention of the ECtHR—what has already been confirmed in the ECtHR judgments in *Vociu v. Rumania,* Application No. 22015/10, *Bujorean v. Rumania,* Application No. 13054/12, *Varga et al. v. Hungary,* Applications No. 14097/12, 45135/12, 73712/12, 34001/13, 44055/13, 64586/13.

[32]ECtHR *Dhahbi v. Italy,* Application No. 17120/09.

considered a specification of the Commission's general powers arising from this Treaty provision. The rules set forth in the RLF communication can be interpreted as a measure to eliminate uncertainty of law resulting from the incompleteness of rules specified in Article 7 with regard to the triggering of the mechanism of RLF (*sensu largo*). Thus, the procedure foreseen in it is meant to produce legal (and at the end of the day, binding) effect, yet the RLF rules (*sensu stricto*) are deprived of a binding force. In the terminology developed by Susan Senden, the RLF communication can be classified as a decisional communication (as contrasted to informational or interpretative ones), i.e. a communication which provides for general rules regarding the way in which the already existing implementing powers will be exercised, in particular, indicating, how the Commission will apply binding law provisions in respective cases and how it will make use of the applicable discretion at its disposal.[33] Decisional communications are not binding but are apt to produce legal effects by virtue of some other rules to which they pertain and to which they pragmatically relate. In the specific RLF (*sensu stricto*) context, the RLF communication derives its legal effectiveness from the fact that it is meant to make sure that the application of Article 7 should commence on a well-reasoned and adequately substantiated basis. As such, the RLF *sensu stricto* could make the application of Article 7 much more informed than without it. Moreover, as it performs an obvious signaling element, the RLF *sensu stricto* guarantees that the Member States concerned would not be surprised with the decision to become subject to measures under Article 7. More than that—they will have a chance to get involved in a dialogue with the Commission where they would be able to submit their own argumentation concerning the rule of law situation.

It is a matter of serious doubt whether the Member States subjected to the RLF *sensu stricto* would be able to challenge the recommendations addressed to them within this procedure before the EU Court of Justice (under Article 263 TFEU, i.e. within the action of annulment of an EU legislative act). The doubt arises from at least two issues:

(a) the formal one, which is based on an argument that Article 263 TFEU overtly excludes annulment actions brought against Commission's recommendations,
(b) the material one, which is based on an argument that, even if Article 263 TFUE were applicable (as—because of the clear intention to produce legal effect—the 'recommendations' under the RLF could be re-interpreted as acts falling within the remit of actions for annulment[34]), at the end of the day, they could not be challenged as they do not represent a final measure, but are rather steps in a procedure to be completed and to involve challengeable legal acts.[35]

[33]Senden (2004), pp. 148–149.

[34]See e.g. the EU Court of Justice judgment in the case C-362/08 *P Internationaler Hilfsfonds eV v. Commission*, ECLI:EU:C:2010:40, para. 52; 22/70 *Commission v. Council*, ECLI:EU:C:1971:32, para. 42.

[35]The argument *per analogiam* based on the EU Court of Justice (the Court of First Instance) judgment in the case T-126/95 *Dumez v. Commission*, ECLI:EU:T:1995:189.

Not being able to challenge the RLF recommendations, the Member States concerned, if only determined enough, would likely disregard them (as it was recently the case with Poland). Since (genuine) recommendations are not binding legal acts, the Commission will not be able to bring an action against the Member States concerned (under Article 258 TFEU) for not fulfilling them. Yet, this non-fulfillment will be a significant evidence in any further proceedings under Article 7.

This conclusion is in the same time an argument supporting the Commission's competence to issue the RLF recommendations. In the context of the entire RLF, they represent an important element of the dialogue between the Commission and the Member State concerned. The fact that the Member State ignored them (if this is the case) becomes an element of the argumentation sued for triggering the Article 7 procedure against this state.

4 The Content of the Rule of Law Under the RLF

To complete the analysis presented in this article, it is quite essential to identify what exactly is meant under the term 'rule of law' in the context of the RLF, regardless of its narrow or broader form. As the term does not have any Treaty definition, it is quite in place to rely on the legal doctrine and the EU Court of Justice's jurisprudence to answer this question.

4.1 The Legal Doctrine

More is known about what the rule of law is not than what it exactly is—especially in national contexts. Yet, basic conditions for the rule of law can be identified in the existing body of literature.[36] It is most often held that the rule of law is achieved whenever the following requirements are met:

(a) law generality—law should be general; particular regulation should be avoided;
(b) law publicity—law should be made public, known to those whom it concerns;
(c) law non-retroactivity—law should not act retroactively;
(d) law cataphaticity—law should be understandable to its primary stakeholders;
(e) law relative stability—law should be kept stable, whenever there are not good reasons to amend it;
(f) systemic consistency—legal norms of the system should be consistent with each other;
(g) law observability—it should be possible for law stakeholders to observe it;

[36]See e.g. May (2014), pp. 33–56; Sanchez-Cuenca (2003), pp. 62–93.

(h) behavioral congruence between legal norms and stakeholders' actions—all stakeholders should effectively observe the law.

Adriaan Bedner divided the features/requirements of the rule of law into three classes:

(a) procedural:

- the presence of the rule by law, i.e. the situation where the state actions are subject to law;
- the law formalization, which requires that it is understandable, stable and predictable);
- the creation of law in democratic procedures, i.e. under conditions requiring that the legislative consent should determine or at least influence legal actions)

(b) substantive:

- the law subordination to justice;
- the protection of individual rights and liberties;
- the respect to human rights and group rights

(c) controlling:

- the independence of judiciary;
- the responsibility of administrative and other independent bodies for reviewing legal process.[37]

Interestingly, most of these requirements are primarily addressed to law-makers. Some of them require a good *ex ante* foresight into the expected perceptions/ reactions of those who would be most likely and/or most strongly concerned with a given piece of law. It is striking that all of these requirements are formulated in procedural terms or, if they concern the content, they are highly abstract. As a result, the question about the 'content' law under the rule of law is quite justified.

One possible answer to this question is that the rule of law is about providing for conditions in which 'right' relationships between the government and citizens as well as between each and every citizen is set. 'Right' means, that the resulting setting is capable to protect and enforce individual rights and to give framework for a large degree of responsibility and accountability in the government. Some answers aspire even higher, as they would consider the 'real' rule of law to guarantee a perfect impartiality of the law-making system.

[37]Bedner (2010), pp. 56–69.

4.2 The EU Court of Justice Jurisprudence

The rule of law was highlighted in the European Union relatively often in various forms. Most importantly in 1986, in its enshrined judgment in the case 294/83 *Parti écologiste 'Les Verts' v. European Parliament*,[38] the Court of Justice held that the Community was a 'community of law'—and reminded that it required the consistency of all law (including national law) with the Treaty serving as a 'basic constitutional charter' (i.e. the systemic anchor of the entire, so defined, legal system). In 1993, the European Council formulated the so called 'Copenhagen Criteria' applicable to all states aspiring for EU membership, in which conformity with the 'rule of law' was enshrined. In 1997, the Treaty of Amsterdam made referrals to rule of law in Article 6 and the new suspension mechanism of Article 7 (so called *Lex Austria*). On some occasions, the Court of Justice upheld the idea that the EU was also subject to the rule of law. In its judgment in the case C-50/00 *P Unión de Pequeños Agricultores v. Council*,[39] the CJ stated that rule of law required consistency of EU secondary law with fundamental rights (see also similarly in joint cases C-402/05 P and C-415/05 *P Yassin Abdullah Kadi and Al Barakaat International Foundation v. Council and Commission*[40]). As it has already been argued, the most recent CJ's jurisprudence has contributed significantly to this rather rudimentary understanding of the concept of rule of law—most importantly in the realm of judiciary. The most recent development of CJ jurisprudence established a link between Article 2 TEU and Article 19(1) TEU as well as the due process standard set forth in Article 47 CFR (concerning the right to an effective remedy and to a fair trial). The CJ construed the EU legal system as the one which is complete and fully capable to enforce all rights conveyed by the EU law onto EU citizens or undertakings, provided that the Member States effectively ensure judicial protection of these rights.[41] In such a complete system, the respective judicial systems, at both national and supranational levels, sport mutual trust to each other.[42] Yet, this trust is subject to the results of a careful double-checking procedure which can be triggered by national courts whenever there are substantiated grounds that the values enshrined in Article 2 TEU are not fully observed or implemented in another Member State.[43] The issue can be expected to be developed further as many cases concerning the rule of law issue are still pending. So far, they have been extensively discussed in a series

[38]ECLI:EU:C:1986:166.

[39]ECLI:EU:C:2002:462.

[40]Judgment of 3 September; ECLI:EU:C:2008:461.

[41]Judgment of 6 March 2018 in the case C-284/16 *Slovak Republic v. Achmea BV*, ECLI:2018:158; see especially para 36.

[42]E.g. Opinion 2/13 of 18 December 2014, *supra* note 2; judgment of 27 February 2018 in case C-64/16 *Associaçao Sindical dos Juízes Portugueses (ASJP)*, ECLI:EU:C:2018:117, para. 39.

[43]Judgment of 5 April 2016 in the case C-404/15 and C-659/15 PP *Aranyosi and Câldâraru*, ECLI:EU:C:2016:198, para 104; judgment of 25 June 2018 in the case C-216/18 PPU *LM*, *supra* note 29, para 23.

of illustrious opinions presented by Advocate General Evgeni Tanchev,[44] who adopted a broader, systemic approach in reviewing judiciary system quality in a Member State.

All these actions have contributed to the understanding of the EU concept of the rule of law. Yet, they definitely are not sufficient to make it possible to construe an independent, EU-specific definition of it. The wording of Article 2:

> The Union is founded on the values of respect for human dignity, freedom, democracy, equality, the *rule of law* and respect for human rights, including the rights of persons belonging to minorities... (emphasis added)

suggests that the rule of law is one of the values on which the EU is founded and that it is somehow different from other values enshrined in this particular provision of the Treaty. We also know (from other provisions of the Treaty as well as from the CJ jurisprudence) that the principle of procedural autonomy applies to the EU Member States. In the procedural realm, its rectifications in CJ's judgments in e.g. cases 21-24/72 *International Fruit Company NV et al. v. Produktschap voor Groenten en Fruit*,[45] C-188/89 *A. Foster et al. v. British Gas plc*,[46] 103/88 *Fratelli Costanzo v. Comune di Milano*[47] indicate that its major aspect is the Member States' free hand in shaping their basic constitutional (institutional) order. This means that also the rule of law (as it has been construed under Article 2 TEU) can be applied in divergent procedural settings of now numerous EU Member States. As a result, uniformity of application of 'the rule of law' (and almost all other standards of EU law) in the European Union is far from an ideal pattern attempted by the EU Court of Justice. In consequence, 'uniform EU law' is—by definition—divergent in real settings, where real interests of EU citizens are at stake. In other words, there is a great deal of intersemiotic discourse of EU Member States' judicial and administrative systems over EU law purported to be 'uniform'. Nevertheless, the already discussed recent developments in CJ's jurisprudence clearly indicated that the substantive concept of rule of law heavily relies on the judiciary independence of the executive.

---

[44] Opinions in cases C-619/18 *Independence of the Polish Supreme Court* of 11 April 2018, ECLI: EU:C:2019:325; C-192/18 (retirement age of judges) of 20 June 2019, ECLI:EU:C:2019:529; C-585/18, C-524/28, C-625/18 *Polish National Judiciary Council, Disciplinary Chamber of the Supreme Court* of 27 June 2019, ECLI:EU:C:2019:551.

[45] Judgment of 12 December 1972; ECLI:EU:C:1972:115.

[46] Judgment of 12 June 1990: ECLI:EU:C:1990:313.

[47] Judgment of 22 June 1989; ECLI:EU:C:1989:256.

5 The International Dimension of the EU Rule of Law Framework

5.1 The Rule of Law Importance for the EU Common Foreign and Security Policy

The fact that the initiative for increased enforcement of the rule of law within the Treaty of Lisbon system was promoted by the foreign affairs services of a group of the EU countries is quite telling about the significance of that idea for the EU external policy. It is enough to say that the TEU (in Article 21(1)) requires the EU foreign service (operating within the framework of the EU Common Foreign and Security Policy, CFSP[48]) to consider the rule of law to be one of its guiding principles (together with democracy, the universality and indivisibility of human rights and fundamental freedoms, respect for human dignity, the principles of equality and solidarity and respect for the Principles of the UN Charter and international law). Pursuant to Article 21(2) TEU, the Union shall define and pursue international common policies and actions which, *inter alia*, consolidate and support democracy, the rule of law, human rights and the principles of international law. As a result, the rule of law has become an idea well pronounced at various levels and in various fora where the EU is represented.

As a matter of fact, in the international sphere, the EU promotes its own model of human rights and—within it—the rule of law. Generally speaking, this model emphasizes the importance of the individual's dignity and individual rights—the ideas deeply rooted in the European Enlightenment. The rule of law can be considered a comprehensive instrument of safeguarding these rights and enforcing them in a uniform manner. Thus, the RLF mechanisms are vital for assuring that—despite the existing procedural divergences in respective EU Member States' legal systems—the EU preserves the integrity of the EU human rights model, and that the EU as an actor of international relations, maintains its high credibility in promoting this model. In other words, the RLF is meant to curb the existing divergence and achieve some uniform standards in the system of enforcement of human rights in order to attract global adherence.

The problem of a proper (i.e. complete and functional) intersemiotic translation of international human rights standards into domestic ones (i.e. the transposition of one legal-pragmatic model of making them reality into another) is pronounced even in systems of common legal tradition and philosophy. With regard to the relationship between legal systems of the Western legal and political tradition, Ernest A. Young noticed, that even when we looked to such systems which, with no doubt, shared common heritage and reflected the same or significantly similar axiological fundaments, we saw 'divergence rather than convergence on many aspects of values and

---

[48]I.e. the subject matter of the provisions of Title V TEU.

political culture'.[49] This not very encouraging conclusion is even more applicable to the relationship between the Western legal and political traditions and its more distant counterparts. The underlying prevalent local social circumstances, moral attitudes and customs may determine a significant gap between the Western concept of human rights and their popular/political acceptance beyond the Western world. This gap may also serve as a political excuse for a national policy of not pursuing any ambitious programme of human rights promotion. Moreover, the recent tensions within the EU which urged the Commission to make recourse to the RLF with respect to Poland were fundamentally caused by the fact that the present Polish government emphasized its different stance to human rights—as it does not seem to share the respect too common to most EU states legal tradition and philosophy stemming strongly from the ideas of the European Enlightenment. Instead, it prefers to derive its legitimacy from rather obscure and unclear ideas of social collectivism and Catholic nationalism.

In order to be effective, international human rights (that is the rights adopted in a context of an international agreement for the purpose of their more or less universal application), must be suitable for their at least relatively equivalent intersemiotic translation—that is their transformation into legal norms expressed in an international statute into legal norms of a given national system.[50] As a result, international standards will only be 'common' either if the transformation system is apt to act effectively and efficiently and/or if translated common standards represent a low enough denominator (which could be detrimental to the international level of human rights protection). Irrespective of the systemic capacity of intersemiotic translation or structural complexity of norms being translated, a firm and welcoming constitutional approach is required to make human rights enshrined in an international law instrument subject to such a translation. The resulting divergence eliminates 'an axiological common ground' to which respective EU Member States could refer in their EU wide and global discourse on human rights. As a result, this discourse could be deprived of important common reference framework which could have brought these counterparties closer to each other and make legal measures reconciliation more likely to achieve.

It is obvious that this problem is not only bilateral. In the globalized world, bilateral reciprocity shortages become aggregated so that they are increasingly likely to cause acute frictions between legal systems which tend to be more often exposed in the area of consular protection and asylum granting. As a result, they may become a source of a wide dispute over the general roles of the state needed to make the international order an effective and efficient system in which various communities and individuals can achieve levels of welfare not achievable under non-cooperative conditions. In respective areas relevant for the formulation and implementation of national and/or regional public policies, such a lack of reciprocity and the resulting inter-systemic friction would reduce effectiveness of these policies, thus reducing an

[49]Young (2005), pp. 161–166 (referring to the *Thompson* judgment, 487, US 830).

[50]See, e.g. Tiefenbrun (2010), pp. 263–280.

aggregate level of total global welfare which—under more concurrence and cooperation—might have reached higher levels.

5.2 International Law Interpretation of the RLF

In legal terms, the modern European human rights concept (including its procedural frameworks such as RLF) represents a departure from a 'traditional bottom line' standard defining inter-relational aspects of international law set forth in the 1927 PCIJ *Lotus* judgment[51] holding that international law (and thus, the human rights-relevant international law) is essentially about relations among states. Today, international law, and especially human rights and the rule of law component of it is a law about global governance which is a concept extending well beyond the relationships amongst states. Global governance can be defined as 'the sum of many ways individuals and institutions, public and private, manage their common affairs'.[52] The practice follows this approach putting in the radar of both international law and human rights (being its significant element) not only states but also non-state actors (especially individuals and their more or less formalized groupings). It does so through the application of international law norms conceived not only as a result of state consent but also of general pressure resulting from a broad consent of all legitimate international law and human rights stakeholders to pursue basic common values of humankind. In modern times such a pressure has become a driving force for shaping international normative agenda.[53]

Having said that, it is important to emphasize that states still play the most important role as international law operators and human rights guarantors (through their own substantive and procedural guarantees producing the rule of law). Thus, at the end of the day, their consent to any conceived norms in these realms still plays the dominant role in legitimating a broad enough and effective (judiciable) recourse to those values in an international scale (in state-setting). To some extent, this pronounced role of states represents an argument usually somehow less pronounced but worth mentioning that only effective assets of international relations really count in international law and human rights promotion.

The essential problem of today's international relations, international law and thus human rights defined in broad terms (i.e. also as a source of potential inspiration for a global governance practice) is at what level of aggregation of their respective standards should be conceived and, consequently, how universally, they can or should be applied and enforced. In such a context, the EU effort to maintain some uniformity in its human rights and the rule of law context can be interpreted as an

[51] [1927] PCIJ 10 Series A, 18.

[52] Commission on Global Governance (1995), *Our Global Neighbourhood: The Report of the Commission on Global Governance*.

[53] See discussion presented in: Thirlway (2014), pp. 8–16.

effort to achieve significant 'weight' able to attract other, non-EU states to follow the European pattern or at least to become an important reference point for the international discussion on the nature, scope of application and the mode of enforcement of human rights.

6 Conclusions

1. The Rule of Law Framework (*sensu largo*) is vulnerable to unguaranteed, discretionary influences of the Member States. This vulnerability arises from its procedural format which requires high thresholds in decision making—with unanimity applicable to the decision which could make it possible for the EU institutions to effectively address any situation in a EU Member States where the rule of law standards have been considered unsatisfactory. With such a mode of the applicable decision-making, RLF procedures are prone to be terminated as a result of collusions made by EU Member States likely to be scrutinized, if at least two of them wish to cooperate with each other in order to abort the RLF procedure brought against one of them.
2. Yet, any serious breaches of an EU Member State of human rights (in the context of ineffective rule of law standards) could single it out within the Union. As a result, in breaches of significant gravity, such a state would not be able to attract cooperation needed for the collusive termination of the RLF. Thus the Framework can have some positive impact on respective EU Member States' behaviour with regard to their respect to human rights.
3. This effect is even reinforced by an active stance of the European Commission which is bound to pursue the RLF effectiveness for the sake of achieving relative uniformity of application of EU law (at large), and making the European Union a credible actor and co-creator of international legal order. The Commission is determined to play an active role also because this allows it to make an important statement on its own institutional powers *vis-à-vis* other EU institutions and the EU Member States.
4. The RLF is an important tool for the maintenance of relative stability of human rights and the rule of law in the EU despite natural divergence propensity resulting from the procedural autonomy of the EU Member States. By achieving this stability, the EU achieves significant political weight in international dialogue concerning human right and the rule of law and preserves a high level of its global credibility in this context. Thus, RLF increases the EU's effectiveness in promoting the European model of their identification and enforcement.
5. It is rather difficult to judge about the universal acceptability of the European evolving concept of human rights. Admittedly, they may be considered attractive because of the universality of their underlying axiology and their comprehensiveness as a legal concept reflexing the Western idea of broadly understood individual and collective welfare. Such general elements can be considered sufficient to serve as a low enough denominator which is widely acceptable to

serve as an element of the 'international order' and to enforce other elements of it. Moreover, high standards of protection of a vast catalogue of human rights in the Western world have contributed to the effectiveness and efficacy of its political and economic systems. They have done so by reinforcing largely adequate mechanisms of public choice generally based on the determination of prevailing preferences *via* political elections, protection of minority groups, and on the well-functioning system of balance of powers. As soon as the prevailing preferences are unveiled, they have to be translated into respective public policies formulated and implemented at various stages of the organization of polity. This has an important bearing on the content of public policies: in their goals, objectives and instruments which—under such a system—take a proper account of human rights.

References

Andersen S (2012) Enforcement of European Union law: the role of the European Commission. Oxford University Press, Oxford

Arnull A (2006) The European Union and its Court of Justice. Oxford University Press, Oxford

Bagińska E, Majkowska-Szulc S (2018) Causation as a requirement for the Member State liability under Art. 7 TEU in conjunction with Art. 2 TEU. In: Hatje A, Tichý L (eds) Liability of Member States for the violation of the fundamental values of the EU. Nomos, Baden-Baden, pp 125–144

Bedner A (2010) An elementary approach to the rule of law. Hague J Rule Law 2(1):48–74

Bonelli M, Claes MN (2018) Judicial serendipity: how Portuguese judges came to rescue the Polish judiciary. Eur Const Law Rev 14(3):622–643

Commission on Global Governance (1995) Our global neighbourhood: the report of the commission on global governance. Oxford University Press, Oxford

European Council in Copenhagen. Conclusions of the Presidency, June 21–22, 1993, document SN 180/1/93 REV 1

European Parliament, Committee on Civil Liberties, Justice and Home Affairs, Report of 17 February 2014 on evaluation of justice in relations to criminal justice and the rule of law, rapporteur Kinga Göncz, document A7-0122/2014

Itzcovich G (2017) On the legal enforcement of values: the importance of the institutional concept. In: Jakab A, Kochenov D (eds) The enforcement of EU law and values: ensuring Member States' compliance. Oxford University Press, Oxford, pp 28–43

Kochenov D (2017) The *Acquis* and its principles: the enforcement of the 'law' vs. the enforcement of 'values' in the European Union. In: Jakab A, Kochenov D (eds) The enforcement of EU law and values: ensuring Member States' compliance. Oxford University Press, Oxford, pp 9–27

Krajewski M (2018) *Associaçao Sindicos dos Juízes Portugueses:* the Court of Justice and Athena's dilemma. Eur Pap 3(1):395–405

May C (2014) The rule of law: the common sense of global politics. Edward Elgar, Cheltenham

Ministry of Foreign Affairs of the Netherlands (2013) Human Rights Policy – Respect and Justice for All. The Hague

Pech L, Platon S (2018) Judicial independence under threat: the Court of Justice to the rescue in the ASJP case. CLMR 55(6):1827–1854

Press release 3244th Council Meeting – Justice and Home Affairs, Luxembourg 6–7 June 2013, document 10461/13 (OR.en)

Prete L (2017) Infringement proceedings in EU law. Kluwer Law Int 6–10:301–304

Sanchez-Cuenca I (2003) Power, rules, and compliance. In: Maravall JM, Przeworski A (eds) Democracy and the rule of law. Oxford University Press, Oxford

Schmidt M, Bogdanowicz P (2017) The infringement procedure in the rule of law crisis. In: Closa C, Kochenov D (eds) Reinforcing rule of law oversight in the European Union. OUP, Oxford, pp 1069–1073

Senden S (2004) Soft law in European Community law. Hart Publishing, Oxford

Thirlway H (2014) The sources of international law. Oxford University Press, Oxford

Tichý L (2018) The nature and requirements for liability of a Member State under Article 7. In: Hatje A, Tichý L (eds) Liability of Member States for the violation of the fundamental values of the EU. Nomos, Baden-Baden

Tiefenbrun S (2010) Decoding international law: semiotics and the humanities. Oxford University Press, Oxford

Tridimas T (2000) The general principles of EC law. Oxford University Press, Oxford

Young EA (2005) Foreign law and the denominator problem. Harv Law Rev 119(148):148–167

Artur Nowak-Far is senior researcher and director of the Institute of Law, SGH-Warsaw School of Economics.

8

Towards a Tyranny of Values: Principles on Defending Checks and Balances in EU Member States

Armin von Bogdandy

Contents

Abstract This contribution develops the framework of European reactions to the undermining of checks and balances in EU Member States. It surveys the normative setting with its various institutional options and contrasting constitutional principles and then applies these principles to the panoply of relevant instruments. The building blocks of this framework are *competence*, *procedure*, *standards,* and *control.* This should help Europe to speak with a principled voice. The contribution shows how

A slightly different and longer version has been published in the *Common Market Law Review* 57 (2020).

A. von Bogdandy (✉)
Max Planck Institute for Comparative Public Law and International Law, Heidelberg, Germany
e-mail: sekreavb@mpil.de

red lines can be drawn that respect constitutional pluralism, and how any action's legitimacy is enhanced if many institutions undertake it jointly.

1 What Is at Stake

In some EU Member States, governing majorities are modifying controlling institutions. These attempts go far beyond the traditional three branches and affect political parties, ombudspersons, the media, NGOs and academia. As such, they critically weaken the domestic checks and balances in a larger sense.[1] Most consider the value of the rule of law to be endangered, but the values of democracy and of respect for human dignity are no less at stake.[2] Indeed, political science sees such measures as symptomatic for illiberal democracies, i.e. for authoritarian tendencies.[3]

This book has been triggered by the remodelling of the Polish Judiciary since 2015.[4] However, the Polish developments are not isolated. Similar tendencies manifest in a series of EU Member States, especially in Hungary.[5] European constitutionalism is perhaps facing a 'constitutional moment':[6] the decision whether it *comprises* illiberal democracies or whether it *fights* them. The first case would herald the end of the European Union's current self-understanding, as 'illiberal democracies' would co-inform the common values of Article 2 TEU in the future. The alternative path requires the Union to counter threats to domestic checks and balances. To achieve this, European constitutionalism must draw and defend 'red lines', which would also imply a considerable constitutional development: European

[1]See Ackerman et al. (2011), p. 264.

[2]On the interrelatedness of these values, see already Habermas (1992), p. 109 et seq.; similarly, Möllers and Schneider (2018), p. 97 et seq. Similarly Commission Proposal for a Regulation of the European Parliament and of the Council on the protection of the Union's budget in case of generalised deficiencies as regards the rule of law in the Member States (COM(2018) 324 final), recital (3).

[3]Lauth and Sehring (2009), p. 165; Kailitz and Köllner (2012), p. 11; Merkel (2013), p. 223 et seq.

[4]For an enumeration of particularly problematic measures, see Proposal for a Council Decision on the determination of a clear risk of a serious breach by the Republic of Poland of the rule of law (COM(2017) 835 final), para. 6 et seq.; on the context, Bachmann (2018), p. 9 et seq.; Sadurski (2019).

[5]Halmai (2018a), p. 85; European Parliament resolution of 12 September 2018 on a proposal calling on the Council to determine, pursuant to Article 7(1) of the Treaty on European Union, the existence of a clear risk of a serious breach by Hungary of the values on which the Union is founded (2017/2131(INL)). On Romania, see Venice Commission, Romania—Opinion on draft amendments to Law No. 303/2004 on the Statute of Judges and Prosecutors, Law No. 304/2004 on Judicial Organisation, and Law No. 317/2004 on the Superior Council for Magistracy (Oct. 22, 2018), CDL-AD(2018)017; European Parliament resolution of 13 November 2018 on the rule of law in Romania (2018/2844(RSP)).

[6]The concept was coined by Ackerman (1991), p. 6, though with a different thrust.

constitutionalism would gain in profile and develop elements of a militant democracy.

This chapter explores the latter path, which leads into unchartered waters. The legality and the legitimacy of the European actions are disputed. Even the Council of the European Union considers one of the European Commission's instruments inadmissible.[7] Some voices, not least the European Parliament, regard European actions as too one-sided.[8] Others accuse the Union of double standards, as it allegedly fails the same values which it demands its Members to respect.[9] Some hold the European Commission as generally 'unsuited' as a guardian of liberal democracy.[10]

Some even detect in these unchartered waters what Carl Schmitt branded as the 'tyranny of values': a defence of values that destroys the very values it aims to protect.[11] In April 2017, the Polish ambassador in Berlin announced that Poland respects all European values and that there merely was 'a problem of interpretation. Brussels is far too strongly informed by liberal left-wing ideology.'[12] In similar terms, Viktor Orbán explained his rejection of Frans Timmermans' nomination as President of the Commission by calling him 'an ideological warrior who accepts no diversity, who tolerates no views which diverge from his own and from liberal democracy, and who wants to force his own conception on all EU Member States'.[13] Such positioning is symptomatic. As Uwe Volkmann observes, in today's European society there are 'different worlds of values which only rotate around themselves and hardly ever intersect'.[14] The predominance of one of these worlds is then quickly considered tyranny by the other.

In the first step, I will explore the constitutional horizon of the question of whether one should intervene in a case such as the Polish one (2). Factors militating against such action are national democracy, the risk of failure, but also the possibility of an unwanted European state (Sect. 2.1), while considerations of the current constitutional self-understanding, Union citizenship and mutual trust speak in favour of such action (Sect. 2.2). The second step develops a legal frame for pertinent instruments of European law, Member States' law and international law (Sect. 3.1),

[7]Council Legal Service, Commission's Communication on a new EU Framework to strengthen the rule of law: – compatibility with the Treaties (10296/14).

[8]Mendelski (2016), p. 390; Franzius (2018), p. 382 and 386; Resolution on the need for a comprehensive EU mechanism for the protection of democracy, the rule of law and fundamental rights (2018/2886(RSP)), recital (K).

[9]Weiler (2016), p. 326.

[10]Schorkopf (2016), p. 159; Janse (2019), p. 43.

[11]Schmitt (2011), p. 48 et seq. The expression 'tyranny of values' was first used by Hartmann (1926), p. 524 et seq.

[12]Quoted after Voßkuhle (2018), p. 17.

[13]Press Release, 'They want to make Soros's man the President of the Commission' (2 July 2019), www.kormany.hu/en/the-prime-minister/news/they-want-to-make-soros-s-man-the-president-of-the-commission.

[14]Volkmann (2018), p. 14.

consisting of the building blocks *legal basis* (Sect. 3.2), *procedure* (Sect. 3.3), *standards* (Sect. 3.4), and *control* (Sect. 3.5).

2 The Principles in Abstract

2.1 Options

The European legal space requires that all institutions exercising public authority within its scope respect its fundamental values. Its legal orders have mutually committed themselves to a constitutional core.[15] This is expressed most clearly in Articles 2, 7, and 49 TEU, but national constitutional law sets out similar requirements.[16] These requirements are complemented by international law, especially Article 3 Statute of the Council of Europe as well as the ECHR.[17] These requirements may not be identical, given European constitutional pluralism, but they certainly rest on largely overlapping core values.[18]

At the same time, it is not clear whether and how public institutions are to defend these fundamental values. Article 7 TEU, which stipulates specific mechanisms, provides much discretion: The Union 'may', but is not bound to defend the European values against its Member States.[19] All the other instruments, too, leave ample scope.[20] There is legal room for considering various options.

From the perspective of Union law, a first option is to avoid any conflict, to do nothing, and—with liberal optimism—to trust into the self-healing powers of liberal constitutionalism. A second option would be to primarily address authoritarian tendencies in the Council of Europe, thus acknowledging the Council's special role regarding questions of Member State constitutional law.[21] This would relieve cooperation within the Union from this conflict. A third option for the Union is to adhere to the established scope of Union law und thus avoid the highly conflictual discussion about values. The Commission acted against Hungary in this sense: it brought the disempowerment of the judiciary to the CJEU as an inadmissible

[15]For an overview see von Bogdandy (2014), p. 980.

[16]BVerfGE 140, 317 – *Identitätskontrolle*; *The Minister for Justice and Equality v. Celmer*, [2018] IEHC 119 (2018).

[17]In detail Uerpmann-Wittzack (2009), p. 131.

[18]Opinion of AG Cruz Villalón in CJEU, Case C-62/14 *Gauweiler and Others*, ECLI:EU:C:2015:7, para. 61.

[19]Communication from the Commission to the Council and the European Parliament on Article 7 of the Treaty on European Union. Respect for and promotion of the values on which the EU is based (COM(2003) 606 final) p. 6; Ruffert (2016), para. 8.

[20]However, there may also be constellations in which there is a duty to take action, Huber (2017), p. 389.

[21]Tuori (2016), p. 237. On the procedure under Art. 20 (c) Statute of the European Council, see Wittinger (2005), p. 130 et seq.

discrimination of elderly judges under the Anti-Discrimination Directive 2000/78.[22] As a fourth option, the Union could leave the issue to its Member States. The Member States in turn could act collectively, as in case of the sanctions against Austria,[23] or individually, e.g., by denying the Member State in question judicial cooperation or by utilising Article 259 TFEU.[24]

Exercising such discretion must be based on valid grounds. The structuring of such grounds is a task of legal doctrine. While such a doctrine cannot recommend any specific outcome, it can rationalise matters. As is the case with most difficult decisions, there are valid reasons both for and against defending the Union's values.

2.2 *Grounds Against Defending the Union's Values*

Powerful arguments suggest caution. One of these, much deployed by the Polish government, refers to the pair of democracy and national identity. Article 2 TEU states democracy as a fundamental value; Article 4 (2) TEU protects the Member States' 'national identities, inherent in their fundamental structures, political and constitutional'. If a democratically elected governing majority modifies these fundamental political and constitutional structures—this most 'sacred' area of national sovereignty—there is strong reason to assume that neither the Union nor other Member States should intervene. From a comparative view, the situation in Poland or in Hungary is far less critical than the one in Russia or Turkey.[25] Furthermore, understanding the Union's values in an exacting manner would create the need to intervene in many Member States. This can hardly be the intention of the TEU.

Another valid argument is the consideration not to damage the Union. Articles 1 and 3 TEU task the Union to develop policies for the good of its citizens. Any attempt to force an elected government under a common constitution can easily result in explosive conflicts. They may even endanger the constitution itself.[26] One need only think of the escalation caused by the actions of the Spanish central state against the governing majority of Catalonia.[27] And European actions against the current governing majority in Poland lack important resources which supported the Spanish central state against the Catalonian government: a clear democratic mandate, a developed national consciousness, and the hard instrument of federal execution. Polish representatives have already declared that they consider European

[22]CJEU, Case C-286/12 *Commission v. Hungary*, ECLI:EU:C:2012:687, para. 24 et seq.; critically Halmai (2017), p. 471.

[23]On this Ahtisaari et al. (2000), para. 116; Schorkopf (2002), Lachmayer (2017).

[24]BVerfGE 140, 317 – *Identitätskontrolle*; Hirsch Ballin (2016), p. 133; Kochenov (2015), p. 153.

[25]Weiler (2016), p. 314.

[26]Dyzenhaus (2012); comparative Federalism is instructive in this respect, Möllers and Schneider (2018), p. 5 et seq.

[27]García Morales (2018), p. 791 et seq.

actions against their remodelling of the judiciary as illegitimate.[28] It appears possible that a European defence of values may fail, which might inflict lasting damage on the Union's authority and demonstrate the frailty of the foundations of the common European house. The Union is not built for such conflict: since its 'constitutional moment' of overcoming the French 'empty seat', the search for consensus is key to its operation.[29]

But success, too, might plunge the Union into serious trouble. If the Union prevails over the combative Polish government, this would imply an enormous proof of power. The Union would significantly gain in stature vis-à-vis its Member States should it succeed in transforming its instruments, so far widely considered as rather ineffective, into a kind of effective federal execution.[30] This could be regarded as a huge step towards the EU's becoming a federal state, since what the Union primarily lacks in this regard is precisely such power. Such a prospect of *Staatswerdung* could cause a backlash from many Member States, which might equally endanger the Union. For all these reasons, the Union's hesitations should not be misconceived as mere opportunism.[31]

2.3 *Grounds in Favour of Defending the Union's Values*

At the same time, there are substantial legal grounds for the Union to defend European values. Three of them appear particularly pertinent: the European self-understanding as a community of values, Union citizenship and the principle of mutual trust.[32]

A first reason for the Union to defend its values results from its self-understanding, stipulated in the Treaties, as a liberal-democratic peace project. According to Article 2 TEU, the Union has been 'founded' on the respect for these values. This applies not only to the Union's supranational institutions, but also to its Member States. Article 2 TEU expresses standards for *any* public action in the European legal space.[33] Respecting and promoting these values is the key requirement for membership, as stipulated in Article 49 TEU. The term 'value' underlines the character of these principles as 'supreme and final normative

[28]See the statement by Polish Prime Minister Mateusz Morawiecki, quoted after Steinbeis (2018); the Vice President of the Polish Constitutional Court has announced that he would consider any judgment of the Court of Justice of the European Union against Poland as illegitimate, see Muszyński (2018).

[29]van Middelaar (2016), pp. 107 et seq., 120.

[30]The Polish compliance with the interim measures ordered by the CJEU in Case C-619/18, *Commission v. Poland*, with regard to the Supreme Court might be an indication.

[31]Cf., e.g., Kochenov and Pech (2016), p. 1062.

[32]On the legal grounds for intervention Closa et al. (2014), pp. 5–7; Hillion (2016), pp. 60–64.

[33]In detail von Bogdandy (2010), p. 13 et seq.

grounds'.[34] In Article 2 TEU, all Member States declare who they are and what they stand for; they articulate the deep logic of their institutional practice and the moral convictions of their citizens. In short: Article 2 TEU positivises the Union's self-understanding as a community of values.

In the light of substantiated evidence that Polish measures violate European values, a European silence would speak volumes. It would question this very community: the common axiological basis would appear either as an unfounded illusion or as a foundation that includes developments such as the Polish ones. In both cases, the self-understanding cultivated so far would hardly prove sustainable. The distance to Trump's USA would diminish. The Union would face a severe identity crisis.

Another legal ground results from the Union's mandate to protect all individuals in the European legal space, which includes protecting Polish citizens against their own government.[35] The CJEU says that 'Article 20 TFEU precludes national measures which have the effect of depriving citizens of the Union of the genuine enjoyment of the substance of the rights conferred by virtue of their status as citizens of the Union'.[36] This includes the 'essence' of EU fundamental rights, which is protected by Article 2 TEU. In *L.M. (Deficiencies in the system of justice)*, which deals precisely with the Polish measures, the CJEU emphasized this link between the essence of a Charter right (the right to a fair trial and an impartial court in Article 47 (2) CFR) and Article 2 TEU and allowed a Polish national to invoke this essence against the internal developments in his home state.[37] With this logic, presumably *any* violation of a value can somehow be tried in court.[38] This is a kind of 'reverse' *Solange* doctrine: outside the scope of application of the Charter of Fundamental Rights, Member States remain autonomous with respect to fundamental rights, *as long as* they guarantee the standard of Article 2 TEU.[39] If this standard is undercut, all public institutions in the European legal space must enforce the essence of the Union's fundamental rights against any measures of the Member State concerned.[40]

The Union's steps against Poland are important not only on a normative, but also on a cognitive level.[41] Such steps disprove the assumption that all Polish citizens stand with the governing majority. Indeed, many Polish citizens fight for liberal

---

[34]Luhmann (1993), p. 19; cf. also Habermas (1992), p. 311 et seq.

[35]Franzius (2018), p. 384.

[36]CJEU, Case C-34/09 *Ruiz Zambrano*, ECLI:EU:C:2011:124, para. 42.

[37]CJEU, Case C-216/18 PPU *Minister for Justice and Equality*, ECLI:EU:C:2018:586. The term 'deficiency' can be found in the case's denomination by the Advocate General as well as in the press release, CJEU, Press Release No. 113/18. In detail von Bogdandy and Spieker (2019).

[38]Spieker (2019), Schmidt and Bogdanowicz (2018), p. 1090.

[39]In detail von Bogdandy et al. (2012), p. 489; von Bogdandy et al. (2015), p. 235; von Bogdandy and Spieker (2019).

[40]Cf. the contributions in Steinbeis et al. (2015), Croon-Gestefeld (2017), p. 371; Blauberger (2016), p. 280; Russo (2014), Kochenov (2013), p. 145.

[41]Mälksoo (2009), p. 653.

democracy in their country.[42] In doing so, they refer to their status as citizens of the Union, as is shown by the European flag accompanying government-critical demonstrations. For Union citizenship, this might be a historic moment: it gains genuine political weight.

A third reason for the Union to defend its values is the principle of mutual trust. In the *L.M. (Deficiencies in the system of justice)* judgment, the Court made a clear point: measures like the Polish ones endanger the fundamental structure of the Union because they undermine mutual trust, without which vital areas of European cooperation cease to function.[43] The principle of mutual trust states: all Member States *must trust* that all Member States respect Union law and its fundamental rights in particular.[44] The status quo of integration can hardly be maintained without mutual trust.[45] But such trust requires defending the values on which it stands.[46]

3 The Principles Applied

3.1 The Toolbox

Many instruments might be used to defend European values. They are of diverse legal nature (political, administrative and judicial, binding and non-binding), they pertain to different legal orders and they are applied by different, sometimes even competing institutions, such as a constitutional court and the CJEU. That calls for a coordinating legal doctrine comprehending several legal orders.

Such a doctrine should not force the different instruments into a Procrustean bed. Instead, it should elaborate their diversity while indicating how to connect them as part of a functional tool box. Coordinated actions are more promising, whereas uncoordinated ones might be counterproductive. In more general terms: a clear and univocal reaction of the many European voices is essential for the protection of the Union's values.

Instruments of Union law are at the centre of attention.[47] This is justified insofar as action by the Union reduces the pressure on Member States to take steps on an individual level: the latter, e.g., a reprisal, can be even more explosive than pressure

---

[42]The current governing majority only received 37.58% of all votes cast, with a voter turnout of 50.92%.

[43]CJEU, *Minister for Justice and Equality*, *supra* note 37, para. 35. In detail, Regan (2018), p. 231.

[44]CJEU, Opinion 2/13 *Adhésion de l'Union à la CEDH*, ECLI:EU:C:2014:2454, para. 191; Lenaerts (2017), p. 805.

[45]CJEU, Case C-411/10 *N.S. and Others*, ECLI:EU:C:2011:865, para. 83; in detail von Bogdandy (2018), p. 487.

[46]CJEU, Case C-578/16 PPU *C.K. and Others*, ECLI:EU:C:2017:127, para. 95.

[47]For an overview see Closa et al. (2014) as well as the accounts given in Closa and Kochenov (2016) and Jakab and Kochenov (2017).

by the Union.[48] Among the instruments of the political institutions, measures taken under Article 7 TEU, the Commission's Rule of Law Framework and the rule of law dialogue of the Council are at the forefront.[49] The Commission's Justice Scoreboard 2018 has become a supervisory instrument, too,[50] as has the Commission's Country Report on Poland within the framework of the European Semester.[51] Regarding some Member States, the Union disposes of additional instruments. The Cooperation and Verification Mechanism in the Treaties of Accession with Bulgaria and Romania is meant to 'see the two countries develop the effective administrative and judicial systems needed'.[52] The Treaty of Accession with Croatia contains a similar instrument.[53] Further instruments are being planned: the Commission wants to make funding subject to respecting EU values[54] and to launch an 'EU Justice, Rights and Values Fund' with an overall budget allocation of 947 million EUR.[55]

In the framework of the European Parliament, there are the plenary debate, the law on sanctioning radical political parties,[56] as well as disciplining instruments within Europe's political alliances.[57]

---

[48]Müller (2015), p. 145.

[49]Conclusions of the Council of the EU and the Member States meeting within the Council on ensuring respect for the rule of law (16134/14).

[50]Cf. Communication from the Commission to the European Parliament, the Council, the European Central Bank, the European Economic and Social Committee and the Committee of the Regions. The 2018 EU Justice Scoreboard (COM(2018) 364 final), p. 4 et seq. On the Justice Scoreboard, Dori (2015), Jakab and Lorincz (2017).

[51]Country Report Poland 2018 accompanying the document Communication from the Commission to the European Parliament, the Council, the European Central Bank and the Eurogroup: 2018 European Semester: Assessment of progress on structural reforms, prevention and correction of macroeconomic imbalances, and results of in-depth reviews under Regulation (EU) No 1176/2011 (SWD(2018) 219 final), pp. 3, 29.

[52]Cf. the corresponding reports by the Commission, most recently Report from the Commission to the European Parliament and the Council, On Progress in Bulgaria under the Cooperation and Verification (COM(2018) 850 final); Vachudova (2016), p. 270; Carp (2014), p. 1.

[53]Act concerning the conditions of accession of the Republic of Croatia and the adjustments to the Treaty on European Union, the Treaty on the Functioning of the European Union and the Treaty establishing the European Atomic Energy Community (2012) OJ L112/21, Art. 36. In detail, Łazowski (2012), pp. 33–36.

[54]Commission Proposal for a Regulation of the European Parliament and of the Council on the protection of the Union's budget in case of generalised deficiencies as regards the rule of law in the Member States (COM(2018) 324 final), Art. 2; see also Halmai (2018b).

[55]Annex to the Communication from the Commission to the European Parliament, the European Council, the Council, the European Economic and Social Committee and the Committee of the Regions, A modern budget for a Union that protects, empowers and defends: The multiannual financial framework for 2021–2027 (COM(2018) 321 final), p. 48.

[56]Regulation (EU, Euratom) 1141/2014 on the statute and funding of European political parties and European political foundations (2014) OJ L317/1, art. 3 and art. 6.

[57]Art. 9 of the European People's Party Statutes, for example, permits the exclusion of both individual and Member State political parties, but does not define a reason for exclusion. Similar provisions are contained in Art. 16 Statutes of the Alliance of Liberals and Democrats for Europe Party.

Then there are the courts.[58] Unlike political bodies, they cannot avoid making decisions. The CJEU can be called upon to decide via the infringement and the preliminary ruling procedures; both can lead to severe financial sanctions. Furthermore, the CJEU can support actions of political institutions: an important example for this is the role it attributes to the qualifications made in the Commission's proposal to institute a procedure under Article 7 TEU.[59] Accordingly, such a proposal is sensible even when the Council and the European Council are unlikely to act.

The Union's institutions apart, those of the Member States can also defend European values. In this context, the tool box of international law is to be considered, from retaliatory measures to the mechanisms of the Vienna Convention on the Law of Treaties[60] to the extreme and contested option of an eventual humanitarian intervention in case a state turns to state terrorism.[61] The governments of the Member States can coordinate such international instruments, as was the case against Austria in 2000.[62] They could also consider, and threaten, to advance integration among themselves, excluding the countries that do not conform with the values.[63]

Member State courts, too, dispose of relevant instruments. They can defend European values against their own state in the light of a 'reverse Solange' doctrine[64] or against another Member State in the light of a 'horizontal Solange' doctrine.[65] The CJEU can support them in this via preliminary rulings. An important question is to what extent national courts can proceed independently from Union law on such matters.[66]

Other pertinent measures are those of the Council of Europe, especially recommendations issued by its political institutions or by the Commission for Democracy through Law (Venice Commission), as well as decisions of the ECtHR.[67] While the Council of Europe far exceeds the EU-centred European legal space, its relevance inside the European legal space flows from Article 6 (3) TEU, Article 52 (3) and Article 53 of the CFR. On an operative level, there is a close institutional connection.[68]

---

[58]On this, see in particular Huber (2017), p. 409 et seq.

[59]CJEU, *Minister for Justice and Equality*, *supra* note 37, paras. 69 et seq.

[60]In detail, see Binder (2013).

[61]Crawford (2013), p. 931; International Law Association (2018), p. 20 et seq.

[62]In detail, see Schorkopf (2002), p. 77.

[63]Franzius (2018), p. 388.

[64]On this, see above, Sect. 2.3. See also the presently pending references on a preliminary ruling in the cases *Miasto Łowicz v Skarb Państwa – Wojewoda Łódzki* (C-558/18); *Prokuratura Okręgowa w Płocku v VX, WW, XV* (C-563/18); *Prokuratura Rejonowa w Słubicach* (C-623/18).

[65]See in particular Canor (2013); a first case of application is the judgment of the Irish High Court in the *Celmer* case, *supra* note 16.

[66]As indicated in BVerfGE 140, 317 – *Identitätskontrolle*.

[67]Cf. on the Venice Commission, Nergelius (2015), p. 291; Grabenwarter (2018), p. 21.

[68]von Bogdandy (2008), p. 69 et seq.

Given that this legal framework comprises instruments of Union law, international law and the law of the Member States, it pertains to European law and not simply to Union law, international or domestic law alone.[69] In the tradition of public law thinking, such a doctrinal framework is to contribute to legal instruments promoting their legitimacy as well as their efficacy. Its most important building blocks are legal basis (Sect. 3.2), procedure (Sect. 3.3), the material standards (Sect. 3.4), and control (Sect. 3.5).

3.2 *Questions of Competence*

Any action to protect European values is prone to escalation. Therefore, it should be in the hands of institutions that can shoulder such a responsibility and manage conflicts. The first aspect responding to this concern is the requirement of a legal basis, in many cases even the need of a specific competence.[70] Thus, the first question is to verify whether its adoption and use are supported by a legal basis.

3.2.1 Article 7 TEU in the Order of Competences

Article 7 TEU plays a key role in this respect, as it might bar other reactions to systemic deficiencies under Article 2 TEU. In this case, the defence of the values would be completely under the control of the governments of the Member States, united in the Union's institutions. Responsibility, therefore, would be crystal clear. The drawback is that the extremely high requirements of Article 7 TEU might leave EU values without defence. Besides this consequentialist consideration, doctrinal arguments likewise militate against interpreting Article 7 TEU as an exclusive mechanism.

A first issue is whether Article 7 TEU prohibits pertinent measures by Member States. Article 3 TFEU does not list Article 7 TEU. Article 4 TFEU, which enumerates the main areas of shared responsibilities, does not feature Article 7 TEU either. However, it lists the space of freedom, security and law. Hence, there could be an argument to assume precedence of measures of Union law vis-à-vis a defence by Member States. Then there is Article 344 TFEU.[71]

The CJEU's case-law seemed to point towards pre-emption, especially in cases like *Melloni*, which excluded the unilateral enforcement of one Member State's

---

[69]On this understanding of European law, see in detail already Mosler (1968), p. 481 et seq.; von Bogdandy (2016), p. 589.

[70]Bast (2006), p. 30 et seq.; Bast (2018), para. 13 et seq.

[71]On the expansive interpretation of this clause, see CJEU, Case C-459/03 *Commission v. Ireland (Mox Plant)*, ECLI:EU:C:2006:345, paras. 123 et seq.

constitutional principles against another.[72] After the German Federal Constitutional Court emphasized its competence to protect the constitutional identity of the German Basic Law against measures taken by other Member States, too,[73] the CJEU has acknowledged that European law leaves room for the national defence of fundamental principles.[74] Since the European values of Article 2 TEU and the identity-informing fundamental principles of the Member State constitutions widely overlap,[75] neither the competences of Article 7 TEU nor other instruments of Union law block Member State institutions from defending European values, according to this case-law. This corresponds to the logic of the European legal space not to monopolise a central question such as value defence in one institution. The considerable need for coordination must be met with other means.[76]

The second issue is whether Article 7 TEU bars actions *taken by other Union institutions*. Article 7 TEU does not contain an explicit statement as to whether other Union institutions may defend European values using other instruments. The general rules apply. It is well established that a specific procedure designed to deal with a certain problem does not exclude developing other instruments,[77] a core statement since the *Van Gend en Loos* judgment.[78] Accordingly, it is, in principle, admissible to develop new instruments,[79] such as the Commission's Rule of Law Framework, or the Justice Score Board.

Nevertheless, Article 7 TEU plays a role. Its wording, the inclusion of the European Council and the extremely laborious procedure in Article 7 TEU indicate that it stipulates the most *intensive* form of defence of values. Therefore, the Union lacks any competence for developing stronger instruments. Hence, the expulsion of a Member State[80] or the dismissal of its government, an instrument the Spanish government used against the Catalan government, are off limits.[81] All instruments complementing those of Article 7 TEU in defending the values of Article 2 TEU must be less severe.[82]

[72]CJEU, Case C-399/11 *Melloni*, ECLI:EU:C:2013:107.

[73]BVerfGE 140, 317 – *Identitätskontrolle*.

[74]At least within the scope of fundamental rights, CJEU, Joined Cases C-404 and C-659/15 PPU *Aranyosi and Căldăraru*, ECLI:EU:C:2016:198.

[75]Cf. Opinion of Advocate General Cruz Villalón in CJEU, *Gauweiler and Others*, *supra* note 18.

[76]On this Sects. 3.3 and 3.4.

[77]Bast (2006), pp. 60–63.

[78]CJEU, Case C-26/62 *Van Gend en Loos v. Administratie der Belastingen*, ECLI:EU:C:1963:1, p. 11.

[79]Bast (2006), pp. 42–67. Cf. also Brauneck (2019), pp. 37 and 59.

[80]On this, see the proposal by Stein (1998), p. 890; Blagoev (2011), p. 191.

[81]Recently in Spain under Article 155 Spanish Constitution. On this, García Morales (2018).

[82]In this sense also CJEU, *Minister for Justice and Equality*, *supra* note 37; see also below, Sect. 3.4.

3.2.2 Instruments of Secondary Law

So far, action under Article 7 TEU is paralyzed by the Council and the European Council. Can other institutions defend the values through other instruments? As has been shown, Article 7 TEU does not prohibit other instruments. But any new instrument needs an appropriate legal basis. This requirement results from the necessity to legitimise any action of public authorities, including 'soft' measures.[83] A new instrument might even need a specific competence.[84]

With a view to the European Parliament, its general tasks allow it to discuss any systemic deficiencies in the Member States,[85] and it has done so for a long time. Its resolutions have gained public attention. However, they have not had much impact yet.

Measures taken by the other institutions could yield more powerful results, which is why the law is more demanding than with respect to the European Parliament, as has been shown by developments in other fields. The CJEU has declared Commission Communications invalid due to lack of competence (!).[86] The Court's requirement of a legal basis is particularly striking in the OMT procedure, whose subject was the mere announcement of a new instrument for purchasing bonds by ECB president Mario Draghi.[87]

The legal service of the Council has disputed the power of the Commission to establish the rule of law mechanism;[88] here, the general problem comes to the fore. However, the admissibility of this mechanism flows from the Commission's right to make requests under Article 7 TEU as well as its general role of a guardian of the Treaties according to Article 17 (1) TEU. On that basis, the Commission can also examine whether the Member States respect the values of Article 2 TEU. The competence to issue corresponding recommendations follows from Article 292 4th sentence TFEU.[89] These considerations also support the Justice Score Board.

Similar questions have emerged in the Council of Europe. One need only think of the sanctions imposed by its Parliamentary Assembly against Russian

---

[83] See Nettesheim (2018), para. 200; Senden (2004), p. 478 et seq. On the legal boundaries, von Bogdandy et al. (2015), pp. 273–275.

[84] In detail Bast (2006), para. 23 et seq.

[85] Bast (2006), para. 28.

[86] CJEU, Case C-57/95 *France v. Commission*, ECLI:EU:C:1997:164; CJEU, Case C-233/02 *France v. Commission*, ECLI:EU:C:2004:173, para. 40; Opinion of Advocate General Michal Bobek in CJEU, Case C-16/16 P *Commission v. Belgium*, ECLI:EU:C:2017:959.

[87] Opinion of Advocate General Cruz Villalón in CJEU, *Gauweiler and Others*, *supra* note 18.

[88] Commission's Communication on a new EU Framework to strengthen the rule of law: – compatibility with the Treaties (10296/14).

[89] Giegerich (2015), pp. 535–536; Toggenburg (2013).

parliamentarians since the annexation of the Crimea.[90] Another example are the opinions from the Venice Commission issued without a request from the Convention state concerned.[91] All these measures constitute reactions to systemic problems and can be treated analogously to the considerations on the instrument tool box of Union law.

3.2.3 The Justiciability of the Values

The defence of values by political institutions has not been very effective so far. As so often in the history of integration, the question arises whether the judiciary can compensate for this. For the CJEU, this is a question of its powers within the procedures of the Articles 257, 258 and 267 TFEU. Article 7 TEU does not block these procedures; Article 269 TFEU only determines that the Court cannot review the material prerequisites of Article 7 TEU. Given the lack of any explicit ban and the CJEU's general role in the *union of law,* there is good reason to assume that values can play a role in procedures under the Articles 257, 258 and 267 TFEU.[92]

The actual crux is the justiciability of the values of Article 2 TEU. The term *value* can be interpreted as the Treaty makers' attributing a vagueness to Article 2 TEU that excludes judicial application.[93] Arguments relating to the separation of powers might support this conclusion. The judicial application of values would immensely extend the courts' sphere of power to highly political conflicts.[94] All of this can be avoided by considering the values not to be justiciable.

However, following the established path of European Union law, the Commission and the CJEU have legally and credibly condensed the values of Article 2 TEU so that they have become accessible to judicial decision making, the value of the rule of law being at the centre. The most important path to condensing the values lies in connecting these values to fundamental rights and the well-established principles of the common constitutional traditions.[95] The effort has proven successful: even from the Polish 'White paper on the reform of the Polish judiciary'—which presents the highly controversial changes in the Polish judiciary as conforming to the values—

---

[90]Reconsideration on substantive grounds of the previously ratified credentials of the Russian delegation (Resolution 1990 (2014) Final version) as well as the extension through: Challenge, on substantive grounds, of the still unratified credentials of the delegation of the Russian Federation (Resolution 2034 (2015) Final version); Steininger (2018), Henderson (2018), p. 393.

[91]von Bogdandy and Sonnevend (2015).

[92]In detail, Spieker (2019), Schmidt and Bogdanowicz (2018), pp. 1069–1073; Hilf and Schorkopf (2017), para. 46; Hillion (2016), p. 59; Franzius (2018), p. 381 (386); a different attitude is expressed by Levits (2018), p. 239 (262); Nicolisi (2015), p. 613 (643); Martenczuk (2018), p. 41 (46).

[93]Kochenov and Pech (2018), p. 512 (520); Nicolisi (2015), p. 643.

[94]On the German discussion, Schmitt (2011), Böckenförde (1990), p. 25.

[95]CJEU, *Minister for Justice and Equality, supra* note 37. On the common constitutional traditions, see Cassese (2017), p. 939 et seq.; Graziadei and de Caria (2017), p. 949 et seq.

one can gather that European values have come to permit concrete legal assessment.[96] Two Commission communications in 2019 bring these developments together.[97]

Two judgments by the CJEU from 2018 are leading the way for the judicial operationalisation of the value of the rule of law. In the case *Associação Sindical dos Juízes Portugueses* (*ASJP*), the Court has operationalized the value of the rule of law by applying it together with another, specific and directly applicable Treaty provision. In the crucial passage, the Court states that 'Article 19 TEU [. . .] gives concrete expression to the value of the rule of law stated in Article 2'.[98] In the *L.M.* (*Deficiencies in the system of justice*) case, it enabled individuals to defend European values.[99] The case dealt with the protection of the separation of powers via an independent judiciary, and it accomplished this via the fundamental right to an impartial court and to a fair trial. The Court's approach is reminiscent of the German Federal Constitutional Court's Maastricht decision, which also made a fundamental principle (democracy) justiciable via an individual right (right to vote, Article 38 (1) of German Basic Law).[100] Since the *L.M.* case, the 'vigilance of individuals concerned to protect their rights' might also protect European values.[101]

Accordingly, the courts, including Member State courts, can decide on the values of Article 2 TEU.[102] The values have become judicially applicable though the doctrinal paths may vary.[103] This expansion of judicial competence mirrors the importance of the values and the judiciary's general role in the European legal space. By now, there is a judicial line of defence beyond the political rationality of Article 7 TEU.

The judicial applicability of European values means that constitutional courts, too, can defend them. However, in many Member States, Union law does not provide a *standard* of constitutional review, according to most constitutional courts concerned.[104] Some reasons for this reticence are of a rather more legal nature, especially the fact that Union law lacks constitutional rank in the domestic sphere. Other considerations are of a more political nature, in particular the consideration

---

[96]Chancellery of the Prime Minister of Poland (2018), para. 166.

[97]Communication from the Commission to the European Parliament, the European Council, the Council, the European Economic and Social Committee and thee Committee of the Regions, Strengthening the rule of law within the Union. A blueprint for action, COM/2019/343 final.

[98]CJEU, Case C-64/16 *Associação Sindical dos Juízes Portugueses*, ECLI:EU:C:2018:117.

[99]CJEU, *Minister for Justice and Equality*, *supra* note 37, para. 47 et seq.

[100]BVerfGE, 123, 267 – *Lissabon*; BVerfGE, 89, 155 – *Maastricht*; see, critically, Nettesheim (2009), p. 2869.

[101]CJEU, *Van Gend en Loos v. Administratie der Belastingen*, *supra* note 78.

[102]See, especially, CJEU, *Associação Sindical dos Juízes Portugueses*, *supra* note 98; CJEU, *Minister for Justice and Equality*, *supra* note 37; now also CJEU, Case C-619/18 *Commission/ Poland*, ECLI:EU:C:2019:531, para. 47; AG Tanchev, Opinion in Case C-192/18 – *Commission/ Poland*, para. 71; AG Tanchev, Opinion in Joined Cases C-585, C-624 and C-625/18 – *A.K. (Indépendance de la chambre disciplinaire de la Cour suprême)*, para. 77.

[103]von Bogdandy and Spieker (2019).

[104]In detail, Paris (2017), p. 798 et seq.; Mengozzi (2015), p. 707; Lacchi (2015), p. 1663.

that the constitutional courts' abstention from applying Union law facilitates a division of tasks that reduces conflicts between the CJEU and the constitutional courts.[105]

These considerations meet with objections. There is enough interpretive scope to include Union law into the purview of constitutional courts,[106] as just decided by the so far reticent German Federal Constitutional Court.[107] Substantively, such a step would result in a more effective implementation of Union law. Moreover, it would strengthen the constitutional courts themselves: they could take a more active role in interpreting Union law and shaping the European legal space.[108]

3.3 Procedure

The pivotal point of the CJEU's *L.M.* (*Deficiencies in the system of justice*) judgment is the fundamental right to a fair trial, Article 47 (2) CFR. It expresses a general legal principle which, in the European legal space, protects not only individuals, but also public authorities.[109] Moreover, it applies not only in judicial procedures, but whenever a legal subject is faced with the exercise of public authority,[110] especially when substantial interests are at stake.[111] This is the case with conflicts concerning systemic deficiencies: the interests in question here are the national reputation, the interest of prosecution, the effective functioning of the national judiciary, financial interests as well as the participation in institutions of the Union. A fair procedure is important not only for the legitimacy of any specific decision, but also for general cohesion in Europe.[112]

Of the many procedural questions, only two will be addressed here. The first one concerns political and administrative procedures. A point of criticism regarding the measures taken by the Commission and the European Parliament is that their motivation is not the defence of Union values, but the sanctioning of an EU-critical stance. To prove this point, it is said that measures comparable to the Polish ones, when taken by EU-friendly governments, do not elicit any reaction.[113]

---

[105]See Paris (2017), p. 814.

[106]In detail Paris (2017), p. 809 et seq.; Griebel (2014), p. 204; Bäcker (2015), p. 411.

[107]BVerfG, Order of 6 November 2019, 1 BvR 16/13 – *Recht auf Vergessen II.*

[108]On this discussion, Voßkuhle (2018), pp. 175 and 197; Komárek (2015), p. 75; Thym (2015), p. 56.

[109]Jarass (2016), para. 12.

[110]In this respect, Art. 47 of the Charter transcends Art. 6 ECHR; see also Alber (2016), para. 10. On the validity of art. 47 para. 2 CFR also from an administrative procedural level, Nowak (2011), para. 44.

[111]On the spill-over effects over administrative procedure, cf. Jarass (2016).

[112]Luhmann (1975), pp. 34 et seq., 48 et seq., 116–120; this was also an insight from the Eurozone crisis, Farahat and Krenn (2018), p. 384.

[113]Mendelski (2016).

Hence, the two institutions are accused of misusing their powers for partisan purposes.

As described above (Sect. 2.1), there is room for discretion when deciding whether to initiate a procedure. The accusation is thus to be dealt with under the doctrine on discretion. This doctrine does, however, not limit parliamentary debate: indeed, it is a general principle that parliaments enjoy full freedom of what to debate.[114] By contrast, the European Commission faces limits.[115] If it uses an instrument of supervision to sanction an integration-critical general attitude, this would amount to an illegal use of discretion. But to identify such improper use, hard evidence is needed. To date, the Commission's actions seem justified by the extraordinary severity of the situations at hand.[116]

With regard to judicial procedures, the core question is as to whether Member State courts have to refer a case to the CJEU if its subject is a possible systemic deficiency in another Member State. A national court can treat such a deficiency both in the light of the European values, as did the Irish High Court in the *Celmer* case,[117] and in the light of the fundamental principles of the national constitution, as in the case 'Identitätskontrolle' of the German Federal Constitutional Court.[118] The German Court has been much criticised for not having made a preliminary reference.[119]

The general question of a constitutional court's obligation to make such a reference has extensively been discussed.[120] When it comes to defending values, such a referral to the CJEU is of particular importance for hedging the relationship between the Member States in question. Only a procedure before the CJEU allows for defending European values in a process which respects the very rule of law because it requires a fair procedure. The Member State concerned must be involved. A national court can hardly provide the government of another state with adequate participation. A procedure before the CJEU appears to provide the only orderly way of deciding critical questions in another legal order. There is, moreover, the consideration that 'Europe should speak with one voice'. Even if national courts refer to *principles of national identity* instead of *European values*, such national principles can be defended better in the framework of European values.[121]

---

[114]CJEU, Case C–230/81 *Luxemburg v. Parliament*, ECLI:EU:C:1983:32, para. 39; Bast (2006), para. 28.

[115]Bleckmann (1997), p. 59 et seq.

[116]In detail, Hoffmeister (2015), p. 195 et seq.

[117]IEHC, *supra* note 16.

[118]BVerfGE 140, 317 – *Identitätskontrolle*.

[119]On the criticism, Burchardt (2016), p. 527 et seq.; Schönberger (2016), p. 422; Nettesheim (2016), p. 424; Sauer (2016), p. 1134; Classen (2016), p. 304; Nowag (2016), p. 1450 et seq.; Rugge (2016), p. 789.

[120]On this, see Paris (2017).

[121]In detail, Spieker (2020).

3.4 *Material Standards*

All *systemic deficiency* instruments contain elements describing a particularly problematic situation. Therefore, similar questions of interpretation and application arise. Three questions will be discussed: the interpretive condensing of the requirements (Sect. 3.4.1), the importance of a comprehensive and moreover collective assessment (Sect. 3.4.2) as well as the question of how concrete a violation must be (Sect. 3.4.3).

3.4.1 Red Lines

As doctrinal treaties, handbooks and commentaries on the German Basic Law show, many important features of a constitution, even of an entire legal order, can be inferred from principles such as human dignity, rule of law and democracy. To this end, German doctrine considers these principles as 'laws of construction'[122] and even 'optimization requirements',[123] thereby justifying a scholarship that has something to say on almost any important issue as well as a judiciary that is confident in its sweeping law-making role. There are hints that the Commission is moving towards a similar expansive understanding of EU values, in particular of the rule of law value.[124] Indeed, the Venice Commission's Rule of Law Checklist with its 53 pages, to which the European Commission refers, almost looks like a detailed manual that provides practitioners with guidance on almost any relevant question.[125]

This cannot be a model for dealing with the values of Article 2 TEU, particularly insofar as they apply to the Member States' legal orders. By using the term *value* in Article 2 TEU, the Treaty makers imply that its provisions are to be understood as vague and, thus, open.[126] And this openness is not an authorisation for the Union's institutions to gradually outline an ever more detailed common constitutional law. While Article 2 TEU has become judicially applicable (see above Sect. 3.2), this does not change the fact that it should not develop into a homogeneity clause similar to Article 28 German Basic Law or Article IV Sec. 4 and Articles XIII to XV of the US Constitution.[127] That would force the constitutional autonomy of the Member

---

[122]Dreier (2015), paras. 5, 8 et seq.; Reimer (2001), p. 26 et seq.

[123]Schulze-Fielitz (2015), para. 44.

[124]Communication from the Commission to the European Parliament, the European Council and the Council, Further strengthening the Rule of Law within the Union State of play and possible next steps, COM(2019) 163 final, p. 1.

[125]European Commission for Democracy Through Law, Rule of Law Checklist, CDL-AD(2016) 007 with its 53 pages just on the rule of law. The European Commission refers to this document as authoritative, see Communication from the Commission, COM(2019) 163 final, p. 8.

[126]Openness is a pivotal point of Schmitt's criticism, Schmitt (2011), pp. 23, 53 et seq.

[127]On this, see Giegerich (2015), p. 499 et seq. For a comparative view, Palermo and Kösserl (2017), p. 321 et seq.

States into a far too narrow corridor, going against European constitutional pluralism.

The 'thickening' of the Article 2 values might endanger European constitutional pluralism. The diversity of Member State constitutions, which is protected by Union law, is enormous. It comprises states with strong, weak or no constitutional courts, markedly different ways of organizing judicial independence, and considerably divergent protections of fundamental rights; it allows for republics and monarchies, parliamentary and semi-presidential systems, strong and weak parliaments, Westminster democracies and consociational democracies, and democracies with strong or weak party structures; and it respects strong or weak societal institutions, unitarian or federal orders as well as anarcho-syndicalist, Catholic, civic, laic, Ottoman, post-colonial, Protestant, socialist and statist constitutional traditions. All these elements play into the various systems of checks and balances, which is why European diversity is particularly pronounced when it comes to this basic feature of any constitutional order. It would be incompatible with this diversity to interpret and apply the values of Article 2 TEU in concrete cases in order to develop them into a kind of DNA of how to set up checks and balances on public authority in the European legal space.

Against this understanding one might argue that the EU Commission has made very detailed requirements on candidate countries,[128] including, for example, extraditing a former Croat general to the ICTY.[129] These detailed requirements, never challenged in Court, might be applicable to Member States after accession as well.[130] Technically, however, these requirements are not linked to Article 2 TEU but to the political Copenhagen criteria. Moreover, candidate countries and Member States have a fundamentally different status, and the accession criteria, finally, are subject to severe criticism themselves.[131]

The constitutional considerations (2) resulted in the conclusion that the instruments for fighting systemic deficiencies serve the cause of ensuring essentials of the European union (*Verbund*), in particular its self-understanding as a community of values, the core of fundamental rights, and the principle of mutual trust, but nothing more. This explains the values' vagueness as well as the extremely high hurdles in Article 7 TEU. The logic of restraint extends to the entire tool box. Consequently, the values are to be interpreted such as to only prohibit particularly problematic measures, without indicating a 'right way', let alone stipulating the basic organisation of Member State institutions. In this sense, they do not constitute 'laws of construction', but rather 'red lines'.[132]

---

[128]See, e.g., European Commission, Communication: Agenda 2000. Vol. I: For a stronger and wider Union, COM(2000) 97 final, p. 42.

[129]For a detailed analysis, see Rötting (2009), pp. 117 et seq.

[130]On the Copenhagen criteria as guidelines for the application of Article 2 TEU, see Hillion (2016), p. 66.

[131]Kochenov (2008), p. 311; Kosar et al. (2019), 443 et seq.

[132]In detail, von Bogdandy et al. (2018), p. 963.

The CJEU's decisions can be understood in this light. The logic of red lines explains a reasoning which may appear rather 'thin' and therefore little convincing at first sight. In most cases, the pertinent value is illustrated only in a general manner, with reference to principles;[133] but there is only little interpretive development in view of the matter concerned. The central aspect is *what cannot be tolerated.* While the lack of interpretive development limits the persuasive power of the judgment, it is by this abstaining that interpretative standards which could considerably limit the Member States' constitutional autonomy can be avoided.[134]

In the seminal *Aranyosi e Căldăraru* judgment, the Court refers only to absolute rights, especially to the prohibition of inhuman treatment,[135] i.e. to norms which are part of the core of European self-understanding.[136] This likewise holds true for the essence of non-absolute rights: In the *L.M.* (*Deficiencies in the system of justice*) judgment, the CJEU states that the newly established disciplinary chamber is problematic, given its appearance as an instrument to cow judges.[137] The judgment outlines further 'red lines' by referring to the qualifications on Poland made in the Commission proposal under Article 7 TEU. Of course, the Court does not treat the proposal as a source of law. Nevertheless, the 'information (. . .) is particularly relevant' and thus serves to assess the Polish measures.[138] This Commission proposal concretely articulates which measures are incompatible with the values and must therefore be revoked for crossing 'red lines'.

This logic of 'red lines' provides indications on how to rebut the presumption, founded in Article 49 TEU, that a Member State complies with European values. Such a doctrine, however, is fundamentally different from a conventional constitutional doctrine of principles that aims at developing from principles an 'overall structure' for the entire legal order.[139] It would rather have to follow the logic of 'negative dialectics', which is characterised by the very fact of not specifying what the ideal situation should look like, but rather what must not be.

---

[133] Cf., in particular, Proposal for a Council Decision on the determination of a clear risk of a serious breach by the Republic of Poland of the rule of law (COM(2017) 835 final), para. 6 et seq., and CJEU, *Minister for Justice and Equality*, *supra* note 37, paras. 62–67. At the same time, it should be underlined that the *L.M.* judgment provides much more justification than the similarly seminal CJEU, *Ruiz Zambrano*, *supra* note 36.

[134] On this way of forming standards, Lepsius (2011), p. 182 et seq.; von Bogdandy and Venzke (2014), p. 254 et seq.

[135] CJEU, *Aranyosi and Căldăraru*, *supra* note 74.

[136] Grabenwarter (2017), p. 3052.

[137] CJEU, *Minister for Justice and Equality*, *supra* note 37, para. 67.

[138] *Id.*, para. 61.

[139] Schuppert and Bumke (2000), pp. 28, 39; on 'guiding principles', Volkmann (2008), p. 67 et seq.

3.4.2 The Comprehensive and Collective Assessment

Most institutions base the determination that a value has been violated on a *comprehensive assessment*. The analysis of the Commission's and the CJEU's pertinent decisions shows that they consider a series of facts to this end, often described in detail, in the light of principles that remain abstract.[140] Such an application, which essentially consists in a comprehensive assessment of developments, events, measures and political statements, is an exercise in discretion and hence inevitably evaluative, and in that sense political. This easily gives rise to the accusation that the decisions are biased or motivated by illicit considerations.[141]

Yet, this practice of assessing is justified by three aspects. Firstly, it is the inevitable consequence of the restrained interpretation, which in turn is justified by the constitutional considerations described in the preceding passage. Secondly, the practice responds to the specific problems of legally capturing authoritarian tendencies. Thirdly, it must be taken into account that the comprehensive assessment is often based on similar perceptions of other institutions and thus takes place collectively (*Einschätzungsverbund*).

The central role of a comprehensive assessment is justified by the very nature of *systemic deficiencies*. Usually, the law is applied to a single action or measure. This mode fails with regard to authoritarian developments, as in most cases only a series of actions and measures *in their entirety* will reach the critical threshold. The actions and measures, taken individually, can often be plausibly justified.[142] The Polish government defends its judicial reforms by means of a legal comparison with 'unsuspicious' countries.[143] In order to establish a 'clear risk of a serious breach' of Article 2 TEU, a comprehensive view of all measures taken by the Polish government with regard to the judiciary is needed, with due consideration of the general political and social conditions of the country. One needs to assess the actions against the judiciary in the context of the actions against other controlling institutions, mainly the parliamentary opposition, the media, science, and NGOs.[144] This contextual approach has been confirmed by the Court of Justice stated in *A.K.*, which

[140]Proposal for a Council decision on the determination of a clear risk of a serious breach by the Republic of Poland of the rule of law (COM(2017) 835 final), paras. 109, 173; CJEU, *Minister for Justice and Equality*, *supra* note 37, para. 68; CJEU, Joined Cases C-585/18, C-624/18 and C-625/18 *A.K. (Indépendance de la chambre disciplinaire de la Cour supreme)*, ECLI:EU:C:2019:982, para. 127, 134, 152.

[141]See above, Sect. 3.3.

[142]Scheppele (2016), p. 105. Nevertheless, some Polish measures against the country's own constitutional court appear as rather clear cases, cf. Iustitia (2018), Gersdorf (2018); Venice Commission, Opinion on Amendments to the Act of 25 June 2015 on the Constitutional Tribunal of Poland, Opinion no. 833/2015, CDL-AD(2016)001, paras. 126, 137, 138.

[143]Chancellery of the Prime Minister of Poland (2018).

[144]This logic of the comprehensive assessment is by no means restricted to the values. The process of establishing a systemic deficiency in the banking sector is similar, cf. Regulation (EU) on European Union macro-prudential oversight of the financial system and establishing a European Systemic Risk Board (2010) OJ L331/1.

dealt with the independence of the Polish Supreme Court's Disciplinary Chamber.[145]

A third aspect contributing to the legitimacy of a comprehensive assessment lies in basing it on concurrent evaluations of other independent institutions, institutions with a recognized authority in questions of values. The regular application takes place in an *Einschätzungsverbund,* i.e., the comprehensive assessment of all circumstances must be widely shared. The more institutions perceive a substantial problem, the stronger the evidence for a systemic deficiency.

It is noteworthy that when it comes to systemic deficiencies, interpretation and application are not presented as being autonomous, but as part of a collective assessment involving many institutions of various legal orders. The Commission and the CJEU, but also many other institutions, recur to other authoritative sources when dealing with such questions, in particular to judgments of the ECtHR and opinions of the Venice Commission.[146] Evaluations of international bodies as well as civic organisations are also significant.[147] In the light of the cherished autonomy of Union law, it appears especially noteworthy that the Commission and the Court give much weight to evaluations under the national legal order concerned; such evaluations even enjoy particular relevance. In the Polish case, an important point is that authoritative Polish voices consider the governing majority's reforms as deeply unconstitutional.[148] Thus, a situation or measure is more likely to qualify as *systemically deficient* the more institutions of the various legal orders share this qualification.

Such a comprehensive assessment is also important in other respects. One need only think of the accusation that the Union itself does not meet the requirements that it demands Poland to fulfil.[149] Certainly, the possibility of the CJEU's judges to be re-elected does not meet the highest standards of judicial independence. However, in pertinent research, it is undisputed that the CJEU is an independent court.[150]

3.4.3 On the Concreteness of the Risk

The political institutions usually assess a general situation and decide whether there is a general risk for the values, for example by the Polish remodelling of its judiciary

[145]CJEU, *A.K. (Indépendance de la chambre disciplinaire de la Cour supreme),* ECLI:EU:C:2019:982, paras. 142, 152.

[146]Cf. Proposal for a Council decision on the determination of a clear risk of a serious breach by the Republic of Poland of the rule of law (COM(2017) 835 final), paras. 18, 32, 95, 116 et seq.; CJEU, Case C-404/15 *Aranyosi and Căldăraru, supra* note 74, para. 90; Opinion of AG Tanchev in CJEU, *Minister for Justice and Equality, supra* note 37, para. 10.

[147]Proposal for a Council decision on the determination of a clear risk of a serious breach by the Republic of Poland of the rule of law (COM(2017) 835 final), paras. 33, 63, 76, 80, 82.

[148]*Id.*, paras. 19, 21, 29, 81, 83, 86; cf. in particular Iustitia (2018), Gersdorf (2018).

[149]Cf. Weiler (2016).

[150]Krenn (2018), p. 2024.

since 2015. For the courts, the question arises whether such abstract risk is enough for a judicial decision, or whether a risk would have to materialise concretely in the case at hand in order to be relevant. The *L.M.* case concerned the question of whether an Irish court must surrender an individual to Poland under a European arrest warrant notwithstanding the general remodelling of the Polish judiciary. The CJEU answered that the national court must verify in a two-step procedure (1) whether there is a systemic deficiency in Poland and (2) if there are 'substantial grounds for believing that the individual concerned will run a real risk of breach of his fundamental right to an independent tribunal and, therefore, of the essence of his fundamental right to a fair trial'.[151]

This two-step review helps to distinguish the legal procedure from the political one under Article 7 TEU. It thus contributes to justifying the CJEU's decision.[152] However, it meets with considerable doubts. Since the measures of the Polish government undermine the independence of the entire Polish judiciary, any case runs the risk of being decided by a compromised judge at some point. Moreover, the CJEU's stipulation that Member State judges must review the independence of their Polish colleagues[153] appears hardly feasible.[154] At least there is a reversal of the burden of proof: in case of a (general) systemic deficiency, it is the Member State in question to give evidence that there is no concrete risk for the individual concerned.[155]

3.5 *Control*

The last building block is the issue of legal protection. It deals with the question of whether and how the instruments' lawfulness as well as the lawfulness of their use can be judicially reviewed. Such review is a core aspect of the European rule of law: the control of public authority by independent and impartial courts is sometimes even considered the crowning element of the rule of law.[156] Article 269 TFEU therefore describes an exception that is to be interpreted narrowly.

Self-evident as this principle might appear, its application is problematic with regard to instruments that do not yield a legal consequence; the protection by the CJEU has long been fragmentary and uncertain in this respect. It appears anything but certain that a Member State can take legal action against a recommendation of the Commission in the framework of the rule of law procedure or against a

[151]CJEU, *Minister for Justice and Equality*, *supra* note 37, para. 75. On this, von Bogdandy et al. (2018), p. 983.

[152]Cf. above, Sect. 3.2.

[153]CJEU, *Minister for Justice and Equality*, *supra* note 37, para. 77 et seq.

[154]Wendel (2019), p. 111; Krajewski (2018), p. 792; Bárd and van Ballegooij (2018), p. 353.

[155]CJEU, *Minister for Justice and Equality*, *supra* note 37, para. 78.

[156]Cf. CJEU, Case C-294/83 *Les Verts v. Parliament*, ECLI:EU:C:1986:166.

classification in the Justice Score Board that damages its reputation. Yet, the more recent case-law of the CJEU is expanding judicial control with regard to such measures.[157] This should make control possible at least when a recommendation of the Commission results in indirect legal consequences, e.g., when it provides a basis for assuming a systemic deficiency.[158] However, there is need for more legal protection, e.g., against recommendations damaging a Member State's reputation.

Another challenge is how to coordinate judicial control between the various legal orders of the European legal space. This leads again to Article 267 TFEU. There is an urgent need for such coordination when defending European values or their equivalents in the national constitutions. The coordination and control of national courts is primarily a task of the CJEU. Yet this does not imply that the CJEU itself is beyond control: it remains subject to the general mechanisms, which assume particular importance with regard to this explosive question. In this respect, the multilevel cooperation of the European courts might find here its finest hour.[159]

4 Towards a Tyranny of Values?

To many people, the European institutions appear distant and foreign. If they urge or even try to force democratically elected governments to revise important political projects, invoking European values, they run the risk of being rejected as self-important, arbitrary and illegitimate actors. Just thumping on the lawfulness of such actions is hardly an appropriate response to accusations of moving towards a tyranny of values. 'Being right' is not sufficient. In order to credibly defend European values, one must make use of fair procedures to convincingly show a broad European public what the values require, why they have been violated and what needs to be done. Defending European values in such a way will not appear as potentially tyrannical, but rather what most European citizens expect the Union to do.[160]

Acknowledgments Translated from German by Annika Müller. I would like to thank the *Dienstagsrunde*, in particular Dr. Laura Hering, Giacomo Rugge, Matthias Schmidt, and Dimitri Spieker, for their valuable critique and support. Unless stated otherwise, all quotes translated from German were translated by the author.

[157] CJEU, Case C-16/16 P *Belgium v. Commission*, ECLI:EU:C:2018:79, para. 44; Case C-258/14 *Florescu and Others*, ECLI:EU:C:2017:448, para. 30; Case C-207/01 *Altair Chimica*, ECLI:EU:C:2003:451, para. 41; Opinion of Advocate General Cruz Villalón in CJEU, *Gauweiler and Others*, *supra* note 18, para. 27 et seq.; Gundel (2018), p. 593; Schmidt-Aßmann (2013), p. 103.

[158] In detail, see above, Sect. 3.4.1.

[159] Voßkuhle (2018), Huber (2017), p. 389.

[160] Special Eurobarometer 489 rule of law, <data.europa.eu/euodp/en/data/dataset/S2235_91_3_489_ENG>.

References

Ackerman B (1991) We the people, Volume 1: foundations. Belknap Press of Harvard University Press, Cambridge

Ackerman R, Desierto D, Volosin N (2011) Hyper-Presidentialism: separation of powers without checks and balances in Argentina and Philippines. Berkeley J Int Law 20:246–271

Ahtisaari M, Frowein J, Oreja M (2000) Report on the commitment of the Austrian Government to the common European values, adopted in Paris on 8 September 2000

Alber S (2016) Art. 47. In: Stern K, Sachs M (eds) Europäische Grundrechte-Charta. C.H. Beck, München, pp 699–730

Bachmann K (2018) Zur Entwicklung der polnischen Demokratie. Aus Politik und Zeitgeschichte 10–11:9–14

Bäcker M (2015) Das Grundgesetz als Implementationsgarant der Unionsgrundrechte. EuR 50:389–414

Bárd P, van Ballegooij W (2018) Judicial independence as a precondition for mutual trust? The CJEU in Minister for Justice and Equality v. LM. New J Eur Crim Law 9

Bast J (2006) Grundbegriffe der Handlungsformen der EU. Springer, Berlin

Bast J (2018) Art. 5 EUV. In: Grabitz E, Hilf M, Nettesheim M (eds) Das Recht der Europäischen Union. C.H. Beck, München

Binder C (2013) Die Grenzen der Vertragstreue im Völkerrecht. Springer, Berlin

Blagoev B (2011) Expulsion of a Member State from the EU after Lisbon: political threat or legal reality? Tilburg Law Rev 16:191–237

Blauberger M (2016) Europäischer Schutz gegen nationale Demokratiedefizite? Leviathan 44:280–302

Bleckmann A (1997) Ermessensfehlerlehre: Völker- und Europarecht, vergleichendes Verwaltungsrecht. Heymanns, Köln

Böckenförde EW (1990) Grundrechte als Grundsatznormen: Zur gegenwärtigen Lage der Grundrechtsdogmatik. Der Staat 29:1–31

Brauneck J (2019) Gefährdung des EU-Haushalts durch rechtsstaatliche Mängel in den Mitgliedstaaten? EuR 54:37–61

Burchardt D (2016) Die Ausübung der Identitätskontrolle durch das Bundesverfassungsgericht. ZaöRV 76:527–551

Canor I (2013) *My brother's keeper*? Horizontal *solange*: "An ever closer *distrust* among the peoples of Europe". Common Mark Law Rev 50:383–422

Carp R (2014) The struggle for the rule of law in Romania as an EU Member State: the role of the cooperation and verification mechanism. Utrecht Law Rev 10(1):16

Cassese S (2017) The 'constitutional traditions common to the Member States' of the European Union. Rivista Trimestrale di Diritto Pubblico:939–948

Chancellery of the Prime Minister of Poland (2018) White Paper on the Reform of the Polish Judiciary. https://www.premier.gov.pl/files/files/white_paper_en_full.pdf

Classen CD (2016) Zu wenig, zu fundamentalistisch – zur grundrechtlichen Kontrolle "unionsrechtlich determinierter" nationaler Hoheitsakte. EuR 51:304–312

Closa C, Kochenov D (eds) (2016) Reinforcing the rule of law oversight in the European Union. Cambridge University Press, Cambridge

Closa C, Kochenov D, Weiler JHH (2014) Reinforcing rule of law oversight in the European Union. EUI Working Paper RSCAS 2014/25

Crawford JR (2013) Overview of part three of the articles on state responsibility. In: Crawford JR, Pellet A, Olleson S (eds) The law of international state responsibility. Oxford University Press, Oxford, pp 931–940

Croon-Gestefeld J (2017) Reverse Solange – Union Citizenship as a Detour on the Route to European Rights Protection Against National Infringements. In: Kochenov D (ed) EU citizenship and federalism: the role of rights. Cambridge University Press, Cambridge, pp 665–683

Dori A (2015) The EU Justice Scoreboard – Judicial Evaluation as a new Governance Tool. MPILux Working Paper 2. http://www.mpi.lu/fileadmin/mpi/medien/persons/Dori_Adriani/The_EU_Justice_Scoreboard_-_Judicial_Evaluation_as_a_New_Governance_Tool.pdf
Dreier H (2015) Art. 20 (Einführung). In: Dreier H (ed) Grundgesetz-Kommentar, 3rd edn. Mohr Siebeck, Tübingen, pp 1–10
Dyzenhaus D (2012) State of emergency. In: Rosenfeld M, Sajó A (eds) The Oxford handbook of comparative constitutional law. Oxford University Press, Oxford, pp 442–460
Farahat A, Krenn C (2018) Der Europäische Gerichtshof in der Eurokrise: eine konflikttheoretische Perspektive. Der Staat 57:357–385
Franzius C (2018) Der Kampf um Demokratie in Polen und Ungarn. DÖV 71:381–388
García Morales MJ (2018) Federal execution, Article 155 of the Spanish Constitution and the crisis in Catalonia. ZöR 73:791–830
Gersdorf M (2018) Opinion on the White Paper on the Reform of the Polish judiciary. http://www.sn.pl/aktualnosci/SiteAssets/Lists/Wydarzenia/EditForm/Supreme%20Court%20-%20Opinion%20on%20the%20white%20paper%20on%20the%20Reform%20of%20the%20Polish%20Judiciary.pdf
Giegerich T (2015) Verfassungshomogenität, Verfassungsautonomie und Verfassungsaufsicht in der EU: Zum 'neuen Rechtsstaatsmechanismus' der Europäischen Kommission. In: Calliess C (ed) Herausforderungen an Staat und Verfassung: Liber Amicorum für Torsten Stein zum 70. Geburtstag, Nomos, Baden-Baden, pp 499–542
Grabenwarter C (2017) Konventionswidrigkeit der Auslieferung bei drohender Todesstrafe – Fall Soering. NJW 70:3052
Grabenwarter C (2018) Die Herausbildung europäischer Verfassungsstandards in der Venedig-Kommission. JöR 66:21–41
Graziadei M, de Caria R (2017) The "Constitutional Traditions Common to the Member States" in the case-law of the European Court of Justice. Judicial Dialogue at its Finest. Rivista Trimestrale di Diritto Pubblico:949–971
Griebel J (2014) Europäische Grundrechte als Prüfungsmaßstab der Verfassungsbeschwerde. DVBl 2014:204–211
Gundel J (2018) Rechtsschutz gegen Empfehlungen der EU-Kommission? Anmerkung zum Urteil des EuGH (GK) v. 20.2.2018, Rs. C-16/16 P (Belgien/Kommission). EuR 53:593–605
Habermas J (1992) Faktizität und Geltung. Suhrkamp, Berlin
Halmai G (2017) The early retirement age of the Hungarian Judges. In: Nicola F, Davies B (eds) EU law stories. Cambridge University Press, Cambridge, pp 471–488
Halmai G (2018a) Illiberal constitutionalism? The Hungarian Constitution in a European perspective. In: Kadelbach S (ed) Verfassungskrisen in der Europäischen Union. Nomos, Baden-Baden, pp 85–104
Halmai G (2018b) The possibility and desirability of rule of law conditionality. Hague J Rule Law 11:171–188
Hartmann N (1926) Ethik. De Gruyter, Berlin
Henderson J (2018) Russia's recent dealings with the Council of Europe and European Court of Human Rights. Eur Public Law 24:393–402
Hilf M, Schorkopf F (2017) Art. 2 EUV. In: Grabitz E, Hilf M, Nettesheim M (eds) Das Recht der Europäischen Union. C.H. Beck, München
Hillion C (2016) Overseeing the rule of law in the EU: legal mandate and means. In: Closa C, Kochenov D (eds) Reinforcing the rule of law oversight in the European Union. Cambridge University Press, Cambridge, pp 59–81
Hirsch Ballin E (2016) Mutual trust: the virtue of reciprocity – strengthening the acceptance of the rule of law through peer review. In: Closa C, Kochenov D (eds) Reinforcing the rule of law oversight in the European Union. Cambridge University Press, Cambridge, pp 133–146
Hoffmeister F (2015) Enforcing the EU Charter of Fundamental Rights in Member States: how far are Rome, Budapest and Bucharest from Brussels. In: von Bogdandy A, Sonnevend P (eds)

Constitutional crisis in the European constitutional area. C.H. Beck/Hart/Nomos, Baden-Baden, pp 195–233

Huber PM (2017) Europäische Verfassungs- und Rechtsstaatlichkeit in Bedrängnis. Der Staat 56:389–414

International Law Association (2018) Final Report on Aggression and the Use of Force, Sydney. http://www.ila-hq.org/images/ILA/DraftReports/DraftReport_UseOfForce.pdf

Iustitia (2018) Response to the White Paper Compendium on the reforms of the Polish justice system. Presented by the Government of the Republic of Poland to the European Commission. http://www.statewatch.org/news/2018/mar/pl-judges-association-response-judiciary-reform-3-18.pdf

Jakab A, Kochenov D (eds) (2017) Protecting European values. Oxford University Press, Oxford

Jakab A, Lorincz VO (2017) International Indices as Models for the Rule of Law Scoreboard of the European Union: Methodological Issues. MPIL Research Paper No. 2017-21. https://papers.ssrn.com/sol3/papers.cfm?abstract_id=3032501

Janse R (2019) Is the European Commission a credible guardian of the values?: A revisionist account of the Copenhagen political criteria during the Big Bang enlargement. Int J Const Law 17:43–65

Jarass H (2016) Art. 47 GRCh. In: Jarass H (ed) Charta der Grundrechte der EU, 3rd edn. C.H. Beck, München, pp 405–427

Kailitz S, Köllner P (2012) Zur Autokratieforschung der Gegenwart: Klassifikatorische Vorschläge, theoretische Ansätze und analytische Dimensionen. Politische Vierteljahresschrift 47:9–41

Kochenov D (2008) EU enlargement and the failure of conditionality: pre-accession conditionality in the fields of democracy and the rule of law. Wolters-Kluwer, Austin

Kochenov D (2013) On policing Article 2 TEU compliance – Reverse Solange and systemic infringements analyzed. Polish Yearb Int Law 33:145–170

Kochenov D (2015) Biting intergouvernmentalism: the case for the reinvention of Article 259 TFEU to make it a viable rule of law enforcement tool. Hague J Rule Law 7:153–174

Kochenov D, Pech L (2016) Better late than never? On the European Commission's rule of law framework and its first activation. J Common Mark Stud 54:1062–1074

Kochenov D, Pech L (2018) Monitoring and enforcement of the rule of law in the EU: rhetoric and reality. EuConst 11:512–540

Komárek J (2015) Why National Constitutional Courts should not embrace EU fundamental rights. In: de Vries S, Bernitz U, Weatherill S (eds) The EU Charter of fundamental rights as binding instruments. Hart, Oxford, pp 75–92

Kosar D, Baros J, Dufek P (2019) The twin challenges to separation of powers in Central Europe: technocratic governance and populism. EuConst 15:427–461

Krajewski M (2018) Who is afraid of the European Council? The Court of Justice's cautious approach to independence of domestic judges. EuConst 14:792–813

Krenn C (2018) Self-Government at the Court of Justice of the European Union: a bedrock for institutional success. Germ Law J 19:2007–2030

Lacchi C (2015) Review by constitutional courts of the obligation of National Courts of last instance to refer a preliminary question to the Court of Justice of the EU. Germ Law J 16:1663–1700

Lachmayer K (2017) Questioning the basic values – Austria and Jörg Haider. In: Jakab A, Kochenov D (eds) The enforcement of EU law and values. Oxford University Press, Oxford

Lauth H, Sehring J (2009) Putting Deficient Rechtsstaat on the Research Agenda: reflections on diminished subtypes. Comp Sociol 8:165–201

Łazowski A (2012) European Union do not worry, Croatia is behind you: a commentary on the Seventh Accession Treaty. Croatian Yearb Eur Law Policy 8:1–39

Lenaerts K (2017) La vie après l'avis: exploring the principle of mutual (yet not blind) trust. Common Mark Law Rev 54:805–840

Lepsius O (2011) Die maßstabsetzende Gewalt. In: Jestaedt M, Lepsius O, Möllers C, Schönberger C (eds) Das entgrenzte Gericht. Suhrkamp, Berlin, pp 159–280

Levits E (2018) Die Europäische Union als Wertegemeinschaft. In: Jaeger T (ed) Europa 4.0. Jan Sramek Verlag KG, Wien, pp 239–270
Luhmann N (1975) Legitimation durch Verfahren, 2nd edn. Suhrkamp, Berlin
Luhmann N (1993) Gibt es in unserer Gesellschaft noch unverzichtbare Normen? C.F. Müller, Heidelberg
Mälksoo M (2009) The memory politics of becoming European: the East European subalterns and the collective memory of Europe. Eur J Int Relat 15:653–680
Martenczuk B (2018) Art. 7 EUV und der Rechtsstaatsrahmen als Instrument der Wahrung der Grundwerte der Union. In: Kadelbach S (ed) Verfassungskrisen in der Europäischen Union. Nomos, Baden-Baden
Mendelski M (2016) Das europäische Evaluierungsdefizit der Rechtsstaatlichkeit. Leviathan 44:366–398
Mengozzi P (2015) A European Partnership of Courts. Judicial Dialogue between the EU Court of Justice and National Constitutional Courts. Il Diritto dell'Unione Europea 701–720
Merkel W (2013) Vergleich politischer Systeme: Demokratien und Autokratien. In: Schmidt MG, Wolf F, Wurster S (eds) Studienbuch Politikwissenschaft. Springer, Berlin, pp 207–236
Möllers C, Schneider L (2018) Demokratiesicherung in der Europäischen Union. Mohr Siebeck, Tübingen
Mosler H (1968) Begriff und Gegenstand des Europarechts. ZaöRV 28:481–502
Müller JW (2015) Should the EU protect democracy and the rule of law inside Member States? Eur Law J 21:141–160
Muszyński M (2018) Polski Trybunał w unijnej rzeczywistości. Rzeczpospolita. https://www.rp.pl/Opinie/303229983-Polski-Trybunal-w-unijnej-rzeczywistosci%2D%2D-Mariusz-Muszynski-o-mocy-wyrokow-TSUE-w-Polsce.html
Nergelius J (2015) The role of the Venice Commission in maintaining the rule of law in Hungary and in Romania. In: von Bogdandy A, Sonnevend P (eds) Constitutional crisis in the European constitutional area. C.H. Beck/Hart/Nomos, Baden-Baden, pp 291–308
Nettesheim M (2009) Ein Individualrecht auf Staatlichkeit? Die Lissabon-Entscheidung des BVerfG. NJW 62:2867–2869
Nettesheim M (2016) Anmerkung. JZ 71:424–428
Nettesheim M (2018) Art. 288 AEUV. In: Grabitz E, Hilf M, Nettesheim M (eds) Das Recht der Europäischen Union. C.H. Beck, München
Nicolisi S (2015) The Contribution of the Court of Justice to the codification of the founding values of the European Union. Revista de Derecho Comunitario Europeo 51:613–643
Nowag J (2016) EU law, constitutional identity, and human dignity: A toxic mix? Bundesverfassungsgericht: Mr R. Common Mark Law Rev 53:1441–1453
Nowak C (2011) Europäisches Verwaltungsrecht und Grundrechte. In: Terhechte JP (ed) Verwaltungsrecht der Europäischen Union. Nomos, Baden-Baden, pp 519–584
Palermo F, Kösserl K (2017) Comparative Federalism. Hart, Oxford
Paris D (2017) Constitutional courts as European Union courts: the current and potential use of EU law as a yardstick for constitutional review. Maastricht J Eur Comp Law 24:792–821
Regan E (2018) The role of the principles of mutual trust and mutual recognition in EU law. Il Diritto dell'Unione Europea 231–248
Reimer F (2001) Verfassungsprinzipien. Duncker & Humblot, Berlin
Rötting M (2009) Das verfassungsrechtliche Beitrittsverfahren zur Europäischen Union. Springer, Berlin
Ruffert M (2016) Art. 7 EUV. In: Calliess C, Ruffert M (eds) EUV/AEUV, 5th edn, pp 166–174
Rugge G (2016) Bundesverfassungsgericht e Corte di Giustizia dell'UE: quale futuro per il dialogo sul rispetto dell'identità nazionale?. Il Diritto dell'Unione Europea pp 789–812
Russo AM (2014) La cittadinanza 'sostanziale' dell'UE alla luce della proposta del gruppo di Heidelberg: verso una 'reverse Solange'?. federalismi.it
Sadurski W (2019) Poland's constitutional breakdown. Oxford University Press, Oxford

Sauer H (2016) "Solange" geht in Altersteilzeit – Der unbedingte Vorrang der Menschenwürde vor dem Unionsrecht. NJW 69:1134–1138

Scheppele K (2016) Enforcing the basic principles of EU law through systemic infringement actions. In: Closa C, Kochenov D (eds) Reinforcing the rule of law oversight in the European Union. Cambridge University Press, Cambridge, pp 105–132

Schmidt M, Bogdanowicz P (2018) The infringement procedure in the rule of law crisis: how to make effective use of Article 258 TFEU. Common Mark Law Rev 55:1061–1100

Schmidt-Aßmann E (2013) Verwaltungsrechtliche Dogmatik. Mohr Siebeck, Tübingen

Schmitt C (2011) Die Tyrannei der Werte. 3rd corrected edn, with an afterword by Christoph Schönberger. Duncker & Humblot, Berlin

Schönberger C (2016) Anmerkung. JZ 71:422–424

Schorkopf F (2002) Die Maßnahmen der XIV EU-Mitgliedstaaten gegen Österreich. Springer, Berlin

Schorkopf F (2016) Wertesicherung in der Europäischen Union. Prävention, Quarantäne und Aufsicht als Bausteine eines Rechts der Verfassungskrise? EuR 51:147–163

Schulze-Fielitz H (2015) Art. 20 Abs. 2 Satz 2 und Abs. 3 (Rechtsstaat). In: Dreier H (ed) Grundgesetz-Kommentar, Band 2, 3rd edn 2015. Mohr Siebeck, Tübingen, pp 186–291

Schuppert GF, Bumke C (2000) Die Konstitutionalisierung der Rechtsordnung. Nomos, Baden-Baden

Senden L (2004) Soft law in European community law. Hart, Oxford

Spieker LD (2019) Breathing life into the Union's common values: on the Judicial Application of Article 2 TEU in the EU value crisis. Germ Law J 20:1182–1213

Spieker LD (2020) Framing and managing constitutional identity conflicts: how to stabilize the modus vivendi between the Court of Justice and national constitutional courts. Common Mark Law Rev 20:361–398

Stein T (1998) Die rechtlichen Reaktionsmöglichkeiten der Europäischen Union bei schwerwiegender und anhaltender Verletzung der demokratischen und rechtsstaatlichen Grundsätze in einem Mitgliedstaat. In: Götz V, Selmer P, Wolfrum R (eds) Liber amicorum Günther Jaenicke. Springer, Berlin, pp 871–898

Steinbeis M (2018) The Deed, not the Doer. Verfassungsblog. https://verfassungsblog.de/the-deed-not-the-doer/

Steinbeis M, Kemmerer A, Möllers C (eds) (2015) Gebändigte Macht: Verfassung im europäischen Nationalstaat. Nomos, Baden-Baden

Steininger S (2018) Managing the Backlash? The PACE and the Question of Participation Rights for Russia. Verfassungsblog. https://verfassungsblog.de/managing-the-backlash-the-pace-and-the-question-of-participation-rights-for-russia/

Thym D (2015) Vereinigt die Grundrechte! JZ 70:53–63

Toggenburg GN (2013) Was soll die EU können dürfen, um die EU-Verfassungswerte und die Rechtsstaatlichkeit der Mitgliedstaaten zu schützen? Ausblick auf eine neue Europäische Rechtsstaatshygiene. ÖGfE Policy Brief. https://oegfe.at/wordpress/wp-content/uploads/2015/07/OEGfE_Policy_Brief-2013.10.pdf

Tuori K (2016) From Copenhagen to Venice. In: Closa C, Kochenov D (eds) Reinforcing the rule of law oversight in the European Union. Cambridge University Press, Cambridge, pp 225–246

Uerpmann-Wittzack R (2009) The constitutional role of international law. In: von Bogdandy A, Bast J (eds) Principles of European constitutional law, 2nd rev. edn. Hart/C.H. Beck/Nomos, Oxford/München, pp 131–167

Vachudova MA (2016) Why improve EU oversight of rule of law. In: Closa C, Kochenov D (eds) Reinforcing the rule of law oversight in the European Union. Cambridge University Press, Cambridge, pp 270–289

van Middelaar L (2016) Vom Kontinent zur Union. Gegenwart und Geschichte des vereinten Europa. Suhrkamp, Berlin

Volkmann U (2008) Verfassungsrecht zwischen normativem Anspruch und politischer Wirklichkeit. VVDStRL 67:57–93

Volkmann U (2018) Wertedämmerung. Merkur 72:5–17
von Bogdandy A (2008) The European Union as situation, executive, and promoter of the international law of cultural diversity – elements of a beautiful friendship. Eur J Int Law 19 (2):241–275
von Bogdandy A (2010) Constitutional principles. In: von Bogdandy A, Bast J (eds) Principles of European constitutional law. Modern studies in European law. Hart, Oxford, pp 11–52
von Bogdandy A (2014) Common principles for a plurality of orders: a study on public authority in the European legal area. I•CON 12:980–1007
von Bogdandy A (2016) European law beyond 'Ever Closer Union' repositioning the concept, its thrust and the EJC's comparative methodology. Eur Law J 22(4):519–538
von Bogdandy A (2018) Ways to frame the European rule of law: Rechtsgemeinschaft, trust, revolution, and Kantian Peace. EuConst 14:657–699
von Bogdandy A, Sonnevend P (eds) (2015) Constitutional crisis in the European constitutional area. C.H. Beck/Hart/Nomos, Oxford/Portland
von Bogdandy A, Spieker D (2019) Countering the Judicial Silencing of critics: Article 2 TEU values, reverse Solange, and the responsibilities of National Judges. EuConst 15:391–426
von Bogdandy A, Venzke I (2014) In wessen Namen? Internationale Gerichte in Zeiten globalen Regierens. Suhrkamp, Berlin
von Bogdandy A, Kottmann M, Antpöhler C, Dickschen J, Hentrei S, Smrkol M (2012) Reverse Solange – protecting the essence of fundamental rights against EU Member States. Common Mark Law Rev 49:489–519
von Bogdandy A, Kottmann M, Antpöhler C, Dickschen J, Hentrei S, Smrkol M (2015) A European response to domestic constitutional crisis: advancing the Reverse-Solange Doctrine. In: von Bogdandy A, Sonnevend P (eds) Constitutional crisis in the European constitutional area. Theory law and politics in Hungary and Romania. C.H. Beck/Hart/Nomos, Oxford/Portland, pp 248–267
von Bogdandy A, Bogdanovic P, Canor I, Schmidt M, Taborowski M (2018) Guest editorial: a potential constitutional moment for the European rule of law – the importance of red lines. Common Mark Law Rev 55:983–995
Voßkuhle A (2018) Die Idee der Europäischen Wertegemeinschaft. Verlag der Buchhandlung Klaus Bittner, Köln
Weiler JHH (2016) Epilogue: living in a glass house: Europe, democracy and the rule of law. In: Closa C, Kochenov D (eds) Reinforcing the rule of law oversight in the European Union. Cambridge University Press, Cambridge, pp 313–326
Wendel M (2019) Rechtsstaatlichkeitsaufsicht und gegenseitiges Vertrauen. EuR 54:111–132
Wittinger M (2005) Der Europarat: Die Entwicklung seines Rechts und der "europäischen Verfassungswerte". Nomos, Baden-Baden

Armin von Bogdandy is Director at the Max Planck Institute for Comparative Public Law and International Law, Heidelberg.

9

A Potential Constitutional Moment for the European Rule of Law: The Importance of Red Lines

Armin von Bogdandy, Piotr Bogdanowicz, Iris Canor, Giacomo Rugge, Matthias Schmidt and Maciej Taborowski

Contents

Abstract This contribution deals with the current European rule of law crisis. It does so by analyzing the recent CJEU's judgment in re *LM* and by considering its possible ramifications for the future of the rule of law in the EU. In particular, it is argued that, as a result of this judgment, the European rule of law as provided for by Art. 2 TEU has become a legally enforceable value. The CJEU has indeed made clear that this value features a set of minimum standards that the Member States cannot bluntly disregard. In the present context, which is characterized by the inaction of the supranational and national political institutions, a prominent role in safeguarding a liberal understanding of the European rule of law is played by the

A. von Bogdandy (✉) · G. Rugge · M. Schmidt
Max Planck Institute for Comparative Public Law and International Law, Heidelberg, Germany
e-mail: sekreavb@mpil.de; rugge@mpil.de; mschmidt@mpil.de

P. Bogdanowicz · M. Taborowski
Faculty of Law and Administration, University of Warsaw, Warsaw, Poland
e-mail: p.bogdanowicz@wpia.uw.edu.pl; maciej.taborowski@brpo.gov.pl

I. Canor
School of Law, Zefat Academic College, Sefad, Israel

School of Law, College of Management, Rishon Le Zion, Israel
e-mail: canor@colman.ac.il

entire European judiciary (the so-called '*Gerichtsverbund*'), including national courts and tribunals.

1 What Is at Stake?

The Union's 'rule of law crisis' is a multi-faceted phenomenon.[1] Of particular concern are Member States where ruling majorities wilfully uproot the separation of powers. The current focus is very much on Poland. The Polish government has taken extensive measures that have undermined the independence of the Constitutional Tribunal. It has strengthened its influence on the National Council of the Judiciary, which selects the judges. It has dismissed more than 150 (out of 700) presidents and vice presidents of ordinary courts. It has forced almost 40% of Supreme Court judges to retire.[2] It has raised the overall number of Supreme Court judges, thereby creating the need for up to 70 new nominations. It has established a new disciplinary chamber as well as an extraordinary appeals procedure before the Supreme Court, which has the potential to subdue independent-minded judges.[3] Yet other Member States should not be forgotten either, such as Hungary. The latter is even said to have become a rather hopeless case—with some involuntary help from Brussels, e.g., through its funds.[4] Hopefully, the recent adoption by the European Parliament of a reasoned proposal under Article 7 (1) TEU will help improve the situation in Hungary. But, should these authoritarian measures remain unopposed, it will be hard to argue in the future that they are at odds with the European values as enshrined in Article 2 TEU.[5]

European institutions have started to react far more determinedly than in the Hungarian case. This is to be welcomed. At the same time, the European reactions raise the stakes dramatically. We might even witness a 'constitutional moment'. This term indicates a situation that deeply impacts on the future path of a constitutional

---

[1]Editorial Comments (2015), pp. 619, 625–627; Editorial Comments (2016), p. 597; Editorial Comments (2017), p. 1309; on the academic debate Bonelli (2017), p. 793.

[2]COM(2017) 835 final, 'European Commission, Reasoned Proposal in accordance with Article 7 (1) of the Treaty on European Union regarding the rule of law in Poland: Proposal for a Council Decision on the determination of a clear risk of a serious breach by the Republic of Poland of the rule of law', at p. 21, para. 116.

[3]Act on the Supreme Court of 8 December 2017, Journal of Laws (2018), item no. 5.

[4]For a dire picture, Charlemagne, The Economist, April 5, 2018. Halmai (2018), p. 85. See also European Parliament, Committee on Civil Liberties, Justice and Home Affairs, 25th June 2018 (Result of roll-call votes), http://www.europarl.europa.eu/committees/en/libe/votes-in-committee.html.

[5]See for a comprehensive description Matczak (2018); 'Opinion on the Draft Act amending the Act on the National Council of the judiciary; on the Draft Act amending the Act on the Supreme Court, proposed by the President of Poland, and on the Act on the organisation of ordinary courts', adopted by the Commission at its 113th Plenary Session (Venice, 8-9 December 2017), http://www.venice.coe.int/webforms/documents/default.aspx?pdffile=CDL-AD(2017)031-e.

order without formally amending it.[6] At issue is whether illiberal democracies become part of the European public order as laid out in Article 2 TEU, or are opposed by it. In any event, the consequences could be truly far-reaching. In the first case, the conventional self-understanding of Europe cannot be maintained any longer, because the European rule of law would cover—and thus legitimize—what is currently happening in Poland and Hungary. This would have tremendous implications, for example for the European stance towards critical developments in other Member States or the Union's external policy (Turkey!). In the second case, the European rule of law would be supplemented by 'red lines'. That would also amount to a 'constitutional moment' because it would add substance and bite to the European values.

To advance the second case, the European institutions are to be commended for reacting fiercely. The Commission's actions, in particular its Article 7 TEU proposal, merit support, also for good legal reasons. At the same time, much will depend on the judicial branch. It is indeed no coincidence that a first, important opportunity to draw such red lines has arisen in the context of legal proceedings, more precisely in the context of what is now known as the *LM* case.[7] Initiated by the Irish High Court through a request for a preliminary ruling, this case concerned the interpretation of Article 1(3) of the European Arrest Warrant Framework Decision (hereinafter: EAW Framework Decision). More specifically, the Irish judge asked whether that provision of the Framework Decision could be so construed as to exclude the execution of a EAW in case of 'cogent evidence that conditions in the issuing Member State are incompatible with the fundamental right to a fair trial because the system of justice itself in the issuing Member State is no longer operating under the rule of law'.

This case will be analysed in greater detail in what follows. It has to be said, though, that no European political measure or judicial decision can, by or of itself, restore the separation of powers in a Member State. They can only contribute to Polish self-healing through its internal constitutional process. However, their importance is not limited to this, as they are crucial for upholding European liberal constitutionalism in the rest of the Union. In fact, it is in this light that the *LM* case must be read. But before examining the case, some introductory remarks are in order.

[6] Ackerman (1991), Vol 1, 6. Note that the original articulation of this term by Ackerman has a more specific meaning. For further analysis, Klarman (1992), pp. 759–797.

[7] Case C-216/18 PPU, *Reference for a preliminary ruling from the High Court (Ireland) made on 27 March 2018 – Minister for Justice and Equality v LM*, (pending), http://www.courts.ie/Judgments.nsf/0/FD843302847F2E228025825D00457F19. This case is based on a referral from the Irish High Court 2013 295 EXT;2014 8 EXT; 2017 291 EXT *The Minister for Justice and Equality v. Celmer*, [2018] IEHC 119, http://www.courts.ie/Judgments.nsf/0/578DD3A9A33247A38025824F0057E747. See also Case C-216/18 PPU, *Reference for a preliminary ruling from the High Court (Ireland) made on 27 March 2018 — Minister for Justice and Equality v LM*, Opinion of Advocate General Tanchev, ECLI:EU:C:2018:517. 28th June 2018.

2 Operationalizing the Value of the Rule of Law

By now, much has happened to operationalize—i.e., interpret, apply and even impose—the rule-of-law value. Confuting many who consider the rule-of-law value of Article 2 TEU an all too vague political statement, the guardians of the Treaties have developed it in a way that allows for a juridical assessment of Member States' activities. To be clear, the institutions have not set out to demarcate the value by creating definitions that can be applied in a formalistic manner, but have rather linked the value of the rule of law to well-established principles. Their application requires much contextualization and circumspection and will inevitably contain political, i.e., discretionary, evaluative and opportunistic, elements. But that is the path of the law, in particular when it comes to 'constitutional moments'.

A ground-breaking contribution to the operationalization of the rule-of-law value can be found in the CJEU's recent decision in the case of *Associação Sindical dos Juízes Portugueses* (*ASJP*). Its interpretation of Article 19 TEU covers the institutional dimension of domestic judicial independence.[8] The European rule of law has thus become justiciable vis-à-vis the Member States.[9] The Commission contributes to this development by compiling relevant principles into a sensible whole, in particular in its Rule of Law Framework.[10] It relies on many sources: the Court's rulings, but also decisions and opinions of other institutions, in particular the European Court of Human Rights and the European Commission for Democracy through Law (the Venice Commission). Such a broad spectrum contributes significantly to the legitimacy of its endeavour.

The Commission's Rule of Law Framework is an important step with regard not only for the interpretation but also, possibly, for the normativity of the rule of law. Although it shows some weaknesses, for example by making it almost indistinguishable from the values of democracy and human rights, it seems a convincing operationalization that is in tune with the *acquis* of European public law. The Commission has reiterated the Framework's interpretation in its Reasoned Proposal under Article 7(1) TEU regarding the Rule of Law in Poland.[11] Moreover, it referred to the rule-of-law value in its 2018 Justice Scoreboard for 'monitoring of justice reforms at EU level' as well as in its last Country Report on Poland under the European Semester.[12] The Commission's recent regulation proposal on 'the

[8]CJEU, Case C-64/16, *Associação Sindical dos Juízes Portugueses*, ECLI:EU:C:2018:117.

[9]CJEU, Case C-477/16 PPU, *Kovalkovas*, ECLI:EU:C:2016:861; Case C-452/16 PPU, *Poltorak*, ECLI:EU:C:2016:858.

[10]COM(2014) 158 final/2, 'European Commission, Communication from the Commission to the European Parliament and the Council: A new EU framework to strengthen the rule of law' p. 4, and Annex I.

[11]*Supra* note 2, p. 1, para. 1.

[12]SWD(2018) 219 final, 'Commission Staff Working Document, Country Report Poland 2018 accompanying the document Communication from the Commission to the European Parliament, the Council, the European Central Bank and the Eurogroup: 2018 European Semester: Assessment

protection of the Union's budget in case of generalised deficiencies as regards the rule of law in the Member States' even provides a definition for the threshold of 'generalised deficiencies' of the rule of law.[13] Operationalization can also be helped by a newly suggested 'Justice, Rights and Values' Fund with a total volume of 947 million euros.[14] Already in force—albeit not yet enforced—is the Union's Regulation on European Political Parties, which permits reviewing whether a European party complies with Article 2 TEU.[15]

Notwithstanding a number of doctrinal issues that remain open, at least the basis for legally assessing Member States using the rule-of-law value is now fairly well-established. From the Polish 'White Paper on the Judiciary', one can deduce that not even the Polish government puts that into question, since it defends its measures on the merits of the European rule of law.[16] The impressive rebuttal of that 'White Paper' by the Polish Judges Association as well as by the Polish Supreme Court also shows a well-established juridical link between the vague rule-of-law value and crucial features of the domestic judiciaries.[17] The European rule of law has thus become an operational principle in European political and legal controversies.

3 The Political Branch in Troubled Waters

Opposing the Polish measures is extremely sensitive because it implies going against a democratically elected government that is transforming basic features of its constitutional order. For that reason it is to be welcomed that the European political

---

of progress on structural reforms, prevention and correction of macroeconomic imbalances, and results of in-depth reviews under Regulation (EU) No 1176/2011', p. 3, 29.

[13]COM(2018) 324 final, 'European Commission, Proposal for a Regulation of the European Parliament and of the Council on the protection of the Union's budget in case of generalised deficiencies as regards the rule of law in the Member States', at Art. 2(b).

[14]COM(2018) 321 final, 'Annex to the Communication from the Commission to the European Parliament, the European Council, the Council, the European Economic and Social Committee and the Committee of the Regions, A modern budget for a Union that protects, empowers and defends: The multiannual financial framework for 2021-2027', p. 48.

[15]OJ 2011 L 317/1, 'Regulation (EU, EURATOM) No. 1141/2014 of the European Parliament and of the Council of 22 October 2014 on the statute and funding of European political parties and European political foundations', at Art. 3(1)c, Art. 6(1).

[16]Chancellery of the Prime Minister of Poland, 'White Paper on the Reform of the Polish Judiciary', 7 March 2018, https://www.premier.gov.pl/files/files/white_paper_en_full.pdf, para. 166.

[17]Iustitia (Polish Judges Association), 'Response to the White Paper Compendium on the reforms of the Polish justice system, presented by the Government of the Republic of Poland to the European Commission', 17 March 2018, https://twojsad.pl/wp-content/uploads/2018/03/iustitia-response-whitepaper.pdf; Gersdorf (First President of the Supreme Court), 'Opinion on the White Paper on the reform of the Polish judiciary, 16 March 2018, https://archiwumosiatynskiego.pl/images/2018/04/Supreme-Court-Opinion-on-the-white-paper-on-the-Reform-of-the-Polish-Judiciary.pdf.

branch has become active. Since the lessons have been learnt from the miserable action national governments undertook against Austria in 2000, the institutional activities are so far concentrated in the Council of Europe's and the Union's institutions. The European Commission in particular tries to position itself as a defender of European values, thereby responding to the harsh criticism levelled against its earlier reluctance. In the Polish case, it has deployed two core instruments for the first time. This is significant in and of itself, as the first usage of an instrument often impacts on its further utilisation. Unfortunately, there is a clear and serious risk of failure, with a possibly calamitous impact on the European rule of law.

One instrument is the Commission's already mentioned 'Rule of Law Framework' of 2014, which was designed as an instrument whose quick implementation can avoid escalating the situation into Article 7 TEU territory. Read as an '*a maiore ad minus*' approach that is permissible under Article 7(1) TEU and Article 292 TFEU,[18] it provides the Commission with a procedure for engaging—through an opinion and later recommendations—in a dialogue with a Member State in case of an observed 'systemic threat to the rule of law'. To date, the use of the Framework has not yielded tangible results, which casts much doubt on the instrument's capacity to impose results. Despite several Commission's recommendations, the Polish authorities have not undertaken any remedial action and have merely made some minor concessions of an illusory nature and clearly no practical consequence.

The Commission then introduced the second instrument to show it 'meant business'. On 20 December 2017, it launched the procedure under Article 7 (1) TEU for the first time ever. It finds that there is a clear risk of a serious breach of the rule of law in Poland, indicates rather precisely which steps need to be taken, and asks that the Council recommend Poland take such steps.[19] It hereby confutes a statement by its former President Barroso, who depicted Article 7 TEU as the 'nuclear option',[20] a statement that evidently delegitimizes the use of this instrument. The legitimacy of its use is corroborated by the European Parliament[21] as well as the Committee of the Regions,[22] which support the Commission and call upon the Council to quickly follow up on the Commission's action.

The Commission's proposal merits close attention. It is detailed and extensive. It integrates the findings of other institutions, such as the Council of Europe or the

---

[18]Giegerich (2015), pp. 499, 535–536. For the opposing view, 10296/14 Legal Service of the Council, 'Commission's Communication on a new EU Framework to strengthen the rule of law: – compatibility with the Treaties', 27 May 2014, http://data.consilium.europa.eu/doc/document/ST-10296-2014-INIT/en/pdf.

[19]*Supra* note 2.

[20]SPEECH/13/684, Barroso (President of the European Commission), 'State of the Union address 2013', 11 September 2013, http://europa.eu/rapid/press-release_SPEECH-13-684_en.htm.

[21]P8_TA-PROV(2018)0055, 'European Parliament resolution of 1 March 2018 on the Commission's decision to activate Article 7(1) TEU as regards the situation in Poland (2018/2541(RSP)'.

[22]RESOL-VI/30, 6391/18, 'Determination of a clear risk of a serious breach by Poland of rule of law – Resolution of the European Committee of the Regions of 22 February 2018'.

United Nations as well as civil-society organizations.[23] This fends off accusations that the findings are partisan. By demonstrating that many institutions share its findings, the Commission makes itself the voice of a broad institutional alliance. At the same time, it underlines the legal dimension of the issue by making its proposal resemble a reasoned opinion in infringement proceedings. The Commission's proposal thus evidently aims to be two things at the same time: a convincing *political* value judgment as well as a *legally* sound analysis. This is not paradoxical; rather, it corresponds to how political institutions should decide.

The legal reasoning of the Commission as to why there is a clear risk of serious breach might appear somewhat 'thin', as it does not really develop what the threshold requires. However, one needs to consider that institutional developments towards an authoritarian regime are regularly hard to grasp from a legal standpoint because legal analysis focusses on individual acts. Taken individually, such measures lend themselves more easily to justification (although most of the Polish measures against the Constitutional Tribunal seem rather clear cases).[24] Indeed the Polish government tries to defend its measures through legal comparison with 'unsuspicious' countries.[25] Therefore, to convincingly determine a 'clear risk of a serious breach' of an Article 2 TEU value, all Polish measures affecting the judiciary must be considered together, with due regard to the overall political and social conditions in the country. Such determination inevitably entails an important discretionary and evaluative dimension, which strictly doctrinal arguments cannot fully guide.

It is now for the Council to act, which would require the approval of four fifths of its members, i.e., 22 Member States. The Council has debated the matter in the General Affairs Council on numerous occasions, most recently in April.[26] But it is distinctly possible that the Council will not decide on the matter, for instance in order to keep the Union united in difficult times (just consider Brexit!). However, such an omission could be used as an argument that the Council—and hence the Member States—do not deem the policies of the Polish government, in particular the changes to the Polish judiciary identified in the Commission's Proposal, an infringement of Article 2 TEU. Accordingly, such policies could more easily be presented as conforming to the founding values of the European Union. They could possibly even be considered an expression of the European rule of law. However, it should not be forgotten that there are also the courts. As so often in European crises, much will depend on the Court of Justice of the European Union as well as on the domestic courts—in short, on the entire judiciary in the European legal space.

---

[23] *Supra* note 2, para. 183 and the respective footnotes.

[24] Iustitia, *supra* note 17, p. 92; Venice Commission, 'Opinion on Amendments to the Act of 25 June 2015 on the Constitutional Tribunal of Poland', Opinion no. 833/2015, CDL-AD(2016) 001, paras. 126, 137, 138.

[25] 'White Paper on the Reform of the Polish Judiciary', *supra* note 16. But see also the rebuttal *supra* note 17.

[26] General Affairs Council, 'Rule of law in Poland', 9 April 2019: https://www.consilium.europa.eu/media/39196/st08130-en19.pdf.

4 The Judicial Branch: 'I Love You, Like I Love Ireland'

Contrary to the Council, courts cannot refrain from making a decision. What might help the courts is the realisation that they will be heavily criticised regardless of how they adjudicate the Polish situation.[27] Still, the courts should seize any opportunity to draw red lines for the European rule of law.[28] Within the complex European judicial system, it is for the CJEU to decide if Poland infringes a European value. Domestic courts should decide this issue only if the CJEU does not do so.

The CJEU might be called upon either via infringement proceedings initiated by the Commission or via preliminary-ruling requests referred to it by national courts, i.e., in top-down or bottom-up proceedings. The traditional path for judicially supervising the Member States is the infringement proceedings, the standard interaction between the two guardians of the Treaties. The infringement procedure should hence also play a vital part in the rule-of-law crisis.[29] The values in Article 2 TEU are subject to the Court's jurisdiction and thus to its mandate to ensure that 'the law is observed' (Article 19(1) TEU), and the Court now seems ready to use this mandate.[30] Article 7 TEU does not preclude parallel infringement proceedings, as the *Van Gend en Loos* precedent exemplifies.[31] How to frame a possible case is more problematic; after all, the Polish situation is triggered by a combination of measures that are as diverse as they are numerous. However, the Court has already held that it can use infringement proceedings to make a finding of general and continuous deficiencies in a Member State,[32] thereby overcoming its normal focus on an individual and concrete setting.

If infringement proceedings are therefore legally viable, one should nevertheless consider that it is a mighty burden for the CJEU to have to decide whether the Polish measures violate the European rule of law. However, this burden can be shared among several courts if the issue is handled via a preliminary-ruling procedure, as

---

[27]The new Vice President of the Polish Constitutional Tribunal has already stated that he would consider any CJEU decision against Poland illegitimate, Muszyński (2018).

[28]The Advocate General in the case indeed addresses the Polish situation. However, he does so only in terms of human rights and thereby fails to fully meet the challenge, *supra* note 7, para. 39.

[29]The Commission initiated two successfull infringement procedures based on Article 19(1) TEU and Article 47 CFR against Poland, see Case C-619/18, *Commission v. Poland (Indépendance de la Cour suprême),* ECLI:EU:C:2019:531 and Case C-192/18, *Commission v. Poland (Indépendance des juridictions de droit commun),* ECLI:EU:C:2019:924. A further infringement procedure is currently pending before the Court, see Case C-791/19, *Commission v. Poland.* See also the pending infringement proceedings against Hungary, Case C-66/18, *Commission v. Hungary (Enseignement supérieur)* and Case C-78/18, *Commission v. Hungary (Transparence associative).*

[30]*Supra* note 8. In the infringement proceedings against Hungary concerning judicial independence, (Case C-286/12, *Commission v. Hungary*, ECLI:EU:C:2012:687) the Commission and the Court were criticized for framing and deciding the case on the grounds of discrimination rather than Article 2 TEU, Halmai (2017), p. 471.

[31]Case C-26/62, *Van Gend en Loos* v. *Administratie der Belastingen*, ECLI:EU:C:1963:1. In detail, Scheppele (2016), p. 105.

[32]Case C-494/01, *Commission* v. *Ireland*, ECLI:EU:C:2005:250, para. 36.

the CJEU then responds to the concerns of national courts. Deciding the issue in a preliminary-ruling procedure would also continue the European tradition that most decisions of deep constitutional impact are taken in the European *Gerichtsverbund*, the European union of courts. Indeed, the *LM*[33] case, which was referred to the CJEU by the Irish High Court, is a first example. As the vivid Polish reactions to this referral show,[34] it has the potential to become a landmark decision on the issue.

The *LM* case originates from a negative appraisal made by the Irish judicial authority as regards the rule of law in Poland. In other terms, it has its origins in a country with which Poland has always had a special relationship. A big hit of Polish rock music of the 1990s, with the title 'I love you, like I love Ireland', is a perfect example of that relationship. As the main vocalist of the group 'Kobranocka' affirmed, 'Ireland [. . .] had a similar history, just like us they fought for independence. We loved them for that. I loved them and love them to this day.'[35] In Polish, to 'love somebody like Ireland' means to love someone deeply. Apart from this curious note, the referral in the *LM* case demonstrates, in broader terms, that it is inevitable that national courts become involved to vindicate the rule of law in the European legal space.[36]

The concrete problem addressed in the preliminary reference was whether Ireland may refuse to surrender a Polish citizen to Poland following a European arrest warrant (EAW) because of a systemic deficiency in the rule of law in that Member State. More specifically, through its referral, the Irish High Court asked the CJEU to interpret Article 1(3) of the EAW Framework Decision, which lays down the obligation to comply with fundamental rights when executing a European arrest warrant.[37] In formulating its questions, the referring court made clear that, in its opinion, the recent reforms of the Polish judiciary jeopardize some fundamental values, such as 'the independence of the judiciary and respect for the Constitution', and amount to 'systemic breaches of the rule of law' as well as 'fundamental defects in the system of justice',[38] thereby prospecting a real risk for the protection of the individual's fundamental right to a fair trial. In the circumstances, instead of asking the CJEU to assess the compatibility of the Polish reforms with the European rule of

---

[33] *Supra* note 8.

[34] See in this respect the statement of the Association of Judges of Ireland in defence of the referring judge https://aji.ie/communications/press-release-2018-03-15/.

[35] Interview with the leader of 'Kobranocka', Andrzej Kraiński, http://gazetapraca.pl/gazetapraca/1,68946,3425292.html (in Polish only).

[36] Canor (2013), p. 383.

[37] O.J. 2002, L 190/1 'Council Framework Decision 2002/584/JHA of 13 June 2002 on the European arrest warrant and the surrender procedures between Member States' as amended by O.J. 2009, L81/24, 'Council Framework Decision 2009/299/JHA amending Framework Decisions 2002/584/JHA, 2005/214/JHA, 2006/783/JHA, 2008/909/JHA and 2008/947/JHA, thereby enhancing the procedural rights of persons and fostering the application of the principle of mutual recognition to decisions rendered in the absence of the person concerned at the trial'.

[38] Joined Cases C-404/15 and C-659/15 PPU, *Aranyosi and Căldăraru*, ECLI:EU:C:2016:198, para. 140.

law, the Irish court asked whether, in situations akin to those in the case pending before it, judicial authorities can refrain from executing a EAW or whether, similarly to how decided in the *Aranyosi and Căldăraru* judgment, they need to carry out a specific and precise assessment as to the exposure of the individual concerned to the risk of unfair trial.

It is worth recalling that, in the *Aranyosi and Căldăraru* judgment, the CJEU had been asked to decide on the possibility for national judges to derogate from the principles of mutual recognition and mutual trust in case of alleged violations of human rights in the Member State issuing a EAW. More specifically, the referring judge had asked the Court whether, to the extent that national judicial authorities possess 'solid evidence' that detention conditions in the issuing Member State are incompatible with fundamental rights, they may or must refuse to execute a European arrest warrant. According to the CJEU, an interpretation of the EAW Framework Decision, which takes into account the absolute prohibition of inhuman or degrading treatment or punishment as set out in Article 4 CFR, implies the obligation for the national judicial authorities not to execute a EAW. However, such a decision can be taken only if 'there are substantial grounds to believe that, following the surrender of that person to the issuing Member State, he will run a real risk of being subject in that Member State to inhuman or degrading treatment'.

In other words, national judicial authorities must run a two-phase test. For starters, they need to assess whether there are systemic or generalised deficiencies as regards the detention conditions in the prison system of the issuing Member State. This appraisal must rely on 'information that is objective, reliable, specific and properly updated', including—but not limited to—'judgments of the ECtHR, judgments of courts of the issuing Member State, and also decisions, reports and other documents produced by bodies of the Council of Europe or under the aegis of the UN'. Then, national judicial authorities must 'make a further assessment, *specific and precise*, of whether there are substantial grounds to believe that the *individual concerned* will be exposed to that risk because of the conditions for his detention envisaged in the issuing Member State'. To carry out this assessment, the executing judicial authority must ask the issuing Member State for all necessary supplementary information, as provided for by Article 15(2) of the EAW Framework Decision.

Now, in the *LM* case, the Irish High Court submitted two questions to the CJEU. First of all, it asked whether, in the presence of cogent evidence of systemic violations of the rule of law in the issuing Member States, the executing judicial authority is in fact obliged to carry out a two-phase test similar to that devised in the *Aranyosi and Căldăraru* judgment. If so, the second question was if the executing judicial authority is to revert to the issuing judicial authority for any further necessary information and, as a result, 'what guarantees as to fair trial would be required'.

After summarising the facts underlying the request for a preliminary ruling and the objectives and principles governing the EAW Framework Decision, the CJEU affirmed that, according to settled case-law (i.e. *Opinion 2/13* and *Aranyosi and Căldăraru*), the principles of mutual recognition and mutual trust among Member States can be abridged only 'in exceptional circumstances'. However, unlike the *Aranyosi and Căldăraru* judgment, which concerned an absolute prohibition

(Article 4 CFR: prohibition of inhuman or degrading treatment or punishment), the *LM* case concerned the right to a fair trial. Hence the question: does a systemic violation of the right to a fair trial amount to an 'exceptional circumstance' that may justify the abridgment of the principles of mutual recognition and mutual trust? The CJEU replied in the affirmative, stating that the independence of the judiciary is part of the essence of the fundamental right to a fair trial and that the defence of the common value of the rule of law depends, in all respects, on the effective protection of that right. Thus, in case of a real risk of violation of the right to a fair trial in the issuing Member State, the executing judicial authorities must refrain, under Article 1 (3) of the EAW Framework Decision, from surrendering the requested person.

As is clear to see, the Court did not rely on the fundamental right to a fair trial, as suggested by the Advocate General, but on the rule of law value itself. Or, to put it better: the CJEU first linked the fundamental right to a fair trial to the value of the European rule of law, and it then adopted such value as normative yardstick against which to respond to the referring court. This emerges, for instance, in paragraph 50 of the judgment, where the Court referred to Article 19 TEU as 'giv[ing] concrete expression to the value of the rule of law affirmed in Article 2 TEU' and cited the precedent in *Associação Sindical dos Juízes Portugueses*. As a result, due to its being a constitutional value common to the EU and its Member States, the European rule of law must be interpreted, applied and safeguarded also by national judges.

Subsequently, the CJEU affirmed that the entire surrender procedure between Member States must be carried out under judiciary supervision and that, for this to happen, national judges must be fully independent. Thus, when the requested person argues that there are systemic or generalised deficiencies which are liable to affect the independence of the judiciary in the issuing Member State, the executing judicial authority must run a two-phase test similar to that devised in the *Aranyosi and Căldăraru* judgment.

It first has to ascertain whether, due to systemic or generalised deficiencies connected to the independence of the judiciary in the issuing Member State, there is indeed a 'real risk' that the requested person's fundamental right to a fair trial be violated. When carrying out this assessment, the executing judicial authority must rely on 'objective, reliable, specific and properly updated' material and consider both the external and the internal dimensions of independence, notably the autonomy of the judges (i.e., the absence of any hierarchical constraint and any form of subordination vis-à-vis other powers) and their impartiality (i.e., the equal distance from the parties to the proceedings and their respective interests). Should it come to the conclusion that there indeed exists a real risk, the executing judicial authority must then assess 'specifically and precisely' whether there are 'substantial grounds' for believing that the requested person will *actually* run that risk. The CJEU justified the necessity of a two-phase test by referring to recital (10) of the EAW Framework Decision. According to this recital, the mechanism of the European arrest warrant can be suspended only when the Council determines, under Article 7(2) and (3) TEU, the existence of a serious and persistent breach by one of the Member States of the principles set out in Article 2 TEU. Thus, lacking such a determination by the Council, national authorities may refrain from executing a EAW only after carrying out an individual and specific assessment of the concrete risks faced by the person concerned.

5 From the *Maastricht Urteil* to the *LM* Case

Despite the generic nature of the preliminary questions put forth by the Irish judge, the CJEU did not miss out on the opportunity to make some specific considerations on the rule of law crisis in Poland and to draw some red lines. Different reasons spoke in favour of an intervention of the Court. To begin with, it was important that these red lines were drawn in a process that itself respected these European founding values, including the right to a fair hearing. Therefore, Poland had to be granted a formal role in the proceedings and be represented by its legitimate government. A domestic court could have hardly provided for that. Second, given that the recent reforms in Poland encroach significantly on the independence of judges and that—as stated in paragraph 54 of the judgment—such independence is 'essential to the proper working of the judicial cooperation system embodied by the preliminary ruling mechanism', the dispute before the Irish High Court presented such a connection with EU law as to justify the intervention of the Court. Third, and more generally, a systemic rule of law problem with judicial independence impinges on the effectiveness of the entire EU legal system; thus, an overall European assessment of the matter was necessary.

That said, one could arguably maintain that the judgment in *re LM* is too abstract. We disagree with this argument. For instance, when explaining the first stage of the two-phase test, the Court specifies that, to assess the existence of a real risk for the rule of law value in a Member State, the executing judicial authority can rely, among other things, on the information laid down in a reasoned proposal by the Commission under Article 7(1) TEU. These acts are, according to the Court, of particular relevance for the purposes of that assessment, especially if they refer to judgments or opinions by other European and international institutions, like in the case of Poland (e.g. the United Nations Human Rights Committee, the European Council, the ECtHR, the Venice Commission etc.). This increases the soundness and legitimacy of the Commission's and, by extension, of the executing authority's findings. Moreover, as regards the disciplinary chamber mentioned in the introduction, the CJEU takes a clear stance against its compatibility with the European value of the rule of law. Finally, within the limits allowed by the specific case, the Court provides national judges with a range of criteria to be followed when carrying out the second stage of the two-phase test. The executing authorities must in fact consider the personal situation, as well as the nature of the offence for which the requested person is being prosecuted and the factual context that form the basis of the European arrest warrant.

Now, from a broader perspective, the judgment in *LM* has (at least) two distinguishing features. First, it involves overcoming the notion that the defence of the European common values is an exclusive preserve of the European political institutions under Article 7 TEU. Second, it posits a pivotal role of the individuals in the protection of the European rule of law value.

As for the first feature, the Court makes clear that the defence of the European common values is also a task for the courts, especially national courts. Consistently with its role in the preliminary ruling procedure, the CJEU does not express a conclusive opinion on the Polish reforms of the judicial system. Rather, it lets the referring court decide if—and to what extent—these reforms amount to a violation of the European rule of law value. For any such decision requires much legitimacy and is likely to be highly contested, it seems wise to share this burden among several courts, national and supranational. In that respect, one might criticize the initial 'if' in paragraph 68 of the judgment for leaving that difficult task too much on the shoulders of the national judge. After all, the formulation 'systemic and generalised deficiencies' is, for all intents and purposes, a European concept, which calls for a more incisive intervention of the CJEU.

As regards the second feature, an increased involvement of national courts implies, by extension, the empowerment of individuals in the protection of the European rule of law value. By linking this value to the essence of the fundamental right to a fair trial, the Court makes a doctrinal move similar to the one the German Federal Constitutional Court undertook in its Maastricht decision. It remains to be seen if the CJEU thereby aims at a similar position as the German court in framing the founding principles of the polity. What is clear, however, is that, from here on, 'the vigilance of the individual' is core not only for the 'supervision' of European law, as famously stated by the Court in *Van Gend en Loos*, but also of the European rule of law value. In addition, upon jointly reading the Court's judgments in *LM* and in *Associação Sindical dos Juízes Portugueses*, it clearly emerges that the European rule of law value can be used as a weapon by the very same judges whose independence is at stake. The recent request for a preliminary ruling of the Polish Supreme court bear witness to that.

At this point, the next question is what impact the *LM* judgment will have in the overall context of the rule of law crisis management. We believe that the impact of this judgment will be colossal and will by far exceed that of the *N.S.*[39] or the *Aranyosi* case.[40] These two latter cases dealt with a particular violation of a certain human right under specific circumstances. The *LM* case, by contrast, deals with a comprehensive violation of the value of the rule of law. It is about a Member State suffering from a systemic deficiency in upholding the rule of law, because the independence of the judiciary has been undermined. That could have the broadest implications and could possibly affect the fundamental principle of mutual trust on which the entire judicial cooperation in the European legal space rests. Not only will criminals not be surrendered on the basis of an EAW but asylum seekers will not be transferred on the basis of the Dublin mechanism; moreover, civil judgments

---

[39]Joined Cases C-411/10 and C-493/10, *N.S. and Others* v. *Secretary of State for the Home Department*, ECLI:EU:C:2011:865.

[40]*Supra* note 38.

originating from this state will possibly not be enforced by the national courts of all the other States.

By significantly reducing horizontal judicial cooperation, the *LM* case could therefore isolate Poland within the European legal space, although hopefully only temporarily. This is a harsh consequence, but a number of reasons speak for it. The respect of the rule of law value is a precondition for membership (Article 49 TEU), for mutual trust,[41] for all fundamental rights, for the entire European edifice.[42] If that is not enough: the future of the European rule of law, as Europe thought it knows it, is at stake if no one opposes the developments in Poland. All this would justify significantly reducing *horizontal* cooperation with Poland.

At the same time, this solution does not foreclose *vertical* cooperation, as it allows national courts to continue using the preliminary-ruling procedure. This is particularly important, because the CJEU and valiant Polish courts can thereby continue to fight jointly for the European rule of law or the rights of Union citizens.[43] In other words, the fact that the independence of the Polish judiciary as a system is compromised does not exclude recognizing the independence of individual courts.

The different functional logic of the preliminary ruling procedure, on the one hand, and horizontal judicial cooperation, on the other hand, allows for this distinction. In a preliminary ruling procedure, the CJEU can assess the referring court in light of its case law on judicial independence, a review that is more difficult in the case of horizontal cooperation. Moreover, the CJEU merely interprets EU law in a preliminary ruling procedure, leaving the national court to apply it to the facts, whereas horizontal judicial cooperation directly affects individuals: while horizontal cooperation subjects an individual to the authority of another Member State, a preliminary ruling procedure can in fact help an individual vis-à-vis the authority to which he or she is already subjected.

This leads to the critical issue of the threshold for non-cooperation. In the *LM* case, the Court decided to follow the approach devised in its *Aranyosi* case-law.[44] Accordingly, non-cooperation requires 'substantial grounds to believe' that the requested person's right to a fair trial 'will run a real risk', for which there is no evidence in the *LM* proceedings. This choice, however, appears inadequate to tackle the rule of law crisis in Poland. Since the Polish government's measures undermine the independence of the entire judiciary, there is little or no point in conducting an individual and specific assessment of the concrete risks the person concerned faces. As things stand, there is always the danger that any case might at some point come before a compromised judge. This circumstance should have prompted the Court to

[41]CJEU, Opinion 2/13, *Opinion on the Draft Agreement on the Accession of the European Union to the Convention for the Protection of Human Rights and Fundamental Freedoms*, ECLI:EU:C:2014:2454, para 168.

[42]*Supra* note 8, paras. 41 and 43.

[43]In detail, von Bogdandy et al. (2012), p. 489.

[44]*Supra* note 7, para. 5.

follow the test developed in *N.S.*,[45] according to which the abstract risk for the individual concerned should suffice to refuse a surrender. From a systemic standpoint, the refusal to surrender on the basis of a merely abstract risk is justified by the urgent need for red lines. From a practical perspective, it is difficult to imagine how the 'dialogue' on judicial independence between the executing authority, on the one hand, and the issuing judicial authority and its government, on the other hand, can meaningfully take place. At the same time, it is clear that once a systemic deficiency has been established, the burden of proof shifts to the country issuing the EAW. *In dubio pro libertate.*

6 Conclusion

For more than two decades, the constitutional developments in Central and Eastern European countries were mainly considered a constitutional sideshow, that depicted countries 'catching up' with their luckier neighbours who had never suffered Soviet occupation. Now, these countries stand in the limelight: much of the future path of European constitutionalism depends on how their peoples decide.

The rest of Europe cannot do a great deal for those countries' constitutionalism. One cannot expect from the deployment of the instruments analysed in this chapter a 'solution' to the crisis. None but the citizens of those countries themselves can restore the separation of powers among their countries' institutions. The decisions taken by EU institutions can only contribute 'to creating a situation where self-healing through domestic processes is still possible'.[46]

However, one needs to look beyond those countries to understand the importance of using these instruments now. European decisions confronting the Polish Government are crucial to uphold a liberal and democratic self-understanding of European constitutionalism throughout Europe. Otherwise, the current Polish undermining of the independence of its judiciary is likely to count towards defining the European rule of law, facilitating similar developments in other places and compromising large parts of European foreign policy. Much is at stake. Yet, as the Polish anthem goes, 'Poland Is Not Yet Lost'; and nor is the constitutional European project, if the institutions act wisely.

References

Ackerman B (1991) We the people: foundations, vol 1, 6. Harvard University Press, Cambridge
Bonelli M (2017) From a community of law to a Union of values. Eur Const Law Rev 13:793–816

[45] *Supra* note 39.

[46] Sonnevend (2017), pp. 123, 145.

Canor I (2013) My brother's keeper? Horizontal Solange: 'An ever closer distrust among the peoples of Europe'. Common Mark Law Rev 50:383–421

Charlemagne (2018) The EU is tolerating – and enabling – authoritarian kleptocracy in Hungary. The Economist, April 5

Editorial Comments (2015) Safeguarding EU values in the Member States – is something finally happening? Common Mark Law Rev 52:619–628

Editorial Comments (2016) The rule of law in the Union, the rule of Union law and the rule of law by the Union: three interrelated problems. Common Mark Law Rev 53:597–605

Editorial Comments (2017) About Brexit negotiations and enforcement action against Poland: the EU's own song of ice and fire. Common Mark Law Rev 54:1309–1317

Giegerich T (2015) Verfassungshomogenität, Verfassungsautonomie und Verfassungsaufsicht in der EU: Zum 'neuen Rechtsstaatsmechanismus' der Europäischen Kommission. In: Calliess C (ed) Herausforderungen an Staat und Verfassung: Liber Amicorum für Torsten Stein zum 70. Geburtstag. Nomos, Baden-Baden, pp 499, 535–536

Halmai G (2017) The early retirement age of the Hungarian judges. In: Nicola F, Davies B (eds) EU law stories. Cambridge University Press, New York, pp 471–488

Halmai G (2018) Illiberal constitutionalism? The Hungarian constitution in a European perspective. In: Kadelbach S (ed) Verfassungskrisen in der Europäischen Union. Nomos, Baden-Baden, pp 85–104

Klarman MJ (1992) Constitutional fact/constitutional fiction: a critique of Bruce Ackerman's theory of constitutional moments. Stanford Law Rev 44:759–797

Matczak M (2018) 10 Facts on Poland for the Consideration of the European Court of Justice. VerfBlog, 13 May 2018. https://verfassungsblog.de/10-facts-on-poland-for-the-consideration-of-the-european-court-of-justice/

Muszyński M (2018) Polski Trybunał w unijnej rzeczywistości. http://www.rp.pl/Opinie/303229983-Polski-Trybunal-w-unijnej-rzeczywistosci%2D%2D-Mariusz-Muszynski-o-mocy-wyrokow-TSUE-w-Polsce.html (in Polish only)

Scheppele KL (2016) Enforcing the basic principles of EU law through systemic infringement actions. In: Closa C, Kochenov D (eds) Reinforcing rule of law oversight in the European Union. Cambridge University Press, Cambridge, pp 105–132

Sonnevend P (2017) Preserving the acquis of transformative constitutionalism in times of constitutional crisis: lessons from the Hungarian case. In: von Bogdandy A, Ferrer Mac-Gregor E, Morales Antoniazzi M, Piovesan F (eds) Transformative constitutionalism in Latin America. Oxford University Press, Oxford, pp 123, 145

von Bogdandy A, Kottmann M, Antpöhler C, Dickschen J, Hentrei S, Smrkol M (2012) Reverse *Solange* – protecting the essence of fundamental rights against EU Member States. Common Mark Law Rev 49:489–519

Armin von Bogdandy is Director at the Max Planck Institute for Comparative Public Law and International Law, Heidelberg.

Piotr Bogdanowicz is Assistant Professor, Faculty of Law and Administration, Warsaw University.

Iris Canor is Professor, School of Law, Zefat Academic College, Israel; School of Law, College of Management, Israel.

Giacomo Rugge is Research Fellow, Max Planck Institute for Comparative Public Law and International Law, Heidelberg.

Matthias Schmidt is Research Fellow, Max Planck Institute for Comparative Public Law and International Law, Heidelberg.

Maciej Taborowski is Assistant Professor, Faculty of Law and Administration, Warsaw University.

Permissions

All chapters in this book were first published by Springer; hereby published with permission under the Creative Commons Attribution License or equivalent. Every chapter published in this book has been scrutinized by our experts. Their significance has been extensively debated. The topics covered herein carry significant findings which will fuel the growth of the discipline. They may even be implemented as practical applications or may be referred to as a beginning point for another development.

The contributors of this book come from diverse backgrounds, making this book a truly international effort. This book will bring forth new frontiers with its revolutionizing research information and detailed analysis of the nascent developments around the world.

We would like to thank all the contributing authors for lending their expertise to make the book truly unique. They have played a crucial role in the development of this book. Without their invaluable contributions this book wouldn't have been possible. They have made vital efforts to compile up to date information on the varied aspects of this subject to make this book a valuable addition to the collection of many professionals and students.

This book was conceptualized with the vision of imparting up-to-date information and advanced data in this field. To ensure the same, a matchless editorial board was set up. Every individual on the board went through rigorous rounds of assessment to prove their worth. After which they invested a large part of their time researching and compiling the most relevant data for our readers.

The editorial board has been involved in producing this book since its inception. They have spent rigorous hours researching and exploring the diverse topics which have resulted in the successful publishing of this book. They have passed on their knowledge of decades through this book. To expedite this challenging task, the publisher supported the team at every step. A small team of assistant editors was also appointed to further simplify the editing procedure and attain best results for the readers.

Apart from the editorial board, the designing team has also invested a significant amount of their time in understanding the subject and creating the most relevant covers. They scrutinized every image to scout for the most suitable representation of the subject and create an appropriate cover for the book.

The publishing team has been an ardent support to the editorial, designing and production team. Their endless efforts to recruit the best for this project, has resulted in the accomplishment of this book. They are a veteran in the field of academics and their pool of knowledge is as vast as their experience in printing. Their expertise and guidance has proved useful at every step. Their uncompromising quality standards have made this book an exceptional effort. Their encouragement from time to time has been an inspiration for everyone.

The publisher and the editorial board hope that this book will prove to be a valuable piece of knowledge for researchers, students, practitioners and scholars across the globe.

List of Contributors

Beáta Bakó
Department of Law, European University Institute, Florence, Italy

Justyna Łacny
Department of Administration and Social Sciences, Warsaw University of Technology, Warsaw, Poland

Artur Nowak-Far
Institute of Law, SGH-Warsaw School of Economics, Warsaw, Poland

Marcin Wiącek
Faculty of Law and Administration, University of Warsaw, Warszawa, Poland

Wojciech Sadowski
Queritius, Warsaw, Poland

Armin von Bogdandy
Max Planck Institute for Comparative Public Law and International Law, Heidelberg, Germany

Stanisław Biernat
Jagiellonian University, Krakow, Poland

Werner Schroeder
Department of European Law and Public International Law, University of Innsbruck, Innsbruck, Austria

Armin von Bogdandy, Giacomo Rugge and Matthias Schmidt
Max Planck Institute for Comparative Public Law and International Law, Heidelberg, Germany

Piotr Bogdanowicz and Maciej Taborowski
Faculty of Law and Administration, University of Warsaw, Warsaw, Poland

Iris Canor
School of Law, Zefat Academic College, Sefad, Israel
School of Law, College of Management, Rishon Le Zion, Israel

Index

www.ingramcontent.com/pod-product-compliance
Lightning Source LLC
LaVergne TN
LVHW080631210926
848485LV00003B/245

* 9 7 8 1 6 4 7 2 8 4 4 6 6 *